Pearls of Yiddish Poetry

Joseph and Chana Mlotek

Pearls of Yiddish Poetry

by
Joseph and Chana Mlotek

edited by
Mark Mlotek

Translated by
Barnett Zumoff

KTAV Publishing House, Inc.
in association with
The Forward Association

ISBN 978-1-60280-156-1

Published by
KTAV Publishing House, Inc.
930 Newark Avenue
Jersey City, NJ 07306
orders@ktav.com
www.ktav.com
(201) 963-9524
Fax (201) 963-0102

CONTENTS

HOW THIS BOOK WAS BORN[1]

In the summer of 1970, shortly after I became the editor of the *Forverts*, Joseph Mlotek, then the Educational Director of the Workmen's Circle, proposed to me that we introduce a poetry contest in the paper. He knew how eager I was to bring in new and interesting features, so he told me about the plan he had conceived, a plan that would be doubly useful: it would arouse the interest of the readers in the treasure of Yiddish poetry and it would draw the readers themselves into participating in it.

I had good reason to have serious doubts about the prospects for success. At that time I was reprinting works from the older Yiddish literature in the *Forverts*, and the response of the readers was very weak. If the classical prose creations hadn't evoked any great interest, what could I expect from poetry? Nevertheless I decided to try. What did I have to lose? If there wasn't a good response, we would discontinue it after a few weeks and no one would miss it.

In the *Notes From The Editor* in the middle of a week, I announced the new section, which appeared for the first time in the *Forverts* of October 25, 1970, under the rubric *Perl Fun Der Yidisher Poezie—Ver Hot Zey Geshafn? fun A. Forsher* (*Pearls of Yiddish Poetry—Who Created Them? by A. Researcher.*) In the present book, it is revealed for the first time that *A. Researcher* was Joseph Mlotek and his wife, Chana Mlotek, who is a well known researcher of Yiddish folksongs.

That rubric was the start of this book. The morning after the first poetry contest appeared, I encountered a Yiddish writer near the *Forverts* building, and he saluted me for the new initiative. He would want it to be successful, he said, but he wanted to warn me that I shouldn't expect any response from the readers. When I got to the editorial office, there were 15 letters on my desk that were addressed to *A. Researcher*. That was the first indication that the new feature was a "hit." How much of a hit it was we first began to comprehend in the succeeding days, when packs of letters kept arriving, both from New York and from the rest of the country and Canada. Later we also began getting letters from overseas.

---

1. This foreword, by the then editor of the *Forverts*, introduced the original book in Yiddish.

And the interest continues to the present time when these lines are being written (December 1972), more than two years after the first rubric of *Pearls* appeared in the *Forverts*. The success has been truly phenomenal.

After a few months, it became apparent that the section had achieved much more than the goals that those in charge of the poetry contest and the *Forverts* Editor had set. In addition to rediscovering the great treasure of Yiddish poetry, the section had uncovered a true folk treasure that would have been lost forever, namely the poems that readers remembered. We had tapped the sources of a mass of Yiddish folksongs and their various versions, had established who the authors were of a number of songs that had previously been thought to be anonymous folksongs, and had discovered the composers of a number of songs whose music had previously been nearly unknown.

For such work as the two researchers Joseph and Chana Mlotek have done, people all over the world get doctorates and other kinds of recognition. We do not have such measures at our disposal. Therefore we have taken the initiative of seeing to it that these great findings should not go lost again (a newspaper, after all, lives no longer than 24 hours.)

On May 27, 1971, I published in the *Forverts* a personal appeal to the readers to help us perpetuate the newly found treasure between hard covers, by subscribing in advance to the planned book of the *Pearls*. Many readers responded immediately with contributions of more than the price of the book. My heartfelt thanks to all of them. They can also be proud to have been partners in a great Yiddish cultural undertaking.

The book you are now holding in your hand contains a selection from the material that has appeared in the *Forverts* during the first 18 months of the section's publication.

Simon Weber

PREFACE

About six years ago, the *Forverts* published a letter to the Editor from a reader, Paul Berman from The Bronx, with a curious request: to help him find the conclusion of a song he remembered from the old country. "I'm talking about a folksong," the reader wrote, "that people used to sing in Poland. The song begins with these words:

> *My mother told me*
> *that there was once*
> *a little house*
> *way down in the valley.*

and here is my request: I am missing the conclusion of this beautiful folksong. I've tried searching in various bookstores, but without success. Distinguished Editor—I would be very grateful if you would try to help me find the end of the folksong. I hope that readers of our beloved *Forverts* will respond to my letter."

The letter interested us for the following reasons: First, it told us that there are readers, ordinary people, who take the trouble to search "in various bookstores" for songs of which they remember only a few lines; second, the letter referred to a song written by a well known poet, Jacob Adler (B. Kovner), which has come into general use as an anonymous folksong. So we thought: How many more such songs by well known poets have been folklorized and their origin is not known, not only by ordinary people but by collectors and compilers of books of folksongs?

Thinking about that, we also recalled another problem: a number of singers and actors have in their concert repertoires songs by famous Yiddish poets, but instead of taking the trouble to find out whose songs they are, they simply say that they are folksongs. That happens often, not only with songs by old-time and half-forgotten authors and composers but even with songs by poets and composers who are still alive and creating.

There have been times when such occurrences are the result of a productive Yiddish life: when a new song by a poet has become popular overnight and people have made it their own and added new variants, not knowing who the author or composer of the song was. It's well known, after all, that six years after

Sholem Aleichem published his lullaby *Shlof, Mayn Kind* (Sleep, My Child) in his *Kol Mevaser Tsu Der Yidisher Folks-Bibliotek* (Announcement of the Jewish People's Library [1892]), five informants from various parts of Russia sent the folklorized song to S.Ginsburg and P. Marek and they published it as one of the more than 300 folksongs that they included in the first large collection of Yiddish folksongs (St. Petersburg, 1901.) The same thing has happened with songs by Abraham Reisen and by the proletarian poets in America, and, even earlier, with the songs of the *Maskilic*[2] poets and folk troubadors.

Such incorporation and folklorization of songs by well known poets happens with all other cultures too, and that, as we have already mentioned, is a sign of a healthy, productive, and creative life that one has to envy.

When we proposed to the editor of the *Forverts,* Simon Weber, the introduction into the newspaper of the section *Pearls of Yiddish Poetry*, one of our goals was in fact to eliminate some of these inaccuracies, and especially to point out that in the future we should pay more attention to details. In addition to that, we set other goals: to revive famous creations of Yiddish poetry that readers had forgotten or perhaps hadn't read before, and to stimulate readers to look into books by Yiddish writers.

In order to interest more readers, we introduced a game: we published poems or parts of poems without the names of the authors and asked the readers to complete the poems and also to tell us who wrote them; a week later, we printed the names of the readers who had answered correctly, and also biographical details about the poets.

Hardly had a few weeks passed after the introduction of that section than we became convinced that we had achieved much more than the goals we had set: we received many letters from readers telling us that they were going to libraries more often to look for the books they didn't have at home and that they had begun asking public libraries to buy Yiddish books, and asking us where they could buy the books they were looking for.

We were especially happy about the response of younger, American-born readers who had become interested in Yiddish poetry, not out of nostalgia like many older readers, but because of the beauty of the poetry itself. Some even began

---

2. Followers of the *Haskalah*, the Jewish Enlightenment that began around the turn of the nineteenth century.

sending English translations that they had done themselves, to interest those young readers who knew no Yiddish.

During the first two years, we published in *Pearls of Yiddish Poetry* about 300 examples of poems written by well known Yiddish poets. For this book, we have chosen only a fraction of those poets, with their poems as we published them in the *Forverts*. The biographical notes make no claim to being comprehensive or original literary essays; we simply wanted to acquaint the readers with the poets and the era in which the poems were written, and to show what recognized literary critics and historians had written about them. We were attempting thereby to stimulate the reader to become more interested in the lives and creations of the poets.

The poems of *Maskilic* and other poets that have been folklorized and are now sung differently from the way they were written, are printed here in their original versions. The interested reader will be able to compare the original texts with the folklorized versions that he or she knows or that are published in collections of folklore. Only the orthography has been changed and a number of Germanisms have been replaced by their proper Yiddish equivalents.

It is important to emphasize that the book is not a comprehensive anthology; the poems and biographies of a number of poets who chronologically should have been represented are not to be found in it.

It is our pleasant duty here to thank a number of people without whose encouragement and help the work would not have gotten done. First of all, we thank the editor of the *Forverts*, Simon Weber, who constantly encouraged us to continue and expand the section. He also took the initiative to create a fund from among the readers who requested in their letters that such a book as this should be published. Without his understanding and help, the work would not have been done by us and therefore the book wouldn't have "been born." He deserves special recognition for acceding to our request by printing the section—for the first time in the history of the *Forverts*—in the modern orthography.

We also thank the distinguished scholar Professor Dov Sadan for his letters of encouragement to do the collection and research work "before it's too late."

And finally, our thanks to our dear children Zalmen and Moishe, whose love for the *Pearls of Yiddish Poetry* made the work easier and sweeter.

Chana and Yosl Mlotek, (December 1972)

Addendum (May 2010)

It is now 38 years since this book was originally published, and 10 years since my beloved husband, Yosl, passed away. New articles of *Pearls of Yiddish Poetry* continue to appear regularly in the *Forverts*. To bring the book up to date, I have added to 32 articles that appeared in the original book 6 newer articles about additional authors omitted in that book, and we are publishing it this year in English translation.

I am grateful that the memory of my husband has lived on through my children and grandchildren. Each year, Zalmen, Debbie, Moish, Audrey and their children Lee, Avram, Missy, Elisha, and Sarah have awarded a Mlotek prize for Yiddish and Yiddish culture to people who have helped keep Yiddish and its culture alive as a living, vibrant expression of our people—as my husband did. I want to especially thank two people: my dear thanks to Samuel Norich, publisher of the Yiddish *Forverts* and the English *Forward*, who has captured the essence of what Yosl and I attempted to do through his Introduction to this book, and my very special thanks to Dr. Barnett Zumoff, a former winner of the Mlotek prize, for his incredibly careful and talented translations. Barney began translating Yiddish poetry at the suggestion of Yosl, and he has gone on to translate almost 20 works to date, each one superbly crafted.

I also want to thank the people who helped us at the beginning of our venture: our father, Leo Gordon, and our brother and sister-in-law, Abram and Dina Mlotek. They helped us index the material that readers sent in and gave us much-needed encouragement, together with our mother, Bessie Gordon, and our sister and brother-in-law, Malke and Bing Gottlieb.

I also want to thank the YIVO Institute for Jewish Research, with which I have been associated for over 50 years, for being the main resource for our nearly a thousand columns.

Lastly, to our readers—a special thank-you for your interest in Yiddish poetry. Your interest and thirst have inspired me to continue the column and to bring out this volume today to hopefully inspire a new generation to drink from the well of our literary and musical treasury.

Chana Mlotek

INTRODUCTION

Decades before Wikipedia and blogs and social networking sites like Facebook and Twitter brought together authors and a vast public in the creation of original content (as we now call it), Chana Mlotek and her late husband Joseph (Yosl) Mlotek were already at it in the pages of the *Forverts*. They had the idea of engaging their readers in recalling and searching out Yiddish songs and poems they remembered from an earlier time. Most of the readers were, by then—the 1970s and the years since—men and women of a certain age. Many were Jews from Eastern and Central Europe who, like Yosl, had survived the destruction of their world and had found refuge, a new life, and a new family in America. Though America was now their home, they still dreamed in the language and images of their childhood and youth "before the war." For most, the landscapes of their youth were no longer physically accessible, but their memories were. They could and did recall the poems and songs that echoed the moments most dear to them, moments with their schoolmates or first love, with parents or comrades-- moments that had given meaning to their lives or shaped who they had become. Sometimes they recalled a fragment, sometimes entire stanzas; whatever it was, it was a "pearl" to them and to others who had come from the same place or the same upbringing. They sent their recalled pearls to Chana and Yosl Mlotek, who published them in their column *Pearls of Yiddish Poetry* in the *Forverts*. Where the recollections of one reader left off, the recollections of another would pick up. Often the Mloteks knew the origin or author of a poem or song that the reader who submitted it did not. Together they pieced together an entire poetic literature, the songs of several generations. Week after week, month after month, year after year, for three decades Chana and Yosl wrote their amazing column together, and in the decade since Yosl's passing Chana has continued it in her heroic way.

Though the Mloteks conceived their column as a popular community project, they were anything but amateurs in this field. Yosl, a son of Polish Jewry, had already, in his teens, found his voice as a journalist and poet in the publications of the Jewish Labor Bund. Chana had had the best Yiddish education that New York could offer. They met in Los Angeles in 1948 when both were awarded scholarships to study Yiddish folklore at UCLA, the first time a course in that subject had been offered anywhere in the U.S. Chana had already been hired by

Max Weinreich, the great scholar of Yiddish language and culture and Research Director of YIVO, to be his secretary, and she later became his research assistant. Later still, she would become the music archivist at YIVO and a sought-after resource for generations of artists and scholars in the field. Soon after they married in 1949, Yosl became the Educational Director of the Workmen's Circle. In that role, in the free summer concerts of Yiddish theater and folksongs he launched in the parks of New York, through his cultural Third Seder, and through his weekly radio programs on WEVD, Yosl enriched the lives of many thousands.

The column they created together in the *Forverts* has now led to four anthologies of Yiddish songs and three recordings. In their unassuming and accessible style, the Mloteks have entertained and educated their readers and have opened or reopened a world of Yiddish song and poetry to a devoted and grateful audience. A selection of some three dozen of the more than 1000 articles they have published in the column has now been ably translated by Dr Barnett Zumoff for inclusion in this volume.

Samuel Norich
Publisher of the *Forverts* and the *Forward*

MIKHL GORDON

(born November 4, 1823 in Vilna; died December 24, 1890 in Kiev)

When Mikhl Gordon, one of the most popular and talented *Maskilic* poets, died in the year 1890 at the age of 67, his poems were already part of the rich folk-treasure that passes from generation to generation. Simon Frug, who was a great fan of Gordon's and saluted his collection of poems in 1889 with a poem of his own, said good-bye to the folk poet after his death in the following words:

> *Sleep sweetly in your tent,*
> *dear, beloved soul.*
> *Take with you to the next world*
> *at least this single consolation,*
> *that your poetry, your Yiddish poetry,*
> *will ring out for many years,*
> *and wherever there lives a Jew*
> *your songs will be sung.*

Now, more than 140 years after his first collection of poems was published in Zhitomir, (*Di Bord un Dertsu Nokh Andere Sheyne Yidishe Lider, Ale Fun a Groysn Hosid*) (The Beard And Other Beautiful Yiddish Poems, All By A Great Khosid—Zhitomir, 1868), one can say without any doubt that it has happened as Frug foresaw: Mikhl Gordon's songs are still sung by Jews throughout the world, though they often don't know or possibly have never heard the name of the author.

When we began the series *Pearls Of Yiddish Poetry* in 1970, we received a letter from an elderly reader who wrote that he remembered from his childhood several lines of a song that his mother used to sing:

> *In the cemetery, from beneath a tombstone,*
> *the bitter voice of a woman can be heard.*
> *It's a mother crying out: Oh woe is me—*
> *what is a stepmother doing to my dear child?*

He wanted to know whether we knew additional words from that song, and asked that we print them.

1

After we had identified the song and had written that these were lines from the song *Di Shtifmuter* (The Stepmother*)*, by Mikhl Gordon, we received letters from other readers who remembered other folklorized variants of the song, and most of them added that they had never previously heard of the author, Mikhl Gordon.

One reader, Charles Rogaski from Wilmington, Delaware, wrote: "You write that the song is surely a hundred years old, and you are correct. Sixty-two years ago, when I was thirteen years old, we poor orphans used to sing the song in kheyder, or in the courtyards where we used to play. Wonder upon wonder: it's already sixty-two years since I've heard or sung the song, but when I read the song now in the *Forverts,* I almost remember the melody as we children used to sing it back home in Kovno, where I come from."

The Stepmother is far from the only song that Mikhl Gordon wrote that has entered folk consciousness as an anonymous song. Another song that many readers surely know and which was popularized by, among others, the famous interpreter of Yiddish folksong Iza Kremer in the 20's and 30's is:

> *If I had the czar's treasures*
> *and his entire kingdom,*
> *they wouldn't be as dear to me*
> *as you are,*
> *my child, my jewel.*

In many collections and records, the song is described as a folksong by an anonymous author. In reality, it's a folklorized version of a song, *Shlof, Mayn Kind* (Sleep, My Child*)*, written by Mikhl Gordon and published in his first collection of songs, which appeared in 1868.

Who was Mikhl Gordon? Not only does the broad readership know very little about him
now, but even in the years when he was alive, creating, and having an influence he was not well known. In one of his songs, he explains why that is so:

> *My songs have gone out into the world*
> *like contraband.*
> *My name isn't on them—*
> *I was afraid of the hasid's hand.*[3]

---

3. According to the first version of *Mayn Haskome* (My Agreement*)*, in a book titled *Magazin* (Magazine), published in Gordon's second collection, *Shirei M. Gordon Yidishe Lider* (Songs from M. Gordon's Poems), Warsaw, 1889. In S. Bernstein's collection *Magazin Fun Yidishe Lider Far Der Yidisher Folk* (Magazine of

His first book didn't come out under his real name but under the name *Fun A Groysn Khosid* (From a Great Hasid). He used an anagram of his name: *Gor Dol Makh Ani*.[4]

Mikhl Gordon was a *Maskil* who in his songs made fun of the *hasidim* and the whole lifestyle of his time. He called on the Jewish folk-masses to break with the old life-style and take up education. That was best expressed in his poem *Shtey Oyf, Mayn Folk* (Arise, My People), in which he called out:

> *Arise my people, you've slept long enough.*
> *Arise and open your eyes,*
> *for it is a plague on you*
> *that you sleep till noon.*
> *Put on clothes like everyone else's—*
> *why do you need your great-grandfather's clothing?*
> *Don't go out in the street in a long khalat[5]*
> *so people will point at you and say: there goes an Asiatic.*

Each verse of his poem mercilessly attacked the fanaticism of the *hasidim*, and he described a *Maskilic* program of how to deal with people. Gordon didn't even spare the language in which he wrote; in that regard, he was no different from the other *Maskilic* writers of his time. He too, like the others, considered Yiddish a "jargon" that Jews had to get rid of as soon as possible:

> *Don't speak a language that no one understands--*
> *your language is alien, confused, and twisted.*
> *The language of the land is clear and pure—*
> *speak it and write it, so everyone will understand.*

In his other poems, such as *Fun Der Khupe* (From The Khupe[6]) and *Mayn Deye* (My Opinion), he attacks, as he himself explains, "the twisted, foolish procedure of matchmaking that parents have inflicted on their children...those untimely

---

Yiddish Songs for the Jewish People). It reads as follows:
> *My songs have gone out into the world*
> *exactly like contraband.*
> *I didn't put my name on them—*
> *I was afraid of an angry hand.*

4. The meaning of the Hebrew words is "I am a stranger, poorer than you."
5. A long black coat, often made of silk, that is worn by Hasidic Jews
6. The marriage canopy in a Jewish wedding

and twisted matches have been the major cause of Jewish poverty." In one poem he tries to explain why he has come out so sharply and satirically against his brothers:

> *I have sung certain songs*
> *not because it's my nature to sing*
> *but because when I see my brothers' mistakes*
> *my heart comes unstrung.*

He criticized because his heart was full of love and concern for his people and not because he wanted to flee from it or reject it. He only wanted to change it, make it better and more beautiful, but not reject it. Like many other *Maskils,* Gordon took seriously the reforms of the Russian government with respect to the Jews, especially those of Alexander II, in whose reign a liberal approach toward Jews began. He expressed his enthusiasm for the new era in his poem *Der Yid in Goles* (The Jew In The Diaspora*)*:

> *Now the nations have gotten smarter—*
> *the dark years will soon pass.*
> *So listen—forget the ancient hatred;*
> *shake hands, with a friendly smile.*

Later Gordon became very disappointed in the "liberal reforms" of the government and also in the so-called education that Jews flocked to.

The two poems that we printed in the poetry contest in the *Forverts* are among the most popular of Mikhl Gordon's folklorized songs. *Di Mashke* (Whisky*)* was published in a folklorized form in M. Kipnis' collection *80 Folkslider* (80 Folksongs*)* as a folksong, which was accepted as such by Peretz Markish. The song also appears as an anonymous folksong in S. Bastomski's collection *Baym Kval* (At The Well, Vilna 1923).

With respect to the satirical song *Di Bord* (The Beard*)*, in which the author makes fun of a fanatical wife who is beside herself because her pious husband has shaved off his beard, it too was folklorized and widely disseminated. In 1951, we printed a study about that song in the *YIVO Bleter*,[7] and showed that it had about a dozen variants and was sung in various districts in Russia, Lithuania, and Poland. Of course, the two songs we are printing in this book: *Di Mashke*

---

7. Chana Mlotek, *The Metamorphosis of Mikhl Gordon's Di Bord (*The Beard*)*, YIVO-Bleter, Volume 35, 1951.

(Whisky) and *Di Bord* (The Beard*)*, have often been sung in forms that are greatly altered from the original texts as Mikhl Gordon wrote them.

When Mikhl Gordon published his second collection, *Yidishe Lider* (Yiddish Songs*)*, in 1889, Simon Frug published a poem in M. Spector's *Hoyzfraynd* (House Friend*)* in which he saluted the poet with these lines:

> *You're among the first of the Jews*
> *who were awakened from sleep*
> *to rap on their doors and windows*
> *to lead them out to the bright world*
>
> *I see your Yiddish Muse clothed*
> *in simple, old-fashioned Jewish clothes,*
> *which are nevertheless skillfully sewn,*
> *both strongly and with proper thread.*
>
> *The old orphan, with no father or mother,*
> *who carries on her back a sack of rhymes.*

This "sack of rhymes" played an enormously important role in the sociocultural awakening and development of the Jewish folk-masses, and it opened a poetic channel for many later poets.

Whisky

So let's drink whisky, brothers—
let's hope we live to drink again.
Let's drink now—enough of eating.
How can you forget about whisky for so long!
If we didn't have whisky,
how would we live in this world?

I must treat whisky honorably.
I stand before it as before an old person,
for it knew my great-grandmother,
and my grandmother used to like it.
From her I inherited the good trait
of draining the whole flask constantly.

When the matchmaker came to my grandfather
to discuss a match between my mother and father,
they talked and talked and nothing came of it,
till whisky entered the picture.
Through whisky the match was agreed on—
my father became my mother's groom.

The marriage took place right away--
they drank whisky all night.
Everyone drank out of big glasses
in honor of the groom and bride.
Through whisky my father married my mother—
through whisky I came into the world.

I still remember that at my circumcision
the whisky never left the table.
Everyone cried *Mazl Tov*!
May the child live and become a rabbi!
That's why I drink most of a glass,
usually without stopping.

As soon as I was weaned from the breast,
I developed a lust for whisky.
I didn't want my mother's cereal,

די משקה

נו, לאָמיר שוין משקה טרינקען, ברידער,
מיר זאָלן דערלעבן — צו טרינקען ווידער;
נו, לאָמיר שוין טרינקען, גענוג שוין עסן,
ווי קענט איר אַזוי לאַנג אָן משקה פֿאַרגעסן!
אָט ווען די משקה וואָלט אונדז געפֿעלט,
ווי וואָלטן מיר לעבן אויף דער וועלט?

די משקה מוז איך ערלעך האַלטן,
איך שטיי פֿאַר איר אויף ווי פֿאַר אַן אַלטן,
דען זי האָט געקענט מיַין עלטער באָבען;
די באָבע פֿלעגט זי ליב האָבן.
פֿון איר האָב איך גענירשענט די מעלה
צו טרינקען ביזן עק און אַלע וויַילע.

בשעת אַ שדכן איז געקומען צום זיידן,
דעם טאַטן מיט דער מאַמען אַ שידוך רעדן,
האָט מען גערעדט און גערעדט, ס'איז געוואָרן נישט,
ביז וואַנען די משקה האָט זיך אַריַינגעמישט;
דורך משקה איז געוואָרן דער שידוך געשלאָסן,
דער טאַטע איז געוואָרן דער מאַמעס חתן.

מען האָט טאַקע באַלד די חתונה געמאַכט,
געטרונקען משקה די גאַנצע נאַכט,
מיט גרויסע גלעזער האָבן געטרונקען אַלע
לכבֿוד דעם חתן, לכבֿוד דער כּלה;
דורך משקה האָט דער טאַטע די מאַמען גענומען,
דורך משקה בין איך אויף דער וועלט געקומען.

איך געדענק נאָך, אַז ביַי מיַין ברית
איז משקה ניט אַראָפּ פֿון טיש;
געשריִען האָבן אַלע מזל־טובֿ!
דאָס קינד זאָל לעבן און זיַין אַ רבֿ!
אָט ד'ריבער טרינק איך אַ רובֿ־פּוס,
דאָס רובֿ טרינק איך גאָר אָן אַ מאָס.

באַלד מען האָט מיך אַנטוויינט פֿון ברוסט,
האָב איך צו משקה באַקומען גרויס לוסט,
איך האָב ניט געוואָלט דער מאַמעס קאַשקע,

I just wanted a little whisky.
I used to take it from a bowl with a spoon
and scream: Mama, give me a little bit more!

At my bar mitzvah, they told me
to drink as much as I wanted.
Of all *mitzvahs* the greatest
is to drink only the best whisky.
When I drink three glasses of whisky,
I forget about all the mitzvahs.

Whenever whisky incites me,
I can commit all kinds of sins;
They can't ever punish me for them
because I've never had enough sleep;
I have no shame, no respect—
I've drunk whisky, and that's an excuse for everything.

When they brought me to the marriage canopy,
I thought: What do I need this kind of trouble for?
But right away they brought in whisky
to say the Seven Blessings with it.
If I hadn't encountered whisky there,
I would have fled right away.

The whisky then said wise things to me:
just stand there quietly, don't suffer—
your wife will eat your heart out,
but just don't forget whisky.
You'll hear your wife's curses,
but through whisky they'll become blessings.

And when your wife makes a face,
drink up a big glass right away.
When she screams at you,
drink up one-two-three.
Let her scream endlessly,
and you just up-end the glasses.

איך האָב נאָר געוואָלט אַ ביסעלע משקה.
כ׳פלעג טרינקען מיט אַ לעפל פֿון אַ שיסל
און שרײַען: מאַמע, גיב נאָך אַ ביסל !

בײַ מײַן בר־מיצווה האָט מען מיר
געהייסן טרינקען גאָר אָן אַ שיעור.
פֿון אַלע מיצוות איז די גרעסטע,
צו טרינקען משקה נאָר די בעסטע.
ווען איך טרינק משקה אַ גלעזער דרײַ,
בין איך פֿון אַלע מיצוות פֿרײַ.

ווען נאָר די משקה רעדט מיך אָן,
מעג איך שוין אַלע עבֿירות טאָן;
מען קען קיין מאָל מיך פֿאַר עפּעס שטראָפֿן,
ווײַל תּמיד בין איך ניט אויסגעשלאָפֿן;
איך האָב קיין בושה, קיין דרך־אַרץ,
כ׳האָב משקה געטרונקען, איז אויף אַלץ אַ תּירוץ.

בשעת מען האָט מיך צו דער חופּה געבראַכט,
וואָס דאַרף איך די צרה? — האָב איך זיך באַדאַכט;
נאָר באַלד האָט מען משקה געבראַכט צו טראָגן,
די שבֿע ברכות אויף משקה צו זאָגן:
ווען איך וואָלט דאָ די משקה ניט אָנגעטראָפֿן,
וואָלט איך פֿון דער חופּה באַלד אַנטלאָפֿן.

דאָ זאָגט מיר די משקה קלוגע דיבורים:
דו שטיי גאַנץ רויִק, האָב קיין יסורים,
דײַן ווײַב וועט דיר דאָס הַאָרץ אויסעסן,
דו זאָלסט נאָר ניט אָן משקה פֿאַרגעסן;
דו וועסט פֿון דײַן ווײַב קללות הערן,
דורך משקה וועלן זיי ברכות ווערן.

און ווען דײַן ווײַב פֿאַרקרימט דעם נאָז,
טרינק דו באַלד אויס אַ גרויסע גלאָז,
ווען זי וועט אויף דיר טאָן אַ געשרײי,
דו טרינק באַלד אויס איינס און צוויי;
זאָל זי זיך שרײַען ניט אויפֿהערן,
און דו זאָלסט נאָר די גלעזער קערן.

That's what happened in ancient times:
the Tree of Knowledge was a grapevine.
Eve talked Adam into
drinking whisky—it's no sin.
If Adam hadn't loved whisky, he would have driven Eve away.

When you feel up or down,
just drink whisky and feel merry;
when times are not good for you,
drink whisky—don't lose your courage.
Through whisky, everyone gets proud and happy—
an underling becomes a king.

I love whisky with its sweet voice.
True, it costs me my last penny;
I don't have any money any more—just a bit of faith.
True, I have very good security,
and as long as I am merry and don't want to worry,
why should I care today about what will happen tomorrow?

When I come to the end of my few years,
I want them to put whisky with me in my grave—
a flask of whisky next to the wall
and a big glass in my right hand.
When the resurrection comes, I'll be here again
and I'll drink whisky right away, in the first hour.

May God just hear my prayer
that the excise tax be repealed soon.
It's my ancestors and their sins that are responsible
for whisky's being subject to such cruel laws.
Our ancestors were saintly people—
they knew nothing of excises and bar payments.

I have heard from pious people
that things will be good when the Messiah comes:
There'll be much whisky for rich and poor
and all the rivers will be full of whisky.
I'd like to live to see the Messiah come—
I'd swim like a fish in the river.

אַזוי איז טאַקע פֿאַר צײַטן געשען;
דער עץ־הדעת איז אַ ווײַנשטאָק געווען.
די חוה האָט דעם אדם אָנגערעדט,
ער זאָל טרינקען משקה, עס איז קיין חטא.
ווען אדם וואָלט חלילה די משקה ניט ליב,
וואָלט ער זײַן חוה אַרויסגעטריבן.

ווען דו ביסט געהויבן אָדער אַרונטער,
טרינק נאָר די משקה און זײַ גאָר מונטער;
ווען דיר איז אַ מאָל די צײַט ניט גוט,
דו טרינק נאָר משקה, פֿאַרליר קיין מוט.
דורך משקה ווערט יעדער שטאָלץ און פֿריילעך;
פֿון אַן אונטער־שמש ווערט אַ מלך.

איך האָב די משקה ליב מיט אָיר אָיר זיס לשון,
אמת, זי קאָסט מיר מײַן לעצטן גראָשן,
איך האָב שוין קיין געלט, נאָר אַ ביסל נאמנות;
אמת, איך גיב גאַנץ גוטע משקנות;
אַבי איך בין לוסטיק און וויל ניט זאָרגן,
וואָס אַרט מיך הײַנט וואָס וועט זײַן מאָרגן?

מײַן ביסעלע יאָרן ווען איך וועל אויסלעבן,
וויל איך, מען זאָל מיר אין קבֿר מיטגעבן
אַ פֿעסעלע משקה נאָענט בײַ דער וואַנט,
אַ גרויסע גלאָז אין דער רעכטער האַנט;
צו תחית המתים בין איך ווידער דאָ
און טרינק באָלד משקה אין דער ערשטער שעה.

דער בורא זאָל נאָר מײַן תפֿילה צוהערן,
אַז דער אַקציז זאָל באָלד בטל ווערן.
עס זענען שולדיק די דורות מיט זייערע עבֿירות,
וואָס משקה האָט נעבעך אויף זיך די גזירות.
צדיקים זענען געווען אונדזערע אָבֿות־אבֿותינו,
זיי האָבן ניט געוווּסט פֿון אַקציז און פּיטיינע *.

איך האָב געהערט פֿון פֿרומע לײַט,
אַז גוט וועט זײַן אין משיחס צײַט:
פֿיל משקה וועט זײַן פֿאַר אָרעם און רײַך,
פֿול משקה וועט זײַן איטלעכער טײַך.
איך וואָלט שוין דערלעבן משיח זאָל קומען,
וואָלט איך ווי אַ פֿיש אין טײַך געשוווּמען.

But be that as it may,
I drink my whisky and pay taxes.
Let water run in the rivers—
I can buy my whisky in a tavern.
I constantly fulfill the mitzvah of drinking whisky,
and keep saying: *l'chaim, l'chaim*!

The Beard
(fragment)

Kokher's[8] wife comes to Poltava.
She sees her husband and doesn't recognize him immediately.
She looks: he's taken off his beard!
She starts to cry and scream.

Are you my husband, are you Kokher?
I don't recognize you—you look like a boy!
Would I have believed it if someone had told me
that my husband would shave off his beard?
Help! May the Beard protect me.

What bad thing did the Beard do to you?
Did it cost you anything?
Did it interfere with your pursuits
or ask you for something to eat?
Help! I can't forget the Beard.

Not long ago, I saw the Beard in a dream,
may it rest in peace.
One hair here and one hair there—
and next to it a scissors.
Help! Bring the Beard to me here.

Show me right away the holy place
where you left the hairs of your Beard.
I'll take them to the synagogue, to the Holy Ark.
Help! Forgive me, Beard, I'll say.

---

8. A made-up name

נאָר זאָל זיך שוין זײַן ווי עס איז,

איך טרינק מײַן משקה און צאָל אקציז.

זאָל זיך אין טײַכן וואַסער לויפֿן,

איך קען מײַן משקה אין שענקל קויפֿן;

די מיצווה פֿון משקה בין איך תמיד מקיים,

און זאָג אַלע ווײַלע: לחיים! לחיים!

די באָרד

קאַכערם ווײַב איז קיין פֿאַלטאַווע געקומען.

זי זעט איר מאַן און דערקענט אים ניט באַלד;

זי קוקט זיך צו, אַז ער האָט זײַן באָרד אַראָפּגענומען,

הייבט זי אָן צו שרײַען און מאַכט אַ געוואַלד.

ביסטו דאָס מײַן מאַן, ביסטו דאָס קאַכער?

איך דערקען דיך ניט, זעסט אויס אַ בחור!

צי וואָלט איך גלייבן, ווען איך וואָלט הערן,

אַז מײַן מאַן וועט זײַן באָרד אָפּשערן.

געוואַלד! די באָרד זאָל מיר ווערן.

וואָס האָט דיר די באָרד געטאָן אַ רעה?

צי האָט זי דיר געקאָסט עפּעס אַ הוצאה?

צי האָט זי דיר געשאַט צו דײַנע אינטערעסן,

אָדער זי בײַ דיר געבעטן עסן?

געוואַלד! איך קען די באָרד ניט פֿאַרגעסן.

גאָר ניט לאַנג האָב איך געזען אין חלום

די גאַנצע באָרד עליה השלום;

אײַן האָר אַהין און אײַן האָר אַהער —

און לעבן איר איז געלעגן אַ שער.

געוואַלד! גיב מיר די באָרד אַהער.

כאָטש ווײַז מיר געשוווינד דעם הייליקן אָרט

ווו דו האָסט געלאָזט די האָר פֿון דער באָרד;

אין שול אין אָרון קודש וועל איך זיי אַוועקטראָגן,

געוואַלד! באָרד, זײַ מוחל, וועל איך זאָגן.

———

ELIAKUM ZUNSER

(born October 28, 1836, in Vilna; died September 22, 1913, in New York)

Right after we started our series *Pearls of Yiddish Poetry*, dozens of letters started coming from readers, recalling lines or whole poems that they remembered
from their youth, but they didn't know the name of the author. Many of the songs
that were sent in were written by Eliakum Zunser, who was also famous under
the name *Elyokum Badkhn*,[9] or, as the people loved to call him: *Lyokem Badkhn*.

Even during his lifetime, Eliakum Zunser was a legend. Rich people hoped that
he would come to their children's weddings and whole families sang his songs.
His songbooks were snapped up as quickly as they appeared in print.

When he came to America in 1889, he began traveling throughout the country for
specially arranged concerts and receptions. A typical thing happened that shows
how very popular he was—Zunser tells about it in his interesting autobiography:
when he arrived in Cleveland and appeared there with his songs *Piramidn* (The
Pyramids*), Tsu Di Shtern (*To The Stars*), Der Nayntsntn Yorhundert (*The Nineteenth Century*), and other of his creations, he sensed a certain dissatisfaction in
the audience. He immediately found out the reason: a rumor had spread that it
wasn't the real Zunser who had come to Cleveland but someone who had come
to fool the audience into thinking that he was the real Eliakum Zunser. In the
street, a large crowd was waiting to beat him up (Zunser even writes that they
had assembled with the "noble intention of lynching me.") He barely escaped
from Cleveland with his life.

Eliakum Zunser started writing rhymes and clothing them in melodies very early
in life. Even before his first book of songs, *Lider Funkhoydesh (*Songs of the
Month), appeared (in 1861), he was already popular, and people used to invite
him to come and amuse them at weddings, circumcisions, and other festive occasions. The little songbook made him even more famous, and they started inviting
him to wealthy weddings in various cities throughout the country. His rhymes
and poems, which he immediately began to sing with suitable melodies, dealt not
only with moralizing to the bride and groom, as with other badkhns; Elyokum
Badkhn also responded to events of the day, ideas that had become popular, and
the most recent occurrences in general Jewish life.

---

9. A wedding entertainer who recited and sang, often in rhyme

Zunser is very modest in his autobiography when he ascribes his popularity only to the fact that he "was the first one in Russia at that time who composed his poems together with song....at that time, the Russian Jews had no other songs than mine, and in that fact lay a large part of my success."

That did play a certain role, but it was surely not the only reason for his success. Zunser, in his explanatory songs, was not, like most *Maskilic* writers at that time, a strict scolder and mocker; he was just a good friend who suffered together with his people.

In a song *Tsu Mayne Fraynd* (To My Friends), Zunser sings about it thus:

> *The development of my songs*
> *is the development of my brothers*
> *since 1825, when I began.*
> *Jews were then fanatical and unread,*
> *so I wrote for them*
> *little pieces that they could understand.*
> *And as the Jews rose higher*
> *and their fanaticism grew weaker,*
> *my songs grew more thoughtful.*
> *They searched for their method,*
> *and recognized their rhythm*
> *at whatever level I took it to.*

Zunser went along, in his homey, *badkhonish* way, accompanied his readers and listeners in all the experiences they had had. In his songs, he expressed their feelings and thoughts as they themselves would have but didn't have the talent for.

Ab Cahan tells, in the first volume of his *Bleter Fun Mayn Lebn* (Pages From My Life), of the impression that his first encounter with Eliakum Zunser made on him, when Cahan was still a young boy in Vilna. It is appropriate to present a long excerpt from his description:

> That evening, I heard Eliakum Zunser at a wedding for the first time. His songs were enormously popular, and I had heard a lot about the wonders he demonstrated as a *badkhn* and as a singer. He used to excite the audience with a new song, which they sang in every house and shop—not only in the Vilna area but throughout Lithuania and Volhynia, and Poland too. The *badkhns* of all countries used to entertain the audiences at weddings with Zunser's songs.

When the ceremony began and he started to speak to the bride, greeting her and explaining things to her, his words were built on her name, the name of the groom, and the names of their parents. From every letter he made a word, and he went thus back and forth, back and forth, again and again, without end. And his phrases came out smooth and interesting, very well done. I couldn't help but admire him. While singing, he tapped out the rhythm with his foot. That and the accompaniment of the klezmers merged into a musical unity that enchanted me. The rhythm of his singing was transmitted to his listeners like electricity. The entire audience sang along wordlessly, and wordlessly tapped out the rhythm.

Zunser's biography is an extraordinarily interesting one. If we had had a Jewish movie industry, the life story of Eliakum Zunser would have been unusually good material for a film. We could have seen, in the form of the life-history of an individual, a piece of Jewish history, with all the suffering and joy of the people: on the one hand, bitter hunger and poverty; the evil decrees of the cantonists[10] and their dark accomplices, the "catchers"[11]; a cholera epidemic that cut down old men and infants in their cradles (including Zunser's four young children); pogroms; and streams of emigration. On the other hand, however, we would have seen the spiritual life of those Jews, their drive to study Torah and raise their children to be good and pious, and their circumcisions, weddings, and other festive occasions, where they tried to forget their everyday worries and troubles and gain a little happiness. There would also have been no lack of the moving recognition and affection that the people showed to their poets, who had given them such dear gifts: hundreds of poems in which they felt their own tears, suffering, and also hopes.

Eliakum Zunser enjoyed great recognition, even in America, where his songs were not as popular as in the old country. Here too, he wrote songs in which he celebrated the freedom that Jews enjoyed here (*Kolumbus un Vashington* [Columbus and Washington]), songs in which he mourned the hard fate of the immigrants in "The Golden Land," where

The worker's life here swims away
in a river of his own sweat.

And songs about peddlers, who are

---

10. The board that designated the quotas for conscripting young children into the Czar's army
11. Men who seized young Jews for the Czar's army

wanderers, like Cain-- day and night
they are exposed to heat or cold,
have no home and no rest,
and are constantly exhausted.

However, other poets arose who expressed the immigrants' loneliness in their new home better than Zunser did. But the people didn't forget him. In 1905, in New York, there was a moving celebration in honor of the 65th anniversary of Zunser's birth. Both the Jewish intelligentsia and ordinary Jews participated. It was a true folk-holiday that expressed everyone's feeling of recognition and affection for the famous folksinger. Among those participating in the program were Abraham Goldfaden, Morris Winchevsky, Morris Rosenfeld, Abraham Liessin, the stars of the Yiddish stage Jacob P. Adler and Morris Moscowitz, the popular lecturer and folk-speaker Tsvi Hirsh Maslianski, and many others.

That was also the last time that Zunser improvised a song in front of a large audience (to the melody of *Shivat Tsiyon* [Return to Zion]), and, moved, thanked the audience for the honor they were bestowing on him.

There are differences of opinion among critics and literary historians about Zunser's literary talent. No one, however, denies Zunser's great accomplishments as a teacher, an explainer and popularizer of ideas to the Jewish folk-masses of his time. Samuel Niger writes that "Elyokum Badkhn and his songs probably did more for the popularization of ideas in his time than the aphorisms in the newspapers, which the masses read very little and understood even less."

Moyshe-Leyb Halpern, the modern poet, expressed after Zunser's death the feelings of many others when he wrote in a poem:

Sleep, sleep, you noble man. Your great love blossoms
and glows in our blood. The song you didn't get to sing
will not go lost. It's true that time
has taken us far away from you....generations away.
The little song that you ignited glows—
it glows and sounds your unsung song in us.

The Flower

Where everyone travels, in the middle of the road,
there is a wonderful flower.
It's been lying there and rotting for several days now.
The wind blows it around,
and it cries out and weeps a great plea:
"Slowly—watch where you're going!
Have mercy—see, you're trampling
a flower with a beautiful blossom!
Someone have pity—
just come here
and pick up a flower that sparkles!
Carry me back
to where I came from,
to where they first planted me.

"For when I see flowers now on every side,
I cry a river of tears.
I remember my previous happiness—
I was the equal of any other flower.
When I blossomed in the emperor's garden
and the sun shone brightly,
dozens of servants tended to me.
Just see what has become of me now:
stepped on and trampled,
soaked,
my flowers deprived of their color;
I lie in the garbage,
the rain pours,
there is no pity for me."

As the flower weeps there and cries out,
every man's heart is moved.
An angel comes from far away
and hears its wailing and pain.
"Tell me, flower, tell me the story—
you move my heart tremendously.
Where did you grow? What's that place called?
How do you come to be here on the road?"

די בלום

וווּ אַלע פֿאָרן, אין מיטן וועג,

ליגט דאָרט אַ טײַערע בלום;

ליגט און פֿוילט שוין אייניקע טעג,

דער ווינט וואַרפֿט איר אַרום;

און זי שרײַט און וויינט מיט גרויס געבעט:

‟פּאַמעלעך, זעט ווי איר גייט!

האָט רחמנות, זעט, איר צעטרעט

אַ בלום מיט אַ פּרעכטיקן קווייט!

רחמנות האָט ווער,

קומט נאָר אַהער —

הייבט אויף אַ בלום, וואָס זי גלאַנצט!

טראָגט מיך אַהין,

פֿון וואַנען איך בין,

וווּ מע האָט מיך צום ערשטן ערפֿלאַנצט.

אַז איך זע איצט בלומען פֿון יעדער זײַט,

גיסט פֿון מיר טרערן אַ טײַך;

איך דערמאָן זיך מײַן גליק פֿון די פֿאָריקע צײַט —

געוווען מיט אַלע בלומען צו גלײַך...

אין קייזערלעכן גאָרטן ווען איך האָב געבליט,

און די זון האָט מיר ליכטיק געשײַנט,

צענדליקע דינער האָבן מיך געהיט —

טאָ זעט נאָר דעם סוף פֿון מיר הײַנט:

דער טרעט אין דער קוועטשט.

צעווייקט און צענעצט,

די בלעטער — אַראָפּ פֿון קאָליר;

איך ליג אויפֿן מיסט,

דער רעגן ער גיסט,

עס איז גאָר קיין רחמנות אויף מיר”.

ווי די בלום וויינט דאָ און שרײַט,

עס צענעמט יעדער מענטשן זײַן הערץ,

קומט אָן אַ מלאך גאָר פֿון דער זײַט

און הערט דאָ איר שרײַען, איר שמערץ.

‟זאָג מיר, דו בלום, זאָג מיר דעם וואָרט,

צענעמסט מיך מײַן הארץ אָן אַ ברעג;

וווּ ביסטו געוואָקסן? ווי רופֿט מען דעם אָרט?

ווי קומסטו אַהער אויפֿן וועג?”

The flower shrieks:
"Oh woe is me, woe!
Don't you remember me at all from before?
I'm from Jerusalem—
'Jew' is my name—
at least *you* should have pity on me!

"For two thousand years, if you had seen me
when I had my kingdom,
you yourself would have marveled at me,
at the beauty of my every petal.
Priests, Levites, innumerable generals—
I boasted of my blossoms then.
Then they suddenly tore me out of my place,
and I have been wandering for nearly two thousand years.

"Wherever I've been,
I've seen murderousness:
they tore me limb from limb,
burned me, cut me, and inflicted other indignities,
and only because I am a Jew!"

Thus did the Jew wander once,
like the flower on the road with its blossom.
One takes his honor, one calls him *zhid*,[12]
one tramples him.
And now he's lost his courage and boldness,
his power and strength.
He has only his faith—that's still his consolation
in the long dark night.
Ah, my heart breaks with pain,
for you too once blossomed!
Such a beautiful flower,
and everyone tramples it.
How can you not have pity?

As soon as the angel hears it mention
its ancient pedigree in Zion,
he places it amid all the flowerpots

---

12. A Slavic pejorative name for a Jew.

טוט זי אַ געשרײַ:

„אוי, ווינד איז מיר, ווײ!

צי דו דערקענסט מיר שוין גאָר ניט פֿון פֿרי'ר?

פֿון ירושלים בין איך,

'ייִד' רופֿט מען מיך,

האָב דו כאָטש רחמנות אויף מיר!

פֿאַר צוויי טויזנט יאָר ווען דו וואָלטסט מיך זען,

בשעת איך האָב מײַן מלוכה געהאָט,

וואָלטסט אַלײן דיך פֿאַרוווּנדערט ווי איך בין געווען,

די שײנהײט פֿון מײַן יעדער בלאַט —

כּהנים, לוויים, יעדערעלער אַן אַ שיעור,

איך האָב דאַמאָלס שטאָלצירט אין פֿלאָר.

דאַן האָט מען פֿלוצלינג אויסגעריסן מיר,

איך וואָלגער מיך באַלד צוויי טויזנט יאָר...

ווּ איך בין געווען,

האָב איך רציחות געזען,

גערוסן מיר גליד פֿאַר גליד;

געבּרענט און געשניטן.

און נאָר מער צרות געליטן —

און נאָר ווײַל איך בין אַ ייִד!"...

אַזוי האָט זיך אַ מאָל געוואָלגערט דער ייִד,

ווי די בלום אויפֿן וועג מיט אַ איר צוועט;

דער נעמט אים אים זײַן כּבֿוד, דער רופֿט אים „זשיד",

דער מיט די פֿיס אים צעטרעט.

און ער האָט שוין פֿאַרלאָרן זײַן מוט און זײַן דרייסט,

פֿאַרלאָרן זײַן קראָפֿט און זײַן מאַכט;

מער ניט די אמונה, דאָס איז נאָך זײַן טרייסט

אין דער לאַנגער, פֿינצטערער נאַכט.

אָך, מײַן הערץ

פֿלאַצט מיר פֿון שמערץ,

דו האָסט דאָך אַ מאָל אויך געבּליט!

אַזוי אַ שיינער צוועט

יעדערער טרעט,

ווי האָט איר עם קיין רחמנות ניט?...

ווי נאָר דער מלאך הערט איר דאָ דערמאָנען

איר אַלטן יִיחום פֿון ציון,

זעצט ער איר צעווישן אַלע וואָזאָנען,

and it begins to blossom again.
And he consoles it with his sympathy:
"Wipe away your tears—the sun will soon start to shine for you.
I won't disrupt your faith, God forbid—
I'll just spruce you up!"
So the flower asks him:
"Tell me your name,
let's know your name."
He answers it:
"My name is Alexander[13],
Czar of Russia."

Return To Zion
(fragment)

Lift up thine eyes round about and behold: All these gather themselves together and come to thee
(Isaiah 49:18)

What do I see through the windowpanes?
They're flying toward me like doves—
my Joseph and my Benjamin are knocking on my door!
O Heaven, God, the wonder!
for I am seeing my children,
the most beloved, the most faithful, coming back to me!
You've been gone so many years
that I thought I was lost,
a desolate widow whose table was deserted.
How have things gone with you
since they captured you?
How are Judah and Ephraim? Tell me about them!

Come back, years of long ago!
I've become young,
I discard my sorrow—
come here, my silk dress!
My house becomes full again,
my heart and limbs grow lighter—
many of my children are coming back with joy!

---

13. Czar Alexander II (1818-1881) promulgated reforms that improved the lot of the Russian Jews

זי הייבט ווידער שוין אָן צו בלוּיִען.

און ער טרייסט איר מיט מיטלייד: „וויש אָפּ דײַנע טרערן,

די זון הייבט דיר אָן שוין צו שײַנען;

איך וועל דיר חלילה דײַן אמונה ניט שטערן,

איך וועל דיר נאָך פוצן און פײַנען!"

פרעגט זי בײַ עם:

„זאָג מיר דײַן שם,

לאָמיך וויסן דעם נאָמען פון זיי;"

ענטפֿערט ער מיר

„דער נאָמען פון מיר

איז אַלכסנדר, קײַזער פֿון ראָסיי".

שיבֿת־ציון

(פֿראַגמענט)

שׂאי סביב עיניך וראי נקבצו באו לך וכר
(ישעיה מט, 18)

וואָס זע איך דורך די שויבן?

עס פֿליִען אָן ווי טויבן

מײַן יוסף, מיטן בנימין קלאַפֿן אין מײַן טיר!

אָ חימל, גאָט, די ווּנדער!

איך זע דאָך מײַנע קינדער,

די ליבסטע, די געטרײַסטע קומען אָן צו מיר!

אַוועק אַזוי פֿיל יאָרן,

געמיינט איך בין פֿאַרלאָרן,

אַן אלמנה אַ פֿאַרוויסטע — לײדיק בײַ מײַן טיש...

מיט אײַך ווי איז געגאַנגען,

צייט מע האָם אײַך געפֿאַנגען?

וואָס מאַכט יהודה און אפרים? ניט מיר אַ נערום!

אַהער קומט, יענע יאָרן!

איך בין יונג געוואָרן,

איך וואָרף אַראָפּ מײַן טרויער, אַהער — מײַן זײַדן קלייד!...

פֿול ווערט מײַן הויז ווידער,

עס הייבט דאָס האַרץ, די גלידער,

פֿיל פֿון מײַנע קינדער פֿאָרן אָן מיט פֿרייד!

Tears of joy are flowing—
let me hug you, kiss you.
Rest your bones with me, beloved guests—
you'll receive every pleasure from me.
You'll know no strange tables, only your mother's hospitality!

These young people
will be blessed by the world.
They've abandoned houses, possessions,
glitter, happiness, and influence.
Educated persons,
highly civilized,
they want to be sacrifices for the entire people!
They've decided,
despite all their regrets,
to remove all the stones
that block their way—
to bear hardships like those in Moses' time,
and their names shall remain with Ezra's[14] till the final days!

The Plow
(fragment)

As for the trafficker, the balances of deceit are in his hand. He loveth to oppress. (Hosea 12:8)
I will yet again make thee to dwell in tents, as in the days of the appointed season. (Hosea 12:10)

The plow
brings good fortune,
the true happiness of life—
I want for nothing.
When morning comes,
I need not borrow or lend—
I needn't worry my head
about my daily expenses.

---

14. Ezra the Scribe, 6th Century BCE Jewish prophet, generally credited with assembling and editing the Torah into its current form.

פֿון שֿימחה טרערן פֿליסן,

לאָזט מיך האַלדזן, קושן,

רוט אײַך אויס בײַ מיר די בײַנער, מײַנע הערצנסגעסט !

איר וועט בײַ מיר קריגן

אַלע פֿאַרגעניגן,

איר וועט ניט וויסן פֿרעמדע טישן, נאָר די מוטערס קעסט !

אָט דיזע יונגע מענטשן

וועמ די וועלט זיי בענטשן,

פֿאַרלאָזן הײַזער, גיטער, גלאַנץ און גליק און פֿראַל !

מענטשן געשטודירטע,

הויך ציוויליזירטע

ווילן זײַן קרבנות פֿאַר דעם גאַנצן כּלל ! ...

זיי האָבן זיך באַשלאָסן

אויף אַלערליי פֿאַרדראָסן,

נאָר אָפּצוווואַרפֿן אַלע שטיינער וואָס ליגט אויפֿן וועג ;

צו יעדן שוועריקייטן

ווי אין משהם ציויטן,

און זייער נאָמען בלײַבט מיט עזראס ביז די לעצטע טעג !

די סאָכע
(פֿראַגמענט)

כנען בידו מאזני מרמה לעשק אהב (הושע יב, 8)

עוד אושיבך באהלים כימי מועד (הושע יב, 10)

אין סאָכע

ליגט די מזל־ברכה,

דער ווארער גליק פֿון לעבן,

קיין זאַך מיר ניט פֿעלט !

עס קומט דער פֿרימאָרגן,

איך דאַרף ניט לײַען, באָרגן,

דער מוח דאַרף ניט זאָרגן

אויף טאָג־הוצאות, געלט.

I've laid by for winter,
in a well stocked bin.
I sow and reap cheerfully—
free in God's world.

Whose riches
can compare to mine?
Who lives quietly, happily,
like me, a farmer in the field?
If God but sends rain,
I feel happiness
and I sow sheaves
as payment to the world.
I provide nourishment to people,
merchants and food sellers,
sailors and commissioners—
and my money is clean.

I am not burdened
by fashion,
as they are in the cities,
the more they earn.
A straw hat and a coat of coarse cloth
I wear for years and years,
and I manage my household
on the same old piece of ground.
My sickle is my treasurer,
my rooster is my alarm clock,
the sun is my timekeeper,
my fan is the wind.

My wife
needs no nanny,
no maid, no housekeeper,
no one to eat me out of house and home.
She needs no hat, no feathers,

ס׳איז אָנגעגרייט אויף ווינטער

אַ זאָסיק אַ געזונטער,

איך זיי, איך שנײַד גאַנץ מונטער —

פֿרײַ אין גאָטעס וועלט...

פֿון רײַכן

ווער קען זיך צו מיר גלײַכן?

ווער לעבט רויִק, גליקלעך

ווי איך, פּויער אין פֿעלד?

גיט נאָר גאָט דעם רעגן,

פֿיל איך גליק און זעגן,

איך פֿיר שוין סנאָפּעס-וועגן,

חיונה פֿאַר דער וועלט.

איך טו לײַט ערנערן,

מאַרקלײַט און שפּײַכלערן,

שיפֿערס, קאָמיסיאָנערן —

און כּשר איז מײַן געלט...

פֿון מאָדעס

האָב איך קיין הכבדות,

ווי אין שטאָט פֿאַרלעבט מען

מער פֿיל מע פֿאַרדינט...

אַ שטרויהוט און אַ סוויטע

טראָג איך אָפּ אַ שמיטה,

און מיט די זעלבע שיטה

פֿירט זיך מײַן געזינט.

דער סערף איז מײַן קאַסירער,

דער האָן — מײַן רעפּוטירער,

די זון איז מײַן צײַטפֿירער,

מײַן פֿעקכער איז דער ווינט...

מײַן דאָמע

ברויכט ניט קיינע אמע,

קיין הויזמעדכען, קיין באָנע,

קיין פֿרעסער אויפֿן קאַרק...

זי דאַרף קיין הוט, קיין פֿעדער,

doesn't walk in the gardens,
doesn't go to the baths
but rather to market on Friday,
no decorative make-up.
She's her own nurse and mistress,
and in the field a free spirit,
strong and healthy.

After some years
a child is born to me.
My income grows,
I buy another parcel of land.
In the city,
the more children, the harder for the father—
he must provide food
and they're a noose around his neck.
For me,
when children grow up,
my work gets easier,
and every single one of them
is a joy for me.

I sew a simple little dress
for my little girl,
and make a match for her
without jewelry or a dowry.
Look at the brides in the city:
even in their abject poverty,
they have to gather everything valuable from their houses,
whatever is there, for dowry,
but it's easy for me to find my girl a groom,
and from hereabouts, too:
I give two goats as dowry
and she is happy with her husband.

Let God but bless
the people who support Zion
and the land will be renewed!
Just bless, O God, those who dig in the earth,
the defenders of the colonies,
the worker-soldiers,

שפּאַצירט ניט אין די סעדער,
פֿאָרט ניט אין די בעדער,
ליבערשט — פֿרייַטיק צום מאַרק...
קיין פֿון קיין פֿאַרמאַסקירטן,
אַליין אי אַם, אי ווירטין,
און אין פֿעלד אַ הירטין,
און איז געזונט און שטאַרק !

מיט יאָרן

מיר ווערט אַ קינד געבאָרן,
ווערט גרעסער מיטן הכנסה,
איך קויף צו ערד אַ שטיק.
אין שטאָט אַ קינד וואָס מערער,
ווערט דעם פֿאָטער שווערער :
ער מוז זייַן אַ דערנערער —
אויפֿן האַלדז אַ שטריק...
בייַ מיר עם וואָקסן קינדער,
ווערט מייַן אַרבעט לינדער,
און יעדערער באַזונדער
איז פֿאַר מיר אַ גליק !

מייַן מיידל

ניי איך אַ פּראָסט קלײדל,
און טו מיט איר אַ שידוך
אָן צירונג, אָן נדן.
זעט אין שטאָט די כלות,
שטעלן פּראָסט בדלות,
ראַמט פֿון שמוב אויס אַלעם,
וואָס נאָר איז פֿאַראָן...
מיר איז לייַכט צו קריגן
אַ חתן גראַד אַ הינג,
און גיב נדן צוווײ צינג,
און לעבט גליקלעך פֿאַר דעם מאָן !

בענטשן

זאָל נאָר גאָט די מענטשן,
וועלכע שטײצן ציון,
צוריק דאָס לאַנד באַנייַט !
בענטש נאָר, גאָט, די ריצער,
די קאָלאָניען-באַשיצער,

the Zerubavels[15] of this era.
When the colonists
number in the millions,
only then will Zion remember
these great people.

---

15. The leader of the Jews returning from the Babylonian exile

די אַרבעטער־שטיצער —
די זרבבלם פֿון דער צייַט.
ווען פֿון די קאַלאַניען
וועט ווערן מיליאַנען,
וועט ציון ערשט דערמאַנען
אַט דיזע גרויסע לייַט!

ABRAHAM GOLDFADEN

(previous surname Goldenfodim)

(Born July 12, 1840, in Old Constantine in the District of Volyhnia, Russia; died January 9, 1908 in New York)

When Abraham Goldfaden died in New York on January 9, 1908, he had one of the largest funerals that had ever taken place in that city of millions of inhabitants. *The New York World*, in its issue of January 11, one day after the funeral, wrote in an editorial:

> A funeral that draws 75,000 mourners, brings commerce to a standstill, and fills the streets so much that 250 policemen were needed to keep order, is remarkable, even in a city with a mass population. Who was the cause of this stream of people? A great financier, a Tammany boss, a railroad magnate with an international reputation, or a bank president who committed suicide?

The newspaper gives this answer:

> He was no more than a modest poet and dramatist, "the Yiddish Shakespeare." It is very doubtful that his name was known in even one Fifth Avenue house, but he was known in all the tenements. It is hard to imagine such widespread mourning west of the Bowery. The residents of the Jewish Quarter still value the old ideals, and they work hard not to be swallowed up in the big-city civilization. Their concepts of greatness are not related to beautiful palaces or large amounts of money in safes. They're still people with heart, from the Old World, with primitive ideas about current-day concepts of greatness and success.

On January 11th, the *New York Times*, too, had an editorial about Goldfaden's funeral, wherein it wrote:

> There may be one or two English poets who can expect to have big funerals when they die. People will assemble to honor the big names, but the proportion of real mourners will be very small in comparison with Goldfaden's funeral. Goldfaden was a poet and a prophet. It may be that many of the people who filled the streets during the funeral were drawn by pure curiosity, but there were many indications of the great respect for and love of that person

and his works, which can hardly be imagined at the funeral of any poet who writes in English here in this country.

Yes, the funeral was a big one, perhaps the biggest that New York had ever seen. But not everyone knew that the person who was being accompanied to his eternal rest with so much sorrow died lonely, in great hunger and poverty. In the last years of his life in New York, the Father of the Yiddish theater, the author of 60 plays and hundreds of songs, lived in loneliness and poverty, though his plays were put on often and many impresarios, directors, and stars gained fame and riches thanks to his talent.

* * *

Goldfaden (whose real name was Avrom Goldenfodim) began to write as a young boy, and he continued to write in Hebrew and Yiddish even while he was in rabbinical school in Zhitomir, from which he was graduated in 1866. He did not become a rabbi. He tried his luck at teaching, lecturing, and publishing a weekly Yiddish newspaper, first in Lemberg (in 1875 and 1876, together with his childhood friend Joel Linetsky) and later in Czernowitz, but without much material success. But he never stopped writing. In 1865, in Zhitomir, his first book of Hebrew poems appeared, and in 1866, also in Zhitomir, his first book in Yiddish: *Dos Yidele* (The Little Jew*)*. His name quickly became well known among the *Maskilim*, and also among the "Broder singers," who sang his songs.

After his failure with the newspaper in Czernowitz, Goldfaden went to Jassy (Romania), where he hoped to publish another newspaper. But a different role was fated for him there: "father of the Yiddish theater." And thanks to him, Jassy became the "cradle of Yiddish theater."

How that happened is interesting. When the Broder singers, who used to perform in a beer garden to entertain the audience, learned of Goldfaden's arrival in Jassy, they invited him to come and sing his songs. He came, but instead of singing joyful songs, as the audience had expected, he stood up and read his serious maskilic poems. It didn't take long for the audience, which had expected to have fun, to start hooting and whistling at the poet-reader. Goldfaden fled in disappointment, but he was convinced that the audience needed to be educated... it was necessary, he thought, to give the audience, in addition to entertaining pieces, pieces with historical content from which Jews could learn about their personal life and the life of their people. But that had to be done with a light touch, playfully, so the audience would enjoy it and would be willing to listen.

Shortly thereafter, he and two talented Broder singers, Israel Grodner and Moyshe Finkel, created in a beer-garden in Jassy a Yiddish theater for which he wrote a two-act play. The audience's enthusiasm encouraged Goldfaden to write other, longer pieces, till he arrived at his famous operettas *Di Kishef-Makherin* (The Witch), *Di Beyde Kuni-Lemls* (The Two Kuni-Lemls*)*, *Dokter Almasada* (Doctor Almasada*)*, *Shulamis*, *Bar Kokhba*, *Akeydes Yitskhok* (The Sacrifice of Isaac*)*, and many, many others.

Goldfaden created itinerant troupes of Yiddish actors; he became not only the writer and composer but also the director and producer. He went from city to city, and everywhere he wrote and played in Yiddish theater. The heartfelt songs and melodies of his plays were immediately seized on by the audiences, and mothers began to sing their children to sleep with *Rozhinkes Mit Mandlen* (Raisins and Almonds*)* from *Shulamis*, and with *Shlof Zhe, Shlof, Mayn Sorele* (Sleep, Sleep, Little Sarah*)* from *The Sacrifice of Isaac*. Everyone started to sing the songs from *The Witch: Hotzmakh Iz a Blinder (*Hotzmakh Is Blind*)*, *Tsu Dayn Geburtstog (*Happy Birthday*)*, and *Heyse Babkelekh (*Little Hotcakes*)*. Nationalistically oriented youths sang with great fervor the songs from *Bar Kokhba*: *Veynt Zhe, Ale Tsiyon's Tekhter* (Weep, All Ye Daughters of Zion), *Gekumen Iz Di Tsayt* (The Time Has Come*)*, and *A Pastekhl Iz Geven Amol In Dem Land Knan* (There Was Once a Little Shepherd in the Land of Canaan*)*. Revolutionary youths too found in Goldfaden's *Bar Kokhba* what they were looking for: encouragement in the fight against national and social oppression. Some theater historians write that because of the play *Bar Kokhba*, in which Goldfaden celebrated the Jewish struggle against the Roman oppressors, the czarist censor prohibited the playing of Yiddish theater in Russia; that was in August 1883. Goldfaden, however, didn't give up his dream of making the Yiddish theater a reality. He went to Warsaw, where it didn't take long before he succeeded, with the secret backing of a Russian theater, in staging Yiddish theater in Warsaw. Great masses of people came to his presentations, and they saw in his theater not only entertainment but also an important factor in the revival of their own national culture.

In 1887, Goldfaden went to New York, where his pieces were being put on successfully. There great disappointment awaited him: because of fear of competition, theater people who wrote and acted in cheap, trashy vehicles interfered with the creation of a Yiddish theater under his management. Goldfaden suffered in New York for two years, and then decided to go back to Europe, disappointed. In 1900, several evenings were organized for him in London, in honor of his 60th birthday. Nokhum Sokolov, Reuben Braynin, and others wrote warm articles about him. They created a fund that helped him in his difficult financial circumstances.

In 1903, Goldfaden, at the invitation of his brothers, again came to New York. A welcoming reception and benefit performance was organized for him, with the following program:

1. The first act of *Shulamis*, with the participation of Boris Thomashefsky, Madam Karp, and others.
2. An act of *Brayndele the Cossack*, with the participation of Jacob Adler, Mrs Adler, and others.
3. An act of *The Two Kuni-Lemels*, with the participation of Bessie Thomashefsky, Sigmund Mogulesco, Morris Finkel, and others.
4. An act of *Bar Kokhba*, with the participation of Jacob Adler, Boris Thomashefsky, and others.

Though the reception was a great success, which encouraged Goldfaden somewhat, new disappointments awaited him here. In 1906, Goldfaden wrote a new play, *Ben Ami*, and sold it to Jacob P. Adler. Adler didn't put the play on—he sold it to Thomashefsky. Several weeks before his death, the play was finally staged, but Goldfaden got no pleasure out of it--he had wanted it played as a drama, without music, but Thomashefsky didn't listen to his demands and did introduce music. On the fifth day after the premiere, Goldfaden became ill, and a few days later he passed into eternity.

In this case, "passed into eternity" is not just a phrase. Goldfaden's theatrical pieces are still staged, 120 years after he wrote them, and are staged with great success. His songs are sung by millions of Jews. In Israel, they put on his *The Witch* in Hebrew, and made a movie of his *The Two Kuni-Lemels*. Many of his songs and tunes have become part of Yiddish folk-music and pass from generation to generation.

Raisins and Almonds

In the Holy Temple, off in a corner,
there sits Bas Tsiyon,[16] the widow, alone.
Rocking her only son, Yidele[17] dearest,
she sings him a beautiful lullaby tone:
ay-lyu-lyu-lyu.

Under Yidele's crib, so very small
stands the purest white kid, not very tall.
The kid to the market's now gone away--
you'll make your living that way:
dealing raisins and almonds—
so sleep now, Yidele, sleep!

This sweet song tells us what we can foresee:
spread throughout the world you'll someday be;
you'll sell your barley and wheat all day,
and you'll grow rich that way;
you'll deal with raisins and almonds,
so sleep now, Yidele, sleep!

There will come a day of money men;
banks and checks will rule the whole world then;
the greatest banker you'll be that day,
and you'll grow rich that way.
So dream of raisins and almonds—
and sleep now, Yidele, sleep!

There will come a time of railroad trains,
running quite far and wide across the plains.
You will ride iron rails all day,
and grow rich in that way.
So dream of raisins and almonds—
and sleep now, Yidele, sleep!

And when you, Yidele, grow very rich,
please remember this song, its lovely pitch;

---

16. Literally, daughter of Zion; figuratively, the mother of the Jewish people
17. Literally, a boy's name; figuratively, the Jewish people

ראָזשינקעס מיט מאַנדלען

אין דעם בית-המיקדש, אין אַ ווינקל חדר,
זיצט די אַלמנה בת-ציון אַליין,
איר בן-יחידל, ייִדעלען, וויגט זי כסדר,
און זינגט אים צום שלאָפֿן אַ לידל שיין: אַלאַ...

אונטער ייִדעלעס וויגעלע
שטייט אַ קלאָר-ווײַס ציגעלע,
דאָס ציגעלע איז געפֿאָרן האַנדלען,
— דאָס וועט זײַן דײַן באַרוף ; —
ראָזשינקעס מיט מאַנדלען,
שלאָף זשע, ייִדעלע, שלאָף ! —

אין דעם לידל, מײַן קינד, ליגט פֿיל נבֿיאות:
אַז דו וועסט אַ מאָל זײַן צעזײט אויף דער וועלט,
אַ סוחר וועסטו זײַן פֿון אַלע תבֿ'אות,
און וועסט אין דעם אויך פֿאַרדינען פֿיל געלט.
ראָזשינקעס מיט מאַנדלען,
שלאָף זשע, ייִדעלע, שלאָף.

עס וועט קומען אַ צײַט פֿון ווערטפּאַפּירן,
קאָנטאָרן וועלן זײַן אין דער גאַנצער וועלט,
דער גרעסטער וועסטו זײַן פֿון די באַנקירן,
און וועסט אין דעם אויך פֿאַרדינען פֿיל געלט.
און אַז דו וועסט ווערן רײַך אאַז"וו.

עס וועט קומען אַ צײַט פֿון אײַזנבאַנען,
זיי וועלן פֿאַרפֿלייצן אַ האַלבע וועלט ;
אײַזערנע וועגן וועסטו אויסשפּאַנען
און וועסט אין דעם אויך פֿאַרדינען פֿיל געלט.
און אַז דו וועסט ווערן רײַך אאַז"וו.

און אַז דו וועסט ווערן רײַך, ייִדעלע,
זאָלסטו זיך דערמאָנען אין דעם לידעלע:

sing of raisins and almonds—all the joy that life brings
from dealing in all kinds of sweet things,
so sleep now, Yidele, sleep!

The Young Soul

Everything is asleep—it's midnight;
not a creature is stirring.
but the silvery moon, all alone,
is strolling among the stars.

Then when sleep makes you tired,
closes everyone's eyes,
an angel flies down
from Heaven at midnight.

In his arms, hugged tightly,
he carries a young soul.
"What do you want from me? Where are you taking me?"
the soul asks him.

"Why are you taking me away from joyous Heaven?
Where are you dragging me so quickly?
I hear a noise, a commotion, a tumult—
I feel a fresh breeze now."

"Don't be afraid, little soul,"
the angel tries to convince it.
"I'll settle you in a fine house—
there you'll live and be happy.

"They'll crown you with a new name—
human being, they'll call you. Do you understand?
You'll live among human beings,
so behave like one there.

"When you begin to understand the world better,
they'll give you a precious amulet,
a new one you haven't seen before;
it's called a 'coin.'

ראָשינקעס מיט מאַנדלען !
— דאָס וועט זײַן דײַן באַרוף —
ייִדעלע וועט אַלץ האַנדלען !
שלאָף זשע, ייִדעלע, שלאָף !

די יונגע נשמה

געשלאָפֿן איז אַלעם, האַלבע נאַכט איז געווען,
קיין שום בריאה האָט זיך גערירט,
נאָר די זילבערנע לבֿנה איינע אַליין
האָט זיך צווישן די שטערן שפּאַצירט.

דעמאָלט, ווען דער שלאָף מיד מאַכט,
פֿאַרשליסט אַלע מענטשנס אויגן,
איז פֿון דעם הימל אין דער האַלבער נאַכט
אַ מלאך אַראָפּגעפֿלויגן.

און אויף די הענט, צוגעטוליעט צו זיך,
האָט ער אַ יונגע נשמה געטראָגן,
— וואָס ווילסטו פֿון מיר ? וווּהין טראָגסטו מיך, —
הייבט אים אָן די נשמה צו זאָגן.

— וואָס נעמסטו מיך צו פֿון פֿריילעכן הימל,
וווּהין שלעפּסטו מיך אַזוי געשווינד ?
עפֿעס הער איך אַ רעש, אַ געוואַלד, אַ געטימל *,
עפֿעס נײַע לופֿט פֿיל איך אַצינד.

— האָב ניט מורא, נשמהלע מײַנס —
הייבט איר אָן דער מלאך אײַנרײדן —
איך וועל דיך באַזעצן אין אַ הײַזל אַ פֿײַנס,
דו וועסט דאָרט לעבן אין פֿרײדן.

מיט אַ נײַעם נאָמען וועט מען דיך קרוינען,
מענטש וועסטו היסן — פֿאַרשטייסט וואָס איך מיין ? —
צווישן מענטשן וועסטו דאָרט ווינען,
און זאָלסט דיך דאָרט מענטשלעך באַגיין.

אַז דו וועסט אָנהייבן בעסער, די וועלט פֿאַרשטיין,
וועט מען דיר געבן אַ טײַערע קמיע,
אַ נײַס, וואָס דו האָסט ביז אָהער ניט געזען,
זי הייסט מיט דעם נאָמען מטבּע:..

"And you'll have to be careful how you handle it—
it's a magnet, it's magic, it's money!
It can give you the world to see—
it can lay waste your world.

"I want to show you right now
a bit of what the coin can do.
Beneath us you see a great city—
look to where I am pointing.

"Look—someone's standing in the cemetery—
he's digging up a corpse.
He's taking the shroud off the bones—
wants to sell it for money.

"Next to the synagogue—look—
there sits an orphan girl, freezing from the cold;
her guardians have driven her out with whips
and have stolen all her money.

"There's a merchant riding in a broad wagon,
with his merchandise wrapped up, hidden.
See how they lead him in chains now—
he's committed great sins for money.

"Look—in a synagogue
very pious people are sitting.
The congregation is sitting there thinking—
they're thinking about selling people for money.

"And someone is leading them by the nose,
doing whatever he pleases with them.
He's the boss of the city, does all kinds of bad things
and buries them—all with his money.

"There sits a man drinking wine with his buddy—
speaking with him in a friendly way and having fun.
Look—he's putting poison into his cup;
he stands to inherit money from him.

און מיט איר דארפסטו זיך היטן ווי צו באגיין,
ווי איז מאַגנעט, זי איז בישוף, זי איז געלט!
זי קען דיר געבן די וועלט צו זען,
זי קען דיר פֿאַרווייסטן דײַן וועלט.

אָט וועל איך דיר אַ ביסל ווײַזן אויפֿן אָרט,
וואָס פֿאַר אַ זאַכן די ממבע טוט אָפּ;
אונטער אונדז זעסטו אַ גרויסע שטאָט דאָרט,
קוק זשע, ווי איך ווײַז דיר אָראָפּ.

זע — אויפֿן בית־הקבֿרות אָט שטײם אײנער,
און האָט פֿון קבֿר אַ מת אויפֿגעשטעלט;
די תּכריכים ציט ער אָפּ פֿון די בײנער,
ער וויל זיי פֿאַרקויפֿן פֿאַר געלט.

נעבן דער שול — זע — דאָרט זיצט
אַ יתומה און פֿריורט נעבעך פֿאַר קעלט;
אָפּעקונעס האָבן איר אַרויסגעשמיצט,
און האָבן באַראַבעווועט איר געלט.

דאָרט פֿאָרט זיך אַ סוחר אין אַ וואָגן אַ ברייטן,
מיט זײַן סחורה פֿאַרזוויקלט, פֿאַרשטעלט,
זע — ווי מען פֿירט אים שוין דאָרט אין קייטן,
ער האָט פֿיל געזינדיקט פֿאַר געלט.

קוק, — אין אַ שטוב זיצן אַ גאַנצע נאַכט
מענטשן פֿרומע, איינס אין דער וועלט;
דאָ זיצט דאָס קהל, מע קלערט, מע טראַכט
מענטשן פֿאַרקויפֿן פֿאַר געלט.

און איינער פֿירט זיי דאָרט בײַ די נעז
און טוט מיט זיי וואָס אים געפֿעלט;
ער איז דער שטאָט־באַלעבאָס, ער טוט אַלעם בייז
און באַגראַבט זיי אַלץ מיט זײַן געלט.

דאָ זיצט איינער און טרינקט מיט זײַן חבֿר ווײַן
און רעדט מיט אים פֿרײַנדלעך און קווועלט;
קוק, — ער טוט אים סם אין בעכער ארײַן,
דאָ דאַרף ער בײַ אים ירשענען געלט.

"There's a rich man sleeping in his bedroom.
Look—murderers surround his house.
They wake him from sleep, grit their teeth:
'Give us the keys to your money!'

"Look—they unsheath their knives
and kill him.
Why are you thrashing about, little soul? What's wrong?
Why are you trembling with fear?"

"No, holy angel—I'm not used to all that.
I can't manage in such a world.
I'm better off at home, I beg you—
I don't see anything good there."

"No, child—you've only seen the faults:
people trying to get rich by injustice.
You can live very peacefully and nicely—
you need but behave justly.

"Love your neighbor as yourself—
don't think everything is about 'me.'
Help him overcome his commonness—
don't begrudge his being richer than you.

"Live justly and with rejoicing—
life, after all, is just a short bridge.
Time carries the years away as a wind carries a straw—
very soon you'll be back here again.

"Go, my child—go for a little walk.
Go dance around a bit.
But don't carouse, don't be mischievous, don't mislead people—
come home unblemished.

"I don't have to tell you the rest;
when you're there you'll figure it out.
Now look: dawn is breaking in the East—
I have to go to my rest now."

דאַרט שלאָפֿט זיך אַ גבֿיר אין זײַן ספּאַלניע אַליין,
קוק, — רוצחים באַלאַגערן זײַן געצעלט;
זיי וועקן אים פֿון שלאָף, קריצן מיט די ציין;
— „דעם שליסל גיב אונדז פֿון דײַן געלט!"

זע, — זיי נעמען שוין מעסערם אַפֿיר,
זיי קוילן אים שוין ביז אַן עק,
וואָס ווארפֿסטו זיך, גשמהלע, וואָס איז מיט דיר?
וואָס ציטערסטו עפּעס פֿאַר שרעק?

— ניין, הייליקער מלאך, איך בין ניט געוווינט צו דעם,
מיט אַזאַ וועלט קום איך ניט אויס;
פֿיר מיך, איך בעט דיך, בעסער אַפּ אַהיים,
איך זע דאָ קיין גוטס ארוים!

— ניין, קינד, דו האָסט נאָר חסרונות געזעהן,
אַז מיט אומרעכט וויל מען וערן אַן עושר;
דו קענסט דיר לעבן זייער רויק און שיין,
דו זאָלסט זיך נאָר פֿירן מיט יושר.

זאָלסט ליבן דײַן חבֿר ווי דיך אַליין,
מיין נישט — אַלצדינג קומט נאָר אין מיר;
העלף אים עפּעס מיט, ווען ער איז געמיין,
פֿאַרגין אים, ווען ער איז רײַכער פֿאַר דיר.

מיט יושר און נחת לעב דיר אַזוי,
דאָס לעבן איז דאָך אַ קליינע בריק;
די צײַט טראָגט די יאָרן ווי דער ווינט אַ שטרוי,
אָט־אָט ביסטו ווײַטער צוריק.

גיי, מײַן קינד, גיי דיר אַ ביסל שפּאַצירן,
גיי טאַנץ דיר אַ ביסל ארום;
נאָר זאָלסט ניט צו הוליען, צו שטיפֿן, פֿאַרפֿירן,
זאָלסט קומען אַהיים אַן אַ מום.

דאָס איבעריקע דאַרף איך דיר מער ניט זאָגן,
וועסט אַליין זײַן דערבײַ, וועסטו קומען דערצו;
וואָרעם זע — אין מיזרח־זײַט הייבט שוין אַן צו טאָגן,
איך דארף שוין גיין אין מײַן רו.

And when the rooster gave his first crow
in the house of a woman in labor,
we heard a cry: "Congratulations!,
a boy—may he live a long life!"

And when the child gave his first sob,
and hadn't yet opened his eyes,
the angel gave him a fillip on the lip
and flew back to Heaven.

The Little Tree

Our distant ancestors planted
a little tree in the wilderness.
That single tree glittered among trees
with its splendor and beauty.
Even the roots and branches,
sweet as dates and figs
like all the fruits of the land,
and the buds and the leaves
we have in our hands
as a legacy from an **uncle.**

>   Chorus:

>   Yes, the little tree was **faith**—
>   we understand that very well,
>   and the uncle was **Moses** himself.
>   The fable fits the Jews very well.

Little birds, free, youthful, pure,
with their gorgeous little feathers,
built themselves little nests
among the little branches.
There they used to fly happily,
singing lovely melodies
that echoed throughout the world.
At that happy tumult,
the **gardene**r up in Heaven
also rejoiced greatly.

און אַז דער האָן האָט געגעבן דעם ערשטן קריי
אין אַ שטוב פֿון אַ קימפּעטאַרין.
"מזל־טובֿ"! — האָט מען געהערט אַ געשריי,
אַ ייִנגעלע צו לאַנגע יאָרן.

און אַז דאָס קינד האָט געגעבן דעם ערשטן כליפּ,
ס׳האָט נאָך ניט געעפֿנט די אויגן,
האָט אים דער מלאך געגעבן אַ שנעל אויף דער ליפּ
און איז צוריק צום הימל געפֿלויגן.

דאָס ביימעלע

אַ ביימעלע האָבן אונדזערע אָבֿות אָבֿותינו
אין דער ווילדער וויסטע געפֿלאַנצט !
מיט פּראַכט און שיינקייט האָט דאָס אײנע
פֿון אַלע ביימעלעך אַרויסגעגלאַנצט,
אויך די וואָרצלען און די ·צוווייגן
זיס ווי מייטלען און ווי צווייגן,
אַזוי ווי אַלע פּירות פֿונעם לאַנד,
אויך די קנאַספּן און די בלעטער —
בירושה פֿון אַ פֿעטער
האָבן מיר עס אין דער האַנט...

כאָר :

יאָ, דאָס ביימעלע איז די אמונה געוועזן !
מיר פֿאַרשטייען עס זייער גוט;
און דער פֿעטער איז דאָך משה אַליין !
דער משל גלײַכט זיך שטאַרק צום ייִד.

פֿייגעלעך, פֿרײַע, יונגיטשקע, ריינע,
מיט זייערע פֿעדערלעך אַ פּראַכט;
האָבן צווישן די צווײַגעלעך די קליינע
יעדעם זיך אַ נעסטעלע געמאַכט.
דאָרטן פֿלעגן זיי פֿריילעך פֿליִען,
זינגען שיינע מעלאָדיִען,
זיי האָבן אַש פֿאַרהילכט די וועלט;
פֿון דעם פֿריילעכן געטומל
האָט דער גערטנער דאָרט אין הימל
אויך פֿאַר גרויס פֿרייד אַנגעקוועלט !

Chorus:

Yes! The **little birds** were the **tribes**—
we understand that very well;
and the **gardener** was **God** himself.
The fable fits the Jews very well.

The golden era didn't last very long—
the little tree *didn't* live happily ever after.
Angry winds from all directions
brought black clouds;
the storm and the weather
tore off all its leaves;
lightning burned it
with its flame.
All the little birds were driven away.—
They can't find a place for themselves.
In the earth there remained only
the lonely, naked trunk.

Chorus:

Yes, the **winds** were the **nations**—
we understand that very well;
it was the **Holy Temple** that burned.
The fable fits the Jews very well.

Now we see the little birds flying around—
they can't find a place for themselves.
When they want to rest a bit,
the **birds of prey** drive them away.
If they want to stay in a certain place,
the **black ravens** come flying
and pluck their little feathers.
If they just want to eat a little seed,
they get pecked in the forehead
and all their blood runs out.

כאָר :

יאָ ! די פֿייגעלעך זײַנען די שבֿטים געווען,
דאָס פֿאַרשטייען מיר זייער גוט —
און דער גערטנער איז גאָר גאָט אַליין,
דער משל גלײַכט זיך שטאַרק צום ייד.

ניט לאַנג האָבן געדווערט די גאָלדענע צײַטן,
ניט תּמיד האָט דאָס בײַמעלע געגליקט...
ווינטן שלעכטע פֿון אַלע זײַטן
האָבן שוואַרצע וואָלקן אָנגערוקט...
דער שטורעם און דאָס שלעכטע וועטער
האָבן אָפּגעריסן אַלע בלעטער...
דער בליץ האָט עס פֿאַרברענט מיט זײַן פֿלאַם !
אַלע פֿייגעלעך פֿאַרטריבן...
אין דער ערד איז נאָר פֿאַרבליבן
דער איינציקער, נאַקעטער שטאַם.

כאָר :

יאָ, די ווינטן, דאָס זײַנען די פֿעלקער געווען...
דאָס פֿאַרשטייען מיר זייער גוט —
געברענט האָט דאָס בית־המיקדש אַליין —
דער משל גלײַכט זיך שטאַרק צום ייד.

יעצט זעט מען די פֿייגעלעך אַרומפֿליִען,
געפֿינען קענען זיי ניט קיין אָרט...
ווען נאָר זיי ווילן זיך אַ ביסעלע אויסרוען,
פֿאָרטרײַבן זיי די רויבפֿייגל פֿון דאָרט...
ווילן זיי נאָר אין אַן אָרט פֿאַרבלײַבן,
פֿליִען אָן די שוואַרצע ראָבן
און פֿליקן זיי די פֿעדערלעך אויס !
ווילן זיי עסן נאָך אַ קערנדל,
כאַפּן זיי אַ פּיק אין שטערנדל
אַז ס'רינט פֿון זיי די גאַנצע בלוט אַרויס...

Chorus:

Yes! The **little feathers** are their money and charm;
we understand that very well.
And the **ravens** are their **enemies** themselves.
The fable fits the Jews very well.

Woe to him who is driven from his home.
Things go well only for the little birds
who remained in the tree,
with a sweet little leaf in their mouth.
Those who have leaves in their mouths
can hope that things will get better.
The sun may yet shine! Who knows?!
The old tree may yet blossom again;
each may come flying
back to his peaceful nest.

Chorus:

Yes! The **nest**, after all, is **Jerusalem**!
We understand that very well.
The little leaf is the **Torah** itself.
The fable fits the Jews very well.

God's Miracles

Once upon a time, the nation
dealt with heathens—the Chaldeans.
"There is only one God,"
declared a certain Hebrew,
and God said to him:
"Listen to me, dear Abraham;
look at the earth and the sky—
that will be my workshop.
I will make you great—
from you will arise
a nation that will be godly.
I'll take care of Nature, I figure,

כאָר:

יאָ! די פֿעדערלעך זיינען זייער געלט און חן —
דאָס פֿאַרשטייען מיר זייער גוט,
און די ראָבן, דאָס זיינען די שׂונאים אַליין —
דער משל גלייכט זיך שטאַרק צום ייד!

ווי דעם, פֿון זיין היים וואָס איז פֿאַרטריבן!
גוט איז נאָר די פֿייגעלעך און וויל,
וואָס פֿון דעם בוים איז פֿאַרבליבן
אַ בלעטעלע אַ זים' אין זייער מויל...
די וואָס האַלטן אין מויל די בלעטער
קענען האָפֿן אויף בעסערן וועטער...
די זון קען נאָר אַ שיין טאָן! ווער ווייסט ?
דער אַלטער בוים קען נאָך אויפֿבליען...
יעדעם קען נאָך קומען צו פֿליען
צוריק אין זיין רויקער נעסט...

כאָר:

יאָ! — די נעסט איז דאָך ירושלים געווען!
דאָס פֿאַרשטייען מיר זייער גוט —
דאָס בלעטעלע איז די תּורה אַליין!
דער משל גלייכט זיך שטאַרק צום ייד!

גאָטס ווּנדער

אַ מאָל האָט זיך די אומה אָנגעקערט
מיט היידן — די כּאַלדעער,
אַז עס איז דאָ אַיין גאָט, האָט ער דערקלערט,
אַיינער אַ העברעער,
און אים האָט גאָט אַ זאָג געטאָן:
— הער מיך אויס, אבֿרהמל,
קוק דעם הימל און די ערד אָן,
דאָס וועט זיין מיין קרעמל;
איך וועל דיר מאַכן גרויס,
פֿון דיר וועט אַרויס
אַ פֿאָלק, וואָס וועט זיין געטלעך,
די נאַטור, מיין איך,
האַלטן וועל איך,

and you will turn pages.
In every generation
I'll show great miracles
only to you,
if you'll just be decent,
good, and fine,
my faithful children.

Before He brought His children
to Him in Jerusalem,
they spent four hundred years
in the land of Egypt.
They were severely oppressed there
till God heard their complaints
and visited miraculous plagues
upon the land:
locusts,
hail,
pestilence,
a dark angel of death,
till Pharaoh himself
told them to leave,
and even gave them money for expenses.
So will I show you
many great and mighty miracles,
if you'll just be decent,
good, and fine
for me, faithful children.

They wandered for forty years
in the hot desolation.
There was no trace of water there,
only sand and bare stones.
The great Moses
drew water from a stone,
and from Heaven they received
delicious wafers.
Many little birds soon came flying to them—
"Cut off our heads
and cook us in your pots,
and may things go well for you!"

און דו וועסט מישן די בלעטלעך.

אין איעדן דור
וועל איך אײַך נאָר
באַוויזן גרויסע וווּנדער,
אז איר וועט נאָר זײַן
וווייל, גוט און פֿײַן,
מיר געטרײַע קינדער.

איידער ער האָט זײַנע קינדער געבראַכט
צו זיך אין ירושלים,
האָבן זיי פֿיר הונדערט יאָר פֿאַרבראַכט
אין דעם לאַנד מצרים.
מען האָט זיי דאָרט זייער שטאַרק געדריקטם,
ביז גאָט האָט דערהערט זייערע קלאָגן,
און האָט אויף דעם לאַנד אָנגעשיקטם
וווּנדערלעכע פּלאָגן:
אַ חיה וואָס פֿרעסטם,
אַ האָגל — אַ פּעסטם,
אַ פֿינצטערן מלאך־המוות,
ביז פרעה אַליין
האָט זיי געהייסן גיין,
און האָט זיי נאָך געגעבן אויף הוצאות.
אַזוי וועל איך אײַך
באַוויזן אַ סך
גרויסע, שטאַרקע וווּנדער,
אז איר וועט נאָר זײַן
וווייל, גוט און פֿײַן,
מיר — געטרײַע קינדער!

אַרומגעגאַנגען זײַנען זיי פֿערציק יאָר,
אין דער היימער וויסטע,
פֿון וואָסער איז דאָרט געוווען קיין שפּור,
נאָר זאַמד און שטיינער פוסטמע;
פֿון אַ שטיין וואָסער האָט זיי געצאַפט
משה דער מיוחס,
און פֿון הימל האָבן זיי געכאַפט
ברייטלעך כצפיחית;
פֿייגעלעך אַ סך
זײַנען צו זיי גלײַך
אַליין צו פֿליִען געקומען:
— שנײַדטם אונדז די קעפ
און קאַכט אונדז אין טעפ,
און לאָז אײַך וווייל באַקומען!

They had barely escaped from Egypt
when Pharaoh came chasing after them.
He and his whole army
came upon them at the shore of the sea.
He would have finished them off,
they would have been lost,
but God whistled,
and the sea, frightened,
congealed in place.
Pharaoh's army
found their graves in that sea,
and from then on, our people
have sung their song joyfully.

"Now when you want to speak to me,
you can do so from Jerusalem.
You'll get my answer there
direct from Heaven."
Thus did their God speak to them
when He departed from them.
"But my contract, the Ten Commandments—
sign it, you Jews!
If you keep it,
I'll make you great
so the whole world will marvel,
but if you forget me,
oh, will I afflict you severely!
And then I'll promptly
forget about you,
will no longer show you miracles,
if you aren't
decent and good for me,
unfaithful children!

אַרויסגעגאַנגען פֿון מצרים זײַנען זיי קאַם,
איז פּרעה זיי נאָכגעלאָפֿן,
מיט זײַן גאַנצער מחנה ביַם ים
האָט ער זיי אָנגעטראָפֿן;
ער וואָלט פֿון זיי געמאַכט אַן עק,
זיי וואָלטן געוועון פֿאַרלאָרן,
האָט גאָט געטאָן אַ פֿײַף, פֿאַר שרעק
איז דער ים פֿאַרגליוועורט געוואָרן.
און פּרעהס מיליטער
האָבן אין דעם מער
געפֿונען זייער קבֿורה;
און אונדזערע לײַט
פֿון יענער ציַיט,
האָבן פֿריילעך געזוּנגען די שירה.

„יעצט אַז איר וועט דאַרפֿן רײַדן צו מיר,
קענט איר פֿון ירושלים,
מיַין ענטפֿער וועט איר באַקומען פֿריַער
פֿון דאָרט מן השמים";
אַזוי האָט געזאָגט צו זיי זייער גאָט,
ווען ער איז פֿון זיי געשידן,

„נאָר דעם קאָנטראַקט — די צען געבאָט,
שריַיבט מיר אונטער, איר יידן.
האַלט איר עם אויס,
מאַך איך אײַך גרויס,
אַז די גאַנצע וועלט וועט קאָכן;
אָבער וועט איר
פֿאַרגעסן אָן מיר —
אוי, וועל איך אײַך שווער באַשטראָפֿן!
און דאַן וועל איך גליַיך
פֿאַרגעסן אָן אײַך
נישט מער באַוויַיזן קיין וווּנדער,
ווען איר וועט נישט זײַן
וווייל און פֿײַן
צו מיר — אומגעטריַיע קינדער!"

I.L. PERETZ

(born May 18, 1852 in Zamosc, province of Lublin;
died April 3, 1915 in Warsaw.)

Quietly, more quietly,
he wants to thank—

Those were the last lines that I.L. Peretz, the father of modern Yiddish literature, was writing on the third day of *khol-hamoed peysakh* in 1915, when his pen suddenly slipped out of his hand and the heart of the great poet stopped forever.

A hundred thousand Jews came to accompany their poet and spokesman to his eternal rest. From Peretz's residence on Ceglane Street in Warsaw to the Gensher cemetery[18], the coffin of the deceased was carried in people's hands. It looked as if the entire city was wrapped in deep sorrow.

H.D. Nomberg, on the next morning, wrote in the Warsaw newspaper *Haynt* (Today*)*:

"…thousands and tens of thousands walked behind and in front of the coffin--- silently, with no words or expressions, just a black coffin was seen on the shoulders of people. Thousands surged and pressed to the open grave that was waiting for the already closed coffin."

The writer P. Katz wrote in the Vilna magazine *Di Vokh* (This Week*)*:

"Whoever didn't personally experience the great days of sorrow for Peretz's death in Warsaw will probably never fully know who and what I.L. Peretz was for the Jewish people. The sad and unexpected news swept across thousands of lips on Sabbath, from early morning till late at night: 'Peretz is dead!'"

The entire Jewish world, without distinction of tendencies or parties, felt orphaned. Vladimir Medem correctly expressed the feelings not only of Bundists but also of all other groups in the Jewish people when he wrote: "He became a piece of life. He wasn't 'one of ours' in the strict sense of the word—he wasn't *anyone's*. He was a member of no party, a follower of no program. He was a seeker; he penetrated into our life."

---

18. The Jewish cemetery on Gensher Street

54

Hundreds of articles, research papers, poems, and books in various languages have been written to date about Peretz and his place in Jewish life and Yiddish literature. Much has been written about his influence on the whole development of modern Yiddish literature, of which he was crowned the father and guide; about his effect on elevating Yiddish to a national language; about his pioneering role in the rise of the modern Yiddish school and in many other areas of Jewish life.

Within the confines of this brief article, we will just touch on one field in which he pioneered that is perhaps less well known: the Yiddish folk-song. It is well known, in connection with his *Folkstimlekhe Geshikhtn* (Folksy Stories*)*, that Peretz loved to read and hear old Jewish stories and legends, *hasidic* themes, and stories of marvels and folk-heroes, but it is less well known that Peretz the intellectual, who wrote with winks and hints, was among the first to become interested in Yiddish folksongs that were created and sung by the lower classes of the people. Even before Ginsburg and Marek began to plan their first anthology of folksongs, which was published in St Petersburg in 1901, Peretz had become interested in these creations of the people and had begun to collect and research them.

I.L. Cahan writes about this in his article *Y.L. Peretz Vi a Zamler Fun Yidishn Folkslid. Bamerkungen Tsu Zayne Kolektsies* (I.L. Peretz as a Collector of Yiddish Folksongs—Remarks About His Collections*)*, in the *YIVO Bleter* (volume 12, pp 1-3, 1937): "Thus in 1895 or 1896, a rumor spread among educated Yiddish readers in Warsaw that the writer Isaac Loeb Peretz, who lived at Ceglane 1, was collecting Yiddish folksongs." Cahan relates that he learned about this accidentally from a conversation he overheard between youngsters in a coffee-house in Warsaw, when one of them asked the other: "How come that such a great writer as Peretz interests himself in such foolish little songs? What does he need them for?"

In another place in the article, Cahan points out that Peretz began to collect folksongs in 1894-5, during the so-called "radical period" of his creative work. He prepared for publication a collection of fifty folksongs; this collection was later discovered in the Dinezon Archive, with the Russian censor's stamp dated July 23rd, 1896. As is well known, Marek and Ginsburg's public call for people to collect and send in folksongs was issued in 1898.

Incidentally, in that same year, 1898, Peretz printed six folksongs in a German magazine in Vienna, *Der Urkval* (The Ancient Source*)*, a monthly that concerned

itself with folksongs. The Yiddish words were transliterated into the Roman alphabet; the Hebraisms and difficult words were explained in German.

How deeply Peretz was involved in collecting folksongs, and how seriously he
dealt with that, can also be seen from the memoirs of a number of Yiddish writers. Abraham Reisen relates that when he was in the army, in 1897, he received
a letter from Peretz in which Peretz asked him to collect folksongs. Peretz gave
his explanation of what a folksong is, and Reisen further relates:

"Naturally I sat right down in the barracks and started recalling the little songs
that my mother sang to me…and when I exhausted the store of folksongs in my
memory, I called in the Jewish soldiers and asked them to sing me the songs that
they knew. In that way, I collected a few dozen Yiddish songs and sent them to
Ceglane 1 in Warsaw."

H.D. Nomberg recounts that "half the time of the Sabbath gatherings at Peretz's
house was spent singing folksongs, in a strange, exalted mood."

It is appropriate to quote a lengthy paragraph from Nomberg's memoirs, because
it best expresses not only Peretz's love for Yiddish folksong but also his deep
understanding of the national value of folk-creation. Nomberg writes:

> The little songs had the effect of prophecy and revelation for Peretz and
> his circle. We all got the impression that a fresh wellspring, bubbling and
> lively, had opened. It was not only that the little songs were entrancing
> with their artless poetry, their inner truth, their deeply heartfelt senti-
> ments—they also awakened and called us to a world that lay completely
> unknown to the Jewish intelligentsia, both the older Torah students and
> the younger educated *Maskilim*. Here a people is living and singing,
> singing of love and yearning, of joy and sorrow! A people that knows
> nothing of all the grimaces, woes, and hair-splitting of our traditional
> and modern intellectuals. The further revolution of thoughts and view-
> points that these revelations evoked can be seen by the reader himself
> if he recalls how widely the conviction was distributed among us (or
> perhaps still is?) that the Jews are on the one hand a 'practical people',
> a chosen people, and on the other hand a sour-tempered people without
> any taste for Nature, simplicity, love, beauty, and poetry.

Peretz was not satisfied with just collecting and singing the folksongs within the
select circle of Yiddish writers and artists who were the members of his house-

hold; he wanted to arouse respect for the creations of the people among a broad circle of readers. Therefore, in 1901 he wrote his famous essay *Dos Yidishe Lebn Loytn Folkslid* (Jewish Life According to Folksong*)* which he published in *Der Yud (*The Jew*)* and later included in his collected works.

When Peretz gave his famous speech at the Czernowitz conference, which he helped organize, he didn't neglect to call on the younger Yiddish writers to draw from the ancient Yiddish folk-treasure. In the speech he said:

"Yiddish does not begin with Isaac Mayer Dik. The *khasidic* tale—that is *breyshis*;[19] '*Sabetai Bal Shem Tov*' and other miraculous tales are folk-poetry; the first folk-poet was Rabbi Nakhman of Bratslav, with his *Zibn Betler* (Seven Beggars.)"

Just as his *Folksy Stories* were inspired by old folk tales and legends, so too were a number of his poems influenced by folk creations. One sees the direct influence of folksong most clearly in his cycle *Oys Romansero* (No Longer a Romeo*)*. I.L. Cahan at that time compared four of Peretz's poems with their pro-totypes and showed that such poems as *Tsi Kh'hob Dikh Lib? Akh, Du Megst Mir Gleybn* (Do I love you? Oh, you can believe me); *Gelibter tayerer khosn* (Dearly beloved bridegroom); *Mamenyu, libenyu, hartsenyu, kroyn* (Mother dear, my beloved, my heart, my crown); etc. were taken directly from folksongs.

It is also appropriate to mention that Peretz's *Dray Neytorins* (Three Seamstress-es*)*, because of its simple and folksy tone, achieved great popularity and was included in anthologies of folksongs.

Nakhman Meisel, in his book *Yitzkhok Leybush Perets un Zayn Dor Shrayber* (Isaac Loeb Peretz and his Generation of Writers), presents 48 poems written to Peretz by 38 Yiddish poets from all over the world. They express not only affec-tion but respect, and great recognition of the poet because he was not only for their generation but even more for the current and future generations. The poems that were written to Peretz in the ghetto and right after the Holocaust make a particular impression. Joshua Shpigel, from the Lodz ghetto, wrote:

Isaac Loeb Peretz! I hear the weeping melody of your fiddle,
the moonlight song on burning walls and floors;
I still see them—your burning, Sabbath-holy Jews,
nourished by your light, which will soothe the red wound.

---

19. Literally, the book *Genesis* in the Bible; figuratively, the beginning

Moyshe Shulshteyn from France, where he went through the seven circles of Hell, came to the Peretz tomb with his prayer:

> *Every night I come to your tomb*
> *and rap on the holy stone,*
> *and I beg, as one begs a savior:*
> *Be my light and my guide.*

And Z. Weinper, like many other poets in America at that same time, also turned his gaze toward Peretz with these words:

> *New generations*
> *arrive and glow,*
> *from somewhere*
> *to somewhere,*
> *singing the songs*
> *of the pale seamstresses*
> *and two brothers...*

And he hears: "In golden times, children forge new links, and they sing: 'they'll rock and rock to sleep the new incarnation of their father's ancient melody.'"

Don't Think...

Don't think the world is a tavern,
created for clawing to the bar with tooth and nail,
for guzzling and gorging while others
look glassy-eyed, faint, from afar;
for swallowing your spittle and clutching your belly,
which is twisting in cramps.
No, don't think the world is a tavern!

Don't think the world is a market,
created for the strong to deal with the weary and weak:
to buy from poor girls their virtue,
from women the milk from their breasts,
from men the marrow from their bones,
and from children their smiles,
those rare guests on their waxen faces.
No, don't think the world is a market!

Don't think the world is a place with no rules,
with free rein for wolves and foxes for robbery and swindling,
with Heaven a curtain so God should not see,
with fog so you can't see your hands,
with wind to drown out the wild cries,
with earth to absorb the blood of the victims!
No, don't think the world has no rules!

The world is not a tavern, not a market, not free of rules!
Everything is weighed and measured!
Not a tear, not a drop of blood, is shed in vain,
no spark in an eye is extinguished!
Tears become rivers, rivers become oceans, oceans become floods!
Sparks become a thunderstorm!
No, don't think there are no rules and no Judge!

Three Seamstresses

Eyes red and lips blue,
not a drop of blood in their cheeks,
foreheads pale and covered with sweat,

מיין נישט

מיין נישט, די וועלט איז אַ קרעטשמע — באַשאַפֿן
מאַכן אַ וועג מיט פֿויסטן און נעגל
צום שענקפֿאַס, און פֿרעסן און זויפֿן, וען אַנדערע
קוקן פֿון ווייַטן מיט גלעזערנע אויגן
פֿאַרחלשט, און שלינגען דאָס שפּייַעכץ און ציִען
צוזאַמען דעם מאָגן, וואָס וואַרפֿט זיך אין קראָמפֿן ! —
אַ, מיין נישט, די וועלט איז אַ קרעטשמע !

מיין נישט, די וועלט איז אַ בערזע — באַשאַפֿן,
דער שטאַרקער זאָל האַנדלען מיט מידע און שוואַכע,
זאָל קויפֿן ביַי אָרעמע מיידלעך די בושה,
ביַי פֿרויען די מילך פֿון די בריסטן, ביַי מעננער
דעם מאַרך פֿון די ביינער, ביַי קינדער דעם שמייכל,
דעם זעלטענעם גאַסט אויפֿן וואַקסענעם פּנים —
אַ, מיין נישט די וועלט איז אַ בערזע !

מיין נישט, די וועלט איז אַ הפֿקר — באַשאַפֿן
פֿאַר וועלף און פֿאַר פֿוקסן, פֿאַר רויב און פֿאַר שווינדל ;
דער הימל — אַ פֿאַרהאַנג, אַז גאָט זאָל נישט זען !
דער נעפּל — מען זאָל אויף די הענט דיר נישט קוקן !
דער ווינט — צו פֿאַרשטיקן די ווילדע געשרייען ;
די ערד — אייַנצוזאַפֿן דאָס בלוט פֿון קרבנות —
אַ, מיין נישט די וועלט איז אַ הפֿקר !

די וועלט איז קיין קרעטשמע, קיין בערזע, קיין הפֿקר !
געמאָסטן ווערט אַלעם, געוווייגן ווערט אַלעם !
קיין טרער און קיין בלוטיקער טראָפּן פֿאַרגייען,
אומזיסט ווערט קיין פֿונק אין קיין אויג נישט פֿאַרלאָשן !
פֿון טרערן ווערט טייַכן, פֿון טייַכן ווערט ימים,
פֿון ימים — אַ מבול, פֿון פֿונקען — אַ דונער —
אַ, מיין נישט, לית דין ולית דייַן !

דריַי נייטאָרינס

די אויגן רויט, די ליפּן בלאָ,
קיין טראָפּן בלוט אין באַק נישטאָ,
דער שטערן בלאָס, באַדעקט מיט שווייס,

breath short and hot—
three girls sit and sew.

The needle shiny, the cloth snowy,
and one thinks: I sew and sew, day and night,
and haven't made a wedding dress!
What comes of my sewing?

I neither sleep nor eat...
I'd give money for Mayer Bal Nes[20]--
perhaps he'd try
to get me at least a widower, an old man,
with many, many children!

The second thinks: I sew and stitch,
and just stitch myself gray braids.
My head burns, my temples pound,
and the machine pounds in rhythym:
ta-ta, ta-ta, ta-ta!

I understand when people hint to me:
no wedding canopy, no ring?
It would be wonderful
to have a love affair at least for a year.
But then, then?

The third spits blood[21] and sings:
I sew myself sick, I sew myself blind,
my breath catches with every stroke.
And he—he's getting married this week—
I wish him no evil!

Ah, forget the way things were!
The community will give me a shroud
and a little bit of ground
where I can rest undisturbed.
I will sleep, sleep!

---

20. The expression means to give charity for poor students.
21. In those days, indicative of pulmonary tuberculosis.

דער אטעם אפגעהאקט און הייס —
עס זיצן דרײַ מיידלעך און נייען.

די נאָדל — בלאַנק, די לײַוונט — שנײַ,
און איינע טראַכט: איך ניי און ניי,
איך ניי בײַ טאָג, איך ניי בײַ נאַכט,
קיין חופּה-קלייד זיך נישט געמאַכט! —
וואָס קומט אַרוים, איך ניי?...

נישט איך שלאָף און נישט איך עס...
איך וואָלט געגעבן אַ׳יף מאיר בעל-נס,
אפֿשר וואָלט ער זיך געמיט:
אַן אַלמן כאָטש, אַן אַלטן ייד,
מיט קינדערלעך אַ שאָק!

די צווייטע טראַכט: איך ניי און שטעפּ,
און שטעפּ מיר אוים גאָר גרויע צעפּ.
דער קאָפּ — ער ברענט, די שלייף — זי האַקט,
און די מאַשין קלאַפּט צו צום טאַקט:
— טאָ-טאָ, טאָ-טאָ, טאָ-טאָ!

איך פֿאַרשטיי דאָך יענעמס וווּנק!
אַן אַ חופּה, אַן אַ רינג,
וואָלט געווען אַ שפּיל, אַ טאַנץ,
אַ ליבע אויף אַ יאָר אַ גאַנץ —
נאָר דערנאָך, דערנאָך?...

די דריטע שפּײַט מיט בלוט און זינגט:
איך ניי מיך קראַנק, איך ניי מיך בלינד,
עס צוויקט די ברוסט בײַ יעדן שטאָך...
און ער — האָט חתונה די וואָך...
איך ווינטש אים נישט קיין שלעכטס!

עט, פֿאַרגעסן וואָס אַ מאָל!...
תכריכים וועט מיר געבן קהל,
אויך אַ קליינטשיק פּיצל ערד,
איך וועל רוען אומגעשטערט,
איך וועל שלאָפֿן, שלאָפֿן!

Hope and Believe

Hope! Spring is not far away.
Butterflies will cavort.
New nests; new birds
will sing new songs.

Believe! The night will soon disappear
and the clouds will dissipate.
The sky will be blue again:
new stars, new suns!
New roses, new flowers
will wake Spring's sweet high—
it will shine, and smell, and sing!
And over our grave too…

Consolation, My People

Consolation, my people—you need consolation.
Strengthen your heart and keep your spirit firm.
Don't be the wind that blows out the fire--
fan the flame, for the night is poison!
Pour oil and trim the wick,
for the night is poison and sleep is death!
Strengthen your heart and keep your spirit firm—
it has shone more than one night
and won more than one battle,
never letting the banner out of its hand!
There it stands—a wall as strong as iron
in the desolate, wildly raging ocean!
Oh, strengthen the people, fan the flame!
Strengthen the people, don't weaken it!
Let the life force
spray all the flaming pillars at night—
night is fading and day awakes!
And send the sunbeam—a golden arrow—
as a greeting to the flaming pillar!
Oh, consolation, my people—you need consolation!
Keep your heart firm and strengthen your spirit!

האָף און גלייב

האָף! נישט ווייַט איז שוין דער פֿרילינג,
ס׳וועלן שמעטערלינגען שפּרינגגען,
ניַע נעסטן, ניַע פֿייגל
וועלן ניַע לידער זינגען.

גלייב, די נאַכט וועט שוין פֿאַרשווינדן
און די וואָלקנם אויך צערינען,
בלוי וועט ווייַטער זיַן דער הימל —
ניַע שטערן, ניַע זונען!
ניַע רויזן, ניַע בלומען
וועקט דעם פֿרילינגם זיסער הויך;
עם וועט שיַינען, שמעקן, זינגען!
און — אויף אונדזער קבֿר אויך...

טרייסט, מיַן פֿאָלק

טרייסט, מיַן פֿאָלק, עם דאַרף די טרייסט,
שטאַרקט דאָם האַרץ, מאַכט פֿעסט דעם גיַסט.
זיַט ניט דער ווינט, וואָס לעשט די פֿלאַם,
נאָר בלאָזט זי אויף, ווייַל נאַכט איז סם!
נאָר בוימל גיסט און פּוצט די קנויט,
ווייַל נאַכט איז גיפֿט און שלאָף איז טויט!
טרייסט, מיַן פֿאָלק, עם דאַרף די טרייסט!
מאַכט פֿעסט דאָם האַרץ און שטאַרקט דעם גיַסט —
עם האָט געליַכט שוין נישט איין נאַכט,
עם האָט געזינגט שוין נישט איין שלאַכט.
און נישט געלאָזט די פֿאָן פֿון האַנט!
עם שטייט — אַן איַיזן-פֿעסטע וואַנט,
אין וויסטן, ווילד-פֿאַרקאָכטן ים!
אַ, שטאַרקט דאָם פֿאָלק! בלאָזט אויף די פֿלאַם!
אַ, שטאַרקט דאָם פֿאָלק, נישט אָפּגעשלאַפֿט!
זאָל שפּריצן העל די לעבנסקראַפֿט
אַלם פֿיַערדיקע זיַל ביַ נאַכט — —
עם זינקט די נאַכט, דער טאָג דערוואַכט!
און שיקט די שטראַל — אַ גאָלדענע פֿיַל —
אַלם גרום דער פֿיַערדיקער זיַל! —
אַ, טרייסט, מיַן פֿאָלק! עם דאַרף די טרייסט!
מאַכט פֿעסט דאָם האַרץ און שטאַרקט דעם גיַסט!

Brothers[22]
(fragment)

White, black, brown, yellow-
blend the colors together!
All men are brothers,
from one father and one mother.

Also, one God created them,
and they have one Fatherland: the world!
All men are brothers—
that has been established.

All men are brothers,
black, white, brown, and yellow.
Only the colors are different—
their natures are the same.

Everywhere the same thrust—
I've heard that a thousand times!
From saying to doing
and from Heaven to Earth!

All men are brothers,
yellow, brown, black, and white.
Peoples, races, and climates—
the whole story is just made up.

Monish
(fragment)

There once was a genius
who knew nothing of the world,
never went to school.
Pious his father and pious his mother—
the family were great scholars,
first-class ones!

---

22. Adapted by Peretz from Schiller's *Ode to Joy*, and often sung to the melody of the chorale in Beethoven's
9th symphony

ברידער

(פֿראַגמענט)

וױיסע, ברױנע, שװאַרצע, געלע —
מישט די פֿאַרבן אױס צוזאַמען !
אַלע מענטשן זײַנען ברידער,
פֿון אײן טאַטן, פֿון אײן מאַמען !

אױך — אײן גאָט האָט זײ באַשאַפֿן,
און — אײן פֿאַטערלאַנד: די װעלט —
אַלע מענטשן זײַנען ברידער,
דאָס איז אײן מאָל פֿעסטגעשטעלט.

אַלע מענטשן זײַנען ברידער,
שװאַרצע, װײַסע, ברױנע, געלבע...
אַנדערש זײַנען נאָר די פֿאַרבן,
די נאַטור איז — די זעלבע:

אומעטום דאָס זעלבע פֿראָלן,
כ'האָב עס טױזנט מאָל געהערט !
און פֿון זאָגן ביז צום טראָגן —
איז פֿון הימל ביז צו דר'ערד !

אַלע מענטשן זײַנען ברידער:
געלע, ברױנע, שװאַרצע, װײַסע...
פֿעלקער, ראַסן און קלימאַטן —
ס'איז אַן אױסגעקלערטע מעשה.

מאַניש

(פֿראַגמענט)

ס'איז געװען אַ מאָל אַן עילוי,
נישט געקענט די װעלט אַפֿילו,
נישט געװען אין קלאַס ;
פֿרום דער טאַטע, פֿרום די מאַמע,
די משפּחה — לומדים סתּמע,
גאָר פֿון עקסטן פֿאַס !

Real geniuses and scholars,
rabbis one and all;
the world rang with their names.
But knowledgeable people said:
Monish, our hero, will outdo them all!

Monish was a good boy,
with a mind as quick as lightning
and filled with Torah.
When a thought entered his mind,
even the Rambam[23] wasn't too hard.
He was a great Torah reciter in the bargain!

And a handsome boy, really splendid!
Hair as black as Night
and bright red lips—like two roses!
Black, arched eyebrows
and eyes as blue as the sky,
with fire burning in them!

Every bone in him was alive,
and he didn't just walk—he soared;
it was a pleasure to look at him!
Girls turned red or pale
when he appeared on the street—
when handsome Monish walked by!

The young rabbi's wife
sits in kheyder all day,
ostensibly listening to them teach!
The soup runs over, the milk scorches,
but she sits with her hands in her lap,
looks at Monish, and beams!

And the neighbor girl, Sheyne Hodl—
the needle falls out of her hand
whenever she hears our Monish!
She gasps for breath

---

23. Acronym for the name of Maimonides

סאַמע גאונים און למדנים,

מיט אַן „אַלף־בית־רבנים",

ס׳קלינגט מיט איר די וועלט;

און מבינים גרויסע זאָגן:

זיי וועט אַלע איבעריאָגן

מאַניש, אונדזער העלד!

מאַניש איז אַ וווילער יונג,

ר׳האָט אַ קעפל פֿײַער־פֿלינק,

אַנגעפֿילט מיט תּורה!

טרעפֿט אויך באַלד אַרײַן אין קאַרב,

מעג דער רמב"ם זײַן ווי דער האַרב!

און דערצו נאָך אַ בעל־קורא!

און אַ שיינער יונג — אַ פּראַכט!

שוואַרצע לאָקן ווי די נאַכט,

קאָרמעזן־ליפן — רויזן צוויי!

שוואַרצע ברעמען ווי די בויגן,

ווי דער הימל בלויע אויגן,

און אַ פֿײַער ברענט אין זיי!

יעדעס ביינדל אין אים לעבט,

און ער גייט נישט, נאָר ער שוועבט;

אַנצוקוקן איז אַ פֿרייד!

מיידלעך ווערן רויט און בלאַס,

אַז ער ווײַזט זיך אויף דער גאַס,

אַז דער שיינער מאַניש גייט!

ד׳יונגע רביצין אין חדר

זיצט אַ גאַנצן טאָג כסדר,

הערט, מפֿולמרשט, ווי מע קנעלט!

ס׳לויפֿט די יויך, די מילעך ברענט,

און זי זיצט פֿאַרלייגט די הענט,

קוקט אויף מאַנישן און קוועלט!

און דער שכנה — שיינע־האָדל

פֿאַלט פֿון האַנט אַרויס די נאָדל,

לאָזט זיך אונדזער מאַניש הערן!

עם פֿאַרפֿעלט איר אַטעם, דאָך,

and her heart gives a twinge,
and hot tears run from her eyes…

Happy is the father who has such a son;
happy the mother who raises him;
happy the generation that posseses him!
Such a person will be born when the Messiah comes!
O Jerusalem, open your gates!
That's what all the rabbis said!

און עס גיט אין הארץ א שטאך,
און — עס קאָפען הייסע טרערן...

— ווייל איז דעם טאַטן, וואָס האָט אזא זון
ווייל איז דער מאמען, וואָס וועט'ן דערציִען,
ווייל איז דעם דור, וואָס אים פאַרמאָגט!
אין משיחם צײַטן ווערט אזוינס געבוירן!
א, ירושלים, עפן דײַנע טויערן! —
דאָס האָבן אַלע רבנים געזאָגט!

SHOLEM ALEICHEM

(pseudonym of Sholem Rabinovich. Born on March 2, 1859 in Pereyeslav in the province of Poltava (Ukraine); died on May 13, 1916 in New York.)

Sholem Aleichem (Sholem Rabinovich) wrote very few poems. He created his undying place in Yiddish literature—and also in world literature—with his humorous stories, novels, and dramas. The small number of poems that did come from his blessed pen showed so much talent, charm, and folksy feeling that they immediately became popular among the broadest circles of the people.

His lullaby *Shlof, Mayn Kind* (Sleep, My Child) was published in 1901, several years after he wrote it, in the first anthology of Yiddish folksongs by Peysakh Marek and Saul Ginsburg, as an anonymous folksong, so widely known and popular was it. His poem *Ikh Vil Nit Geyn In Kheyder* (I Don't Want to Go to Kheyder*)* was sung by Ludwig Satz and other Yiddish actors. Concerning his lullaby, it is appropriate to examine it more closely. It was published for the first time in 1892 in the *Kol Mevaser Tsu Der Yidisher Folks-Bibliotek* (Introduction to the Yiddish Library), which Sholem Aleichem began publishing in 1888 and in which he began to gather the most important Yiddish writers. In a note to the poem, Sholem Aleichem wrote that he had created the lullaby to the melody of Lermontov's *Spi Mladenyets, Mayi Prikrasni, Bayushki Bayu* (Sleep, My Young Hero, My Beautiful One, Sleep Tight.) Later on, Sholem Aleichem made the acquaintance of the Jewish composer David Kovanovsky, who created an original melody to the poem. The song became so popular that people began to sing it in various districts, as often happens with popular songs, with different melodies, added verses, and altered words, and the original author was forgotten. What is extremely interesting is that six years after the poem was published, in 1898, when Marek and Ginsburg began their work of collecting Yiddish folksongs, the poem was sent to them from five separate districts as a folksong. And so indeed was it published in their book, as we have already mentioned, as an anonymous folksong. After the 1905 revolution, Sholem Aleichem wrote a parody of the lullaby under the title *Shlof Alyekse* (Sleep, Alexei*)*, in which he made fun of Czar Nikolai and his heir Alexei. That song too immediately became very popular. Here are a few verses of the parody:

Sleep, Alyekse, my heir,
my radiant person!

Sleep, my only son, my kaddish-sayer,
sleep, sleep—don't cry!

You'll grow to be very wise,
wiser even than I,
and a king of kings
with a land called Siberia.

God willing, you'll possess
sacks full of annuities,
many taverns and prisons,
and no end of churches.

And policemen and Cossacks,
guards at the door,
who can hack and shred
and whip without end.

You'll count contributions,
silently—shh.
Promise them a constitution,
but screw them!

Sholem Aleichem wrote the song in Russian and in Yiddish, and it was sung in both languages. The Jewish revolutionaries also created another song, based on the same theme, in which they sang:

A young Siberian is your father—
sleep, sleep, lyu-lyu.

After the First World War, in 1918, the Jews in Poland created another parody of the same song, in which they ridiculed the terrible situation in which they found themselves: "For the dollars that our father in America sends, we'll be able to buy sacks of German marks, and the emissaries that have come to help impoverished Jews eat the chicken and soup themselves."

Sholem Aleichem's lullaby was also adapted in the ghettos of Poland during the second World War. At that time, a song was written, sung to the same melody, that said:

Sleep, my child, my little martyr—
close your little eyes.
You know nothing, my dear one, of a Fuehrer.
Sleep in sweet repose.

*   *   *

The poem *Epitaph*, which was inscribed on Sholem Aleichem's gravestone, was first written by him in 1905. In a letter to his son-in-law, the Hebrew-Yiddish writer I.D. Berkowitz, Sholem Aleichem wrote: "I'm sending you an inscription for the headstone on my grave that I've written during these 'black days,' and I ask you to translate it in rhyme, as I wrote it; and if you can't achieve that, ask, in my name, our friend Schneur, who is a very devil in the field of song." Sholem Aleichem himself later rewrote the epitaph with certain changes, and included it in his will. In another variation, which we found among Sholem Aleichem's manuscripts, there is the following verse, which Sholem Aleichem apparently decided not to include:

He loved all of mankind,
and the Jews most of all.
He was always traveling,
but now he is resting in peace.

Sleep, My Child

Now sleep my solace, my dearest one--
my darling son, let Night sleep bring.
Now sleep, my crown, my *kaddish*,
and lyulinke, lyu, lyu I'll sing.

Your mother's at your cradle-side,
she sings a song and weeps.
Some day, I'm sure, you'll understand,
but now, this night, just sleep.

Your father's in America,
my darling little son.
You're still a babe, so sleep on now—
just sleep now little one.

They say America is for all
such a wondrous joy,
and it's really Paradise
for Jews, both man and boy.

[We know of no dark exile there,
or cruel decrees, my son.
No troubles there or wailing cries,
so sleep now, little one.

They say that there the lucky Jews,
no Evil Eye, are rich.
They are all satisfied with life—
you can't tell which is which.][24]

They eat white challah every day;
imagine—challah, son of mine!
I'll cook you soup for supper meal,
so sleep now, dream a world so fine.

And meanwhile what is there to do
but simply hope and pray.

---

24. The two bracketed verses were self-censored by Sholem Aleichem and later restored; they are not in the Yiddish text presented here

שלאָף מײַן קינד

שלאָף, מײַן קינד, מײַן טרײסט, מײַן שײנער,
שלאָף, מײַן זונעניו!
שלאָף, מײַן קרױן, מײַן קדיש אײנער,
ליולינקע ליו-ליו.

בײַ דײַן װיגל זיצט דײַן מאַמע,
זינגט אַ ליד און װײנט;
װעסט אַ מאָל פֿאַרשטײן מסתּמא,
װאָס זי האָט געמײנט.

אין אַמעריקע * איז דער טאַטע
דײַנער, זונעניו!
ביסט אַ קינד נאָך, שלאָף לעת-עתּה,
שלאָף זשע, שלאָף ליו-ליו.

דאָס אַמעריקע* איז פֿאַר יעדן,
זאָגט מען, גאָר אַ גליק,
און פֿאַר ייִדן אַ גן-עדן,
עפּעס אַן אַנטיק.

דאָרטן עסט מען אין דער װאָכן
חלה, זונעניו,
ייַכלעך װעל איך דיר דאָרט קאָכן,
שלאָף זשע, שלאָף ליו-ליו.

נאָר דערװײַלע לאָמיר האָפֿן,
אױ, װאָס קאָן מען טון?
כ'װאָלט שױן לאַנג צו אים געטראָפֿן —
װײס איך ניט װוּהין.

גאָט װעט העלפֿן, װעט ער שיקן
בריװעלעך, זונעניו!
גאָר אין גיכן אונדז באַגליקן,
שלאָף זשע, שלאָף ליו-ליו.

ער װעט שיקן צװאָנציק דאָלער,
זײַן פּאָרטרעט דערצו,

---

* אין טעקסט שטײט „אַמעריק".

I would have gone to him long since,
but do not know the way.

If God commands, he'll write to us
sweet letters, darling son.
He'll make us happy very soon,
so sleep, my little one.

He'll send us twenty dollars,
and a picture of his face.
God willing, then he'll send for us
and bring us to his place.

He'll do everything,
my son, just for us two,
and will come to greet us,
so sleep my son, lyu, lyu.

He'll grab you up and kiss you,
stay silent in his joy,
and I'll cry rivers of tears
for my lovely, dearest boy.

Until the joyous letter comes,
we'll sleep, my son, we two,
for sleep's a wondrous remedy
and let us sing, my son, lyu, lyu.

Songs From Kheyder

Bad people come and go—
love and good times are constant.
After summer passes,
autumn winds are right behind.

In the house it's dark and wet—
it's cold and muddy in the street.
The nights are getting longer
and hearts are no less heavy.

און וועט נעמען, לעבן זאָל ער,
אונדז אַהינצוצו.

ער וועט אַלץ פֿון אונדזערט וועגן
שאַפֿן, זונעניו,
און וועט פֿאַרן אונדז אַקעגן,
שלאָף זשע, שלאָף ליו-ליו.

ער וועט כאַפֿן דיך צום קושן,
טאַנצן אַזש פֿאַר פֿרייד;
איך וועל קוועלן, טרערן גיסן,
וויינען שטילערהייט.

ביז עס קומט דאָס גוטע קוויטל,
דאַרף מען, זונעניו!
שלאָפֿן, ס'איז אַ טײַער מיטל, —
ליולינקע ליו-ליו.

לידער פֿונעם חדר

שלעכטע קומען און פֿאַרבײַטן
שטענדיק ליבע, גוטע צײַטן;
נאָכן זומער שטײט שוין הינטן,
באַלד דער אָסיען מיט די ווינטן.

און אין שטוב איז פֿינצטער, נאַס,
קאַלט און בלאָטיק אויף דער גאַס,
און די נעכט, זיי ווערן גרעסער,
אויף דעם האַרצן אויך ניט בעסער.

Now he stands not far away,
his assistant at his side
with a stick and a lantern.
Damn him!

The rebbe is constantly whipping
big and small, the whole kheyder.
He teaches earnestly, pressures everyone,
but no one wants to learn.

We're drawn to the ice outside—
the ice is smooth, the snow is white!
We want to skate, have fun,
but he drives us crazy with *Four Fathers*,

Four Fathers and *Nzikin*, [25]
and his whip beats on backs
from morning to night
till we're all worn out.

We want to eat, and even more, to sleep,
and we carry weapons here:
all kinds of sticks and stones,
crying out like soldiers!

They tell us to sing out joyfully
and cry out loudly: "O Lord, my King!"
Whoever doesn't want to sing out loudly,
even a peasant, gets a pinch.

At home we fall down—
we want to sleep. Then he comes again,
the rebbe, to our dreams—
comes to our dreams and speaks to us:

"Listen, mischievous ones, I think
it's time for Gemora!
Tell me what Rabbi Popa[26] said--
tell me or I'll bury you!"

---

25. The fourth of the six books of the Mishnah
26. One of the rabbinical disputants in the Talmud

און ער שטייט שוין דאָ ניט ווײַט,
דער באַהעלפֿער בײַ דער זײַט,
מיט אַ שטעקן, אַ לאַמטערן,
— אײַנגעזונקען זאָל ער ווערן !

און דער רבי שמײַסט כּסדר
גרויס און קליין, דעם גאַנצן חדר,
לערנט ערנצט, ברעכט די ביינער,
לערנען אָבער וויל נישט קיינער ;

ס'ציט אַהינצו אויפֿן אײַז,
ס'אײַז איז גלאַט, דער שניי איז ווײַס !
ווילט זיך גליטשן, אַ קאַטשאָוועם !
און ער דולט אונדז מיט „פֿיר אָבֿות" ;

מיט „פֿיר-אָבֿות" מיט „נזיקין"
טאַנצט דער קאָנטשיק אויפֿן רוקן...
פֿון פֿאַר טאָג ביז שפּעט בײַ נאַכט,
ביז מע ווערט שוין גוט פֿאַרשמאַכט.

ווילט זיך עסן, נאָך מער שלאָפֿן,
און מיר גייען דאָ מיט וואָפֿן :
שטיינער, שטעקנס אַלערליי,
ווי סאָלדאַטן מיט געשריי !

און מע הייסט אונדז זינגען פֿריילעך,
שרײַען הויך : „אַדוני מלך" !
ווער עס וויל ניט זינגען הויך,
כאַפּט אַ קניפּ, אַ קולאַק אויך.

אין דער היים מע פֿאַלט אַנידער,
מע וויל שלאָפֿן, קומט ער ווידער,
אוי, דער רבי, ער קומט צו חלום,
קומט צו חלום, גיט אַפֿ שלום :

„הער נאָר, שיינעץ, ס'איז אַ סבֿרא,
ס'איז שוין צײַט צו דער גמרא !
זאָג, וואָס וויל רב פּפּא האָבן ?
זאָג ! ניט, וועל איך דיך באַגראָבן !"

In the morning, back to kheyder,
today as yesterday, as always.
The whip thrashes our bones,
but no one wants to learn.

The good rays of the sun
shine through the dark windows;
Nights get short and days get longer—
our hearts now feel lighter.

Wait, children, hope for tomorrow.
You should hope, you mustn't worry!
Have hope and faith
in our Jewish victory!

Good people come and go—
desolate, bad times are constant.
After autumn, after winter
comes spring, dear children!

Epitaph

Here lies a simple Jew,
a humorist and Yiddish writer.
His works for men and women too
made their lives much brighter.

All his life he laughed at things—
the whole world was his field of play.
But while the world was doing well,
he was near his dying day.

Precisely when the whole wide world
was joyful through and through,
he himself was at death's door,
which only dear God knew.

אין דער פֿרי, צוריק אין חדר,
הײַנט װי נעכטן, אַזוי כּסדר ;
און דער קאָנטשיק דרעשט די ביינער,
לערנען אַבער װיל ניט קיינער.

*

פֿון דער זון די גוטע שטראַלן,
דורכן טונקעלן פֿענצטער פֿאַלן ;
קלײַנע נעכט, די טעג שוין גרעסער,
אויף דעם האַרצן װערט שוין בעסער.

װאַרט זשע, קינדער, האָפֿט אויף מאָרגן,
איר דאַרפֿט האָפֿן, טאָרט ניט זאָרגן !
די אמונה, דער בטחון —
אונדזער ייִדישער נצחון...

גוטע קומען און פֿאַרבײַטן,
תּמיד שלעכטע, װיסטע צײַטן ;
נאָכן אסיען, נאָכן װינטער
קומט דער פֿרילינג, ליבע קינדער !

עפּיטאַפֿיע

דאָ ליגט אַ ייִד אַ פּשוטער,
געשריבן ייִדיש-טײַטש פֿאַר װײַבער,
און פֿאַרן פּראָסטן פֿאָלק האָט ער. —
געװען אַ הומאָריסט אַ שרײַבער.

דאָס גאַנצע לעבן אויסגעלאַכט,
געשלאָגן מיט דער װעלט כּפֿרות !
די גאַנצע װעלט האָט גוט געמאַכט,
און ער — אוי װײ — געװען אויף צרות !

און דװקא דעמאָלט װען דער עולם האָט
געלאַכט, געקלאַטשט און פֿלעגט זיך פֿרייען,
האָט ער געקרענקט — דאָס װייס נאָר גאָט —
בסוד, אַז קיינער זאָל ניט זעען.

SIMON FRUG

(born in 1860 in Bobrovi-Kut, Kherson province, Ukraine;
died on September 22nd, 1916, in Odessa)

When Simon Frug began to write Yiddish in 1888, he had already been famous and recognized as a Russian poet for eight years. Immediately after publishing his first Russian poems in the St. Petersburg Russian-Yiddish magazine *Razsoviet,* he drew the attention not only of the Yiddish intelligentsia that had grouped themselves around that magazine, but also of the broad Jewish folk-masses. The editors of the magazine brought the young poet from his home city of Kherson to St. Petersburg, where he became surrounded by much praise and recognition. His Russian poems on Jewish national themes created a reputation for Frug as the first great national Yiddish poet.

Chaim Nachman Bialik, who, like many other yeshiva students, had read Frug's poems in the Volozhin yeshiva, said about them: "For me, Frug was not writing in Russian—as I read his poems, I felt in every word the language of our ancestors." Inspired, the later-to-become great national poet exclaimed: "Now that's a poet! The Divine Spirit and the angels pay attention to his poems."

In his Russian poems, Frug lamented Jewish suffering and persecution, which reached their peak in the bloody pogroms of 1881; he revived motifs and heroes from the Biblical era, and brought consolation and encouragement to his people.

In 1885, his first collection of Russian poems was published. Two years later, another collection was published, and both books were received by Russian literary critics with great praise.

Under the influence of the newly appearing Yiddish literature, Frug began to write in Yiddish. He didn't start with poems, but with satirical serialized stories, in order to teach and draw morals, as was the way of many *Maskilim.* Simon Dubnow writes about that period in Frug's creativity that the famous poet "… who at that time had been elevated to the acme of Russian culture by great Russian critics, lowered himself for a while to the 'jargon,' at first light-heartedly, but later more seriously and deeply."

Frug himself did not believe at that time that one could write good poetry in Yiddish. He saw his "Yiddish Muse" as an old lady "…pale as the wall, with bluish, dried-out lips and sick, nearsighted eyes...skinny, withered, gloomy, in rags and tatters." He compared the Jewish people to a poor man who had once had his own language and culture but now carried in his sack bread "...of all, all sorts; an old orphan without a mother or father who carries on his shoulders a sack full of rhymes." He complained that while writing his Yiddish poems "...with all his strength, with his last tooth/ bit into and ripped apart the jargon/ chewed the dear language of our mothers/ peppered it with pauses and salted it with rhymes/ to soften it at least a little/ and to smother that dear aroma/ of the Vilna markets and the Dinaburg butcher shops."

His poems demonstrated the opposite. M. Pines, in his *Geshikhte fun der Yidisher Literatur* (History of Yiddish Literature, Warsaw, 1911), wrote that Frug's poems showed the people to what extent Yiddish, which had been declared a coarse and inharmonious dialect, "...can, in the hands of a talented and skillful poet, become an instrument for the sweetest finest, and most harmonious sounds."

Frug was distinguished from all the other Yiddish poets by the refined form of his poems, by their rhythm and their sound. Samuel Niger writes: "Such chiseled verse, such condensation of expression, such purity of tone, is rare, even in Peretz or Frishman."

N.B. Minkoff feels that one could call Frug the father of modern Yiddish poetry: "...in the sense of his pioneering spirit," he writes, "Frug played a role in Yiddish poetry analogous to that of Mendele in Yiddish prose." He brought in from Russian poetry new elements: beautiful sound, flexibility, and rhythm that were new and refreshing in Yiddish poetry."

Concerning Frug's nature poems, which were also new to Yiddish poetry, Bal-Makhshoves[27] writes: "He felt in nature the great world-soul, the life that pours in a thousand streams, the only source from which a healthy people draws life and love for living...that's why the sound of his poetic fiddle was so wonderfully new, wonderfully fresh."

Frug derived his love of nature from the pastoral environment in which he had grown up. He was born in a village (Bobrovi-Kut in the province of Kherson) that was one of the first Jewish agricultural colonies in Russia. There he spent his childhood, studied in *kheyder*, played in the open air, and felt a closeness to the Jews who worked "...in rain, in storms, in heat, and in cold," whom he later

---

27. Pen name of Israel Elyashev, 1873-1924

celebrated and blessed: "...long life to the hands with calluses, the foreheads from which sweat runs."

Frug was the first poet who awakened and called for Jewish national freedom in Palestine, even before the Lovers of Zion and later the Zionists:

> *Enough, enough of kneading clay—*
> *arise, your mother is calling you home.*
> *Fly like an eagle--*
> *a new path is beginning.*
> *Raise your great, ancient banner,*
> *the banner, the banner of Zion.*

In another poem, he calls upon the people to gather all its strength to free itself from the grave in which it lies buried:

> *With strength, with fervent belief,*
> *from its long, deep sleep it awakes.*
> *It will, alone and by itself,*
> *drive away the dark, cold night.*

And the poet prays:

> *O dear God, Thou mighty God—*
> *punished with great woe and suffering,*
> *with poverty and sorrow, shame and mockery,*
> *Thy people has become a beggar.*

> *Have mercy, let it at least*
> *see a bit of happiness in the world.*
> *Give it a field of its own, its own,*
> *on which to plow and sow.*

> *Give it a forest, a garden—*
> *let it forget its ancient suffering.*
> *Let it feel how dear it is*
> *to eat its own little piece of bread.*

In his poem *Der Kos* (The Cup*)* (translated by Peretz), he asks, via the mouth of a child:

Is the cup bottomless,
that we suffer without end?
How long we have been suffering in exile,
and the cup refuses to become full!
Perhaps through the years
the tears in the cup dry up?

His poem *Es Shaynt Di Levone, Es Glantsn Di Shtern* (The Moon Shines, The Stars Sparkle*)* was sung as a national hymn. Dubnow says correctly that "… judging from his inclinations, Frug was a Zionist long before that movement began. His well known *Tsiyon's Marsh* (The March Of Zion*)* rang out even longer ago, at the cradle of 'The Lovers of Zion.'"

Among the national poems that became famous, one should mention Frug's song *Hot Rakhmones* (Have Mercy*)*, written after the Kishinev pogrom. Jews throughout the world sang:

Brothers, sisters—have mercy!
Great and terrible is the need.
Give to the dead for shrouds,
give to the living for bread.

Frug was also the first to celebrate the beauty of Jewish holidays: old, beautiful traditions and Jewish heroes lived again in his poems about *peysakh, khanike,* etc. He also wrote beautiful Nature and children's poems. In one poem, he says:

The woods and fields all 'round about,
the clouds and stars, the rivers and lakes—
all of Nature was my teacher.
She taught me both to sing and to play,
she taught me both to think and to feel,
she showed me ugliness and beauty.

Frug also did not overlook the Jewish workers' struggle for freedom in Russia; he encouraged them through his poetry. The most famous of the poems is *Di Fon* (*The Banner*), which has woven into its threads

all the pain and suffering,
all the fresh wounds
of the deep prison cells,

the black depths,
the hungry villages,
and the stuffy cities.

Composers created music for a large proportion of Frug's poems, and some of those songs have been incorporated into textbooks and are sung in Yiddish schools throughout the world.

As a Russian poet, Frug has long been forgotten. No one remembers or reads any longer his Russian poems, of which he and the Russian-Jewish intelligentsia were so proud. He has remained alive precisely in the language of the Vilna marketplace and the Dinaburg butcher shops.

The Song of Work

For you, my poor brothers and sisters,
scattered throughout the world,
who creep along, lost, on a thousand roads
in the rain, the storm, the heat, and the cold—

for you, the eternal groaner and sigher,
the depressed, complaining, lamenting Jew,
my fresh, lively, joyful song
is sounding and singing, echoing and ringing.

Life flows in a thousand streams,
and in the end comes to the ancient, eternal shore.
For one, Earth is a blooming garden,
and for a thousand it's a hard, muddy road.

A song of praise for effort and work!
Sing, greet them from the heart—lovingly, warmly.
Blessed be the hands with calluses,
the foreheads from which sweat runs.

Blessed be the workshop and the spindle,
the hammer, the plow, the sickle, and the saw.
For one, the Earth is a blooming garden,
and for a thousand, it's a hard, muddy road.

Delicious, brothers, are the nobleman's dishes!
Most delicious of all are the pieces of bread
derived from your own honest labor,
with sweat and efforts, but not needless ones.

Delicious is the nobleman's sleep in his room,
on soft pillows, white as snow.
More delicious is a peaceful evening after work
in the field, on a stack of fresh hay.

The sun shines much brighter after a rain;
warmth is sweeter, more welcome after the cold.
Those who have suffered misfortune
understand what it means to be happy.

ליד דער אַרבעט

פֿאַר אײַך, מײַנע אָרעמע ברידער און שוועסטער,
וואָס זענען צעזייט און צעשפּרייט אויף דער וועלט,
וואָס קריכן און בלאָנדזשען אויף טויזנטער וועגן,
אין רעגן, אין שטורעם, אין היץ און אין קעלט,

פֿאַר דיך, אוי, דו אייביקער קרעכצער און זיפֿצער,
פֿאַרשוואַרצטער, פֿאַרקלאָגטער, פֿאַריאָמערטער ייד,
טוט שאַלן און זינגען און הילכן און קלינגען
מײַן פֿריש, מײַן לעבעדיק-פֿרייילעכע ליד.

אין טויזנטער שטראָמען גיסט זיך דאָס לעבן
און קומט פֿאָרט צום אַלטן, צום אייביקן ברעג....
די וועלט איז פֿאַר איינעם אַ בליִענדער גאָרטן,
פֿאַר טויזנט — אַ שווערער, אַ זומפֿיקער וועג.

אַ, לויב און געזאַנג דער מי און דער אַרבעט!
זינגט, גריסט זיי פֿון האַרצן, ליבנד און היים!
געזונט זאָלן זײַן די הענט מיט מאָזאָליעם,
דער שטערן, פֿון וועלכן עס גיסט זיך דער שוויים!

געבענטשט זאָלן זײַן די ווערקשטאַטס, דאָס שפּינדל,
דער האַמער, די סאָכע, דער סערפּ און די זעג!
די וועלט איז פֿאַר איינעם אַ בליִענדער גאָרטן,
פֿאַר טויזנט — אַ שווערער און זומפֿיקער וועג.

געשמאַק זענען, ברידער, דעם שררהם מאַכלים!
געשמאַקער פֿון אַלעם — דאָס שטיקעלע ברויט,
וואָס צים זיך פֿון אייגענער, ערלעכער אַרבעט
מיט שוויים און מיט מי, אַבי נאָר אָן נויט.

געשמאַק איז דעם שררהם שלאָף אין זײַן צימער,
אויף ווייכינקע קישעלעך, ווײַם ווי דער שניי;
געשמאַקער — אַ שלומער פֿאַרנאַכט, נאָך דער אַרבעט
אין פֿעלד, א.זוו אַ קאָפּיצע פֿרישינקן היי.

פֿיל ליכטיקער שײַנט די זון נאָך אַ רעגן;
די ווארעמקייט — ליבער און זיסער נאָך קעלט;
נאָר די, וועלכע האָבן דאָס אומגליק גענאָסן,
פֿאַרשטייען וואָס גליקלעך זײַן הייסט אויף דער וועלט,

The arrow is made of steel, the plow of iron—
they're very simply made and not too pretty.
But we make swords and shields out of them,
and indeed holy crowns as well.

The sickle is made of steel, the plow of iron—
they're none too decorative.
But in them lies our strength and our life,
and we can't take a single step without them.

So sing in praise of work and toil—
Sing, greet them from the heart—lovingly, warmly.
Blessed be the hands with calluses,
the foreheads from which sweat runs.

Sand and Stars

The moon shines, the stars sparkle,
the night soars over mountains and valleys.
The ancient book lies open before me—
I read it, read it a thousand times.

I read the holy, dear words.
I hear a voice: "I swear:
my people, you'll be like the stars in the heavens,
like sand on the shores of the sea."

Lord of the Universe! They never go lost,
not a single word of Your promises.
Your holy will must be fulfilled—
everything comes in its time and place.

And one thing has already come true—
I feel that, I know it for sure.
We've become like sand that is unprotected,
sand that everyone treads upon.

Yes, dear God, it's true: like sand and like stones,
scattered to shame and mockery.

די פֿײל איז פֿון שטאָל, דער האַמער — פֿון אײַזן,
גאַנץ אײנפֿאַך געמאַכט און ניט איבעריק שײן,
מיט זיי אָבער מאַכט מען דאָס שוועַרד און דעם פֿאַנצער
און טאַקע די הייליקע קרוינען אַליין.

דער סערפּ איז פֿון שטאָל, די סאַקע — פֿון אײַזן:
קיין צירונג קיין גרויסע זעַנען זיי ניט;
אין זיי אָבער ליגט אונדזער קראַפֿט, אונדזער לעבן,
אָן זיי איז אוממעגלעך איין איינציקער טריט.

טאָ לויבט זשע און זינגט דער מי און דער אַרבעט!
זינגט, גריסט זיי פֿון האַרצן, ליבנד און היים!
געזונט זאָלן זײַן די הענט מיט מאַזעליעם,
דער שטערן, פֿון וועלכן עס גיסט זיך דער שווייס!

זאַמד און שטערן

עס שײַנט די לבנה; עס גלאַנצן די שטערן;
די נאַכט שוועבט אויף בערג און אויף טאָל...
דאָס אַלטיטשקע ביכעלע ליגט פֿאַר מיר אָפֿן,
איך לייען עס, לייען עס טויזנטער מאָל.

איך לייען די הייליקע, טײַערע ווערטער,
מיר הערט זיך אַ שטימע: ״איך שווער —
מײַן פֿאָלק, דו וועסט זײַן ווי די שטערן אין הימל,
ווי זאַמד אויפֿן ברעג פֿונעם מער...״

רבונו של עולם! עס ווערט ניט פֿאַרפֿאַלן
פֿון דײַנע הבטחות קיין איינציק וואָרט:
מקוים מוז ווערן דײַן הייליקער ווילן,
אַלץ קומט אין זײַן צײַט, אויף זײַן אָרט.

און איינס איז שוין טאַקע מקוים געוואָרן —
דאָס פֿיל איך, דאָס ווייס איך געוויס;
מיר זעַנען געוואָרן ווי זאַמד, וואָס איז הפֿקר,
וואָס יעדערער טרעט מיט די פֿיס...

יאָ, גאָטעניו, אמת, ווי זאַמד און ווי שטיינער,
צעשפּרייט און צעוואָרפֿן אויף שאַנד און אויף שפּאָט...

But the stars, the bright, the clear—
the stars, the stars—where are they, God?!

Have Mercy

Streams of blood and rivers of tears
boil and flow deep and wide…
our ancient great misfortune
has spread its hand over us.

Do you hear the moaning of mothers there,
and the cries of the children?
Dead men lie in the streets
and sick ones fall down next to them.

Brothers, sisters, have mercy!
Great and terrible is the need.
Give to the dead for shrouds
and give to the living for bread.

From a distance it's hard to feel
distant tears, strangers' weeping,
distant misfortune, strangers' misfortune,
strangers' blood. No, brother, no!

A thousand hearts with a single pain—
a thousand houses with a single door.
All, all—a single sorrowing
sick orphan are we…

Brothers, sisters, have mercy!
Great and terrible is the need.
Give to the dead for shrouds
and give to the living for bread!

Streams of blood and rivers of tears
boil and flow endlessly…
The fear of death looks through the window
and hunger knocks on the door.

נו, אָבער די שטערן, די ליכטיקע, קלאָרע —
די שטערן, די שטערן — וווּ זענען זיי, גאָט ?!...

האָט רחמנות

שטראָמען בלוט און טײַכן טרערן
זידן, פֿליסן טיף און ברייט...
אונדזער אַלטער, גרויסער אומגליק
האָט זײַן האַנט אויף אונדז פֿאַרשפּרייט.

הערט איר דאָרט, ווי מוטערס קלאָגן
און פֿון קינדער דאָס געשריי?
טויטע ליגן אויף די גאַסן,
קראַנקע פֿאַלן נעבן זיי...

ברידער, שוועסטער, האָט רחמנות!
גרויס און שרעקלעך איז די נויט —
גיט די טויטע אויף תּכריכים,
גיט די לעבעדיקע ברויט!...

פֿון דער ווײַטן שווער צו פֿילן:
ווײַטע טרערן — פֿרעמד געוויין,
ווײַטער אומגליק — פֿרעמדער אומגליק,
פֿרעמדעס בלוט... נײַן, ברידער, נײַן!

הערצער טויזנט — און אײַן ווייטאָג
טויזנט הײַזער — און אײַן טיר;
אַלע, אַלע — אײַן פֿאַרקלאָגטער
קראַנקער יתום זענען מיר ...

ברידער, שוועסטער! האָט רחמנות!
גרויס און שרעקלעך איז די נויט —
גיט די טויטע אויף תּכריכים,
גיט די לעבעדיקע ברויט!...

שטראָמען בלוט און טײַכן טרערן
זידן, פֿליסן אָן אַ שיעור...
אימת-מוות קוקט אין פֿענצטער
און דער הונגער קלאַפּט אין טיר...

Our hands are too weak to fight—
great and severe is our weakness.
Look you with consolation and love—
with a good, warm Jewish heart.

Brothers, sisters, have mercy!
Great and terrible is the need.
Give to the dead for shrouds
and give to the living for bread.

My Song

I've been a cantor without a platform
for nearly twenty-five years now.
Still my prayers always ring out
and I have a beautiful chorus too,

a great chorus of all sorts,
with all the voices in the world—
millions of birds in the garden
and millions of flowers in the field.

The grapevine prays *Dew* and *Rain* with me,
each in its proper season.
The forests sing *Hallelujah* with me,
singing and ringing on all sides.

The storm helps me blow *tkies*[28]—
it has a magnificent *shofar*.[29]
To hear it is a real pleasure
when it blows on an autumn night.[30]

The sun, the source of life, sings to me,
the wind sings *Hosannas* by the river,
and with a very new melody
I want to sings those songs to you.

---

28. The sound made by blowing a *shofar*
29. Ram's horn, which is blown on various religious occasions
30. As on Rosh Hashone

שלאָף איז אונדזער האַנט צו שטרײַטן,
שטאַרק און שװער איז אונדזער שמאַרץ...
קום זשע, דו, מיט טרײַסט און ליבע,
גוטעס, הײסעס ייִדיש האַרץ !

בּרידער, שװעסטער, האָט רחמנות !
גרױס און שרעקלעך איז די נױט —
גיט די טױטע אױף תּכריכים,
גיט די לעבעדיקע בּרױט !...

מײַן ליד

איך בין אַ חזן אָן אַן עמוד
כּמעט שױן פֿינף און צװאַנציק יאָר.
דאָך קלינגען מײַנע תּפֿילות תּמיד
און כ׳האָב דערצו אַ שײנעם כּאָר.

אַ גרױסן כּאָר פֿון אַלע סאָרטן,
פֿון אַלע שטימען אױף דער װעלט;
מיליאָנען פֿײגעלעך אין גאָרטן,
מיליאָנען קװיטעלעך אין פֿעלד.

דער װײַנשטאָק איז מיט מיר מתפּלל
אױף טל־זומטער אין דער צײַט,
די װעלדער זאָגן מיט מיר הלל;
עס קלינגט און זינגט פֿון יעדער זײַט.

דער שטורעם העלפֿט מיר בּלאָזן תּקיעות —
ער האָט אַ שופֿר גאָר אַ פּראָכט —
און הערן ממש איז אַ חיות
זײַן בּלאָזן אין אַן אָסיען־נאַכט;

מיר זינגט די זון מכלכּל־חיים,
הושענות שלאָגט דער װינט בּײַם טײַך...
און מיט אַ ניגון גאָר אַ נײַעם
װיל איך די לידער זינגען אײַך.

But my heart seems to be
locked in chains and I want to cry.
Whatever I start to sing with,
I end up with *min hamatser.*[31]

Pure and Bright Are the Heavens

Pure and bright are the heavens—
the wind whistles fresh and joyful.
"Sing to me, sing me a summer song,"
pleads the pale, weak child.

"Come with me to the valley, to the garden—
weave me a wreath
from the flowers that grow there
and blossom, beautiful and big."

Ah, my child, do you see?
My harp hangs broken on the wall,
long unused to playing
in my weak, sick hand.

Long unused to sweet joys
is my sick heart.
Summer, winter, autumn, and spring—
the old hurt remains.

---

31. Out of the Depths

מײַן הארץ איז אָבער ווי אין רינגען
געפֿאַסט, און ווײנען ציט עס מיך;
מיט וואָס איך הייב ניט אָן צו זינגען, —
מיט „מן המצר" ענדיק איך...

רייַן און ליכטיק איז דער הימל

רייַן און ליכטיק איז דער הימל;
פֿריש און פֿרײַלעך ווײט דער ווינט...
— זינג מיר, זינג אַ זומער־לידל! —
בעט דאָס שוואַכע, בלייכע קינד:

— קום מיט מיר אין טאָל, אין גאָרטן,
פֿלעכט אַ קרענצעלע מיר אויס
פֿון די בלומען, וועלכע וואַקסן
דאָרט און בלײַען, שיין און גרויס...

אַך, מײַן קינד! דו זעסט? — צעבראָכן
הענגט מײַן האַרפֿע אויף דער וואַנט;
אָפּגעווינט שוין לאַנג פֿון שפּילן
איז מײַן שוואַכע, קראַנקע האַנט;

אָפּגעווינט פֿון זיסע פֿריידן
איז שוין לאַנג מײַן קראַנקע האַרץ.
זומער, ווינטער, האַרבסט און פֿרילינג
בלײַבט אין אים דער אַלטער שמאַרץ.

ABRAHAM REISEN

(born April 1, 1876 in Koidenov, province of Minsk, White Russia;
died March 31, 1953 in New York)

During the dedication of I.L. Peretz Square in New York, in 1952, Abraham Reisen met his thousands of readers and fans for the last time. For the last time, he was able to see and feel something no other Yiddish writer had had the privilege of achieving: how warm streams of affection flowed toward him from three generations--the first generation, even back in the old country and then here in America in the early immigrant years, who seized upon his poems like a new Torah of hope and consolation; the second generation of Yiddish readers, who grew up between the two World Wars, during the blossoming of Yiddish literature; and the third generation, the generation of our children.

We were with the children from our schools; we saw their little hands waving the Peretz banners when the name of their most beloved poet, Abraham Reisen, was called out; we saw their celebration and joy, and we murmured softly: blessed be the poet who can be a wondrous bridge between generations, whom so many storms have tried to overthrow--blessed be he.

After that, we thought: where does that affection of the people for the poet come from? Whence the heartfelt closeness? Whence the love in the eyes of children brought up in homes where the language of Reisen's poetry is no longer the language in which they express their joys and sorrows? There can be only one answer: that was how the people was repaying its bard with some of the great love he had bestowed on them. The people, just like a child, always senses where real love and warmth are coming from. And when Reisen sang:

> *I have a heart full of love,*
> *I am rich with love.*
> *Good people or bad—*
> *all are the same to me.*

everyone knew that that was not just a poem by him—it was also his life.

His heart was full of love for everyone, but he always gave first place to the poor, the insulted, and the weak. He was the bard and celebrator of poor and ordinary people, those who shuffle along next to the wall of life and not in the tumult of

100

the great fairs. His heroes were the cobblers, shopkeepers, teachers, and poor artisans struggling in distant, strange cities; servant girls hiring themselves out to rich ladies to help sick mothers; Yiddish intellectuals in cold, lonely little rooms; and *yeshiva* students wandering around at strangers' tables.

Reisen introduced all of them into Yiddish literature, not as faceless masses but as people, individuals with their own yearnings and dreams. He has a moving story about a shopgirl, Lize, who is dying of sorrow because no one pays any attention to her. She is only one of many and has nothing to distinguish her from the others around her. Nevertheless, Lize has a life of her own, dreams of her own, yearnings. She is, after all, *Lize,* and not just one of many. So she goes around full of sadness till one carnival-night, when she decides to dress up as a Gypsy; she decorates herself in the most attention-getting and most colorful clothing. Now she is different from everybody else. People notice her, start to talk about her as an *individual,* not just one of many.

Reisen, with his blessed eye, forces the world to look at and listen to every one of us, as if to say:

"Look—there's a *person* living near you, and every person is an entire world."

Reisen was perhaps one of the most human poets, not only in our Yiddish literature but also in world literature. For that reason, it is no wonder that he stood so close, all his life, to the labor movement, which wanted to convert his poetry into action. His poem *Di Vant* (The Wall*)* was sung at secret gatherings in forests, in the ghettos and concentration camps of Poland, and at demonstrations in the streets of New York by Jewish workers who were battling for better living conditions. His poem *Hulyet, Hulyet, Beyze Vintn* (Frolic, Frolic, Angry Winds*)* brought hope for Spring into the hearts of tens of thousands. Into the line *"Winter will last a long time,"* Jewish workers inserted the word *"not."* Instead of *"Summer is still far away,"* they began to sing *"Summer is not far away,"* and it became one of the most popular revolutionary songs. His words of consolation, *"I hear the song of love and peace/ the mighty song; and every sound of the song announces:/ the sun has risen"* ignited belief and the will to fight for a world of *"love and peace."*

In the memoirs of the Bundist leader Leybetshke Berman it is related that at the secret gatherings of the Bund in the old country one could often hear, in addition to the slogan "Long live Socialism!," an exclamation by an enthusiastic youth: "Long live Abraham Reisen!"

Years ago, before we had Yiddish secular schools for our children, a critic wrote this about Reisen: "If we had Yiddish schools, the children would learn Reizen's poems by heart and would recite and sing them." Those who are close to the Yiddish schools today know that not only do the children know Reisen's poems by heart but it is impossible to imagine the Yiddish school without Reisen, without his poems and stories.

And a remarkable thing: Reisen never wrote any special children's literature of the type wherein a "tree" becomes a "little tree," a "dog" becomes a "doggie", and a "man" becomes a "little fellow"; his poems and stories are just as near and dear to children as to adults, because from them stream beauty, an elevated tone, and sincerity. Reisen, who knew people very well, understood that beauty and an elevated tone do not have to be dressed up for children with a special children's vocabulary in order to reach their ears and heart. For that reason, every teacher has more than once blessed Reisen for helping, with his great artistic writings, to bring the new generation so close to our rich heritage, for introducing a festive note into the day-to-day reality of Jewish-American life, and for igniting love for our Yiddish language in their hearts.

Reisen was not a fighter—he was a poet, a teacher, and a friend. But it seems to us that he made one exception: he was an uncompromising fighter for the honor and rights of Yiddish. From the Czernowitz Conference of 1908 to the year 1953, Reisen never stopped fighting against all enemies of our Yiddish language, without exception. He didn't spare the assimilationists who spoke insultingly about "the ugly jargon," and he also didn't have any use for those who wanted to choke Yiddish for the sake of Hebrew. Reisen remained faithful to the Peretz tradition on the Yiddish scene, and for that reason his name has been and will remain for us a beacon in our battle for our language, Yiddish.

*   *   *

In 1894, when Reisen was 18 years old, he published in the *Filadelfier Shtot-Tsaytung* (Philadelphia City Newspaper*)* his *Troyerike Motivn, Gevidmet Oreme-Layt* (Sorrowful Themes, Dedicated to Poor People.) In the succeeding 59 years of his artistic flowering, the poet dedicated hundreds of wonderful themes to the poor, in whom he heard "the sorrow of the world."

> *And what the whole world has experienced,*
> *suffered in all eras,*
> *has ridden past me quietly.*

The poet carried in himself all the sorrows of the world, as well as all the hopes of the suffering world for freeing itself of sorrows. Reisen taught us that we should grasp those sorrows and carry with us his great belief in and love for mankind.

We should teach our children and grandchildren what Reisen taught us in his poem about Mendele, the grandfather of Yiddish literature:

> *In his little purse there lies a great treasure.*
> *Let's not leave it out in the rain!*
> *Let's protect it, now and in time of storms!*
> *Ah, the little purse is our fortress...*

And may that shining fortress on which the name of Reisen is also incised continue to shine and illuminate the coming generations.

The Wall

Our eyes full of rage, suffused with blood,
our hearts beat forcefully and courageously.
We're standing next to a large stone wall
with axes and hammers and iron rods in our hands.
        We're breaking the wall!

The wall is of stone and quite strong and thick;
it blocks the road to life and joy.
It blocks the bright sun and makes
dark night out of joyous day.
        We're breaking the wall!

And if from the wall there falls
a stone or a brick and strikes someone's head,
the others remain standing there fearlessly
and continue to work—they don't run away.
        We're breaking the wall!

The work must continue, the work is hard.
Gather together, brothers—come here, all of you,
let each of you lend a firm hand.
We'll break the high, dark wall—
        we'll break, we'll break the wall!

O Faster, Messiah

O faster, Messiah, we cannot wait long—
the world all around us is plotting our fate.
Our hunger and need are like poisonous snakes—
no law, only fear and anguish we see.
The world cannot feed the Earth's population,
so come soon, Messiah, upon your white steed.

"O come soon, Messiah!" our voices ring out—
the chains of our slavery are clanging all 'round.
There's innocent blood everywhere that you look--
it spurts 'neath the lash, wherever we are.

די וואַנט

די אויגן — פֿול צאַרן, פֿאַרגאָסן מיט בלוט,
די הערצער — זיי שלאָגן מיט קראַפֿט און מיט מוט —
מיר שטייען ביי אַ הויכער, געמויערטער וואַנט, —
מיט העק און מיט האַמערס, און איעזנס אין האַנט —
מיר ברעכן די וואַנט !

די וואַנט איז געמויערט גאָר פֿעסט און גאָר דיק,
פֿאַרצוימט אונדז די וועגן צום לעבן, צום גליק;
פֿאַרשטעלט אונדז די ליכטיקע זון און זי מאַכט
פֿון פֿריילעכן טאָג אונדז אַ פֿינצטערע נאַכט —
מיר ברעכן די וואַנט !

און פֿאַלט פֿון דער שטיינערנער וואַנט וועז אַראָפּ
אַ שטיין, צי אַ ציגל, טרעפֿט וועמעז אין קאָפּ, —
די איבעריקע בלייבן דאָך שטיין גאָר אָן שרעק
און אַרבעטן ווייטער, מען לויפֿט נישט אַוועק —
מיר ברעכן די וואַנט !

די אַרבעט דאַרף דויערן, די אַרבעט איז שווער —
פֿאַרזאַמלט זיך ברידער, קומט אַלע אַהער;
זאָל יעדערער צולייגן פֿעסטער זייַן האַנט,
מיר וועלן די הויכע, די פֿינצטערע וואַנט —
צעברעכן, צעברעכן די וואַנט !...

אַ, גיכער, משיח

אַ, גיכער, משיח, אַ, גיכער שוין קום !
עס רינגלט די גאַנצענע וועלט שוין אַרום,
ווי גיפֿטיקע שלאַנגען דער הונגער און נויט,
און הפֿקר און פֿחד, און אַנגסטן און טויט.
עס וויל שוין ניט אַלעמעז שפֿייזן די ערד —
אַ, קום שוין, משיח, אויפֿן ווייַסינקן פֿערד.

אַ, קום שוין, משיח ! עס דריקט עס אומעטום
די קייטן פֿון קנעכטשאַפֿט אַרום און אַרום:
עס האָט שוין קיין אָרט דאָס אומשולדיקע בלוט,
וואָס שפֿריצט און וואָס גיסט זיך פֿון אונטער דער רוט.

The swords are blood-reddened from horrible wars,
so come soon, Messiah, upon your white steed.

To the Little Hammer

Oh bang little hammer, oh bang!
Hit nail after nail harder!
There's no bread in the house,
just endless troubles and pain.

Oh bang little hammer, oh bang!
The clock will soon strike twelve.
Our eyes are closing—
give us strength, dear God, help!

Oh bang, little hammer, oh bang!
Strike the nails harder and faster.
By morning I must finish
the rich man's daughter's shoes.

Oh bang, little hammer, oh bang!
Don't slip out of my hand!
You're my only source of food—
without you I'll die of hunger!

A Winter Song

Frolic, frolic, angry winds—
freely rule the world!
Break the branches, bend the trees,
do whate'er you want!

Drive the birds out of the woods
and chase them far away.
Those that cannot fly away,
just kill them on the spot.

Rip the shutters off the windows—
knock out the windowpanes!

עס ראָסטעט פֿון מענטשעלעכע בלוט שוין דער שוועָרד —
אָ, קום שוין, משיח, אויפֿן וויַיסינקן פֿערד!...

צום העמערל

אָ, העמערל, העמערל, קלאָפּ!
שלאָג שטאַרקער אַ טשוועק נאָך אַ טשוועק!
קיין ברויט איז אין שטוב שוין נישטאָ,
נאָר צרות און לייד אָן אַן עק!

אָ, העמערל, העמערל, קלאָפּ!
דער זייגער, ער שלאָגט שוין באַלד צוועלף:
די אויגן, זיי מאַכן זיך צו —
גיב פּוחות — אָ, גאָטעניו, העלף!

אָ, העמערל, העמערל, קלאָפּ!
שלאָג שטאַרקער די טשוועקעס, שלאָג גיך,
ביז מאָרגן מוז פֿאַרטיק שוין זיַין
דער גבֿירהטעס טעכטערלס שיך!

אָ, העמערל, העמערל, קלאָפּ!
ניט גליטש פֿון מיַין האַנט זיך אַרוים!
מיַין איינציקער שפֿיַיזער ביסטו,
פֿון הונגער אָן דיר גיי איך אוים!...

אַ ווינטערליד

הוליעט, הוליעט, בייזע ווינטן,
פֿריַי באַהערשט די וועלט!
ברעכט די צוויַיגן, וואַרפֿט די ביימער,
טוט וואָס איַיך געפֿעלט!

טריַיבט די פֿייגל פֿון די וועלדער
און פֿאַריאָגט זיי פֿאָרט;
די וואָס קענען וויַיט נישט פֿליִען,
טייט זיי אויפֿן אָרט!

ריַיסט די לאָדן פֿון די פֿענצטער,
שויבן ברעכט אַרוים!

If a candle's burning in the dark,
rage and blow it out!

Frolic, frolic, angry winds—
now has come your time!
Winter still will last quite long
and summer's far away!

A Family of Eight

A family of eight,
but just two beds.
When the night comes,
where will they sleep?

Three with the father
and three with the mother,
little hands and feet
entwined.

And when the night comes,
they have to make the beds.
Then mother starts to plead
for Death to take her.

She really means it!
It's no wonder!
Though it's also crowded in the grave,
at least she'll lie there alone.

What Does It Mean To Me

What does the rain mean to me?
What is it trying to tell me?
Its drops on the windowpanes
roll down like sad tears.
My boots are torn
and it's muddy out in the street.

ברענגט אַ ליכטל' ערגעץ טונקל, —
לעשט מיט צאָרן אויס!

הוליעט, הוליעט, בייזע ווינטן,
איצט איז אייער צייט!
לאַנג וועט דויערן דער ווינטער,
זומער איז נאָך ווייט!...

אַ געזינד זאַלבע אַכט

אַ געזינד זאַלבע אַכט,
און בעטן נאָר צוויי, —
און קומט אָן די נאַכט,
וווּ שלאָפֿן דאַן זיי?

דרײַ מיטן טאַטן
און דרײַ מיט דער מאַמען —
הענטלעך און פֿיסלעך,
געפֿלאָכטן צוזאַמען.

און קומט אָן די נאַכט,
מ'דאַרף מאַכן די בעטן,
דאַן הייבט אָן די מוטער
דעם טויט אויף זיך בעטן.

זי מיינט מיט אָן אמת, —
עס איז נישט קיין וווּנדער:
אויך ענג איז אין קבֿר,
דאָך ליגט מען באַזונדער...

מאַי־קאָ משמע־לן?...

מאַי־קאָ משמע־לן דער רעגן?
וואָס זשע לאָזט ער מיר צו הערן? —
זײַנע טראָפּנס אויף די שויבן
קײַקלען זיך ווי טריבע טרערן.
און די שטיוול איז צעריסן
און עס ווערט אין גאַס אַ בלאָטע;

Winter will soon come
and I don't have a warm overcoat.

What does the candle mean?
What is it trying to tell me?
The tallow drips and runs down,
and soon there'll be nothing left of it.
Just so do I flicker here in the shul
like a candle, weak and dark,
till I go out,
quietly, in the East corner.

What does the clock mean?
What is it trying to tell me
with its yellow number-face
and its loud chimes?
It's a hired tool, has no life, no feelings.
When the hour comes, it must strike,
with no will of its own.

What does my life mean?
What is it trying to tell me?
Idling and wasting away in my youth
and growing old before my time;
wasting and swallowing tears;
sleeping on my hard fist;
killing time in this world
and waiting for the next one.

I and the World

If things were bad with all the world
and things were good for me alone,
I'd surely then invite the world
to share the comforts of my home.

I'd comfort it, give my caress,
and say: "Don't worry so, dear world,"
until it slowly came around
and stood up straight upon the ground.

באַלד וועט אויך דער ווינטער קומען —
כ׳האָב קיין וואַרעמע קאַפּאָטע...

מאַי־קאָ משמע־לן דאָס ליכטל ?
וואָס זשע לאָזט עם מיר צו הערן ?
ס׳קאַפּעט און עם טריפֿט איר חלבֿ
און ס׳וועט באַלד פֿון איר ניט ווערן.
אַזוי צאַנק איך דאָ אין קלײַזל,
ווי אַ ליכטל, שוואַך און טונקל,
ביז איך וועל אַזוי מיר אויסגיין
אין דער שטיל, אין מיזרח־ווינקל...

מאַי־קאָ משמע־לן דער זײגער ?
וואָס זשע לאָזט ער מיר צו הערן,
מיט זײַן געלבן ציפֿער־בלעטל,
מיט זײַן קלינגען, מיט זײַן שווערן ?
ס׳איז אַן אָנגעשטעלטע כּלי,
האָט קיין לעבן, קיין געפֿילן,
קומט די שעה, דאַן מוז ער שלאָגן,
אָן זײַן רצון, אָן זײַן ווילן...

מאַי־קאָ משמע־לן מײַן לעבן?
וואָס זשע לאָזט עם מיר צו הערן ?
פֿוילן, וועלקן אין דער יוגנט,
פֿאַר דער צײַט פֿאַרעלטערט ווערן,
עסן „טעג" און שלינגען טרערן,
שלאָפֿן אויפֿן פֿויסט דעם האַרטן,
טײמט דאָ די עולם־הזה
און אויף עולם־הבא וואַרטן...

איך און די וועלט

ווען די גאַנצע וועלט וואָלט לײַדן
מיר אַליין זאָל גוט זײַן בלויז:
וואָלט איך דאָן די וועלט די גאַנצע
אײַנגעלאַדן אין מײַן הויז.

איך וואָלט טרייסטן זי און צערטלען,
און געזאָגט: ניט זאָרג זיך וועלט.
ביז זי וואָלט צו זיך געקומען
און זיך אויף די פֿיס געשטעלט.

If all the world were happy now
and only I were full of pain,
I'd come to it and make demand:
"Now you must make me whole again."

But things are bad for both of us—
the world's in pain and I too now.
The world has no one who can help,
nor is there one to show me how.

ווען די וועלט געווען וואָלט גליקלעך,
איך אַליין בלויז פֿול מיט לייד,
וואָלט איך דאַן צו איר געקומען
און געפֿאָדערט: גיב מיר פֿרייד!

אָבער אַז מיר ביידע ליַידן,
סיַי די וועלט, סיַי איך אַליין,–
האָט די וועלט ניט וואָ צו קומען
און איך האָב ניט וואָ צו גיין...

MORRIS WINCHEVSKY

(pseudonym of Lipe Ben-Tsion Novakhovets;
born on August 9, 1856 in Yanove, in the vicinity of Kovno, Lithuania;
died on March 18, 1932, in Bronx, NY)

Morris Winchevsky, who was crowned "the grandfather of Jewish socialism" and of the Yiddish social poem, declared his credo in one of his earliest poems:

I would sing in all rhythms
to wake you to the battle!
I would ring all the bells
to announce the time has come!

As a pioneer of Jewish socialist thought and struggle, Winchevsky did not omit a single literary form or rhythm to sing to and awaken the Jewish workers and folk-masses to the struggle for a better life. He was a fiery publicist, a sharp writer of light fiction and satires, a talented writer of literary prose, a poet, a playwright, a writer of fables, and a translator. And though as early as 1911, at his 55th birthday banquet, he considered himself a forgotten poet, pleading:

Clear away the dead flowers
from the dead bouquet;
the day will not come back
for the forgotten poet—

the day of his fame never passed. His own poetry lives on in the influence he had on Yiddish poetry in general with his themes and his singing rhythms.

When Morris Winchevsky came to New York in 1894, he had long been famous here and beloved by the Jewish workers and folk masses. They knew his poems from the old country, and read his creations in the Yiddish socialist and anarchist press in America. Many of his poems were recited at demonstrations and labor festivals. Though the poet and fighter was only 38 years old, he had already been crowned the grandfather of Jewish socialism and had participated in socialist activity in nearly a dozen European countries: Russia, Germany, Austria, France, Denmark, Holland, Belgium, Switzerland, and finally England, where he developed broad political and literary activity.

However, Winchevsky was and remained a *Jewish* socialist. His relationships with the greatest socialist and anarchist leaders of the time only strengthened his desire to work among Jews, as a Jewish socialist, and to write and create in the language of his people—Yiddish. As early as 1879, he wrote, in London, the first socialist brochure in Yiddish, *Yihi Or* (Let There Be Light*)*. He had started to write his socialist poems and articles in Hebrew, but he quickly perceived that to be able to influence the people for whom he was creating he had to write Yiddish. He became the first Yiddish social poet.

Two principal themes are expressed in his poems: empathy and lamentation for the fate of the poor and suffering together with sharp satire about the oppressors and users; and a call to battle, to awakening a new world, in which

> *the world will grow more beautiful,*
> *love greater and hatred less*
> *between women and men,*
> *between one land and another.*

With the first theme, there were such famous poems as *In Regn, In Vint, Un In Kelt* (In The Rain,Wind, and Cold) (What are two little infants doing in the street/ in the rain, wind, and cold?); *Dray Shvester* (Three Sisters) (In England there's a city named Leicester/ in London there's a square by that name); *A Meydele in der Siti* (A Girl In The City) (Near the Exchange, the temple of swindling/ I daily see a poor child); *London Bay Nakht* (London At Night) (You little lamps and lanterns,/ tell me what you think about at night, /standing there and burning); and one of his first poems, *Dos Lid Funem Hemd*, an adaptation of Thomas Hood's *Song of the Shirt* (With slender fingers, skinny and twisted, with eyes that are nearly blind from work).

Most of these poems were written between 1884 and 1891, in London, where the poet saw "frightful poverty in all its nakedness, tatters, and debasement ...through the contrast between the millions of pounds sterling and the billions of puds[32] of troubles." He could not free himself from the "billions of puds of troubles" that his eyes and his heart took in, even in his purely lyrical poems:

> *How long will slavery last?*
> *Who knows, ah, who knows how long?*
> *I only know that so long*
> *will my poem and dirge mourn.*

---

32. A Russian measure of weight: about 40 lbs.

And although Winchevsky writes in the same poem that his poems "don't have a ring to them" and that they "lack melody," people seized on the poems, which had a new rhythmic tone, and clothed them with melodies. He writes about that in his book *Lider un Gedikhte* (Songs and Poems) (New York, 1910): "That I didn't make the poems to be sung was true on my part, but the people sang them and sang them a lot, and I must confess that that gave me many happy moments. That was especially the case with the tunes that came to me from across the Atlantic, directly from the hearts of my brothers and sisters in Russia, during the exciting times of the battles for freedom."

Among the poems for rousing and calling to battle that became popular on both sides of the ocean, some of which are still sung today by folk-choruses and stage artists, are: *Di Tsukunft* (The Future) (Oh, the world will grow younger); *Es Rirt Zikh* (Things Are Moving) (Do you hear, children, how things are moving/ how they are moving everywhere); *Kamf-Gezang* (Battle Song) (Unfurl the red banner); *A Bezem un a Ker* (A Broom and a Sweep) (Enough! I don't want to feed/the idlers any more); *Der Frayhayt-Gayst* (The Spirit of Freedom) (In the streets, among the masses/ of oppressed folk-races); *The Marseillaise* (Arise, ye oppressed masses/ and put an end to slavery—Winchevsky's translation of the French original); and others.

B.J. Bialostotsky, in *Fir Zaynen Zey Geven* (They Were Four), in the *Dovid Edelshtat Gedenk-Bukh* (The David Edelshtat Memorial Book, 1953) and N.B. Minkoff, in *Pionern fun der Yidisher Poezie in Amerike* (Pioneers of Yiddish Poetry in America) comment concerning Winchevsky's influence on the proletarian poets and on Yiddish poetry in general. Bialostotsky, for example, shows that the famous poem Mayn Yingele (*My Little Boy*) was written by Rosenfeld under the influence of Winchevsky's poem *Kleyn Etele* (Little Etele); not only the themes but also the rhythms are similar:

I know a little girl,
a child of a working man;
her little face
brings joy to the family.

She blossoms, the beautiful girl,
even in a time of poverty;
her father considers her little dress
more important than his bread.

He often sits by her little bed
sadly, on his chair,
and thinks about his little Etele
with his eyes red and full.

Bialostotsky points out two other themes of Rosenfeld's that are reminiscent of Winchevsky's themes and rhythms: Rosenfeld's "It was both snowing and raining/ and walking through the streets" is reminiscent of Winchevsky's *In Rain and Wind and Cold;* also Rosenfeld's poem about the poor blind man in New York's East Side is reminiscent of Winchevsky's poem about the blind musician in London's Whitechapel:

Rosenfeld:

On Grand Street, not far from Sokerstein's store,
a blind man with long gray hair sits every day,
groans with hunger and weariness,
and plays his fiddle sorrowfully.

Winchevsky:

In Cheapside[33], not far from the statue,
there daily stands on the sidewalk
a blind man, who holds in his skinny hands
an old, used instrument
and plays a terribly sad tune.

It is also appropriate to mention a folksong that can be found in a number of song anthologies as an anonymous song and that is popular among the younger and older generations in America, but has its origin in a song of Winchevsky's written in 1890, namely the popular song *Ale Brider* (All Brothers*)*. The song was published by A. Litvin in his regular column in *Di Tsayt (*The Times*)*, under the title *Di Kolokotke* (The Rattle), as "a very popular Bundist song." In reality, the song comes from a poem of Winchevsky's, *Brotherhood,* published in *Di Kolokotke*, organ of the United Patriots, edited by "A Fellow From Minsk" in *Arbeter Fraynd*, London, August 29, 1890. The original text of the poem is as follows:

---

33. A poor district in London

Brotherhood

Yes, we're all united,
whether we have much or little;
we're all brothers
and we pray from the same *siddur.*
Whether we cut pants patterns
or coupons from bonds,
we're all together,
the poor man and the rich.

Short side-curls, long side-curls,
Jews with and without money;
thin or obese bellies,
pure hearts or wild ones,
pious heads or heads of sinners,
heads with *yarmlkes* or top-hats--
we're all a single people,
like soldiers in one regiment.

Pious or secular, all united,
like the groom and his bride;
like the broomstick and the broom,
like the *tsitsis* and its cords,
like the *mezzuzah* and the door,
like the shirtwaist and the blouse,
like the Torah and Rashi,
like *kugl* and *kashe*
like jewels and their glitter,
like musicians and dancers a-twitter.

Things Are Moving
(fragment)

Do you hear, children, how things are moving,
how they are moving everywhere?
How the workingman is preparing
for the fight with capitalism
and the fight to the death with the flayers,
the avaricious ones, the money-tyrant?

אַחדות

יאָ, מיר זײַנען אַלע אייניק!
צי מיר האָבן פֿיל צי ווייניק,
און מיר זײַנען אַלע ברידער,
און מיר דאַוונען פֿון איין סדור,
ס'זײַ מיר שנײַדן פאַנטאַלאָנעס,
ס'זײַ מיר שנײַדן אָפ קופֿאָנעס,
אייניק זײַנען אַלע מיר,
גלײַך דער אביון מיטן גבֿיר!

קורצע פּאות, לאַנגע פּאות,
ייִדן מיט און אָן מטבעות,
דאָרע און געפֿילטע קישקעס,
הוילע הערצער און מאַנישקעס,
פֿרומע קעפּ און קעפּ פֿון זינדערס,
קעפּ אין יאַרמלקעס, צילינדערס.
אַלע זײַנען מיר איין פֿאָלק,
ווי סאָלדאַטן אין איין פֿאָלק.

פֿרום און לינק, פֿאַראייניקט אַלע,
ווי דער חתן מיט דער כלה,
ווי דער בעזעם מיטן שטעקן,
ווי די ציצית מיט די עקן,
ווי די טיר מיט דער מזוזה,
ווי די טאַליע מיט דער בלוזע,
ווי דער חומש מיט די רש"י,
ווי דער קוגל מיט דער קאַשע,
ווי דער תכשיט מיטן גלאַנץ,
ווי דער כלי־זמר מיטן טאַנץ.

עס רירט זיך
(פֿראַגמענט)

הערט איר, קינדער, ווי עס רירט זיך,
ווי עס רירט זיך איבעראַל?
ווי דער אַרבעטסמאַן מושטירט זיך
צו דעם קאַמפֿ מיט קאַפּיטאַל, —
צו דעם טויט־קאַמפֿ מיטן שינדער,
דעם האַבון, דעם געלט־טיראַן,

Do you hear, children, how things are moving
for the robbed workingman?

Do you hear, children, how things are moving?
Do you notice that the end is near?
Forward, children, we're marching
lustily, under the red banner!
Freedom ignites our hearts,
without trumpets or drums.
His brothers, you see, children,
are going to free the workingman!

Everywhere, on both sides
of the Atlantic, things are moving!
He'll no longer allow
his blood sucker to ride on his back.
No longer will he allow himself
to be harnessed like a blind horse.
He wants to be free, dear children—
the workingman wants to have a full stomach!

See, children? He wants to
put an end to slavery,
wants to enjoy all the things
his hands create.
Children, he's a discoverer :
he's thought up a way
to live happily, children—
he, the simple workingman.

The Future
(fragment)

Oh, the world will grow younger
and life will grow easier.
Every mourner will become a singer--
they'll become brothers soon!
Just let the people grow wiser
and chase away the deceivers,

הערט איר, ווי עם רירט זיך, קינדער,
דער באַרוימטער אַרבעטסמאַן ?

הערט איר, קינדער, ווי עם רירט זיך,
מערקט איר, אַז דער סוף קומט אָן ?
פאַרווערטם, קינדער, עס מאַרשירט זיך
לוסטיק ביַי דער רויטער פאָן !
פריַיהייט איז דער הערצער-צינדער,
אָן טרומיט און באַראבאַן,
זיַינע ברידער, זעט איר, קינדער,
גייט באַפריַיען דער אַרבעטסמאַן !

איבעראַל פֿון ביידע זיַיטן
פֿון אָטלאַנטיק רירט ער זיך !
ער וויל מער ניט לאָזן ר,יַיטן
זיַינע בלוטזוינער אויף זיך.
ער וויל מער ניט, ווי אַ בלינדער
פֿערד, ביַי זיי גייין אין געשפאַן,
ער וויל פריַי זיַין, ליבע קינדער,
זאָט זיַין וויל דער אַרבעטסמאַן !

זעט איר, קינדער, ער וויל מאַכן
פֿון דער שקלאַפֿעריַי אַן ענד,
וויל גענימן אַל די זאַכן,
וואָם עם מאַכן זיַינע הענט,
קינדער, ער איז אַ דערפֿינדער,
ער האָט אויסגעטראַכט אַ פּלאָן,
ווי צו לעבן גליקלעך, קינדער,
ער — דער פראָסטער אַרבעטסמאַן.

די צוקונפֿט

(פראַגמענט)

אָ, די וועלט וועט ווערן יינגער,
און דאָם לעבן ליַיכטער, גרינגער,
יעדער קלאַגער וועט אַ זינגער
ווערן, ברידער, באַלד !
לאָז דאָם פאָלק נאָר ווערן קליגער,
און פאַריאָגן דעם באַטריגער,

the fox and the tiger,
from their beautiful forest.

Oh, the world will grow more beautiful,
love greater and hatred less
between women and men,
between one land and another.
Oh, the world will grow freer,
freer, more beautiful, younger, newer,
and truth will be dear to it,
dear as a friend.

Oh, the world will soon grow bolder
and there will be no master,
not the crown and not the purse,
and not the soldier's sword.
So take courage in the ranks
to bring freedom,
to liberate and renew
our old world!

Three Sisters

In England's a city called Leicester[34],
in London's a square by that name.
Three sisters work there in the square,
and all have achieved certain fame.

The youngest sells flowers all day,
the second one shoelaces sells,
and late in the night comes the eldest—
her body itself she sells.

The younger ones look at their sister—
no hatred at all in their eyes.
The world and the town and the square
all three of them strongly despise.

---

34. Pronounced 'Lester'

אים, דעם פֿוקס, און אויך דעם טיגער
פֿון זײַן שיינעם וואַלד.

אָ, די וועלט וועט ווערן שענער,
ליבע גרעסער, שׂינאה קלענער,
צווישן פֿרוּיען, צווישן מענער,
צווישן לאַנד און לאַנד;
אָ, די וועלט וועט ווערן פֿרײַער,
פֿרײַער, שענער, יונגער, נײַער,
און אין איר די וואָרהייט טײַער,
טײַער ווי אַ פֿרײַנד.

אָ, די וועלט וועט ווערן דרײַסטער
און עס וועט ניט זײַן אַ מײַסטער,
ניט די קרוין און ניט דער טיײַסטער, —
ניט דעם זעלנערס שווערד.
אַלזאָ מוזיק אין די רייען,
אין די רייען, צו באַפֿרײַען,
צו באַפֿרײַען און באַנײַען
אונדזער אַלטע וועלט!

דרײַ שוועסטער

אין ענגלאַנד איז אַ דאָ אַ שטאָט לעסטער,
אין לאָנדאָן איז דאָ אַזאַ סקווער,
אין סקווער שטייען טעגלעך דרײַ שוועסטער,
די מיידלעך — זיי קען ווער ניט ווער.

די קלענסטע פֿאַרקויפֿט דאָרטן בלומען,
די מיטלסטע — בענדלעך פֿון שיך,
און שפֿעט אין דער נאַכט זעט מען קומען
די עלטסטע, וואָס האַנדלט... מיט זיך.

די יונגערע ביידע באַטראַכטן
די עלטערע שוועסטער אַן האַם;
דען אַלע דרײַ מיידלעך פֿאַראַכטן
די וועלט, מיט דער שטאָט, מיט דער גאַס.

At night when the younger ones reach
their nest, as they call their poor place,
they secretly moisten the flowers
with tears running down from their face.

A Broom and a Sweep
(fragment)

Enough! I don't want to feed
idlers any more.
Enough trembling before barons—
give me a broom!

Get out, my lords and noblemen,
you with sweaters and fat bellies
who tell me how to live and threaten me.
You with linen robes--you go too!
I don't need middlemen any more—
a broom and a sweep!
No middlemen, no middlemen, no middlemen!
No more!

I don't need preachers any more—
a broom and a sweep!
No preachers, no gracious lords,
no idlers any more!

און דאך װען די קליינע צװײ קומען
צום נעסט, װאָס זײ רופן אַ היים,
באַנעצן זײ בענדלעך און בלומען
מיט טרערן, װאָס בלײַבן געהײם.

אַ בעזעם און אַ קער

(פֿראַגמענט)

גענוג! איך װיל ניט פֿיטערן
קײן לײדיק־גײערס מער,
גענוג פֿאַר פֿירשטן ציטערן, —
אַ בעזעם מיר אַהער!

אַרױס, מײַן לאָרד און אַדלמאַן,
דו סװעטער — דיקער בױך,
דו מוסר־זאַנגער, טאַדלמאַן,
דו קיטלמאַן, גײ אױך!

איך דאַרף ניט מער קײן מיטלמאַן,
אַ בעזעם און אַ קער!
קײן מיטלמאַן, קײן טיטלמאַן, קײן קיטלמאַן,
ניט מער!

איך דאַרף ניט מער קײן פֿרײדיקער,
אַ בעזעם און אַ קער!
קײן פֿרײדיקער, קײן גנעדיק־הער,
קײן לײדיק־גײער מער!

DAVID EDELSHTAT

(Born May 9, 1866, in Kaluga, Russia;
died October 17, 1892, in Denver, Colorado)

When David Edelshtat died on October 17, 1892, in the Denver Sanitarium for Lung Diseases, he was barely 26 years old. He had been active in Yiddish literature for only four years (he had previously written in Russian), but his death evoked profound sorrow among the Jewish workers and folk-masses throughout the world, as if a prophet had been taken from them, an old and beloved leader, a guide and folk tribune. Poets wrote poems mourning his premature death. Newspapers and magazines printed memorial articles, and ordinary Jews in the streets and shops wept.

A poet of the time, N.B. Babad, on the day of Edelshtat's death, expressed the feelings of everyone with a poem in which he said:

> *He is dead! And a noble, honest hand,*
> *a hand that always faithfully*
> *served all the poor people and suffering friends,*
> *has ceased writing and living.*

> *Yes, dead is the fighter, fallen in battle*
> *in the bitter struggle for his holy goals.*
> *Edelshtat died young—before his time—*
> *but his spirit lives and will live!*

> *Yes, dead is the singer, the freedom-prophet,*
> *far, far from his comrades and brothers.*
> *Yes, the lyre is dead, but the poet lives—*
> *the sweet, heartfelt poems live!*

What was and still remains the unusual power of Edelshtat's poetry?

H. Leivick, who celebrated Edelshtat in one of his most beautiful ballads, gives this answer to the question in an article about Edelshtat: "Edelshtat's poetry resounded with the hopes for a 'divine humanity,' where every individual's suffering is not drowned in regal, dictatorial, uniform abstractions but is seen as if it were the direct suffering of all people together. That was pure, profound humanism; that was the wellspring of Edelshtat's poems. That virtue will stand by him forever. Despite all the current catastrophes, the murderousness and ruination in the world, it will remain his virtue throughout the generations."

The famous anarchist writer and leader Rudolf Rocker wrote: "Edelshtat was one of those great souls who are ready to dedicate themselves because they are deeply convinced that the highest thing a man can achieve is to dedicate his whole life to a great cause that is not just his cause but that of all mankind. To that cause he was faithful till the chronic illness that sent him prematurely to the grave ripped the pen from his hand."

Edelshtat was connected to the anarchist movement. Several months after the *Freie Arbeter Stimme* (Free Worker's Voice) was founded (in July 1890), he became its editor (in January 1891), and he actually laid the spiritual foundation of the journal.

Edelshtat's poems *In Kamf* (In Battle) and *Tsu Arbeter-Froyen* (To Working Women) are only two of a very large number of poems that are sung to this day with as much holy excitement and emotion as they were long ago. Among his most popular poems are: *Mayn Tsavoe* (My Will) (O dearest friend, when I have left this world/ bring to my grave our flag of red), *Tsum Yidishn Proletarier* (To The Jewish Proletarian) (My brothers wearing threefold chains/ as thinkers, Jews and slaves), *Yitsies Mitsrayim* (The Exodus From Egypt) (In the ancient land of Egypt/ lived a king of evil soul), *Der Ovntglok* (The Evening Bell) (O Muse, call me not with your magical fingers), *Vakht Oyf* (Awake) (How long, oh how long/ will you keep being slaves), *Mayn Letste Hofnung* (My Last Hope) (In storm and battle/ gone my years), and many, many others.

In the year 1952, on the occasion of the 60th anniversary of his death, there appeared a "David Edelshtat Book", edited by Benjamin Jacob Bialostotski, with dozens of articles, reviews, recollections, and poems about Edelshtat's great contribution to Yiddish proletarian poetry and to the life of Jewish workers.

Edelshtat's contemporary, Joseph Bovshover, on the day of Edelshtat's death, wrote a moving poem in which he mourned the poet's premature death in these words:

Edelshtat! You have died—
you no longer feel the worldly pain.

But your death has wounded my heart
terribly, terribly!

You have died, but I am consoled
because your great spirit lives.
When I sing your songs
they will console me.

And I know that the time will come
when freedom will shine;
then everyone will lay
a wreath of flowers on your grave.

In Battle

They hate us and drive us all 'round the earth--.
they plague us, oppress us, and more.
Because we can value the true worth
of people who suffer and are poor.

They shoot us and hang us, where'er we be—
they hound us from birth to our graves.
But truth for all workers we will see,
and freedom for all the wretched slaves.

And they cannot frighten us any more—
we fear neither prison nor death.
We're ready to fight in the last war—
we'll fight to our final struggling breath.

Though they forge us fetters of strongest steel
and tear off our limbs from the whole,
it's only our bodies they can steal,
but never our holy human soul.

O tyrants, the flow'rs wake from coma--
immortal they bloom near and far.
The petals' exciting aroma
is spreading to everywhere you are.

They bloom in each man's thoughtful, open mind
who loves justice, truth, and the light.
The blessings of Nature urge mankind
to battle, to struggle for the right,

to free from their pain all the tyrants hate,
to free them from hunger and cold—
for mankind a Heaven we'll create,
a world free and beautiful and bold.

A world where there'll be no more shedding tears,
nor innocent blood more will flow—
where man's hope will shine through the ages,
and love there forevermore will glow.

אין קאַמף

מיר װערן געהאַסט און געטריבן,
מיר װערן געפּלאָגט און פֿאַרפּאָלגט —
און אַלעם דערפֿאָר, װײַל מיר ליבן
דאָס אָרעמע שמאַכטנדע פֿאָלק.

מיר װערן געשאָסן, געהאַנגען,
מען באַרױבט אונדז דאָס לעבן און רעכט,
דערפֿאָר, װײַל מיר אמת פֿאַרלאַנגען
און פֿרײַהײט פֿאַר אָרעמע קנעכט!

אָבער אונדז װעט ניט דערשרעקן
געפֿענקעניש און טיראַנײַ,
מיר מוזן די מענטשהײט דערװעקן
און מאַכן זי גליקלעך און פֿרײַ.

שמידט אונדז אין אײַזערנע קײטן,
װי בלוטיקע חיות אונדז רײַסט,
איר װעט אונדזער קערפּער נאָר טײטן,
אָבער ניט אונדזער הײליקן גײַסט!

טיראַנען! איר קענט אים ניט טײטן,
דאָס איז אַן אומשטערבלעכע בלום,
אירע שמעקנדע, פֿלאַמענדע קװײטן
בלײַען שױן איצט אײצט אומעטום!

זײ בלײַען אין דענקנדע מענטשן
װאָס ליבן גערעכטיקײט, ליכט,
אַלײן די נאַטור טוט זײ בענטשן
צום קאַמף, צו די הײליקע פֿליכט:

באַפֿרײַען די אָרעמע שקלאַפֿן,
װאָס שמאַכטן אין הונגער און קעלט
און פֿאַר דער מענטשהײט באַשאַפֿן
אַ פֿרײַע, אַ ליכטיקע װעלט,

װוּ עס זאָל ניט גיסן קײן טרערן,
ניט פֿליסן אומשולדיקעס בלוט,
און מענטשן, װי גלענצנדע שטערן,
שײַנען מיט ליבע און מוט!

You tyrants—you think you can kill us all,
but new fighters soon will be born.
We'll fight and we'll stand straighter, taller,
and freedom will have a bright new morn.

Awake!

How long, Oh how long, will you keep being slaves
and wearing the shameful steel chains?
How long will you heap all the glorious riches
on those who have robbed you of your bread?

How long will you stand with your heads bowing down,
All abased, with no home, full of pain?
The day has now dawned, just wake up, ope your eyes,
recognize all your mighty, steely strength!

Achieve all your freedom, on barricades fight--
declare war on tyrants and kings!
Your courage, decisions, my brave fighting comrades,
will bring you the victory you crave.

Your chains and their thrones both will soon disappear
beneath blows from brave workers' swords.
With sweet-smelling flowers and sun's golden radiance,
our freedoms will beautify the earth.

The world then will live, love, and blossom again,
and glow in a bright golden May.
My brothers, enough of your bowing to tyrants--
now swear that you all will soon be free!

The chime of our freedom is ringing out now—
assemble the long-suff'ring slaves.
Inspired, fight the battle, my fearless dear brothers—
redeem all your holy human rights.

איר קענט אונדז דערמאָרדן, טיראַנען!
נײַע קעמפֿער וועט ברענגען די צײַט, —
און מיר קעמפֿן, מיר קעמפֿן ביז וואַנען,
די גאַנצע וועלט וועט ווערן באַפֿרײַט.

וואַכט אויף

ווי לאַנג, אַ ווי לאַנג וועט איר בלײַבן נאָך שקלאַפֿן?
און טראָגן די שענדלעכע קייט!
ווי לאַנג וועט איר גלענצנדע רײַכטימער שאַפֿן
פֿאַר דעם, וואָס באַרויבט אײַער ברויט??

*

ווי לאַנג וועט איר שטיין, אײַער רוקן געבויגן,
דערנידעריקט, היימלאָז, פֿאַרשמאַכט!
עס טאָגט! וואַכט אויף! עפֿנט די אויגן!
דערקענט אײַער אײַזערנע מאַכט!

*

פֿריידיקט די פֿרײַהייט פֿון קאַמף־באַריקאַדן!
דערקלערט די טיראַנען אַ קריג!
מיט און אַנטשלאָסנקיים, בראַווע קאַמעראַדן,
וועלן אײַך פֿירן צום זיג!

*

קייטן און טראָגען, אַלעם מוז פֿאַלן
אונטער דעם אַרבעטערס שווערד!
מיט דופֿטנדע בלומען, מיט גאָלדענע שטראַלן
וועט פֿרײַהייט באַצירן די ערד!

*

און אַלעם וועט לעבן, ליבן און בליִען,
אין פֿרײַהייטס גאָלדענעם מײַ!
ברידער, גענוג פֿאַר טיראַנען צו קניִען!
שווערט, אַז איר מוזט ווערן פֿרײַ!

*

קלינגט איבעראַל אין די פֿרײַהייטס־גלאָקן!
פֿאַרזאַמלט די לײַדנדע קנעכט!
און קעמפֿט באַגײַסטערט, קעמפֿט אומדערשראָקן,
פֿאַר אײַערע הייליקע רעכט!

To The Working Women

Working women, suffering women,
women who languish at home and in the factory,
why are you standing to one side? Why don't you help build
the temple of freedom, of human happiness?

Help us carry the red banner
forward, through storms, through dark nights!
Help us spread truth and light
among ignorant, lonely slaves.

Help us to raise the world out of its filth,
to sacrifice everything dear to us,
to fight together like mighty lions
for freedom, for equality, for our principles.

More than once have noble women
made hangmen and thrones tremble.
They showed we could trust them
with our banner through the bitterest storms.

Remember your Russian sisters,
murdered for freedom by the czar, that vampire,
deathly exhausted in their stony nests,
buried in snow in desolate Siberia.

Remember the names, the holy names:
Perovskaya, Helfman, Ginsburg, and others--
thousands who used to be ashamed
to obediently carry the yoke of slavery.

They stood in the storm so heroically,
carried hope and light into the darkness!
They took revenge on the wild tyrants,
looked death in the face proudly!

Do you remember them? Then let their lives
inspire you! May you successfully
learn and think, fight and strive
toward freedom and happiness for the working people!

צו די אַרבעטער־פֿרויען

אַרבעטער־פֿרויען, לײַדנדע פֿרויען,
פֿרויען, וואָס שמאַכטן אין הויז, אין פֿאַבריק,
וואָס שטייט איר פֿון ווײַטן ? וואָס העלפֿט איר ניט בויען
דעם טעמפּל פֿון פֿרײַהייט, פֿון מענטשלעכן גליק ?

העלפֿט אונדז טראָגן דעם באַנער דעם רויטן,
פֿאַרוווערטס, דורך שטורעם, דורך פֿינצטערע נעכט !
העלפֿט אונדז וואַרהייט און ליכט צו פֿאַרברײַטן,
צווישן אומוויסנדע, עלנטע קנעכט !

העלפֿט אונדז די וועלט פֿון איר שמוץ דערהייבן,
אַלעם אַפּפֿערן, וואָס אונדז איז ליב,
קעמפֿן צוזאַמען, ווי מעכטיקע לײבן,
פֿיר פֿרײַהייט, פֿיר גלײַכהייט. פֿיר אונדזער פּרינציפּ !

ניט איין מאָל האָבן שוין נאָבעלע פֿרויען
געמאַכט ציטערן העגקער און טראָן.
זיי האָבן געצייגט, אַז מען קען זיי פֿאַרטרויען
אין ביטערסטן שטורעם די הייליקע פֿאָן.

דערמאָנט זיך אַן אײַערע רוסישע שוועסטער,
דערמאָרדעט פֿיר פֿרײַהייט פֿון צאַר דעם וואַמפּיר,
פֿאַרמאַטערט ביז טויט אין די שטיינערנע נעסטער,
פֿאַרגראָבן אין שניי אין דעם ווּיסטן סיביר.

געדענקט איר די נעמען, די הייליקע נעמען :
פּעראָווסקאַיאַ, העלפֿמאַן, גינזבורג און נאָך
טויזנטער, וואָס פֿלעגן זיך שעמען
צו טראָגן געהאַרכזאַם דעם שקלאַפֿניאָך ?

זיי זײַנען אין שטורעם 'זוי העלדיש געשטאַנען,
געטראָגן אין פֿינצטערעניש האָפֿנונג און ליכט !
ראָכע גענומען פֿון ווילדע טיראַנען,
שטאָלץ געקוקט דעם טויט אין געזיכט !

געדענקט איר זיי ? דאַן זאָל זייער לעבן
באַגײַסטערן אײַך ! איר זאָלט מיט דעם דערפֿאָלג
לערנען און דענקען, קעמפֿן און שטרעבן
צו פֿרײַהייט און גליק פֿיר דאָס אַרבעטער־פֿאָלק !

My Will

O dearest friend, when I have left this world,
bring to my grave our flag of red—
the freedom flag, the flag unfurled,
besplotched with blood of workers dead.

And there beneath the banners hanging,
sing me my song, my freedom song—
my song that rings with fetters clanging,
the song of slaves, of human wrong.

I'll hear it even though I'm in my tomb,
my freedom song, my song so true.
I'll shed hot tears from Mother Earth's womb
for all the slaves, Christian and Jew.

And when I hear the clanging swords so brave
in final battle for the right,
I'll sing to all from out the cool grave
to give them courage for the fight.

מײַן צוואה

אָ, גוטע פֿרײַנד, ווען איך וועל שטאַרבן,
טראָגט צו מײַן קבֿר אונדזער פֿאָן —
די פֿרײַע פֿאָן מיט רויטע פֿאַרבן,
באַשפּריצט מיט בלוט פֿון אַרבעטסמאַן!

און דאָרט אונטער דעם באַנער רויטן,
זינגט מיר מײַן ליד, מײַן פֿרײַע ליד!
מײַן ליד „אין קאַמף", וואָס קלינגט ווי קייטן
פֿון דעם פֿאַרשקלאַפֿטן קריסט און ייִד.

אויך אין מײַן קבֿר וועל איך הערן
מײַן פֿרײַע ליד, מײַן שטורעמליד,
אויך דאָרט וועל איך פֿאַרגיסן טרערן
פֿאַר דעם פֿאַרשקלאַפֿטן קריסט און ייִד!

און ווען איך הער די שווערדן קלינגען
אין לעצטן קאַמף פֿון בלוט און שמאַרץ —
צום פֿאָלק וועל איך פֿון קבֿר זינגען
און וועל באַגײַסטערן זײַן האַרץ.

JOSEPH BOVSHOVER

(born September 30, 1873, in Lubavich, in the Province of Mogilev,
White Russia; died December 25, 1915, in Poughkeepsie, NY)

When we speak and write about proletarian poetry in the United States, we mention, in a single breath, four poets who represent the era of creation of social
poetry, though there were many more than four. They are: Morris Winchevsky,
David Edelshtat, Morris Rosenfeld, and Joseph Bovshover. Bovshover was
the youngest of the four, and, some literary critics maintain, the most talented.
"Bovshover was," a Soviet critic wrote in the 1930s, "the most talented revolutionary poet in the era of the birth of the Jewish labor movement. The form of
his battle songs was very different and much better than those of his older comrades." Also B.J. Bialostotski, in his essay *Fir Zaynen Zey Geven* (They Were
Four), in the David Edelshtat Memorial Book, describes Bovshover as a poet "…
whose poetry is hotter and generally more zestful" than that of the other three.

Because not many of Bovshover's poems were sung, most of them are less well
known by the general population than those of the other three proletarian poets.
However, a number of Bovshover's poems were recited at various labor gatherings and celebrations, and took the listeners by storm with their fervor and
calls to battle. Among the most popular were *Di Revolutsion* (The Revolution)
and *A Gezang Tsum Folk* (A Song to the People), which Zalman Reizn, in his
Leksikon fun der Yidisher Literatur (Lexicon of Yiddish Literature), called "…a
pearl of Yiddish poetry." Choruses in Europe and America sang that poem to
Jacob Shaeffer's music.

His poem *Revolution* had a tremendous power that tore at the reader or listener
like a storm:

> *I come because tyrants*
> *have transformed the people into subjects of thrones;*
> *I come because peace*
> *grazes on gunpowder and the lead from cannons;*
> *I come because the world is divided*
> *and the bond of mankind is torn asunder;*
> *I come because they want to make locking up the whole world*
> *the spirit of the times.*

That was a mighty call for battle against enslavement and exploitation, not only in the shop, against a single evil foreman or boss, but to put an end to, to over-throw, to destroy, the whole regime of "...false laws and ways." One senses in these lines the approach of a storm, the approach of the longed-for revolution that will "...crush into ash all of those that oppress the weak."

Just as strong and poetically beautiful is his poem *A Song to the People*, in which he calls out:

> *Raise your eyes and see*
> *a loaded ship upon the sea,*
> *and see in the dark forests*
> *the smoke of locomotives.*

Such chiseled verse, such rhythm, and such a picture of the riches created by those who "...saw and plane, weave and sew and knit" had never been drawn in Yiddish poetry till Bovshover.

So it is no wonder that the inspired worker-masses gave the young poet praise and recognition. But the life of the poet was a tragic one, and it also ended tragically. After a number of his poems had been published in his own English translation, Bovshover was greatly praised by the editor of the magazine *Liberti* (Liberty), Benjamin Tucker, who was one of the most important anarchist lead-ers at that time. He wrote that Bovshover was a rising star in English poetry.

Literary historians and others who write about Bovshover believe that the ex-aggerated praise greatly confused the young poet. He began to show signs of mental illness, and friends put him a psychiatric hospital in the year 1899. In the hospital, he sank into a severe depression, from which he seldom emerged dur-ing the fifteen years he was there.

In his book *Noente Geshtaltn* (Nearby Images), Itsik Manger draws a moving picture about how two enthusiastic fans of the poet go to the hospital to see the sick Bovshover. The doctor asks:

"Does Bovshover want to see you? Many workers come to see him."

"Is there any hope that he'll get well, doctor?"

"Get well?" the doctor answers. "Who knows? I'm afraid not. His condi-tion has been getting worse for several years. Sometimes he gets wild and agitated and thinks the whole world is against him; he thinks Shelley is his footstool, that he himself is Goethe or Shakespeare, that he is greater than Apollo, Dionysus, and Prometheus together."

"Maybe I could see him, Doctor? We've come specially from New York, spent a whole free Sunday for that."

Manger subsequently depicts how the two young workers see their beloved poet walking in the garden in a deep depression. But their love and admiration for him does not get any less. They stand there, looking at and admiring the poet who produced mighty lines such as:

I come like a proud comet,
like the sun at daybreak;
I come like an angry storm
with lightning and thunder.

N. B. Minkoff, who published three volumes about the pioneers of Yiddish poetry in America, ends his essay about Bovshover with these words: "The tragically and prematurely deceased poet wrote for only a total of seven years. Edelshtat's poetry appeared when he was 26 years old; Bovshover began spinning his social poetry where his older comrades left off, or nearly left off. In his first poems, he continued their tradition, but in him the abstract element and the leaning toward classical forms were stronger. It was in those forms that he achieved his full maturity. His best poems were inspired visions, written harshly, with fiery breath. Some of his depictions rise to great stature, like those of the great masters. With the prematurely silenced tragic poet's death, Yiddish poetry lost one of its greatest poetic hopes just at the point where it was about to be fulfilled."

A Song to the People

Raise your eyes, O people so lonely and poor—
raise your eyes to the East, West, North, and South,
and see the gathered treasure, the fruits of your labors,
and the left-over riches from previous generations.

Raise your eyes and see on the ocean the golden ships,
and see in the forest the smoke from locomotives,
and see how they soar and come quickly from a distant region
and bring to our land products and merchandise to trade.

Raise your eyes and see the great walled factories
where workers saw and plane and weave and sew and knit,
and forge and file and turn and carve and smooth and polish,
and make the merchandise and the riches for human use.

And see the dumb robots, the giant iron slaves,
that spare human strength and help create the riches.
And see how the wild, mighty force of Nature is subdued,
for deep is human intelligence and full of secrets.

אַ געזאַנג צום פֿאָלק

הייב אויף דיינע אויגן, אַ פֿאָלק, וואָס דו ביסט
אַזוי עלנט און אָרעם,
הייב אויף דיינע אויגן צו מיזרח און מערבֿ,
צו צפֿון און דרום;
און זע די געזאַמלטע אוצרות, און זע
פֿון דיין אַרבעט די פּירות,
און זע דעם געבליבענעם רייכטום פֿון
פֿריִער געוועזענע דורות.

הייב אויף דיינע אויגן און זע אויפֿן ים
די געלאָדענע שיפֿן,
און זע אין די טונקעלע וועלדער דעם רויך
פֿון די לאָקאָמאָטיוון,
און זע ווי זיי שוועבן און קומען געשווינד
פֿון אַ געגנט אַ ווייטן
און פֿירן אין אַנדערע לענדער פּראָדוקטן
און סחורות צו בייטן.

הייב אויף דיינע אויגן און זע די
געמויערטע גרויסע פֿאַבריקן,
וווּ אַרבעטער זעגן און הובלען, און וועבן,
און נייען און שטריקן,
און שמידן און פֿיילן, און טאָקן און שניצן,
און גלעטן און פּוצן,
און שאַפֿן די וואַרע, און שאַפֿן דעם רייכטום
צום מענטשעלעכן נוצן.

און זע די מאַשינען, די בלאַנקע, די רייזיקע
אייַזערנע שקלאַפֿן,
וואָס היטן די מענטשעלעכע כּוחות און העלפֿן
די רייַכטימער שאַפֿן,
און זע, ווי די ווילדע, די מעכטיקע קראַפֿט
דער נאַטור איז באַצוווּנגען,
ווייַל טיף איז דער מענטשעלעכער שׂכל אין
אירע געהיימניס געדרונגען.

And to the distant, merry, blooming fields raise your eyes
and see the golden stalks standing there, bowed down with their weight,
and see the beautiful gardens and the trees hung with fruits,
where birds fill the branches, fill the air with song.

And see how the juicy wine grapes are trodden in the cold,
how wine is poured into casks to get older and tastier
so it can later fizz in goblets to gladden the human heart,
awakening hope and love, chasing pain and woe.

And see how all of Nature is ready to sweeten your life
and fulfill demands in your breast and strivings in your heart.
Courageously, in gigantic multitudes, stretch out your skinny hands.
Enough of being robbed! Enough of being deceived!

Raise your eyes, O people—come out of your dark tombs.
Raise your eyes to the East, West, North, and South
and take the inherited riches and the fruits of your labor,
and while creating—live,
and while enjoying—create in the freer generations!

און וויַיט אויף די בליַענדע, לוסטיקע פֿעלדער
הייב אויף דיַינע אויגן

און זע, ווי עס שטייען די גאָלדענע זאנגען
פֿון שווערקייט געבויגן,

און זע אין די פּרעכטיקע גערטנער די ביימער
מיט פֿרוכטן באַהאַנגען,

און פֿייגל דערפֿילן די צווײַגן, דערפֿילן
די לופֿט מיט געזאַנגען.

און זע, ווי די זאַפֿטיקע ווײַנטרויבן ווערן
געטראָטן אין קעלטער,

דער ווײַן ווערט געגאָסן אין פֿעסער צו ווערן
געשמאַקער און עלטער,

אום שפּעטער צו זידן אין בעכער, די מענטשלעכע
האַרץ צו דערפֿרייען,

דערווועקנדיק האָפֿנונג און ליבע, פֿאַריאָגנדיק
שמערצן און ווייען.

און זע, ווי די גאַנצע נאַטור איז באַרייט צו
פֿאַרזיסן דיַין לעבן,

און פֿיל אין דיַין ברוסט אַ פֿאַרלאַנגען און פֿיל אין
דיַין האַרצן אַ שטרעבן,

און מוזיק אין ריזיקע מחנות שטערעק אויס דיַינע
הענט, די פֿאַרדאָרטע, —

גענוג שוין צו זײַן די באַרויבטע! גענוג שוין
צו זײַן די גענאַרטע!

הייב אויף דיַינע אויגן, אַ פֿאָלק, גיי אַרויס פֿון
די פֿינצטערע קבֿרים,

הייב אויף דיַינע אויגן צו מיזרח און מערבֿ,
צו צפֿון און דרום

און נעם די גאוירשנטע אוצר:ת, און נעם
פֿון דיַין אַרבעט די פּירות,

און שאַפֿנדיק — לעב און געניסנדיק — שאַף
אין די פֿרײַערע דורות! —

Revolution

I come like a proud comet, like the sun when the dawn begins to break;
I come like angry weather bringing lightning and thunder;
I come like glowing lava from cloud-covered volcanoes;
I come like the storm from the North, which wakens and frightens the oceans.

I come because tyrants have transformed peoples into kingdoms;
I come because they graze peace on gunpowder, lead, and cannons;
I come because the world is divided and the bond between peoples is ruptured;
I come because they want the spirit of the times to be: locking up the boundless world.

I come because I was born in the desert of domination;
I come because the rulers have awakened and nourished my rage;
I come because the human breast cannot kill the seeds of life;
I come because one cannot cast freedom eternally into chains.

I led the enslaved people in earlier times;
I helped them exchange their shameful slavery for freedom;
I was in the vanguard of helping to renew the world,
and I'll walk today with the peoples and help free them completely.

And you, holy sacks of money, anointed, crowned bandits—
I will destroy you and your false laws and customs,

רעוואָלוציאָן

איך קום ווי אַ שטאָלצער קאָמעט, ווי די זון, ווען עם
הייבט אָן צו טאָגן ;
איך קום ווי אַ בייזער געוויטער, פֿון בליץ און פֿון
דונער געטראָגן ;
איך קום ווי אַ גלוטיקע לאַווע פֿון וואָלקן־באַדעקטע
וווּלקאַנען ;
איך קום ווי דער שטורעם פֿון צפֿון, וואָס וועקט און
דערשרעקט אָקעאַנען.

איך קום, ווייַל עם האָבן טיראַנען פֿאַרוואַנדלט די
פֿעלקער אין טראַנען ;
איך קום, ווייַל מען פֿיטערט דעם פֿרידן מיט פֿולווער
און בלייַ און קאַנאָנען ;
איך קום, ווייַל די וועלט איז צעטיילט, און דער בונד
פֿון דער מענטשהייט צעריסן ;
איך קום, ווייַל מען וויל פֿאַר דעם צייַטגייַסט דעם
ענדלאָזן וועלטרוים פֿאַרשליסן.

איך קום, ווייַל איך בין אין דער מידבר פֿון הערשאַפֿט
געבאָרן געוואָרן ;
איך קום, ווייַל עם האָבן די הערשער געוועקט און
דערצויגן מייַן צאָרן ;
איך קום, ווייַל די מענטשלעכע ברוסט קען די זריעה פֿון
לעבן ניט טייטן ;
איך קום, ווייַל מען קען ניט קען די פֿרייַהייט אויף אייביק
פֿאַרשמידן אין קייטן.

איך האָב די געקנעכטעטע פֿעלקער געפֿירט אין די
פֿריִערע צייַטן
און האָב זיי געהאָלפֿן די שענדלעכע קנעכטשאַפֿט
אויף פֿרייַהייט פֿאַרבייַטן.
איך בין מיט דעם פֿאָרשריט געגאַנגען, די וועלט
אים געהאָלפֿן באַנייַען,
און גיין וועל איך הייַנט מיט די פֿעלקער, און וועל זיי
אין גאַנצן באַפֿרייַען.

און אייַך, איר געהייליקטע געלטזעק, געזאַלבטע,
געקרוינטע באַנדיטן,

and your hearts, pining for human blood, I will stab,
and your golden crowns and scepters I will shatter!

Your colorful purples, which the people has celebrated
with foolish joy and enthusiasm, I will tear into pieces like rags—
your frozen world will lose its proud sparkle,
just like the snow that falls from icebergs, melted by the sunshine.

I will destroy your cobweb morals and ancient lies,
and your dark butterflies I will choke like flies.
Your heavens and your devils and gods
I will destroy, and I will purify the Earth and the Ether.[35]

You can choke me, shoot me, or hang me—your efforts are in vain;
I'm not afraid of prison or the scaffold or the gallows!
I'll arise from the earth and cover it with weapons
till you fade away forever, till the grave erases you!

---

35. The imaginary fluid through which planets and stars were thought to move

איך וועל אײַך פֿארניכטן מיט אײַערע פֿאלשע
געזעצן און זיטן,

און אײַערע הערצער, וואָס שמאַכטן נאָך מענטשנבלוט,
וועל איך דערשטעכן,

און אײַערע קרוינען און סצעפּטער, די גאָלדענע,
וועל איך צעברעכן !

איך וועל אײַער פֿאַרביקן פּורפּור, ווי שמאַטעס אין
שטיקלעך צעפֿליקן,

צו וועלכע דאָס פֿאָלק האָט געגויבלט אין נאַרישער
פֿרייד און אַנציקן, —

פֿאַרלירן וועט אײַער פֿאַרפֿאַרענע וועלט אירע
בלענדשײַן דעם שטאָלצן,

אַזוי ווי דער שניי, וועלכער פֿאַלט פֿון די אײַזבערג,
פֿון זונשײַן צעשמאָלצן ;

פֿאַרניכטן וועל איך אײַער שפּינוועב־מאָראַל און
די אוראַלטע ליגן,

און אײַערע פּויפּסטן, די פֿינצטערערע, וועל איך
דערשטיקן ווי פֿליגן,

און אײַערע הימלען, און אײַערע שדים, און אײַערע
געטער,

איך וועל זיי צעשטערן, און רײן וועל איך מאַכן די
ערד און דעם עטער ! —

און מעגט איר מיך ווערגן, און שיסן, און הענגען —
אומזיסט אײַער מי !

מיך שרעקט ניט קיין קערקער *, מיך שרעקט קיין שאַפֿעט
ניט, מיך שרעקט ניט קיין תּליה !

אַרויסזוואָקסן וועל איך פֿון דר׳ערד און איך וועל זי
מיט וואָפֿן באַדעקן,

ביז איר וועט אויף אייביק פֿאַרזינקען, ביז אײַער וועט
דער קבֿר פֿאַרמעקן !

MORRIS ROSENFELD

(born December 28th, 1862, in Baksha, in the province of Suvalka;
died June 22nd, 1923, in New York.)

Many hundreds of articles, reviews, and books have been written about the life
and works of Morris Rosenfeld. There is not another poet who elicited both so
much praise and so much criticism. As early as the year 1897, there began in the
magazine *Der Nayer Gayst* (The New Spirit) a discussion, which continued for
months, about Morris Rosenfeld's place in Yiddish literature. The participants
in the discussion were such well known personalities of the time as L. Budianov, Leon Kobrin, Jacob Milkh, Alexander Harkavy, and others. Budianov and
Milkh, who were typical representatives of the Jewish cosmopolitan intelligentsia of the time, didn't know what to make of Rosenfeld's national poems, so
they criticized him as a poet in general. Budianov complained that one could not
speak of a national poet when the Jews were not a nation at all.

Milkh, in the same vein, "established" that there was no such thing as Jewish
civilization or culture. "That ended with the Talmud," he ruled categorically, so
one could not say that Rosenfeld expressed the national feelings of his people in
his poetry.

The discussion, in various forms and variations, was repeated in later years. The
broad Jewish folk masses on both sides of the ocean, however, paid little attention to that discussion. Morris Rosenfeld became their most beloved and most
popular poet; he lamented their pain about the sweatshop, the dark tenement-
houses, their poverty, and their woes, he was their *Trern Milyoner* (Tear Millionaire), who collected every tear of the lonely Jewish immigrant and brought it
to the world with a warning that a tear "boils and won't stop seething," and that
"the pale operator" would not always sit hunched over his machines in silence.

More than any proclamation or any agitation speech by the best speaker, Rosen-
feldian lines like the following called them to battle to put an end to the frightful
conditions:

Why do you take the meat for yourself
and push the bones to me?
What do you think, what? That I'm a dog,
a dog with aristocrat's teeth?

A dog that runs around in the street
and sleeps in the gutter,
and when someone jokingly throws him a bone
he is overjoyed?

Oh tremble lest I be a lion—
don't play jokes on me,
for I'll pick myself up
and tear you to pieces!

There was no Jewish worker who didn't identify with Rosenfeld in his poem *Mayn Yingele* (My Little Boy), and didn't feel, as he did, that sitting in the sweat-shop at his machine, his self was rotting away and he was becoming a machine himself.

He was the only one of the four great proletarian poets (Winchevsky, Edelshtat, Bovshover, and himself) who also wrote often about Jewish national feelings, and those poems remained in the national memory of the people. His poems about *Khanike* candles (*likhtelekh*) "...that tell little stories (*geshikhtelekh*) about bloody events, ability, courage, and wonders from long ago" survived the words of the intelligent, cosmopolitan writers that "...Jews are not a nation, so Rosenfeld cannot be a national poet."

Rosenfeld was the first Yiddish poet whose poems, thanks to Professor Leo Wiener of Harvard University, were translated into English, and then into many other European languages. They elicited great interest and praise everywhere.

His suffering during the last years of his life, when he became blind and did not receive appropriate recognition by the newer writers and critics, received artistic redress in H. Leivick's drama *Der Poet Iz Gevorn Blind* (The Poet Has Gone Blind.)

The Tear Millionaire

Oh, not some golden tuning-fork
bestirs my silent voice to sing.
A call from the boss
cannot make my voice ring—
only the slave's groan when he is weary
can wake the songs in me.
Then full of flame my words go forth
to try and right poor people's wrongs.

And that is why I melt away—
just see my life evaporate.
What can poor folks ever do,
how can they earn, if not too late?
For every tear they pay a tear,
for that's the only way they know,
and I'm a millionaire of tears,
collecting all the tears and woe.

The Sweatshop
(Fragment)

The machines are so wildly noisy in the shop
that I often forget who I am.
I get lost in the frightful tumult—
my self is destroyed, I become a machine.
I work and work and work endlessly—
I create and create and create.
Why? For whom? I don't know and I don't ask.
What business has a machine thinking?

I have no feelings, no thoughts, no understanding.
The bitter, bloody work suppresses
the noblest, most beautiful, best, richest,
deepest, and highest things that life possesses.
Seconds, minutes, and hours go by--the days and nights sail past quickly.
I run the machine as if I wanted to overtake them—
I race mindlessly, endlessly.

דער טרערן־מיליאָנער

אָ, ניט קיין גאָלדענע קעמערטאָן
שטימט אָן מײַן קול צום זינגען,
עס קען דער װוּנק פֿון אויבנאָן
מײַן שטים ניט מאַכן קלינגען;
דעם שקלאַפֿם אַ קרעכץ, װען ער איז מיד
נאָר װעקט אין מיר די לידער, —
און מיט אַ פֿלאַם לעבט אויף מײַן ליד,
פֿאַר מײַנע אָר׳מע ברידער.

דערפֿאַר פֿאַרגיי איך אָן אַ צײַט.
דערפֿאַר װעפֿט אויס מײַן לעבן:
װאָס קענען מיר די אָר׳מע־לײַט
פֿאַר אַ באַלוינונג געבן?
זיי צאָלן טרערן פֿאַר אַ טרער, —
דאָס אַלעם, װאָס זיי קאָנען: —
איך בין אַ טרערן־מיליאָנער
און װיין אויף די מיליאָנען.

די סוועטשאַפ

(פֿראַגמענט)

עס רוישן אין שאַפ אַזוי װילד די מאַשינען,
אַז אָפֿט מאַל פֿאַרגעס איך אין רויש דאָס איך בין:
איך װער אין דעם שרעקלעכן טומל פֿאַרלאָרן,
מײַן איך װערט דאָרט בטל, איך װער אַ מאַשין:
איך אַרבעט און אַרבעט, און אַרבעט אָן חשבון,
עס שאַפֿט זיך, און שאַפֿט זיך, און שאַפֿט זיך אָן צאָל
פֿאַר װאָס? און פֿאַר װעמען? איך װייס נים, איך פֿרעג
װי קומט אַ מאַשינע צו דענקען אַ מאָל?

ניטאָ קיין געפֿיל, קיין געדאַנק, קיין פֿאַרשטאַנד גאָ
די ביטערע, בלוטיקע אַרבעט דערשלאָגט
דאָס איידלסטע, שענסטע און בעסטע, דאָס רײַכסטע
דאָס טיפֿסטע, דאָס העכסטע װאָס לעבן פֿאַרמאָג
עס שװוינדן סעקונדן, מינוטן און שטונדן,
גאָר זעגל־שנעל פֿליִען די נעכט מיט די טעג;
איך טרײַב די מאַשין גלײַך איך װיל זיי דעריאָג, —
איך יאָג אָן אַ שׂכל, איך יאָר אָן אַ ברעג.

The clock in the shop never rests—
it shows everything, strikes constantly, wakes us constantly.
Someone once explained it to me:
"In its showing and waking lies understanding."
But I seem to remember something, as if from a dream:
The clock awakens life and understanding in me,
and something else—I forget what. Don't ask!
I don't know, I don't know! I'm a machine!

At times, when I hear the clock,
I understand its showing and its language quite differently;
It seems to me that the pendulum urges me:
"Work, work, work a lot!"
I hear in its tones only the boss's anger, his dark look.
The clock, it seems to me, drives me,
gnashes its teeth, calls me "machine," and yells at me: "Go!"

But when the wild tumult dies down
and the boss goes away for his lunch hour,
dawn begins to break in my mind
and things tug at my heart.
Then I feel my wound,
and bitter, burning tears
soak my meager lunch, my bread.
I feel choked up and I can't eat any more—I can't!
Oh, frightful toil! Oh, bitter poverty!

The human being that is sleeping within me
begins to awake—
the slave that is awake in me
seems to fall asleep.
Now the right hour has struck!
An end to loneliness—let there be an end to it!
But suddenly the whistle, the "boss," sounds an alarm!
I lose my mind, I forget who I am.
There's tumult and struggling—my self is lost.
I don't know, I don't care—I am a machine!

דער זייגער אין װערקשאפ, ער רוט ניט אפילו,
ער װײזט אלץ און קלאפט אלץ און װעקט נאָך אנאנד;
געזאָגט האָט מענטש מיר אַ מאָל די באדײטונג:
זײן װײזן און װעקן, דאָרט ליגט אַ פארשטאנד;
נאָר עטװאָס געדענקט זיך מיר, פּונקט װי פֿון חלום;
דער זייגער, ער װעקט אין מיר לעבן און זין,
און נאָך עפּעס, — איך האָב פֿארגעסן, — ניט פֿרעגט עס!
איך װײס ניט, איך װײס ניט, איך בין אַ מאשין!...

און צײטנװײיז װען איך דערהער שױן דעם זייגער,
פארשטײ איך גאנץ אנדערש זײן װײזן, זײן שפּראך, —
מיר דאכט, אַז עס נוקעט מיר דאָרטן דער אומער,
כ׳זאָל ארבעטן, ארבעטן, מערער, אַ סך!
איך הער אין זײן טאָן נאָר דעם באָסעס װילדן בײזער,
זײן פֿינצטערן קוק אין די װײיזער די צװײי; —
דער זייגער, מיר סקרוכעט, מיר דאכט, אַז ער טרײַבט מיך
און רופֿט מיך „מאשינע!" און שרײַט צו מיר: „ניי!"

נאָר דאן, װען ס׳איז שטילער דער װילדער געטומל,
אװעק איז דער מײַסטער, אין מיטאָגצײַט־שטונד,
דאַן פֿאנגט אָן אין קאָפּ בײ מיר לאנגזאם צו טאָגן,
אין הארצן צו ציִען, — איך פֿיל דאַן מײַן װוּנד; —
און ביטערע טרערן, און זודיקע טרערן
צעװײיקן מײַן מאָגערן מיטאָג, מײַן ברױט, —
עס װערגט מיך, איך קען ניט מער עסן, איך קען ניט!
אַ, שרעקלעכע פּראצע! אַ, ביטערע נױט!

דער מענטש, װעלכער שלאָפֿט אין מיר הײבט אַן דערװאכן;
דער קנעכט, װעלכער װאכט אין מיר שלאָפֿט דאכט זיך אײַן; —
אצינד איז די ריכטיקע שטונדע געקומען!
אַ סוף צו דעם עלנט, אַ סוף זאָל עס זײַן!...
נאָר פּלוצלונג — דער „װיסטל", דער באָס — אַ טרעװואָגע!
איך װער אַן דעם שׂכל, פֿארגעס, װוּ איך בין, —
עס טומלט, מען קעמפֿט, אַ, מײַן איך איז פֿארלאָרן, —
איך װײס ניט, מיך ארט ניט, איך בין אַ מאשין...

My Little Boy

I have a darling little boy,
a lovely son so fine,
and when I see him, seems to me
the whole wide world is mine.

But seldom, seldom do I see
my lovely boy awake;
I see him only when he sleeps--
it makes my poor heart break.

My work drives me away by dawn—
I get home late at night.
A stranger to me is my boy—
a stranger to my sight.

I come depressed and sad back home—
the darkness there abounds.
My wife so pale then tells me how
he plays, with joyous sounds.

How sweet he speaks, how wisely asks:
"O mother, dearest ma,
when will he bring a penny home
for me, my darling pa?"

I hear his words and rush to heed—
yes, yes, it has to be!
My father's love burns bright in me—
my child just has to see!

I stand right near his little bed
and listen quietly.
His lips move now—he's dreaming sweet:
"Dear pa, you've come to me."

I kiss his dear blue eyes just once—
they open and see me.
They see me standing next to him,
but sleeping soon is he.

מײַן ייִנגעלע

איך האָב אַ קלײנעם ייִנגעלע,
אַ זונעלע גאָר פֿײַן!
ווען איך דערזע אים דוכט זיך מיר,
די גאַנצע וועלט איז מײַן.

נאָר זעלטן, זעלטן זע איך אים,
מײַן שײנעם, ווען ער וואַכט,
איך טרעף אים אימער שלאָפֿנדיק,
איך זע אים נאָר בײַ נאַכט.

די אַרבעט טרײַבט מיך פֿרי אַרויס
און לאָזט מיך שפּעט צוריק;
אָ, פֿרעמד איז מיר מײַן אײגן לײַב!
אָ, פֿרעמד מײַן קינדס אַ בליק!

איך קום צעקלעמטערהײט אַהײם,
אין פֿינצטערניש געהילט, —
מײַן בלײכע פֿרוי דערצײלט מיר באַלד,
ווי פֿײַן דאָס קינד זיך שפּילט,

ווי זיס עס עס רעדט, ווי קלוג עס פֿרעגט:
„אָ, מאַמאַ, גוטע מאַ,
ווען קומט און ברענגט אַ פּעני מיר
מײַן גוטער, גוטער פּאַ?"

איך הער עס צו און אײַל — עס מוז, —
יאָ, יאָ, עס מוז געשען!
די פֿאָטער-ליבע פֿלאַקערט אויף:
עס מוז מײַן קינד מיך זען!...

איך שטײ בײַ זײַן געלעגנערל
און זע, און הער, און שאַ!
אַ טרוים באַוועגט די ליפּעלעך:
„אָ, ווו איז, ווו איז פּאַ?"

איך קוש די בלויע אײַגעלעך,
זײי עפֿ'נען זיך — „אָ, קינד!"
זײי זעען מיך, זײי זעען מיך,
און שליסן זיך געשווינד.

"Your daddy's here, my darling son—
a penny here for you."
Again he's dreaming, oh so sweet:
"Dear pa," he says anew.

I stand there feeling sad and blue—
I'm bitter to the core.
"When you awake, my dearest son,
you'll find me here no more."

My Resting Place

Don't look for me where myrtle's greening--
you won't find me there, my dear.
At my machine, where life's lost meaning,
there's my resting place, I fear.

Don't look for me where birds are singing--
you won't find me there, my dear.
A slave am I where chains are jingling--
there's my resting place, I fear.

Don't look for me where fountain's splashing--
you won't find me there, my dear.
Where tears are flowing, teeth are gnashing,
there's my resting place I fear.

And if you truly, deeply love me,
come to me my sweet, my dear,
and bring your glow to skies above me—
make it sweet, my place right here.

„דאָ שטייט דיין פּאַפּאַ, טײַערער,
אַ פּענעלע דיר, נאָ!"
אַ טרוים באַוועגט די ליפּעלעך:
„אַ, וווּ איז, וווּ איז פּאַ?"

איך בלײַב צעוווייטיקט און צעקלעמט,
פֿאַרביטערט און איך קלער:
„ווען דו דערוואַקסט אַ מאָל, מײַן קינד,
געפֿינסטו מיך ניט מער"...

מײַן רוע-פּלאַץ

ניט זוך מיך, וווּ די מירטן גרינען!
געפֿינסט מיך דאָרטן ניט, מײַן שאַץ;
וווּ לעבנס וועלקן בײַ מאַשינען,
דאָרטן איז מײַן רוע-פּלאַץ.

ניט זוך מיך, וווּ די פֿייגל זינגען!
געפֿינסט מיך דאָרטן ניט, מײַן שאַץ;
אַ שקלאַף בין איך וווּ קייטן קלינגען,
דאָרטן איז מײַן רוע-פּלאַץ.

ניט זוך מיך, וווּ פֿאָנטאַנען שפּריצן!
געפֿינסט מיך דאָרטן ניט, מײַן שאַץ;
וווּ טרערן רינען, ציינער קריצן,
דאָרטן איז מײַן רוע-פּלאַץ.

און ליבסטו מיך מיט וואַרער ליבע,
טאָ קום צו מיר, מײַן גוטער שאַץ!
און הײַטער אויף מײַן האַרץ די טריבע,
און מאַך מיר זיס מײַן רוע-פּלאַץ.

ABRAHAM LIESSIN

(pseudonym of Abraham Walt; born on May 19th, 1872 in Minsk; died on November 5th, 1938, in New York.)

Abraham Liessin is one of the poets whose poems used to be passed secretly from hand to hand at illegal meetings of Jewish socialists in czarist Russia. He was active in secret Jewish socialist groups even before the founding of the Bund. There formed around him a circle of young Jewish socialists who called themselves "Walties" because they considered Liessin-Walt their spiritual leader who was fighting against the assimilationist and cosmopolitan tendencies of other Jewish socialists. Liessin-Walt ignited his listeners at the secret meetings with his speeches, which were rooted in Jewish history, in the morality of the Jewish prophets, and in stories of generations of Jewish martyrs who sacrificed themselves for their religion, to sanctify the Holy Name.

His *Lid Oyfn Vaytn Tsofn* (Song of the Distant North), or, as it is also known, *Di Lena* (The Lena), accompanied exiled Jewish revolutionaries on their road to Siberia and in the cold, snowy steppes. Also his national poems, in which he celebrates Jewish valor and readiness for self-sacrifice, became very popular. They were recited at meetings of secret groups, and melodies were composed to them. A manuscript of his poems was circulated secretly, from hand to hand, in various cities in Russia, among both the intelligentsia and the ordinary workers.

In 1866, Liessin came to America and became active in the Jewish socialist movement. In the Workmen's Circle, he was the leading fighter for Yiddish education and cultural activity. He was one of the first staff writers for the *Forverts*. From the year 1913 till his death in 1938, Liessin was the editor of *Di Zukunft* (The Future*)*; under his editorship, the *Zukunft* became the world address for the greatest and best creators of Yiddish literature. His song *Der Kremer* (The Shopkeeper) is still sung by Jewish artists on the concert stage. He was also the composer of the *Arbeter Ring* (Workmen's Circle) *Hymn*.

In his memoirs *Epizodn* (Episodes), in Volume 3 of *Historishe Shriftn* (Historical Writings), reprinted in *Zikhroynes un Bilder* (Memories and Pictures), Liessin tells how as a child he used to stand in the synagogue Friday evenings and listen to stories that Jews told about the Russian Revolution: "I, a nine-year-old boy, stood near my father's coat tails, swallowed the stories, and glowed." Those stories became interwoven in his mind with the histories that he used to read in his father's books about "...the great martyrology of Jewish history and the burning streams of Jewish tears and blood contained in the ancient yellowed pages." The new fighters and martyrs for Russia's freedom awoke in the boy, the later fiery speaker, publicist, and poet, "...the same excitement," that he "...felt on reading the old Jewish chronicles—he felt the pain of *kidush hashem* (martyrdom)". That admiration for Russia's freedom-fighters, and for the Jewish martyrs of long ago, molded Liessin's life and creativity. When he joined the socialist propagandists in Minsk, he immediately began to complain: "Why do you come to Jews like foreigners, with Gentile books? Come to them as one of their own, with Yiddish literature, and you'll get a great deal more accomplished."

Those were new and bold words, which sounded quite strange to the ears of the young Jewish revolutionaries in Russia, and later in America. After all, any mention of the history of the martyrs and heroes of the Jewish people sounded to them like the "Jewish nationalism" from which they wanted to free themselves.

But Liessin's empathy for the suffering of the Jewish people and their desire to bring forth a world order of justice and freedom for all peoples, were intimately connected and had never been in contradiction with each other, as in other peoples. On the contrary, one complemented the other.

Even in his first poems (from 1889), the poet admires all those who underwent

all kinds of suffering
in desolate Siberia, that accursed prison,
in every tower of incarceration.

He laments the recent graves of those "...who shone like radiant stars, carried the holy fire." They were all his friends and comrades "...with bright mind and holy spirit, each and every one of them valiant."

Together with them, however, he also sees how

Eliezer, the son of Ennin, flames forward
there with Yokhanon the Galilean,
and Simeon raises against the enemy's legions
the sparkling sword so great.
I go around with the heroes in the flames
on defense walls built in the clouds.

In his later poems, he revived forgotten scenes and heroes from Jewish history, and through them called on the fighters of all eras:

You who remain, carrying the banner high--
take strength , brothers. Hold, oh hold, the front!

He celebrated Judah the Maccabbee and his fellow warriors. He lamented the martyrs' deaths of Rabbi Akiba and his students, the martyrs who died in the bonfires of the Inquisition, and the thousands of nameless Jews who died in all the holy sacrifices, for *kidush hashem.*

And everywhere I see the neck stretched out,
the trial, the waking dream,
in the reflection of every era we've discovered,
in the echo of every generation.
It is, after all, my four-thousand-year-old neck,
still ready for the slaughterer.

It is for that reason that it is so natural that Liessin would also admire the pioneers of the Bund who "…went out with red lanterns on a gray, secret morning," because they were

the announcement of salvation that awakens and exalts!
And everywhere their light shows itself,
it tears apart the lead
and illuminates bigger and bigger circles.

And for that reason he constantly returned to the theme of Hirsh Lekert, who became the symbol of renewed Jewish valor:

A poor ghetto child, the lowest of the low,
a life so short, a life so bitter,
which again conjured up out of our grayness
the noblest romance about a wondrous knight,
an avenger of the honor of the desecrated.

For that reason, too, the love of Yiddish, the language of the Jewish people:

I endured every danger with them
for hundreds of years,

and I absorbed their rage and sorrow.
I forged, through the generations,
the miracle of will despite pain,
to live for sacred teachings
and die steadfastly for them.

In his essay about Liessin, *Yidishe Shrayber Fun Tsvantsikstn Yorhundert* (Yiddish Writers of the Twentieth Century), Samuel Niger correctly notes: "It makes no difference whether one sacrifices himself for his belief in God, for the sake of his people, for the ideals of justice and freedom---it makes no difference what one gives his life for, he gives it up with pure intentions, with purified belief, and our poet of heroism gives him his heartiest blessings."

In his above-mentioned memoirs, Liessin says that even as a young man he felt that "...after all, the religious martyrs of yesterday would have been the secular martyrs of today," and the secular martyrs of today "...would have been the religious martyrs of yesterday."

That feeling later became the central theme of both the literary and societal activity of the great poet and publicist: he saw Jewish history as a constant chain of persistence, belief, and martyr-like readiness for "Holy Torahs."

Liessin's last poem was his elegy on the death of his closest friend and comrade, Boruch Charney Vladeck, who died suddenly on October 30th, 1938. Several days later, on November 5th, Liessin too "...fell from his post, exhausted, and the cold of death stopped his warm heart."

Hirsh Lekert

Noiselessly, in the wee hours,
they take him from the prison, like thieves,
and under heavy guard, locked in a carriage,
take him, accompanied by horsemen in silent procession,
take him carefully, in the stillness of dawn
so no one will be in the streets,
to the military field somewhere outside the city,
where his dark scaffold already awaits him.

And in the field an army is hiding,
standing with rifles and looking at the gallows
to see the Jewish cobbler-boy hanged
for the glory of the czar and von Wahl.[36]
Four battalions have been assembled quietly,
as if all Vilna were getting ready to attack.

Here comes the carriage, and he emerges—
redness appears high in the eastern sky.
He sees the scaffold clearly before him,
and close by it, his grave, freshly dug for him.
His heart is lamenting, he steps back—
everything swims before his eyes.
How dearly life smiles, how beautiful the world is,
how few good things he's seen—and already has to go to his grave!

Just one moment of weakness, painful and difficult—
then once again the proud revolutionary.
He goes to the scaffold, to his fate, cheerfully—
hears the judgment with courage and dignity, steadfastly,
and angrily rejects the offer to recant.
With contemptuous, mocking gaze he takes the measure
of the stiff, official, piously staring face
of the government rabbi, frightened to death.

Now they bind his wrists, now he sees the noose,
now the great moment is coming!
How he despises them, them and their punishment!

---

36. The governor of Vilna, whom Hirsh Lekert had attempted to assassinate

חירש לעקערט

(פֿראגמענט)

זיי האָבן רוישלאַז, אין די שעהען אין די שפּעטע,
פֿון טורמע, ווי גנבֿים, אים ארויסגענומען,
און אונטער שטאַרקער וואַך, פֿארהאַקט אין אַ קאַרעטע,
געפֿירט, באַגלייט פֿון רײַטער, אין פֿאַראַד אין שטומען —
געפֿירט אים פֿאַרזיכטיק, אין טויטקייט פֿון באַגינען,
אַז קיינער זאָל זיך אויף די גאַסן ניט געפֿינען.

און ביזן „מיליטער-פֿעלד", ערגעץ הינטער שטאָט,
ווּ פֿינצטער האָט דערוואַרט אים שוין דער עשאַפֿאָט.
און אויפֿן פֿעלד איז אן ארמיי געווען פֿארבאַרגן,
געשטאַנען אונטער ביקסן מיטן בליק צום תּלין,
צו זען דעם שוסטערריונג דעם ייִדישן דערוואָרגן
צום רום צום העררלעכן פֿון קייסער און פֿאַן-וואַליען;
פֿיר באַטאַליאַנען האָט מען שטיל צונויפֿגעטריבן,
ווי שטורעמען גאַנץ ווילנע וואָלט מען זיך געקליבן.

אָט קומט שוין די קאַרעטע און ער גייט ארויס,
ווען הויך אין מיזרח-הימל ברעכט די רויטקייט אויס.
דערזעט ער דײַטלער שוין פֿאַר זיך דעם עשאַפֿאָט
און האַרט דערבײַ די גרוב, פֿאַר אים געגראָבן פֿריש;
צעיאַמערט זיך זײַן האַרץ, ער מאַכט צוריק אַ טראָט,
און פֿאַר די אויגן גיט זיך זיך אַלעם ווילד אַ מיש —
ווי ליב דאָס לעבן געוואָרן שמייכלט, ווי די וועלט איז שיין,
ווי וויייניק גוטם געזען און מוז אין גרוב שוין גיין!

נאָר איין מינוט פֿון שוואַכקייט, ווייטיקדיק און שווער,
און ווידער שוין דער שטאַלצער רעוואָלוציאָנער.
ער גייט צום עשאַפֿאָט, צום גורל זײַנעם, מונטער,
און האָרט דעם פּסק אין מוט אין ווירדיקן, אין פֿעסטן,
און לאַכט דעם אָנבאָט פֿון פֿארראַט מיט האַס ארונטער,
און נעמט מיט בליקן שפֿאַטישע פֿאַראַכטעלער מעסטן
דעם שטײַפֿן, אָפֿיציעלן, פֿרום-צעענגלאַצטן פּנים
פֿון טויט-צעשראָקענעם ראַבינער, דעם קאַזיאַנעם.

אָט בינדט מען אים די העגט, אָט זעט ער שוין די שטריק,
אָט קומט שוין, קומט שוין אָן דער גרויסער אויגנבליק.
ווי טוט ער זיי פֿאַראַכטן — זיי און זייער שטראָף!

How they look at him in astonishment, the slaves!
And now, finally, the noose—thrown onto his nose
by the hangman, badly, clumsily.
With his hands bound, he catches it with his head
and shakes it down onto his neck.

And soon, in the morning gloom, from the gallows-knot
a lonely, blue, cold corpse swings.

There he lies now, a corpse buried in his grave,
and above him the army moves quickly.
Thousands of feet pound the grave
and flatten the earth on it.
With his memory already forgotten,
the hangmen disperse to eat breakfast.

The Shopkeeper
(fragment)

The little shopkeeper sits in his little shop,
the hundredth little shop on the street.
He sits and waits for a customer—
outside it's dark and wet.

Customers seldom appear—
he sits and shivers from the cold.
He sits and dreams dreams
and thinks about the world.

He thinks about kings and peoples,
and knows all about them.
The shopkeeper reads the Hebrew paper
and sees politics clearly.

He has plans; his mind
flashes like lightning.
How much better he'd do things
if he were the baron!

ווי קוקן זיי אויף אים פֿאַרחידושטע, די קנעכט !
און אָט שוין פֿאַלט די פּעטליע אויף זײַן נאַז צום סוף,
געוואָרפֿן פֿון דעם תּלין אומגעלומפּערט-שלעכט ;
טאָ כאַפּט ער, העענט געבונדן, פֿלינק זי מיטן קאָפּ
און טריײסלט זי אַליין שוין אויפֿן האַלדז אַראָפּ.

און באַלד אין מאָרגן-גרינקײַט, הויך אין תּליה-קנופּ,
צעוויגט זיך עלנטיק אַ בלויער, קאַלטער טרופּ.

אָט ליגט ער שוין אַ בר-מינן אין גרוב פֿאַרשאָטן,
און איבער אים דער חייל לויפֿט אין מאַרש אין גיכן ;
עם האָבן טויזנטער סאָלדאַטסקע פֿיס געטראָטן,
און מיט דער פֿלאַכער ערד דעם קבֿר אויסגעגליכן ;
און זיכער, אַז זײַן זכר וועט שוין זײַן פֿאַרגעסן,
צעפֿאָרן זיך די העענקערס פֿרישטיק אָפּצועסן.

דער קרעמער

(פֿראַגמענט)

דער קרעמערל זיצט אין זײַן קרעמל,
דאָם הונדערטסטע קרעמל אין גאַס ;
ער זיצט און ער וואַרט אויף אַ קונה ;
אין דרויסן איז פֿינצטער און נאַס.

עם ווײַזן זיך זעלטן די קונים ;
ער זיצט און ער שוידערט פֿאַר קעלט,
און גענעצט און חלומט חלומות,
און טראַכט זיך מפֿוח דער וועלט.

ער טראַכט וועגן מלכים און פֿעלקער
און ווײַס בײַ זיי אַלץ אויף אַ האָר ;
דער קרעמערל לעזט די „הצפֿירה"
און זעט די פּאָליטיקע קלאָר.

עם טוען אים פּלענער, ווי בליצן,
דעם מוח אַזוי אַ צינד אָן :
ווי וואָלט ער עס בעסער געמאַכט שוין,
ווען ער וואָלט געווען דער באַראָן !

"Oh, if I had the power!
My enemies would bite the dust
and I'd create a country
just from our people!

"A Jewish country, people!
Can you fully grasp that?
For that means a country of geniuses,
a country of veritable angels!

"A Jewish country, people!"
He jumps up from his bench
shaken, excited, and inflamed
by the great, proud thought.

But suddenly a customer appears,
as big as a chick pea,
and asks for a bit of butter—
distracts him from the matter.

The shopkeeper yawns and yawns
and shivers even harder from the cold.
The customer has interfered with his celebration
and the world resumes its everyday course.

In The Distant North

In the land where the Lena flows,
with its mighty, cold waters,
there stands a little tent
hidden in the eternal snows.

There it stands, a plaything for the storm,
lost in the middle of the field.
There he languishes in his icy loneliness,
the sick, dying hero.

Bloodily the winter,
the blind, roaring force,

„אָ, וואָלט איך געהאַט נאָר דעם פּוח!
די ערד וואָלטן שׂונאים געקײַט,
און טאַקע אַ מלוכה געשאַפֿן,
און טאַקע פֿון אונדזערע לײַט!

„אַ ייִדישע מלוכה, רבותים!
צי קענט איר דאָס גרונטיק פֿאַרשטיין?
דאָס הײסט דאָך אַ מלוכה פֿון גאונים,
אַ מלוכה פֿון מלכים אַליין!

„אַ ייִדישע מלוכה, רבותים!" —
ער טוט אַ שפּרונג אויף פֿון זײַן באַנק,
צערודערט, צערייצט און צעפֿלאַקערט
פֿון גרויס, פֿון שטאָלצן געדאַנק.

נאָר פּלוצלינג באַווײַזט זיך אַ קונה,
אַזוי ווי אַן אַרבעס די גרויס,
און בעט פֿאַר אַ קאָפּיקע פּוטער,
און שלאָגט אים פֿון ענין אַרויס.

עם גענעצט און גענעצט דער קרעמער,
און שוידערט נאָך שטאַרקער פֿאַר קעלט;
צעשטערט האָט דער מיסחר זײַן יום־טוב,
און וואָכעדיק ווערט אים די וועלט.

אויפֿן ווײַטן צפֿון

אין לאַנד, וואו עם קײַקלט די לענאַ
איר מעכטיקן וואַסער, דעם קאַלטן —
דאָרט שטײט זיך אַ קליייניקע יורטע,
אין אייביקע שנייען באַהאַלטן.

זי שטײט דאָרט אַ שפֿיל פֿאָרן שטורעם,
פֿאַרוואָלגערט אין מיטן דעם פֿעלד —
דאָרט שמאַכט אין זײַן אײַזיקן עלנט
דער קראַנקער, דער שטאַרבנדער העלד.

עם ציט זיך צעיושעט דער ווינטער,
די בלינדע, די ברומענדע מאַכט;

goes on, shielded by the night,
the muffled, eternal night.

The dying is prolonged, prolonged—
difficult, long, and endless,
and an oppressive, painful sleep
torments the pale martyr.

He dreams of springtime,
when the heavenly dome is blue.
There, in his distant home,
the sun shines upon the world;

It shines for all,
and all feel light-hearted.
Newly grown blades of grass caress,
and trees are blossoming green.

Everyone strolls outside
and balm flows in their breasts.
Life celebrates a holiday,
the holiday of love and joy.

But one, a lonely one, sits there—
silent, despondent, to one side.
Her heart, her broken heart,
takes no part in everyone's joy.

She sits and thinks about the Lena,
about the cold, dark North.
There stands a little tent,
hidden in the eternal snows.

It stands there, a plaything for the storm,
lost in the middle of the field.
There he languishes in his icy loneliness,
the sick, dying hero.

עס ציט זיך פֿאַרפֿאַנצערט דער חושך,
די טויבע, די אייביקע נאַכט.

עס ציט זיך, עס ציט זיך די גסיסה,
די שווערע, די לאַנגע אָן סוף,
און ס׳מאַטערט דעם בלייכן מאַרטירער
אַ דריקנדער, פֿיַנלעכער שלאָף.

און ס׳חלומט זיך אים פֿון אַ פֿרילינג,
ווו בלוי איז דער הימל-געצעלט;
דאָרט איצט אין דער הײם אין דער וויַטער
צעשיַנט זיך אַ זון אויף דער וועלט.

דאָרט שיַנט איצט די זון פֿאַר די מענטשן,
און ליכטיק איז יעדנס געמיט,
און גרעזעלעך יונגינקע צערטלען,
און בײמער — אין גרין און אין בליט.

און אַלע שפּאַצירן אין דרויסן,
און באַלזאַם צעגיסט זיך אין ברוסט;
און ס׳פֿיַערט דאָס לעבן זיַן יום-טובֿ,
דעם יום-טובֿ פֿון ליבע און לוסט.

נאָר איינע, אָן אײנזאַמע, זיצט דאָרט,
פֿאַרצאָגט, אָן אַ זיַט, שטומערהייט;
איר האַרץ איר צעבראָכענע, נעמט ניט
קיין אָנטייל אין אַלעמענס פֿרייד.

זי זיצט און זי טראַכט פֿון דער לענאַ,
פֿון טונקעלן צפֿון פֿון קאַלטן;
דאָרט שטייט זיך אַ קליינינקע יורטע,
אין אייביקע שנייען באַהאַלטן.

זי שטייט דאָרט אַ שפּיל פֿאַרן שטורעם.
פֿאַרוואָלגערט אין מיטן דעם פֿעלד —
דאָרט שמאַכט אין זיַן איַיזיקן עלנט
דער קראַנקער, דער שטאַרבנדער העלד.

Yiddish

In sleepless nights she used to come to me
with her dear grace.
Where she came from
has remained her secret.
In the quiet pre-dawn hours,
she'd come in gently trembling—
a whisper of some sort of prayer,
a shimmer from some sort of glow.

Her eyes would shine to me
with a soft, trusting light.
She'd lay her hand on my head
and cool my fevered brow.
The room would turn white and peaceful
at her wondrous touch
when the two wings on her back
shimmered with whiteness.
I'd hear her voice,
beautifully melodious,
like the voice of my mother
reading from the Yiddish Bible on Sabbath long ago:

"I don't come to you radiant with God's word,
as my sister used to long ago,
sanctified by ancient, great times
and with lightning and thunder in her voice.

"I don't come to you, as she did, from a sunny height,
reflecting the purity of the blue heavens.
I don't have the softness of green meadows
or the wild, desolate beauty of proud mountain cliffs.

"I come to you, my child, from silent exiles
in crowded, sealed-off ghettos.
I possess only the charm of pious prayers,
only the beauty of dying to sanctify His name.

ייִדיש

אין שלאָפֿלאָזע נעכט פֿלעגט זי קומען
צו מיר אין איר ליבער גענאָד.
פֿון וואַנען זי האָט זיך גענומען —
דאָס איז שוין פֿאַרבליבן איר סוד.
זי פֿלעגט אין פֿאַרמאָגן אין שטילע
מיט צימער, מיט צאַרטן, אַריַין —
אַ פֿליסטער פֿון עפּעס אַ תּפֿילה,

אַ שימער פֿון עפּעס אַ שיַין.
און אויפֿלײַכטן פֿלעגן מיר אויגן
מיט ווייכן, פֿאַרטרויילעכן ליכט;
אַ האַנט אויף מײַן קאָפּ פֿלעגט זי לייגן
און קילן דעם פֿלאַם פֿון געזיכט.
פֿלעגט וויַים אַזוי ווערן אין צימער
און גרינג פֿון איר וווּנדער-באַריר,
ווען וויַים פֿלעגן געבן אַ שימער
צוויַיי פֿליגלען פֿון הינטן ביַי איר.
און פֿול מיט מעלאָדישקייט גוטער,
פֿלעגט האַרציק זיך הערן איר קול,
אַזוי ווי דער קול פֿון מײַן מוטער
ביַים טיַיטש-חומש שבת אַ מאָל:

„איך קום ניט צו דיר פֿון גאָטס וואָרט אַ באַשטראַלטע,
אַזוי ווי מײַן שוועסטער פֿלעגט קומען אַ מאָל —
פֿאַרהיילליקט פֿון ציַיטן פֿון גרויסע, פֿון אַלטע,
מיט בליצן און דונערן-אָפּקלאַנג אין קול.

„איך קום ניט, ווי זי, פֿון אַ זוניקער הויכקייט,
אין הימל אין בלויסטן זיך שפּיגלענדיק רייַן;
איך האָב ניט פֿון היגלען פֿון גרינע די ווייכקייט,
פֿון פֿעלדזנבערג שטאָלצע — דעם וויסט-ווילדן חן.

„איך קום צו דיר, קינד מײַן, פֿון גלותן שטומע,
פֿון געטאָס פֿאַרפּאָקטע, פֿאַרהאָקטע אין קלעם;
איך האָב נאָר די חנען פֿון תחינות, פֿון פֿרומע,
איך האָב נאָר די שיינקייט פֿון קידוש-השם.

„און טראָג איך אין זיך ניט די בליצן, וואָס בלענדן,
דעם פֿלאַמיקן זונגאָרם, וואָס וווּנדער באַוויַיזט,
טאָ האָב איך דעם שימער פֿון שטערן-לעגענדן,
די ליבע לבנה-באַלויכטונג פֿון גיַיסט.

"Though I don't carry within me the blinding lightning
or the flaming sunbeams that perform miracles,
I do carry the sparkle of starry legends,
the precious moonlight of the soul.

"From Worms, from Mainz, and from Speyer,
through Prague and Lublin to Odessa,
a single flame kept spreading,
a single miracle.
Our mortal enemies always hovered there—
thousand-eyed Death lurked nearby.
There, desolate and sorrowful,
I accompanied your ancestors.

"I endured every danger with them
for hundreds of years,
and I absorbed
their rage and sorrow.
I forged, through the generations,
the miracle of will, despite pain,
to live for sacred teachings
and die steadfastly for them.
If pure holiness
derives only from torture and pain,
then I, my child, am the one for you—
I am your holiest one.

"Though honoring God hasn't brought me pain,
or prophetic visions either,
the lust to sin of the priest who shamefully kneeled before Baal
is also foreign to me.

"And though foreign to me is the enthusiasm of the victor
that history has wreathed with sunbeams,
so too is the cruelty of the warrior
who lives by the bloody sword.

"I haven't had titans
who sparkle to the heavens like lonely icebergs in the sky,
but our people has been completely purified by misfortune
and sanctified by pain.

„פֿון װאָרמס, פֿון מײַנץ און פֿון שפּײַער,
דורך פּראָג און לובלין, ביז אָדעם,
האָט אַלץ זיך געצױגן אײן פֿײַער,
האָט אַלץ זיך געצױגן אײן נם.
האָט שטענדיק דער בלוטפֿײַנד געהױערט,
געלױערט פֿילאױיגיק דער טױט —
אָט דאָרט האָב איך, װיסט און פֿאַרטרױערט,
די עלטערן דײַנע באַגלײט.

„איך בין מיט זיי הונדערטער יאָרן
געגאַנגען דורך יעדער געפֿאָר,
און אײַנגעזאַפּט האָב איך דעם צאָרן
און אײַנגעזאַפּט האָב איך דעם צער.
און אױסגעשמידט האָב איך דורך דורות
דעם װוּנדער פֿון װילן און װיי,
צו לעבן פֿאַר הײליקע תּורות
און שטאַרבן מיט פֿעסטקײט פֿאַר זיי.
און אױב נאָר די קדושה די רײנע
שײַנט אָפּ פֿון עינויים אין פּײַן,
טאָ בין איך דאָר, קינד מײַן, די אײנע,
טאָ בין איך די הײליקסטע דײַן".

"און האָט ניט קײן גאָטס–כּבֿוד געטאָן פֿאַר מיר װייען,
קײן זעונג פֿון נבֿיא אין מיר ניט געגליט, –
דערפֿאַר איז מיר פֿרעמד אױך די זינד–גלוט פֿון כּהן,
װאָס האָט זיך אין שאַנד פֿאָרן בעל געקניט.

"און אױב מיר איז פֿרעמד די אַנטציקונג פֿון זיגער,
װאָס האָט די געשיכטע מיט שטראַלן געװעבט,
טאָ פֿרעמד איז מיר אױך די אַכזריות פֿון קריגער,
װאָס האָט אױף פֿאַרבלוטיקטע שװערדן געלעבט.

"איך האָב ניט געהאַט די טיטאַנען, װאָס גלאַנצן,
װי אײַנזאַמע שניי–בערג, אין הימל אַרײַן;
געװען איז שױן אָבער די אומה אין גאַנצן
געלײַטערט אין אומגליק, געהײליקט אין פּײַן.

"I used to absorb the blood and tears
and the cries of pain,
and the more I heard the last agonized cries of dying martyrs,
the holier I became.

"I've sung a song of Torah
to a child in his cradle—
after that, the melody resounded
in his soul, all his life.

"I used to glow in hearts
when the reader spoke in shul,
and shout exultantly
when the *magid* preached.

"I sent along fervent prayers
with Jewish mothers—
I prepared great, silent martyrs
with holiness,
led them through their hours of darkest need
with the women's Bible,
and lovingly adorned those heroic deeds
that they call living.

"A treasure for the people
was preserved in me:
the folk-soul, fresh and pious,
an incomparable, immeasurable treasure.

"And furthermore, my child,
carry on the teachings of generations, altered though they may be:
to live and die for sacred teachings
and to be a stubborn people of martyrs.

"און אויפֿנעמען פֿלעג איך די בלוטן און טרערן,
און אויפֿנעמען פֿלעג איך דעם וווייטיק–געשריי,
און הייליקער ווערן, וואָס מער איך פֿלעג הערן
פֿון שטאַרבענדע קדושים דעם לעצטן אוי–ווי.

"איך האָב שוין צום קינד אין די וויגן
פֿון תּורה געזונגען אַ ליד;
דערנאָך האָט געקלונגען דער ניגון
אַ לעבן לאַנג אים אין געמיט.

איך פֿלעג זיך אין הערצער צעשטראַלן
בײַם אַלשיך פֿון זאַגער אין שול;
בײַם מגיד אין וואָרט פֿלעג איך שאַלן
מיט גבֿורה מיט זאַפֿטיקער פֿול.

איך האָב מיט געבעטן מיט הייסע
די ייִדישע מוטערס באַגלייט;
מאַרטירערינס שטילע און גרויסע
אין הייליקייט האָב איך געגרייט.
איך האָב מיט דער צאַינה–וראינה
דורך פֿינצטערסטער נויט זיי געפֿירט,
און ליבלעך די העלדנטאַט יענע,
וואָס הייסט בײַ זיי לעבן, געצירט.

און אײַנגעהיט איז פֿאַר דער אומה
געבליבן אַן אוצר אין מיר:
די פֿאָלקס–זעל – אַ פֿרישע, אַ פֿרומע,
אַן אוצר אָן ערך און שיעור.

"און ווײַטער, מײַן קינד, צי די לערע פֿון דורות,
אַפֿילו וווען איך אין פֿאַרענדערטן שײַן –
צו לעבן און שטאַרבן פֿאַר הייליקע תּורות,
אַ האַרטנעקיק פֿאָלק פֿון מאַרטירערער צו זײַן.

"If you seek to brighten the ghettos with beauty,
then know that no beauty is as beautiful
as the beauty of the human soul often is
and the beauty of the folk-soul itself always is.

"Look for that quiet beauty in me,
and do not fear that someday I'll be gone.
Will even the people live forever?
Will even life itself live forever?

"As long as I'm so dear to you, my child,
and as long as we're still together here,
and as long as the fire still burns in your blood,
don't let the hour of inspiration go by."

That's how she used to speak,
and everything was brightened by her love.
In her call I would hear
the sorrow of the world calling.
And then, in the quiet, exalted dawn,
something would happen:
I'd feel enlightened
and I'd see hidden wonders;
pure and illuminated in white,
my song would rise for her;
timely words would rise and fall, syllable after syllable,
and I'd break out into tears of loving, creative joy.
Weeping, I'd swear to her to remain a link in the chain—
to carry on farther and farther through the generations
the miracle of will despite pain,
to live for sacred teachings and die steadfastly for them.

"און זוכסטו מיט שיינקייט די געטאָס באַהעלן,
טאָ ווייס, אַז קיין שיינקייט איז ניט אַזוי שיין,
ווי אָפֿט מאָל די שיינקייט פֿון מענטשעלעכע זעלן,
ווי שטענדיק די שיינקייט פֿון פֿאָלקזעל אַליין.
"און זוך זי אין מיר, אָט די שיינקייט די שטילע,
און שרעק זיך ניט טאָמער–ווען וועל איך פֿאַרגיין:
וועט אייביק דען לעבן די אומה אַפֿילו?
וועט אייביק דען לעבן דאָס לעבן אַליין?

"און כּל–זמן איך בין דיר, מײַן קינד, אַזוי טײַער,
און כּל–זמן מיר זײַנען צוזאַמען נאָך דאָ,
און כּל–זמן עס ברענט אין דײַן בלוט נאָך דאָס פֿײַער,
ניט לאָז זי פֿאַרבײַ, די באַגײַסטערטע שעה."

זי פֿלעגט אַזוי ריידן. און ווערן
פֿלעגט אַלץ פֿון אַ ליבשאַפֿט באַהעלט;
איך פֿלעג אין דעם רוף אירן הערן
דעם רופֿנדן צער פֿון דער וועלט.
פֿלעגט דאַן אין באַגינען דעם שטילן
געהויבענעס עפּעס געשעַן,
און דורכגעלויכט פֿלעג איך זיך פֿילן
און וווּנדער פֿאַרהויילענע זעַן.
און לויטער, אין דורכלויכט אין ווײַסן,
פֿלעגט אויפֿגיין פֿאַר איר מײַן געזאַנג;
דאָס צײַטיקע וואָרט פֿלעגט זיך רײַסן
און פֿאַלן, אַ קלאַנג נאָך אַ קלאַנג.
און אויסברעכן פֿלעגן מיר טרערן
פֿון ליבנדער, שאָפֿנדער פֿרייד,
און ווײַנענדיק פֿלעג איך איר שווערן
אַ רינג צו פֿאַרבלײַבן אין קייט –
צו ציִען אַלץ ווײַטער דורך דורות
דעם וווּנדער פֿון ווילן און ווי,
צו לעבן פֿאַר הייליקע תּורות
און שטאַרבן מיט פֿעסטקייט פֿאַר זיי.

The Eternal Jew
(fragment)

Between peoples the terrible wars
go on, generations without end.
Beneath my feet the battlefield trembles and roars,
but still along the road my way I wend.

Through deserts and swamps, past bramble and bone,
I walk and I walk and I'll keep to my tract.
With none other than Satan the Destroyer alone
I've concluded an eternal pact.

Fire shall not burn me
nor water engulf me.
Spears shall be unable to pierce me
and bullets shall bounce off my body.

I feel stronger than the troubles of life,
than human anger and crime;
stronger than fire, water, or strife,
stronger even than Time.

Before my eyes, through the thousands of years,
the greatest kingdoms have disappeared.
The strongest peoples have been destroyed
and great cities have been plowed with salt.

Enormous mountains have been overshadowed
and eternal forests are rotted and trampled.
Mighty cliffs are softened and kneaded—
I still live and endure.

I live and I live and I'll still keep on living—
through thousands of years I will fight.
I'll still keep living and struggling and striving—
the sharp tooth of Time has grown dull.

דער אייביקער ייִד

(פֿראגמענט)

עס ציט זיך דורך ענדלאָזע דורות און ציט
דער גוואלדיקער פֿעלקער-געשלעג ;
עס ציטערט דאָס שלאַכטפֿעלד מיר אונטער די טריט —
איך גיי מיר אַלץ ווײַטער מײַן וועג !

דורך זאַמד און דורך דערנער, דורך שטיין און דורך בײַן,
איך גיי און איך גיי און איך וועל נאָך אַלץ גיין,
איך האָב מיטן שׂטן המשחית אַליין
געשלאָסן אַן אייביקן בונד :

דאָס פֿײַער, עס זאָל מיך ניט ברענען,
דאָס וואַסער, עס זאָל מיך ניט שלינגען,
דער שפּיז זאָל מיך שטעכן ניט קענען,
די קויל זאָל צוריק פֿון מיר שפּרינגען.

איך פֿיל, איך בין שטאַרקער פֿון אַלע יסורים,
פֿון מענטשלעכער בייזקייט און שטרײַט,
און שטאַרקער פֿון וואַסער, פֿון פֿײַער, פֿון שטורעם,
און שטאַרקער אפֿילו פֿון צײַט.

עס זײַנען פֿאַר מיר, דורך די טויזנטער יאָרן,
די מלוכות די גרעסטע געגאַנגען פֿאַרלאָרן,
די פֿעלקער די שטאַרקסטע פֿאַרטיליקט געווארן,
און וועלט-שטעט צעאַקערט אין זאַלץ ;
און ריזיקע בערג זײַנען לאַנג שוין צעשטאַטן,
און אייביקע וועלדער — צעפֿוילט און צעטראַטן,
און מעכטיקע פֿעלדזן — צעוויקט און צעקנאַטן,
— איך לעב און געדײַע נאָך אַלץ !

איך לעב און איך לעב און איך וועל נאָך אַלץ לעבן
דורך טויזנטער יאָרן פֿון שטרײַט ;
איך וועל נאָך אַלץ לעבן און קעמפֿן און שטרעבן, —
און טעמפּ איז דער צאָן פֿון דער צײַט !

S. ANSKY

(pseudonym of Shloyme-Zaynvl Rappaport; born in 1863 in Tshashnik,
White Russia; died on November 8, 1920 in Warsaw)

S.Ansky, whose real name was Shloyme-Zaynvl Rappaport, began his multifaceted literary and cultural-societal activity as a *Maskil* who propagandized the ideas of the *haskole* among Jewish youth in Russia. Later he became close to the *narodnikes*[37] and began to wander among the peasants, coal-miners, and ordinary people, among whom he carried out educational work in the spirit of the Russian people's movement. He began to print articles and stories in the magazine of the *narodnikes*, *Russkoye Bagatsvo* (Russian wealth), and later, in 1892, he left Russia and lived for a time in Germany, Switzerland, and France. Through all that time, he was extending his studies, and manifested a special interest in the folklore of the peoples among whom he lived.

When Ansky went back to Russia at the beginning of the 20th century, the second and most important stage of his creative life began. Under the influence of his childhood friend Dr Chaim Zhitlovsky, he turned his attention back to Jewish life and the Yiddish language. He grew close to the socialist revolutionaries and wrote a number of revolutionary songs, which became very popular. His song *Di Shvue* became the hymn of the Bund. His song about the salty ocean that included within it all human tears, suffering, and pain became one of the most popular songs among the Bundists. Another, perhaps more important, turning point in his life was when he made the acquaintance of the great historian Simon Dubnow and the leaders of the Jewish Historical Ethnographic Society in St. Petersburg, who got him interested in Jewish folklore.

It was only because of his deep interest in and understanding of his people that Ansky attained his real calling as a cultural researcher and artist. In the years 1912-1914, he organized a group of Jewish youngsters and set out "to return to the people," this time not to the Russian peasants but to his own people: under the aegis of Baron Horatio Ginsberg, he conducted the first Jewish ethnographic expedition to collect Jewish folk creations. The researchers/collectors visited almost 70 cities and returned with great treasures: thousands of photographs of synagogues, many thousands of written folktales, songs, legends, record-books, documents, miscellaneous Jewish artifacts, phonograph records, etc.

---

37. Men of the people

Ansky became famous throughout the world for his masterpiece, *The Dybbuk*, which was staged for the first time by the Vilna Troupe on December 9, 1920, the thirty day anniversary of his death. That work, which like many of Ansky's other creations was rooted in Jewish folklore, was translated and staged in many theaters all over the world. In New York, an opera based on *The Dybbuk* was staged in 1951. One of the crowning achievements of the *Habimah* theater was *The Dybbuk*, which it put on for the first time, in Hebrew, in Moscow in 1922, under the direction of Vachtangov, with music by Joel Engel.

To The Bund
(fragment)

In the salty ocean of human tears
there is a terrifying pit.
It cannot get any deeper or darker—
it's marked out by a bloody stream.

The pit has been dug for thousands of years
by faith and hatred and pain,
and for thousands of years, drop by drop,
tears have poured into it.

And now the pit is full. These are Jewish tears,
but make no mistake about them:
a bloody tear belongs to a poor man—
a rich man's is white as snow.

But to you, workers and poor people,
belongs the pit,
and to your 'brothers,' the rich robbers,
belongs the surface foam.

The ocean's now full, overflowing its shores.
Where are the heroes, the people
who will dare courageously
to throw themselves into the pit, into the battle?

Who will finally liberate the workers
from hunger and eternal suffering,
and who will show them the path to freedom,
to brotherhood, equality, and happiness?

The hero will liberate the world and heal it—
he'll reach the depths of the pit!
Long live the Jewish Workers' Bund
of Russia, Lithuania, and Poland!

צום בונד

(פֿראַגמענט)

אין זאַלציקן ים פֿון די מענטשלעכע טרערן
געפֿינט זיך אַ שרעקלעכער תּהום;
ער קען שוין ניט טיפֿער, ניט פֿינצטערער ווערן,
אים צייכנט אַ בלוטיקער שטראָם...

דעם תּהום האָבן טויזנטער יאָרן געגראָבן
אמונה און שׂינאה און פֿײַן,
און טויזנטער יאָרן אַלץ טראָפּן נאָך טראָפּן
עס גיסן זיך טרערן דערײַן.

און פֿול איז דער תּהום... דאָס איז יידישע טרערן
נאָר האָט ניט קיין טעות אין זיי:
אַ בלוטיקער טרער טוט דעם קבצן געהערן,
דעם נגיד — אַ ווײַסער ווי שניי.

נאָר אײַך, בעלי-מלאָכות, אביונים, קבצנים,
געהערט דאָך דער בלוטיקער תּהום,
און אײַערע „ברידער", די רײַכע גזלנים,
געהערט נאָר פֿון אויבן דער שוים.

שוין פֿול איז דער ים און פֿאַרפֿלייצט אַלע ברעגן.
וווּ זײַנען די העלדן, די לײַט,
די, וועלכע עס וועלן זיך מוטיק דערוואַגן
צו וואַרפֿן אין תּהום זיך, אין שטרײַט?

דעם אַרבעטער ווער זשע וועט ענדלעך דערלייזן
פֿון הונגער און אייביקער לייד
און ווער וועט דעם וועג אים צו פֿרײַהייט באַווײַזן,
צו ברידערשאַפֿט, גלײַכהייט און פֿרייד?

דער העלד וועט די וועלט אי באַפֿרײַען, אי היילן,
ער׳ט גרייכן דעם תּהום ביזן גרונט!
עס לעבע פֿון רוסלאַנד, פֿון ליטע און פּוילן
דער יידישער „אַרבעטער-בונד"!

The Tailor

The house is small, the house is old—
in every corner, garbage and mold.
It's dark, sad, and cold.
A sick tailor sits and sews.
The tailor sews,
his needle goes,
his mind reels,
great need he feels:
there's no bread, no bread!

His face yellow, despondent, lost in thought—
the needle moves day and night.
From time to time a dry cough
stops his hand, racks his chest.
The tailor sews,
his needle goes,
his mind reels, great need he feels:
there's no bread, no bread!

In the house it's sad and empty.
From the cradle a sigh, from the bed a cough.
A little lamp burns weakly—
a light rain taps on the roof.
The tailor sews,
his needle goes,
his mind reels,
great need he feels:
there's no bread, no bread!

         * * *

"What are you doing here in the world, tailor?"
"I'm living."
Terrible cold clamps his heart. Accursed cold!
If this is living, what is death?
The tailor sews,
his needle goes,
his mind reels,
great need he feels:
there's no bread, no bread!

דער שנײַדער

די שטוב איז קליין, די שטוב איז אַלט,
אין יעדן ווינקל מיסט און קויט.
ס'איז פינצטער, אומעטיק און קאַלט,
אַ קראַנקער שנײַדער זיצט און נייט.
דער שנײַדער נייט,
די נאָדל גייט,
דער מוח דרייט,
ס'איז גרוים די נויט,
ניטאָ קיין ברויט, ניטאָ קיין ברויט.

*

דאָס פנים געל, פאַרצאָגנט, פאַרטראַכט,
די נאָדל רודערט מאָג און נאַכט,
פֿון צײַט צו צײַט אַ פוסטער הוסט
האַלט אויף די האַנט, רײַסט אויף די ברוסט.
דער שנײַדער נייט,
די נאָדל גייט,
דער מוח דרייט,
ס'איז גרוים די נויט,
ניטאָ קיין ברויט, ניטאָ קיין ברויט.

*

אין שטוב איז אומעטיק און פוסט,
פֿון וויג אַ זיפֿץ, פֿון בעט אַ הוסט,
אַ קליינער לעמפל ברענט זיך שוואַך,
אַ דראָבנער רעגן קלאַפּט אין דאַך.
דער שנײַדער נייט,
די נאָדל גייט,
דער מוח דרייט,
ס'איז גרוים די נויט,
ניטאָ קיין ברויט, ניטאָ קיין ברויט.

*

„וואָס טוסטו, שנײַדער, אויף דער וועלט?"
„איך לעב"... — אַ שוידערלעכע קעלט
נעמט אָן בײַם האַרץ, פאַרפלוכטע נויט!
אַז דאָס הייסט לעבן, וואָס איז טויט?!
דער שנײַדער נייט,
די נאָדל גייט,
דער מוח דרייט,
ס'איז גרוים די נויט,
ניטאָ קיין ברויט, ניטאָ קיין ברויט.

The Emigrant's Song

We're wandering, we're wandering,
from one land to another one,
through hunger and through cold.
We're deeply lost, we're bitter now,
we're wailing and we're trembling now,
we strangers in the world.

We're lost amid the human stream,
without a home or native land,
no fam'ly and no house;
oppressed we are by everyone,
we're blown by storm winds everywhere,
we strangers in the world.

We're stopped at all the border lines,
and trampled like the roadway's dust—
no money, strength, or help.
Oh where, oh where, where can we go,
what goals are we all striving for,
we strangers in the world.

Our exile's been two thousand years,
in ancient and in modern times--
a treasure keeps us strong.
A treasure that is quite unique,
the power of a wanderer
that permeates the world.

We have with us that treasure still,
that wondrous power guides us still,
replaces all we lack.
Eternal seeds we keep with us
of holiness, belief, and faith
to sow throughout the world.

Our worker's hand is strong and sure,
our revolution's rocky hard,
heroic valor have we all.

עמיגראַנטן־ליד

מיר וואַנדערן, מיר וואַנדערן
פֿון איין לאַנד אין דעם אַנדערן
דורך הונגער און דורך קעלט,
פֿאַרוואָגלטע, פֿאַרביטערטע,
פֿאַריאָמערטע, צעציטערטע,
מיר, גרים פֿון דער וועלט !

אין מענטשנשטראָם פֿאַרלאָרענע
אַן היים און לאַנד געבאָרענע,
אַן הויז און אַן געצעלט ;
פֿון אַלעמען געשלאָגענע,
פֿון שטורעמווינט געטראָגענע,
מיר, גרים פֿון דער וועלט.

בײַ גרענעצן פֿאַרכאַטענע,
ווי שטויב פֿון וועג געטראָטענע,
אַן מאַכט, אַן הילף, אַן געלט. —
ווּהין, ווּהין זשע שוועבן מיר ?
צו וועלכע ציֵלן שטרעבן מיר ?
מיר, גרים פֿון דער וועלט ?

פֿון גלות טויזנטיאַריקן
פֿון נייעם און אַמאָליקן
האָט אונדז זיך אָפּגעשטעלט
אַ רייכטום גאָר אַן אַנדערער, —
אַ כוח פֿון אַ וואַנדערער,
וואָס גייט אום אין דער וועלט.

אַ גרויסן אוצר טראָגן מיר,
אַ שטאַרקע מאַכט פֿאַרמאָגן מיר,
שטאָט אַלץ דעם, וואָס אונדז פֿעלט :
מיר טראָגן זוימען אייביקע
פֿון הייליקע, פֿון גלייביקע,
צו זייען אויף דער וועלט.

מיר טראָגן קראַפֿט אין אַרבעטסהאַנט,
פֿון פֿעלדזנשטיין אַ ווידערשטאַנד
און גבורה פֿון אַ העלד ;

We carry to the working place,
through fire, blood, and human hate
the bright new coming world.

A brand new world, a greater one,
a more beautiful and better one,
we will create for all.
Our courage is the building-block,
our spirit and our precious blood,
we burgers of the world.

מיר טראָגן אין דער אַרבעטסגאַס
דורך פֿײַער, בלוט און מענטשנהאַס
אַ קומענדיקע וועלט!

אַ נײַע וועלט, אַ גרעסערע,
אַ שענערע, אַ בעסערע
וועט ווערן אויפֿגעשטעלט;
מיר בויען זי מיט אונדזער מוט,
מיט אונדזער גײַסט, מיט אונדזער בלוט,
מיר בירגער פֿון דער וועלט!

M.M. WARSHAWSKY

(born on November 26, 1848, in Odessa; died in 1907 in Kiev)

At one time, there was no place on earth where Jews of East European origin lived where the songs of M.M. Warshawsky were not sung. Probably only one in a thousand of those who sang his songs had ever heard the name of their writer. Seldom has such a far-ranging prophecy come true as in the case of the prediction of the popularity of Warshawsky's songs: Sholem Aleichem, who was the first to discover Warshawsky's talent and helped him to publish his book *Yidishe Folkslider* (Yiddish Folksongs) in 1901, wrote in his Introduction: "I am quite convinced that it will not take very long till Warshawsky's *Yiddish Folksongs* become true folksongs, which one will be able to hear everywhere, in every Jewish house, wherever one still hears a Yiddish word, where they are not ashamed of our Jewish folk-language, which people call 'the jargon'".

Sholem Aleichem's prophecy was more than fulfilled; even where people no longer spoke Yiddish in their daily lives; even in many cases when they were ashamed of our "poor jargon," one could hear Warshawsky's songs sung. Now, more than 100 years after the book was published in Kiev, Warshawsky's songs are often the only open identifying signs of the deep national feeling that many of the Jews of Russia carried hidden within them. Warshawsky's famous song about the Yiddish alphabet, "…you'll grow up some day/ and then you'll surely know/ all the sadness in the holy alphabet/ all the tears and woe" received a new lease on life there: Jews in Soviet Russia , in the 1950s, sang:

> *Study, little boy, with enthusiasm,*
> *and you'll know how to be a Jew;*
> *don't think about any other matters—*
> *just look into your prayer-book.*
> *One more thing, my child, I want to say:*
> *that you should hold your Jewish name dear;*
> *don't change it,*
> *even if they drive you into the fire.*
> *If they start to beat you and drive you,*
> *say this to them:*
> *Komets alef, o—komets beyz, bo.*

(Quoted from Simon Weber's article *Yidish Lid Vos Vert Geheym Farshpreyt in Rusland* (Yiddish Song That Is Sung Secretly in Russia); *Forverts* , November 1, 1962)

* * *

Let us now tell a little about how our great Sholem Aleichem discovered Warshawsky and convinced him to publish a book of his songs:

> In a conversation with a licensed lawyer in Kiev (M. M-r), he told me that he had traveled that week with a colleague of his, also a licensed lawyer, M.M. Warshawsky from Kiev to the court in Vasilkov, and that Warshawsky had sung him little Jewish songs in 'jargon' the whole way, the kind that melt in one's bones.

> "Whose songs were they?" I asked. "Where can one get them and where are they published?"

> "They're his own songs, and they're not published anywhere. He himself writes the words and the music to them, and he himself sings them. Everything himself."

> "So why are you keeping quiet about it? Bring him here, that bird!"

> A few days passed and the bird was brought to him. The guest didn't need to be coaxed very long—he sat down at the piano and accompanied himself as he sang his beautiful songs, with so much feeling and humor and such a beautiful, hearty voice that I just hugged him and kissed him.

> "You wretch! Why don't you allow these songs to be published? If I didn't know that they were your own, I'd swear that I had once heard my mother singing them."

> The power and charm of Warshawsky's songs do indeed lie in what Sholem Aleichem said in his comment: "…as if I had once heard my mother singing them."

Even before Warshawsky's first book was published, many Jews were already singing his songs. They considered them true folksongs, created by their mothers and grandmothers.

We are sure that more than one of our readers will be very surprised when we list a number of well known songs, which they know too, and tell them that all of them were created, not by "the folk" but by M.M. Warshawski. Here's one of those songs:

> *Stronger, better!*
> *Make the circle better!*
> *God has made me great and strong--*
> *revel, children, all night long—*
> *my youngest daughter's married! (Repeat)*

Here's another:

> *The in-laws are marching in, children,*
> *so let's rejoice: sha, sha!*
> *The groom is quite a wonder,*
> *and his family shouts 'Hurrah!'*

and still another, which has been incorporated into our modern *hagode*:

> *Malke, my darling,*
> *may good health be thine.*
> *Fill up the goblet,*
> *the goblet with wine!*

And what about *Akhtsik Er Un Zibetsik Zi* (Eighty He and Seventy She)? and *Kinder, Mir Hobn Simkhes Toyre* (Children, It's Simkhes Toyre*); Groyser Got, Mir Zingen Lider* (Great God, We're Singing Songs); and *Di Yontevdike Teg* (The Days of Holiday)?

All of those songs, and many, many others were created by none other than M.M. Warshawsky. Like other folk-poets before him, and also after him, he created both the words and the music. He used to sing the songs at house parties and meetings with friends, and they soon spread to cities and villages where Jews lived. As happens with popular songs, people often changed the text, eliminating words that were not easy to say and exchanging them for other words, and most important—they quickly forgot that they had been written by a writer named Mark Markovich Warshawsky.

When Sholem Aleichem met Warshawsky and they discussed things, it became apparent that not only couldn't Warshawsky write musical notation but it even

came hard to him to write Yiddish words on paper. So Sholem Aleichem asked
him to dictate the words to him and he wrote them down. After that, he looked
for a musician, who wrote down the melodies. Sholem Aleichem also went with
Warshawsky to various Jewish gatherings, at which he would recite his humorous stories and Warshawsky would sing.

Sholem Aleichem recounts:

> Not a single evening event or Zionist gathering took place that they didn't
> drag us to...I had to recite something and Warshawsky had to sing some-
> thing, though neither my recitations nor Warshawsky's songs had anything
> to do with Zionism. But it became so much the custom that we couldn't do
> anything about it! After they had talked and debated themselves out, they
> would set up a table, move in all the chairs, seat Sholem Aleichem at the
> head of the table, and the scene would turn into Kasrilevke[38]. But the real
> festivities would first begin when Warshawsky sat down at the piano."

Right now, as we are printing these biographical notes about Warshawsky, it is
over 100 years since the first edition of his collected songs was published. Since
then, other editions have been published, and there's not a single book of popular
Yiddish songs in which the songs of M. M. Warshawsky do not appear.

---

38. A fictional small town that Sholem Aleichem depicted in many of his tales

The Hebrew Alphabet (*Oyfn Pripetshik*)

On the cozy hearth, there's a lovely fire--
crackling flames we see,
and the *rebbe*'s teaching children lovingly
the Hebrew ABC.

Listen children dear, and remember please,
what you learn today.
Say the alphabet and say it once again--
start with letter "a."

Study children dear—put your heart in it;
listen carefully.
He who's first to learn the Hebrew alphabet
gets a flag from me.

And my children dear, have no fear of it;
though it's hard to start.
He who knows the Torah, reads it easily,
will have a happy heart.

Dearest children mine, you'll grow up some day,
and then you'll surely know
all the sadness in the holy alphabet,
all the tears and woe.

When you get to feel, as a grown-up Jew,
exile's crushing weight,
reading from the ancient holy alphabet
will help you bear your fate.

On the cozy hearth, there's a lovely fire--
crackling flames we see,
and the *rebbe*'s teaching children lovingly
the Hebrew ABC.

דער אַלף־בית

אויפֿן פּריפּעטשיק ברענט אַ פֿײַערל
און אין שטוב איז הייס,
און דער רבי לערנט קלײנע קינדערלעך
דעם אַלף־בית.

זעט זשע, קינדערלעך, געדענקט זשע, טײַערע,
וואָס איר לערנט דאָ;
זאָגט זשע נאָך אַ מאָל, און טאַקע נאָך אַ מאָל:
קמץ־אַלף — אָ !

לערנט, קינדער, מיט גרויס חשק,
אַזוי זאָג איך אײַך אָן;
ווער ס'וועט גיכער פֿון אײַך קענען עבֿרי,
דער באַקומט אַ פֿאָן.

לערנט, קינדער, האָט ניט מורא,
יעדער אָנהייב איז שווער;
גליקלעך דער וואָס האָט געלערנט תּורה,
צי דאַרף דער מענטש נאָך מער?

איר וועט, קינדער, עלטער ווערן,
וועט איר אַליין פֿאַרשטיין,
וויפֿל אין די אותיות ליגן טרערן
און ווי פֿיל געוויין...

אַז איר וועט, קינדער, דעם גלות שלעפֿן,
אויסגעמוטשעט זײַן,
זאָלט איר פֿון די אותיות כּוח שעפֿן,
קוקט אין זיי אַרײַן!

אויפֿן פּריפּעטשיק ברענט אַ פֿײַערל
און אין שטוב איז הייס,
און דער רבי לערנט קלײנע קינדערלעך
דעם אַלף־בית...

The Circle (The Bride's Family)

Musician, strike the cymbals—
who can compare to me?
Oh, oh, God is great,
He gives blessings to my house:
my youngest girl is marrying today—
my youngest daughter's married,
my youngest daughter's married.

Faster, louder,
you're my queen and I'm the king.
Oh, oh, I have seen
with my very own eyes
that God has blessed my house:
my youngest daughter's married.

Faster, louder,
the circle, make it wider.
God has blessed my family
and brought me happiness.
Frolic, children, all night long—
my youngest daughter's married.

Faithful uncle Yossi
and dear old auntie Sossi—
to celebrate this marriage rite
they've sent me countless flasks of wine
from the holy land of Palestine—
my youngest daughter's married.

Motl! Shimen!
The poor folk have come.
Set the finest table for them:
expensive wines and delicious fish.
Oh, oh, daughter, give me a kiss—
my youngest daughter's married.

Ayzik, you rascal—
watch grandma do the *kazik!*[39]

---

39. Name of a dance

די ראָד (פלהס צד)

שלאָגט, כלי־זמר, אין די טאַצן,
ווער וועט אַצינד מיך שאַצן?
אוי, אוי! גאָט איז גרוים!
ער האָט דאָך געבענטשט מײַן הויז...
די מיזינקע גיב איך אויס —
די מיזינקע אויסגעגעבן!
די מיזינקע אויסגעגעבן!

שטאַרקער!... פֿרײלעך!
דו, די מלכּה, איך, דער מלך,
אוי, אוי, איך אַליין
האָב מיט מײַנע אויגן געזען,
ווי גאָט האָט מיר מצליח געווען —
די מיזינקע אויסגעגעבן!

שטאַרקער!... בעסער!...
די ראָד, די ראָד מאַכט גרעסער!
גרוים האָט מיך גאָט געמאַכט,
גליק האָט ער מיר געבראַכט,
הוליעט, קינדער, אַ גאַנצע נאַכט! —
די מיזינקע אויסגעגעבן!

דער טרײַער פֿעטער יאָסי
און די גוטע מומע סאָסי
האָבן מיר צום חתן־מאָל
טײַערע ווײַנען אַן אַ צאָל
מיר געשיקט פֿון ארץ־ישׂראל —
די מיזינקע אויסגעגעבן!

מאָטל!... שמעון!...
די אָרעמע־לײַט זענען געקומען,
שטעלט זיי דעם שענסטן טיש,
טײַערע ווײַנען, טײַערע פֿיש,
אוי־זווי, טאַכטער, גיב מיר אַ קיש! —
די מיזינקע אויסגעגעבן!

אײַזיק!... מזיק!...
די באָבע גייט אַ קאָזיק.

Look, just look (no Evil Eye),
she stamps her feet and strides around.
What joy, what happiness:
my youngest daughter's married.

Itsik, you witty one!
Why so quiet with your violin bow?
Yell at the musicians:
Are they playing or sleeping?
Pluck the strings with might and main—
My youngest daughter's married!

The Goblet (*Tayere Malke*)

Malke, my darling,
may good health be thine!
Fill up the goblet,
the goblet with wine.

This beautiful goblet,
just look at it shine.
My *zeyde* drank from it
and now it is mine.

Both bad years and good years
have come to our life.
We've kept our old goblet
through storm and through strife.

The children all loved it,
as you've heard them say,
but I have been chosen
to keep it today.

Malke my darling,
may good health be thine.
To whom shall I drink
from this goblet of wine?

קיין עין־הרע זעט נאָר, זעט,
ווי זי טופּעט און ווי זי גייט,
אוי, אַ שׂימחה, אוי, אַ פֿרייד ! —
די מיזינקע אויסגעגעבן !

איציק !... שפּיציק !...
וואָס שוויַיגסטו מיט דעם שמיציק ? !
אַיִף די כּלי־זמר טו אַ געשריַי :
צי שפּילן זיי, צי שלאָפֿן זיי,
ריַיסט די סטרונעס אַלע אויף צוויי ! —
די מיזינקע אויסגעגעבן !

דער בעכער

טיַיערע מלכּה —
געזונט זאָלסטו זיַין ! —
גיס אָן אין בעכער,
אין בעכער דעם וויַין.
בים־באָם ! בים־באָם !
בים־באָם ! בים־באָם !

פֿון דעם דאָזיקן בעכער,
ער גלאַנצט אַזוי שיין,
האָט געטרונקען מיַין זיידע,
מיַין זיידע אַליין.

ס'איז געווען שלעכטע ציַיטן,
ווי עס מאַכט זיך אַ מאָל,
נאָר דעם בעכער האָט ער געהאַלטן —
איַיזן און שטאָל !

ער האָט משׂמח געווען אַלע קינדער,
באַקאַנט איז דאָס דיר,
פֿונעם טאַטן איז דער בעכער
געקומען צו מיר !

טיַיערע מלכּה, —
געזונט זאָלסטו זיַין ! —
פֿאַר וועמען זאָל איך טרינקען
דעם דאָזיקן וויַין ?

I'll drink to the praise of
the Jews' inner fire.
They struggle and struggle,
and never they tire.

I want us to drink
from the goblet this day
to those who have gone now
forever away.

I'll drink to my enemies,
but don't let them know.
Our goblet spurts tears now—
just see how they flow.

Sing louder and stronger:
"Great God, You are One!"
Now hide our old goblet—
our song it is done!

The Miller's Tears

Oh, how many years
have passed
since I've been the miller in this place.
The wheels, they turn around,
the years, they pass along,
and I am gray and full of years.

Were there some good days—
I'm trying to recall—
did I have some happiness—some?
The wheels they turn around,
the years, they pass along,
no answer to my query comes.

לחיים וויל איך טרינקען
פֿאַר דעם פֿינטעלע ייד,
וואָס מוטשעט זיך תמיד
און ווערט קיין מאָל ניט מיד !

לחיים וויל איך טרינקען,
און מאַקע אָן אָן עק,
פֿאַר די וואָס זענען געפֿאָרן
אויף אייביק אַוועק !

איך וואָלט טרינקען פֿאַר מײַנע שׂונאים,
נאָר זאָג זיי ניט אויס !
קוק — טרערן שפּריצן פֿונעם בעכער,
פֿון דעם בעכער אַרויס !

זינגט העכער און העכער :
גאָט, דו ביסט גרויס !
באַהאַלט, מלכּה, דעם בעכער,
דאָס לידל איז אויס !
בים־באַם !   בים־באַם !
בים־באַם !   בים־באַם !

דעם מילנערס טרערן

אוי, וויפֿל יאָרן
זענען פֿאַרפֿאָרן,
זינט כ׳בין אַ מילנער אָט אַ דאָ...
די רעדער דרייען זיך,
די יאָרן גייען זיך —
איך בין שוין אַלט, און גרייז און גראָ ;
די רעדער דרייען זיך,
די יאָרן גייען זיך,
איך בין שוין אַלט, און גרייז און גראָ.

ס׳איז טעג פֿאַראַנען,
כ׳וויל מיך דערמאַנען,
צי כ׳האָב געהאַט אַ שטיקל גליק ?...
די רעדער דרייען זיך,
די יאָרן גייען זיך,
קיין ענטפֿער איז ניטאָ צוריק.

My faithful Mintsi,
my child, my Shprintsi,
Oh, oh, I wail: oh lack-a-day!
The wheels they turn around,
the years, they pass along,
and you have also gone away.

Deprived of happiness,
have I remained:
no wife, no child—I'm all alone.
The wheels, they turn around,
the years, they pass along,
and I'm as lonely as a stone.

I've heard them say
they want to get rid of me—
out of the village and the mill.
The wheels, they turn around,
the years, they pass along,
without an end, without a will.

Where will I live?
Who'll take care of me?
I'm old—and tired, too.
The wheels, they turn around,
the years, they pass along,
and with them
passes the Jew.

מײַן טרײַע מינצי,
מײַן קינד, מײַן שפּרינצי,
אױ־װײ, אַ יאָמער, אױ, אַ שרעק!
די רעדער דרייען זיך,
די יאָרן גייען זיך,
מיט זיי זענט איר אױך באַלד אַװעק.

פֿון גליק פֿאַרטריבן,
בין איך געבליבן
אָן װײַב, אָן קינד, אָט דאָ אַליין...
די רעדער דרייען זיך,
די יאָרן גייען זיך,
און עלנט בין איך װי אַ שטיין.

איך האָב געהערט זאָגן,
מ'װיל מיך פֿאַריאָגן
אַרױס פֿון דאָרף און פֿון דער מיל...
די רעדער דרייען זיך,
די יאָרן גייען זיך,
אױ, אַן עק און אַן אַ ציל...

װוּ װעל איך װײנען?
װער װעט מיך שױנען? —
איך בין שױן אַלט, איך בין שױן מיד...
די רעדער דרייען זיך,
די יאָרן גייען זיך,
און אױך מיט זיי גייט אױס דער ייד...

YEHOYASH

(pseudonym of Yehoyash-Solomon Blumgartn;
born on September 16, 1872 in Verzhbolove (Virbaln), in the Suvalk district;
died on January 10, 1927, in New York)

In the year 1888, a 16-year-old boy who had just come to Warsaw from his little town, Verzhbolove, knocked on I. L. Peretz's door. Like many other young men of the time, he had come to Peretz bringing all his possessions--a packet of poems in Hebrew and Yiddish. The young man recited and his heart was pounding: would the door he had just opened lead him into the temple of Yiddish literature or would it close for him? From time to time, he furtively raised his eyes to glance at Peretz, and he noticed that the poet, the later "Father of Modern Yiddish Literature," was listening intently. The young man became hopeful and recited another poem.

When he finished reciting, Peretz embraced him and said that he found the poems charming and that he saw in him a great talent. The young man beamed. The dreams of his hopes were opening for him: he would be a Yiddish poet.

That was the beginning of the creative path of Yehoyash-Solomon Blumgartn, who became famous in the Yiddish world under the Biblical name of Yehoyash.

When Yehoyash arrived in New York in 1890, the proletarian poets Winchevsky, Edelshtat, Rosenfeld, and Bovshover were already famous. There were also many other poets who sang about the loneliness of the Jewish immigrant, about the sweatshop, and about the struggle for a better and more beautiful world. Yehoyash was one of the few Yiddish poets who did not write any songs of battle, and maybe for that reason he was less well known to the broad masses of readers. In his poems, he revealed universal motifs, a love of nature, insights into Jewish history, and a quest to achieve poetic perfection.

Peretz Hirshbeyn says in his memoirs that people looked at Yehoyash at first as some sort of exotic flower, wondered: "Who is he?", and sniffed around him, touched him with their fingers, and understood him poorly. "We smelled the odor of dried flowers."

It was not long before recognition came. His poems were printed prominently in most of the newspapers and literary magazines throughout the world. They were translated into English, Polish, Russian, German, and French, and especially into Hebrew. They were included in Hebrew and Yiddish readers and anthologies. Jacob Fichman, who in 1911 put together an anthology of Yiddish poetry, *Di Yidishe Muze* (The Yiddish Muse), wrote this about Yehoyash: "Yehoyash, in his Yiddish poetry, introduced many universal motifs, ideas, and images…in his best poems, there is a reflection of the *zeitgeist*, the deepest experience of the Jewish intelligentsia and its tragic contradictions."

A few years earlier, in the Warsaw magazine *Hazomir* (Song), I.L. Peretz had published a review of the first volume of Yehoyash's poems, which was published in New York in 1907. Peretz had said enthusiastically:

"Yehoyash is the beginning of the new Yiddish poetry. He has come from the people, so he has seen and felt more. At a time when Mendele was depicting the community, Dinezon was describing the household, Spector was photographing the town and the village, and Sholem Aleichem was painting the portrait of the Jew who was starting to wander, Yehoyash saw what was crushed into crumbs among the entire people and put the crumbled, scattered pieces together so that it might become a force."

As early as 1907, Yehoyash set about realizing his dream of translating the Bible into Yiddish, but he did not stop writing his own poems, fables, children's poems, legends, travel impressions, and reportage.

The younger poets who entered Yiddish literature before and after the first World War and often criticized the older writers looked up to Yehoyash, however. The group "*In Zikh*," comprising Nokhem Borekh Minkoff, Aaron Glants-Leyeles, and Jacob Glatstein, among others, wrote in its manifesto, in 1919, that Yehoyash "…is the most important figure in all of Yiddish poetry today, a poet who never stops searching, who has the ability—we don't know what will be in the future—who is at the very zenith of his creative ability to feel and write in new forms and new ways. We consider him one of our closest."

Composers wrote music to many of his poems, and the songs were sung on concert stages, in the Yiddish schools, and by Yiddish choruses. Leo Low wrote a cantata to his song *Rosh Hashone Leyelones* (The New Year of the Trees).

Others of Yehoyash's songs that are sung include: *Der Zingamaring Iz Gegangen In Vald* (The Zingamaring Went Into the Forest), with music by M. Posner; *Nisht Geshlofn Nor Gevakht* (Not Asleep but Awake), with music by N. Zaslavski; *Di Bin* (The Bee), *Fun Dem Kleynem Kemerl, Zingendik a Zemerl* (From The

Little Chamber, Singing a Little Song), with music by Israel Glatstein; *Gefaln Iz a Shotn Af Mayn Shvel* (A Shadow Fell Across My Doorstep), with music by Lazar Weiner; *Kumt A Foygl Tsu Mayn Shoyb* (A Bird Comes to My Window Pane), with music by S. Golub; *A Folks-Motiv* (A Folk-Motif [Mother Dear, Mother Darling, My Necklace Please Untie]), with music by Mikhl Gelbart; *Ovnt-Klangen* (Evening Sounds); *Der Fidler* (The Fiddler), with music by Samuel Bugatch; and *O Kinderlekh Libe* (O Dear Children), with music by Vladimir Heifetz; and many others.

His poem *Paganini* was one of the most beloved recitations by various actors and amateurs in America before and after the first World War. Yehoyash said it was a theme from Heinrich Heine's *Florentinische Nachte* (Florentine Nights), written in prose. The poem was so popular that a parody appeared in *Der Kundes* (The Mischievous One) in 1909, written by Charles Zunser, a son of Eliakum Zunser, who signed it with the name *The Kaleputsker Melamed* (The Teacher From Kaleputsk).

For the last ten years of his life, Yehoyash was principally occupied with his translation of the Bible. We will not attempt in this short biographical note to give a complete evaluation of the cultural-historical importance of that translation. We are satisfied just to quote two famous authorities: the literary critic Samuel Niger and the poet, critic, and master of the language Jacob Glatstein. Niger wrote: "The spirit of prophecy rests on Yehoyash's translation of the Bible…this is the greatest creation in Yiddish, the principal classical model of the language for the generations to come." Glatstein wrote: "It's precisely in our generation that we are first able to evaluate what Yehoyash accomplished with his Bible interpretation. Yehoyash created the greatest protection against the death of our Yiddish language: he rescued thousands of Yiddish words from oblivion and gave them eternal life in the shadow of the Bible."

A *Yom Kippur* Tale

I've finished my *yom kippur* prayer,
intensely and with many tears.
They're ready for *kol nidre* now,
repenting for their years.

But empty is the East-wall place
of Nissan, our beloved rabbi.
The *gabay*[40] sends the *shames*[41] quick
to find the reason why.

The minutes, hours, drag along
like creeping, slimy snakes.
An awful fear besets the *shul*
and every heart now quakes.

The cantor wears his long white coat
and riffles through the prayer-book.
The waxen candles spray their light—
the night takes on a gloomy look.

And now the *shames* has come back.
"What's going on there, quickly tell!"
The *shames* gasps and tells his tale:
"I heard outside, from basement cell,
a sweet *kol nidre* tune.
A person there, a child he rocked:
'Oh sleep now, sleep now soon'"

I went downstairs to take a look
and almost died of fright.
Reb Nissan stood and rocked the child—
he crooned with sweet delight.

---

40. The lay director of the synagogue
41. The rabbi's assistant

אַ יום־כּיפּור־מעשהלע

שוין תּפֿילה זכּה אָפּגעזאָגט
מיט טרערן און כּוונות...
דער עולם צו כּל־נדרי שוין
מאַכט זיפֿצנדיק הכנות...

דאָך לײדיק איז די מיזרח־שטאָט
פֿ|ן אַלטן רבֿ ר' ניסן;
דער גבאי שיקט דעם שמשׂ שנעל
די סיבה זיך דערווײסן...

מינוטן, שעהען ציִען זיך
ווי קריכעדיקע שלאַנגען,
אַ וויסטע. אָנגסט באַפֿאַלט די שול
און דריקט דאָס האַרץ מיט צוואַנגען...

דער חזן שטײט אין קיטל בלאַס
און מישט די מחזור־בלעטער...
די וואַקסליכט שפּריצן אין דער שטיל,
די נאַכט ווערט שפּעט און שפּעטער...

נו, אָט איז שוין דער שמשׂ דאָ:
„זאָגט, וואָס פֿאַסירט האָט, שנעלער?"
דער שמשׂ סאָפּעט און דערצײלט:
„אין שולגאַס פֿון אַ קעלער,

דערהער איך פּלוצלינג אַ געזאַנג,
אַ זיס כּל־נדרי־ניגון,
ווי אימעצער וואָלט דאַוונענדיק,
אָן עופֿעלע פֿאַרוויגן...

„איך גײ אַראָפּ און טו אַ קוק,
איך בין פֿון שרעק פֿאַרגאַנגען...
ר' ניסן שטײט און וויגט אַ קינד
מיט הײליקע געזאַנגען..."

The mother'd gone away to *shul*
to pour out all her heart.
The baby cried, poor thing, all night--
it tore one's heart apart.

And now, guess what? The famous man,
the ancient one with scholar's charms,
had heard the voice and took the child
with love into his arms.

He'd wrapped the little baby up
in his *talis* white and blue,
and sang him sweet *kol nidre* tunes
while crooning lyu-lyu-lyu.

Folk Motif

O mother darling, mother dear,
my necklace please untie.
The Emp'ror soon will travel here—
God forbid I catch his eye!

O daughter mine, my dearest one,
don't let your heart oppress.
I don't want the Emp'ror to fancy you—
you'll wear no beads or dress.

O mother darling, mother dear,
please comb my hair an unkempt way,
or else the Emp'ror soon will send
his men to take me his way.

O daughter mine, my dearest one,
his men won't take you anywhere.
I don't want the Emp'ror to fancy you—
just tie a braid in your long hair.

O mother darling, mother dear,
please smudge my girlish face.

„די מאמע איז אַוועק אין שול
איר האַרץ דאָרט אויסצוגיסן,
און ס'קינד האָט, נעבעך, שרײַענדיק
די גאַל זיך אײַנגעריסן...

„נו, קלערט איר וואָס? דער גרױסער רב,
דער גרײַז, דער עוקר הרים,
דערהערט דאָס קול און נעמט דאָס קינד
מיט ליבשאַפֿט אויף זײַן אָרעם...

„ער האָט דאָס קליינע נפֿשל
אין טלית אײַנגעטוליעט,
און זינגענדיק כּל-נדרי אים
געניאַנטשעט און געליולעט...”

פֿאָלקסמאָטיוו

— מאַמעניו מײַנע, מאַמעניו-האַרץ,
בינד אָפּ פֿון מײַן האַלדז די קאָרעלן,
דער קייסער וועט קומען צו פֿאָרן אַהער.
און כ'וועל אים חלילה געפֿעלן...

— טאָכטערל מײַן, טאָכטערל גאָלד,
דײַן הערצעלע זאָל זיך ניט פֿלאָגן,
איך וויל ניט דער קייסער זאָל האָבן דיך האָלט,
און דו וועסט קיין צירונג ניט טראָגן...

— מאַמעניו מײַנע, מאַמעניו-האַרץ,
מײַן צאָפּ טו מיר מיאוס פֿאַרקעמען,
דער קייסער וועט קומען צו פֿאָרן אַהער,
און שיקן שטאַפֿעטן מיך נעמען...

— טאָכטערל מײַן, טאָכטערל גאָלד,
ער וועט קיין שטאַפֿעטן ניט שיקן,
איך וויל ניט דער קייסער זאָל האָבן דיך האָלט,
און קניפּ דיר אַ קאָלטן אַ דיקן...

— מאַמעניו מײַנע, מאַמעניו-האַרץ,
מײַן ווײַסע געזיכט טו פֿאַרשמירן,

The Emp'ror soon will travel here
to take me to his kingly place.

O daughter mine, my dearest one,
you must not be so rash.
I don't want the Emp'ror to fancy you—
I'll black your face with ash.

O mother darling, mother dear,
my eyes now fill with tears.
The Emp'ror soon will travel here—
my sleep is haunted by my fears.

O daughter mine, my dearest one,
now fly like arrows from a bow.
I fear that if he sees your eyes
he'll fancy you—so go now, go!

Paganini

About the great Paganini
there used to be a legend:
that hidden in his violin
lay the lovely soul

of the wondrously beautiful girl
he loved with all the flame
of his poet's soul.
And, stimulated by that great love,

the young violinist,
the wizard of the strings,
used to draw sighs from the heart
and tears from the eyes.

People used to hear the weeping,
like the pleading of a girl.
The image of her sad face
used to float into the air.

דער קייסער וועט קומען צו פֿארן אהער,
און וועט אין זײַן פֿאלאַץ מיך פֿירן...

— טאַכטערל מײַן, טאַכטערל גאָלד,
האָב נאָר ניט קיין מורא אין האַרצן,
איך וויל ניט דער קייסער זאָל האָבן דיך האַלט,
און וועל דיך מיט סאָזשע פֿאַרשוואַרצן...

— מאַמעניו מײַנע, מאַמעניו-האַרץ,
כ'טו ביטערע טרערן פֿאַרגיסן,
דער קייסער וועט קומען צו פֿארן אהער,
ווי קען איך די אויגן פֿאַרשליסן?...

— טאַכטערל מײַן, טאַכטערל גאָלד,
אַנטלויף ווי אַ פֿײַל פֿונעם בויגן,
כ'האָב מורא דער קייסער וועט קריגן דיך האַלט,
ווען ער וועט נאָר זען זען דײַנע אויגן...

פּאַגאַניני

אויף דעם גרויסן פּאַגאַניני,
פֿלעגט אַרומגיין אַ לעגענדע,
אַז באַהאַלטן אין זײַן פֿידל
איז געלעגן די נשמה

פֿון דעם וווּנדערשיינעם מיידל,
וואָס געליבט מיט אַלע פֿלאַמען,
פֿון זײַן דיכטער-זעלע האָט ער —
און דערשטאָכן פֿון גרויס ליבע...

פֿלעגט דער יונגער פֿידל-שפּילער,
דער מכשף פֿון די סטרונעס,
שלעפֿן זיפֿצן פֿון די הערצער,
צִיען טרערן פֿון די אויגן —

פֿלעגט זיך הערן, ווי דאָס וויינען,
ווי דאָס בעטן פֿונעם מיידל,
פֿלעגט זיך טראָגן אין דער לופֿטן,
איר באַטריבטער בלייכער פּנים...

The fiddle speaks, the fiddle pleads,
and the beautiful girl complains—
tries to still the jealousy
of the agitated artist.

Her sounds get faster,
race quickly and angrily—
noisily and stormily
comes Paganini's answer.

Faster, louder, angrier, wilder,
till the fiddle breaks apart
with a red stream of blood
gurgling from the dying girl.

With a knife in her heart,
his beloved lies on the ground—
looks with sightless eyes
at the murderer Paganini.

Suddenly—listen! The bass notes
groan heavily and full of doubt.
In a sea of depression,
a soul sinks and drowns.

On his knees is Paganini,
squeezing the hand of the dead girl.
He looks with wild, desolate gaze
at the bloody stiletto.

It's too late now—his regret
overflows into a prayer,
into a hot, quiet confession.
And the angels sing.

Gentler, softer, paler, weaker,
grows the sobbing of the strings.
A choked groan, a wail,
and then it fades out to a murmur.

ס'רעדט די פֿידל, ס'בעט די פֿידל,
און דאָס שיינע מיידל טענהט,
זוכט די אײפֿערזוכט צו שטילן,
פֿון דעם אױפֿגעקאָכטן קינסטלער —

שנעלער װערן באַלד די קלאַנגען,
יאָגן האַסטיק מיט רציחה,
און עס פֿילדערט און עס שטורעמט,
פּאַגאַנינים בײזער ענטפֿער...

שנעלער, העכער, בײזער, װילדער...
ביז די פֿידל פּלאַצט פֿונאַנדער,
אין אַ בליטיקשטראַם אַ רױטן,
און דאָס כאָרכלען פֿון אַ גוסס.

מיט אַ מעסער אינעם האַרצן,
אױף דער ערד ליגט די געליבטע,
קוקט מיט שטאַר פֿאַרגלאָזטע אױגן,
אױף איר מערדער פּאַגאַניני...

פּלוצלינג האַרכט... די טיפֿע טענער,
קרעכצן שװער און שװואַרץ־פֿאַרצװײפֿלט,
אין אַ ים פֿון מרה־שחורה,
זינקט און טרינקט זיך אַ נשמה...

אױף די קני שטײט פּאַגאַניני,
דריקט די הענט דעם טױטן מײדל,
קוקט מיט װילדע װיסטע בליקן,
אױף דעם בלוטיקן סטילעטטאָ...

ס'איז צו שפּעט שױן... זײַן חרטה
גיסט זיך איבער אין אַ תּפֿילה,
אין אַ הײסן שטילן װידוי —
און עס װיינען די מלאָכים.

מילדער, װייכער, מאַטער, שװאַכער,
װערט דאָס כליפּען פֿון די סטרונעס,
אַ פֿאַרשטיקטער קרעכץ... אַ יאָמער...
דאַן פֿאַרגײט עס אין אַ מורמל...

Slowly the sounds sigh away—
The fiddle is barely breathing now.
Suddenly—has a flock of birds
started singing in the summer forest?

From the fiddle there comes
a sound like girlish laughter.
Paganini kisses and caresses
the arms of his beloved…

He kisses her black eyes,
plays with her black hair,
whispers into her ear
the secrets of his great love…

From the blue summer sky,
the tiny stars observe,
and around the green tree
they tremble with pleasure.

                              *   *   *

The artist's fiddle used to cry
and used to laugh—
always weaving into tears
the incarnation of the girl.

Using magic, they say,
he imprisoned her soul in his fiddle
after he had murdered
his very own beloved.

לאַנגזאַם זיפֿצן אויס די קלאַנגען,
קוים וואָס ס'אַטעמט נאָך די פֿידל...
פּלוצלינג... האָט אַ מחנה פֿייגלעך
זיך אין זומערוואַלד צעזונגען ?...

פֿון דער פֿידל רײַסט אַרוים זיך,
ווי אַ מיידלשער געלעכטער ;
פֿאַגאַניני קושט און צערטלט
אין די אָרעמס זײַן געליבטען...

קושט די שוואַרצע אויגן אירע,
שטיפֿט און שפּילט מיט אירע לאָקן ;
רוימט איר אײַן אין אויער סודות,
פֿון זײַן גרױסער הייסער ליבע...

פֿונעם בלאָען זומער־הימל,
קוקן צו די קליינע שטערן,
און אַרום די גרינע ביימער
שאָקלען, טרייסלען זיך פֿון תענוג...

*

פֿלעגט דעם קינסטלערס פֿידל ווײנען,
פֿלעגט זי לאַכן — שטענדיק האָט זיך
דורכגעוועבט דורך אַלע טרעלן,
יענער גילגול פֿונעם מיידל...

מיט אַ כּישוף — זאָגט מען — האָט ער
אײַנגעשפּאַרט בײַ זיך אין פֿידל
איר נשמה, ווען דערמאָרדעט
האָט ער די געליבטע זײַנע...

CHAIM NACHMAN BIALIK

(born January 9, 1873 in Radi, Volhynia, Ukraine; died July 4, 1934 in Vienna.)

In a poem written in Yiddish in 1911, the then already most recognized Hebrew-Yiddish poet meditates about what his death will look like. The poet imagines all possible deaths—from his soul departing

> *like a butterfly,*
> *dancing and trembling*
> *around a tallow candle*

to its sudden disappearance

> *into a black abyss,*
> *as if it would always be surrounded*
> *by darkness, death, and silence.*

More than any frightful and debasing death, however, the poet fears that he is destined

> *to die while still alive,*
> *in a paper shroud*
> *in a book-closet,*

> *and while still alive,*
> *I'll stand on my grave*
> *and recite the orphan's* kaddish,
> *I—for myself.*

No other Jewish poet has made so deep an impression on the people with his poetry as did Bialik with his poem *B'Ir Haharige* (In The City of Slaughter), about the terrible pogrom in Kishinev in 1903, which he wrote in both Hebrew and Yiddish. The entire Jewish people sat *shiva* for the murdered innocents: old men and children, men and women. But instead of a comforting word to assuage the pain and woe of the unhappy survivors, one heard the poet's voice of sorrow and rage. Instead of weeping tones echoing in the air of the Jewish world with Simon Frug's plea

Brothers, sisters, have pity!
Great and terrible is the need—
Give to the dead for shrouds
and give to the living for bread!

Bialik threw his words of rage into the faces of the victims, for "hiding a few dozen of themselves in some hole and praising God's name amid the garbage."

"Instead of consoling us," writes Samuel Niger in his introductory essay to the volume *Lider un Poemen* (Songs and Poems), "the poet 'forged a heart of iron and steel' and lectured us about ourselves, that we 'fled like mice, hid like bed-bugs, and died like dogs'....waited for someone to come and console us---so he came with curses."

The people, however, felt the poet's love behind the words of sorrow and rage, and they responded to him with love and honored him. Under the influence of Bialik's *In The City of Slaughter*, self-defense groups arose in many cities, and with weapons in their hands they opposed the pogromists.

The critic I. Rappaport, among others, says about this in his essay about Bialik (in the book *Zoymen In Vint* (Seeds in the Wind), Buenos Aires, 1961) that "when the storm of pogroms was nearing Odessa, it was decided to publish Bialik's shattering opus in a Russian translation (for the Russified Jewish youth) in order to help mobilize the youth and prepare them mentally for physical resistance. The writer Bal Makhshoves wrote this about the poem: "One can say that Bialik is the only one in the history of Yiddish literature who in one night and with one poem achieved such tremendous and well earned popularity among all classes of the Jewish people."

Also his poem *Dos Letste Vort* (The Last Word), which was written (in Yiddish) with prophetic fervor, made the same shattering impression. Young men and women knew by heart and recited the great poem, in which the poet sang:

I go, I come—I will heal wounds.
Together with you I will bleed.
Where necessary, I will bind the wounds,
and where necessary, I will lick the blood
that drips from your wounds.
I will console, plead, weep, waken---
and I will not let you go down!

I go, I come—I bring consolation;
I bring news of vengeance.
I am blessed by God with spirit—
I will gift you with my soul.

And when the poet sees that he:

is met by mockery and shame,
that you have closed the door to him,
that God's hand has been rejected
and God's word is mocked

there come once again the poet-prophet's words of rage, saying that he has no
words of consolation for the people:

I have a word, a terrible word
that will lift you from your spot,
that will turn light into darkness for you
and will poison your heart.

*   *   *   *

And God says to me: "Now go down
to the pot maker's house and buy a pot,
and throw it down while saying,
at the top of your lungs so everyone will hear:
'Just so will you be broken!'"

The Last Word and *In the City of Slaughter* awakened national feeling and national pride in the Jewish youth, and for that reason Bialik was crowned the
national poet of the Jewish people.

Most of his other poems, too, were saturated with national feelings and responsi-
bilities. Immigrants who came to Israel from Soviet Russia related that Bialik's
poem *B'Sade [In Feld]* (In the Field) was circulated surreptitiously, in Russian
translation, among the Jewish youth, who identify with the national aspirations
of the Jewish people. It's as if Bialik had written the powerful lines for them:

No, not like a bird that flies out of the cage with song,
and not like a lion who rips himself from behind bars into the world—

but like a dog, beaten, exhausted, and tortured for a very long time,
I have fled to the rustling field, ashamed and abased.

* * *

I stand before the field, the rich, rustling, joyous broad field,
and only now feel my poverty, which drills these thoughts into my head:
it was not I that plowed this field, not I that sowed it with seed—
not I, not I that will gather the loaded sheaves of grain.

It's not I that prayed to God for a warm rain for them,
not I that wearily watered the field with the sweat of my brow,
not I that rejoiced at the bountiful growth of the sheaves--
it's not my joyous, ringing song that will sound for them at harvest-time.

And yet you are dear to me, fields; from them I remember my brothers
working there far away in my own dear abandoned land.
Perhaps their voices will sound at the same moment in answer
to the distant and lonely brother who lives in exile, in shame!

These deeply personal poems, too, are saturated with national responsibility. Perhaps that is best expressed in his *Hamasmid* (The Diligent Student). There he mourns the yeshiva student whose youth passes in love and beauty and who cries out: "Lord of the Universe, on what is Your mighty power wasted?"

The poet, however, knows the great national significance of the yeshiva, from which there came

down to us.....geniuses from attics
and candles from dark corners.

Bialik knows that the personal sacrifice that the Talmudic student makes is not in vain. It has helped the people forge the "eternal spirit" of national survival:

Here is born, through fire and radiance,
the soul of the people and its eternal life.

* * *

What is different, then, in the flames and voices
that carry the heart so boldly to Heaven?
Who placed magic in those pages—
with what power are they imbued
to ignite flames in the darkened eyes,
to strike sparks in dejected hearts?

Bialik also wrote magnificent poems in which he told about his unhappy childhood, about the poverty in which he lived, about his father the shopkeeper, who
"while he was pouring a glass of whiskey for a peasant was looking into an open
volume of *Mishna*," and about his delicate mother, upon whom fell the entire
burden of making a living when he became an orphan at the age of seven.

Bialik's folksy poems have a special place in his poetry. Just like Peretz, Bialik
became deeply interested in Jewish folk creations, folksongs, and stories and
legends, because he understood their historical cultural value. His folksy poems
in Hebrew and Yiddish had all the charm of naïve folk poetry, but also all the
virtues of good artistic poetry. Among his poems written in Yiddish one finds
Oyf Dem Hoykhn Barg (On The Tall Mountain), *Unter Di Grininke Beymelekh*
(Under the Green Little Trees), and *Mayn Gortn* (My Garden); and among
those written in Hebrew are *Tsvishn Pras Un Khidekl* (Between the Pras and the
Khidekl);[42] *In Mayn Gortn* (In My Garden*)*; *S'iz Aroys a Naye Mode (*A New
Fashion Has Appeared); *Nit Bay Tog Un Nit Bay Nakht* (Not By Day and Not
By Night); *Ver S'Hot Perl* (One Has Pearls); *Eyns, Tsvey, Dray, Fir* (One, Two
Three, Four); and many others.

About his poems in Yiddish, Samuel Niger says: "Bialik's Yiddish, like his Hebrew, is not frozen into traditionality but is fresh and lively, rooted in the tradition of the language. And those deep, juicy, lively roots of his Yiddish, and his
Hebrew, are not accidental roots. They draw their nourishment from the entire
spiritual legacy of his people."

In a poem dedicated to Akhad Ha'am, whom Bialik considered his mentor, the
poet says:

And if it comes to pass in our generation that we discover
the Divine Spirit in one of our people, with brightly radiant soul—
then She has not allowed Herself to be so revealed in anyone
as She has revealed Herself in you, through your great soul.

---

42. Two rivers mentioned in the Bible

Those were words that were surely in large measure true as well of himself, the
great Hebrew-Yiddish poet.

Under The Green Little Trees

Under the green little trees
play little Moyshes and Shloymes,
with *tsitsis, kapotes,* and *peyes*—
little Jews fresh from the egg.
Little bodies—straw, smoke, and little feathers--
blow them into little limbs.
They catch light winds
and birds carry them away.

But one thing they have: little eyes.
The eyes have two pupils
that glow and sparkle and dance,
and they think about something prophetic and wonderful,
let their minds wander,
about the days of yesteryear and about birds.
Oh God protect, little Jewish children,
your kosher little eyes!

In The City of Slaughter
(fragment)

Of steel and iron, cold and hard and mute,
forge a heart for yourself, O man, and come!
Come to the city of slaughter so you can see with your own eyes
and touch with your own hands
the poles, fences, building, and walls,
the stones in the streets, the blocks of wood,
the black, dried-out blood and brains
of your brothers' heads and throats.
And wander around amid the ruins,
past broken walls and twisted doors,
past smashed ovens and broken chimneys,
bare black stones and half-burned bricks
where fire, axes, and iron bars
yesterday played a wild tune at the bloody wedding.
And creep through attics under punctured roofs
and look through all the dark holes—

אונטער די גרינינקע ביימעלעך

אונטער די גרינינקע ביימעלעך
שפילן זיך משהלעך, שלמהלעך,
ציצות, קאַפּאָטקעלעך, פּאהלעך,
ייִדעלעך פֿריש פֿון די אייעלעך.
גופֿעלעך — שטרוי, רויך און פֿעדערלעך.
נעם און צעבלאָז זיי אויף גלידערלעך,
כאַפֿן זיי אויף גרינגע ווינטעלעך
און סע צעטראָגן זיי פֿייגעלעך.

נאָר איין זאַך פֿאַרמאָגן זיי, אייגעלעך,
די אויגן פֿאַרמאָגן צוזוויי פינטעלעך,
וואָס גליִען און פֿינקלען און טוקן זיך,
און עפּעס ווי נבֿיאיש און וווּנדערלעך
פֿאַרטראַכטן זיך טיף און פֿאַרזוקן זיך
א ייף נעכטיקע טעג און אויף פֿייגעלעך —
אוי! מיר זאָל זיַן, ייִדישע קינדערלעך,
פֿאַר אייַערע כּשרע אייגעלעך!

אין שחיטה-שטאָט

(פֿראַגמענט)

...פֿון שטאָל און אייַזן, קאַלט און האַרט און שטום,
שמיד אויס א האַרץ פֿאַר זיך, דו מענטש, — און קום!
קום גיי אין שחיטה-שטאָט, זאָלסט זען מיט דיַנע אויגן,
זאָלסט אָנטאַפּן מיט דיַנע אייגענע הענט,
אויף צוימען, סלופּעס, מויערן און ווענט,
אויף שטיינער פֿון דער גאַס, אויף אַלע העלצער,
דאָס שוואַרץ-פֿאַרטריקנט בלוט מיט די געהירן
פֿון דיַנע ברידערס קעפּ און העלדזער.
און אומבלאָנדזשען זאָלסטו צווישן חורבֿות
דורך וועגן צעבראָכענע מיט אויסגענומטע טירן,
פֿאַרבייַ צעשטירדצטע אויוונס, האַלבע קוימענס,
אַנטבלויזטע שוואַרצע שטיינער, האַלב פֿאַרברענטע ציגל,
ווו פֿיַער, האַק און אייַזן האָבן נעכטן
אויף דער בלוט-חתונה א ווילדן טאַנץ געשפּילט;
און קריך דורך בײדעמער, דורך לעכעריקע דעכער,
און קוק זיך אײַן אין אַלע שוואַרצע לעכער —

they're open, black, mute wounds
that you can't expect will heal in this world.
You'll walk in streets flooded with feathers—
you'll bathe in a river, a desolate river
that comes from people's bloody sweat.
You'll walk on mountains of tattered possessions—
there are entire lives, entire lives,
broken forever like shattered pottery!
You'll walk, you'll run, you'll get lost in ruins:
brass, silver, fur coats, books, silk, and satin—
all tattered and torn into tiny pieces,
and trampled Sabbaths, holidays, and dowries,
prayer shawls, phylacteries, parchment, pieces of Torah pages,
and clear-white wrappings for your soul.
Look, look! They wrap themselves around your legs!
Kiss them out of the garbage
and wipe the dust off your shoes.
You're running away? You're running away to light and air?
Run away, run away—Heaven is laughing at you!
The sun will stab your eyes out with spears.
Acacia plants, bright with fresh greens and whites,
will poison you with their odor of blood and hemorrhage.
Your head will be covered with flowers and feathers,
and little pieces of glass,
glittering in the gutter with a thousand sparkles,
will dance to meet your angry gaze.
For God has given you, with a gentle hand, a pair of twins:
a slaughter and a Spring—
the garden bloomed, the sun shone,
and the slaughterer slaughtered.

דאָס זײַנען אָפֿ׳נע, שוואַרצע, שטומע וואונדן,
וואָס וואַרטן מער אויף קיין רפֿואה אין דער וועלט...
אין גאַסן וועסטו גיין, מיט פֿעדערן פֿאַרפֿלייצטע —
די באַדסט זיך אין אַ טײַך, אַ ווײַסן טײַך,
וואָס האָט זיך אויסגעלאָזט פֿון מענטשנס בלוטיקן שווייס ;
דו טרעטסט אויף גאַנצע בערג צעפֿליקטע האָב-און-גוטס —
דאָס זײַנען גאַנצע לעבנס, גאַנצע לעבנס,
צעבראָכענע אויף אייביק ווי וואַ שאַרבן !
דו גייסט, דו לויפֿסט, דו פֿלאַנטערסט זיך אין חורבן,
מעש, זילבער, פֿוטער, שמות, זײַד און אַטלעם,
צעריסענע, צעפֿליקטע אויף פֿיץ-פֿיצלעך,
מיט פֿים צעטראָטענע שבתים, ימים-טובֿים, נדנם,
טליתים, תפֿילין, פֿאַרמעט, שטיקער תּורה,
יריעות הייליקע, קלאָר-ווײַסע וויקעלעך פֿון דײַן נשמה,
זע, זע, זיי וויקלען זיך אַליין אַרום דײַן פֿום
און קושן דיר די טריט פֿון מיסט אַרויס
און ווישן אָפּ פֿון דײַנע שיך דעם שטויב...
דו לויפֿסט ? צו ליכט און לופֿט און אַנטלויפֿסטו ?
אַנטלויף, אַנטלויף — דער הימל לאַכט פֿון דיר !
די זון וועט דיר מיט שפּיזן אויסשטעכן די אויגן,
אַקאַציען, מיט פֿרישע גרינס און ווײַס באַצווייגן,
וועלן סמען דיך מיטן ריח פֿון בלום בלוט און בליטן,
דײַן קאָפּ מיט בלימעלעך און פֿעדערן באַשיטן,
און שטיקלעך גלאָז פֿון מיטן גאַס מיט טויזנט גלאַנצן
וועלן דיר אַנטקעגן אויף דײַן בייז-וואונדער טאַנצן...
דען גאַט האָט דיר מיט מילדער האַנט געשענקט אַ צווילינג :
אַ שחיטה מיט אַ פֿרילינג ;
דער גאָרטן האָט געבליט, די זון האָט געלויכטן —
און דער שוחט האָט געשאַכטן...

ZALMAN SCHNEUR

(born February 1887 in Shklov; died February 20, 1959 in New York)

Zalman (Zalkind, Zale) Schneur occupies a dominant position in modern Hebrew poetry, where he is often mentioned in the same breath as Chaim Nachman
Bialik and Saul Chernikhovsky, and in Yiddish prose, which he enriched with
such monumental works as *Shklover Yidn* (Jews of Shklov), *Feter Zhame* (Uncle
Zhame), *Noyekh Pandre* (Noah Pandre), *Der Keyser and Der Rebbe* (The Emperor and the Rabbi), *Der Mamzer* (The Bastard), and other powerful stories and
novels.

Among Schneur's most popular creations are his folksy poems *Margaritkelekh*
(Little Daisies) and *Ita*, which are among the first poems he wrote. *Tra-la-lo-lo*
(which became popular under the name *Little Daisies*) was written in 1909, in
Paris. Thanks to the beautiful melody that was set to it, it became popular in all
Jewish communities.

The second poem, *Ita*, which Schneur designated a folk-poem, was also written
in the same year, in Berlin. The two cities, Paris and Berlin, were not the only
ones in which the young and restless poet spent his youthful years. At the age
of thirteen, he left his parents' home in Shklov and went to Odessa, which was
the center of the Russian Jewish intelligentsia. There the young Schneur made
the acquaintance of Bialik, Mendele Moykher Sforim, Ravnitsky, Dubnow, and
other Hebrew and Yiddish writers. Several years later he went to Warsaw, where
he began to work in a Hebrew publishing house. At that time he also published
his first Hebrew and Yiddish poems—the Hebrew ones in a children's magazine,
Oylem Kotn (Small World), and the Yiddish ones in M. Spektor's *Yidishe Folkst-
saytung* (Yiddish People's Newspaper). He didn't stay in his job very long, and
just as he had in Odessa, he starved for several years in Warsaw. I.L. Peretz gave
him a job as his personal secretary, and dictated the first version of *Di Goldene
Keyt* (The Golden Chain) to him. In Warsaw, he became friendly with David Frishman and began working in his Hebrew magazine, *Ha Dor* (The Generation),
in which he published poems and light fiction. From Warsaw, Schneur went to
Vilna, where he began writing and publishing his first lengthy Hebrew work: a
novel, *Mavet* (Death), and a number of poems that made a great impression on
intelligent Hebrew readers. There he also began to write and publish a number
of Yiddish stories and poems. In 1906, he went to Paris to study at the Univer-

sity, but he didn't stay there very long; his energy and temperament carried him through all the larger cities of Europe and North America and back to Warsaw and Odessa, the centers of Yiddish literature. His Hebrew poems were received with tremendous enthusiasm by Bal-Makhshoves and others.

Bal Makhshoves writes this about him:

"We are in the presence of the first Yiddish poet who is youth itself…in Yiddish poetry, Schneur is the first to personify youth so strongly. His poetic imagination is like a mighty waterfall that flows before your eyes with wild strength. Healthy hot eroticism, as healthy and hot as the feelings of an animal, penetrates the poetic waterfall with glowing fire."

And Bal-Makhshoves continues in the same vein:

"His imaginings of a person's life in this gray world are so strongly saturated with the feelings of kingly power, of the strongest eroticism, and so closely bound to the nerves of a beautiful, powerful, earthy person, that the poet appears to us, willy-nilly, in the kingly image of a Greek god."

Little has been written among us about his Yiddish poems. Zalman Reizin writes in his *Leksikon Fun Der Yidisher Literatur un Proze* (Lexicon of Yiddish Literature and Prose) (Vilna, 1929) that "an overall evaluation of his Yiddish poetry will be possible only when the songs and poems he has published piecemeal in Yiddish over the past 20 years are collected in book form."

Zalman Reizin characterizes Schneur's Yiddish poems in these words: "Just as in his Hebrew ones, Schneur was the poet of healthy youth that has already tasted despair and loneliness." "Schneur's poems," says Reizin, "introduced a fresh, laughingly unworried tone into Yiddish poetry."

In his lengthy poem *Karshn* (Cherries), these poetic characteristics are expressed in the clearest way:

> *Ripe cherries and ripe girls*
> *with eyes much blacker than cherries;*
> *girls climb up after cherries and laugh—*
> *clean, bare feet meander through the grass,*
> *the thin, elastic branches snap,*

the leaves rustle and the shadows lurk—
apparently they help us laugh.

And after Schneur tells about the boy's chasing the girl "who jumps down from
a tree like a young fawn", he paints a picture such as had not been painted in
Yiddish literature before:

You hug her and act nonchalant;
a kiss on her angry little mouth, her neck,
a kiss there between her thick braids—
it's so warm there, so soft,
like under a dove's wing.
Then you let her go. She's tired, she's thirsty.
You look to one side, so modestly and calmly,
and see only a small, glowing ear;
you divert your kisses to juicy cherries.
Oh, sweet and delicious are the cherries,
a world full of cherries.

At the time of the second World War, Schneur was living in New York, and he
wrote a number of powerful poems about the Holocaust. In his dramatic poem
Sar Yisroel (The Prince of Israel), he throws an angry accusation into the faces
of the peoples of the world who had replied to our outcries with silence:

Why are you so silent?
Your ears are acutely awake
to every distant groan
of one of your citizens,
but deaf to the laments
of an entire people!

And when murmuring folk voices are heard in response:

We are still thinking about it.
The time hasn't come yet--
you have to wait!
Don't annoy the world with your complaints.

the poet answers:

Think, think!
Let it only not get too late
for us—and also for you!
World, O Christian world,
they're after you, not us!
You peoples are the end—
we are just a means...
today it's us, and tomorrow—you!
Poland knows that already,
France feels it already,
the North and the West see it already.
World, O world—
you remain silent even now?
Your silence is your sentence!

Tra-La-Lo-Lo

In the woods near the creek there grew
lovely small daisies,
like little suns with white rays,
white ones, tra-la-lo-lo.

Little Khave was walking, quietly, dreamily,
and let down her golden blond braids.
Her neck was bare and she was singing softly
a little song: tra-la-lo-lo.

A slender young man came toward her,
with hair black as pitch.
His eyes were flaming and merry,
and he said to her: "tra-la-lo-lo."

"What are you looking for, little girl? What did you lose?
What are you trying to find in the grass?"
"I'm looking for daisies," said Khavele, blushing,
blushing with tra-la-lo-lo.

"You're still looking? I've already found
the prettiest daisy in the woods,
a daisy with braids and with sapphire eyes,
with eyes that go tra-la-lo-lo."

"No, I already have daisies—I forgot.
I'm looking for...there's a spring not far from here."
"The spring is stopped up—without me you'd remain thirsty
at the little spring, tra-la-lo-lo."

"I really don't want to drink—I'm looking for shade;
the sun is so boiling hot."
"My hair is darker and cooler than the shade
in the woods, tra-la-lo-lo."

"Thirsty, my girl—tired, my love?
May I take your hand?
May I stroke it and kiss it,
or only go tra-la-lo-lo?"

טראַ־לאַ־לאַ־לאַ

אין װעלדל ביים טײַכל דאָרט זײַנען געװאָקסן
מאַרגאַריטקעלעך עלנט און קלײן ; —
װי קלײנינקע זונען מיט װײַסינקע שטראַלן,
מיט װײַסינקע טראַ־לאַ־לאַ־לאַ.

געגאַנגען איז חוהלע שטיל און פֿאַרחלומט,
צעלאָזן די גאָלד־בלאָנדע צעפּ, —
דאָס העלדזל אַנטבלױזט און געמורמלט־געזונגען
אַ לידעלע : טראַ־לאַ־לאַ־לאַ.

דאָ קומט איר אַנטקעגן אַ בחור אַ שלאַנקער,
מיט לאָקן, מיט שװאַרצע װי פּעך ;
ער פֿלאַמט מיט די אױגן און ענטפֿערט איר לוסטיק,
און ענטפֿערט איר : טראַ־לאַ־לאַ־לאַ.

— װאָס זוכסטו דאָ, מײדל ? װאָס האָסטו פֿאַרלױרן,
װאָס װילסטו געפֿינען אין גראָז ?
„איך זוך מאַרגאַריטקעס" — פֿאַררױטלט זיך חוה,
פֿאַררױטלט זיך טראַ־לאַ־לאַ־לאַ.

— דו זוכסט נאָך ? און איך האָב שױן טאַקע געפֿונען
די שענסטע מאַרגאַריטקע אין װאַלד,
אַ מאַרגאַריטקע מיט צעפּ און מיט אױגן סאַפֿירן,
מיט אײנגעלעך טראַ־לאַ־לאַ־לאַ.

— נײן, כ'האָב שױן מאַרגאַריטקעם. איך האָב זיך פֿאַרגעסן —
איך זוך... דאָ ניט װײַט איז אַ קװאַל...
— דער קװאַל איז געשלאָסן, אָן מיר בלײַבסטו דורשטיק
בײַם קװאַלכעלע, טראַ־לאַ־לאַ־לאַ.

— איך װיל גאָר ניט טרינקען. איך זוך מיר אַ שאָטן,
די זון באַקט אַרײַן אַזױ הײס...
— מײַנע האָר זײַנען שװאַרצער און קילער װי שאָטנס
אין װעלדעלע — טראַ־לאַ־לאַ־לאַ.

דורשטיק מײַן מײדעלע, מיד איז מײַן קלײנינקע,
צי מעג מען זי נעמען בײַם האַנט ?
צי מעג מען זי גלעטן, צי מעג מען זי קושן ?
צי מעג מען נאָר ? טראַ־לאַ־לאַ־לאַ.

"Please leave me alone, my mother says we mustn't—
my mother is old and strict."
"Where mother, what mother? Here there are only trees,
just little trees, tra-la-lo-lo."

"They'll see us!" "No one sees us." "They'll hear us!" "No one hears us--
the woods are both blind and deaf.
Hug me, my sweet, you see that I'm calm—
I'm just kissing you, tra-la-lo-lo."

"Do you love me?" "I love you." "Are you embarrassed?" "I am."
"Oh love me and be embarrassed and keep still—
see how my pitch black hair mixes with your golden locks,
tra-la-lo-lo."

*   *   *

The sun has set, the boy's disappeared,
and Khavele still sits in the woods.
She looks into the distance and murmurs dreamily
the little song: tra-la-lo-lo.

Ita
(fragment)

Listen to this story, which happened
in a village in Lithuania.
There was a girl there
whose name was Ita.

Eyes of blue and pale hands,
and braids like black snakes.
Any man who saw her
practically fainted away.

He'd go around like a shadow,
whispering: "Ita, Ita."
Listen to this story, which happened
in a village in Lithuania.

— אַ, לאָז מיך, מען טאָר ניט! די מאַמע זאָגט מ'טאָר ניט,
מײַן מאַמע איז אַלט און איז בײַז.
— װו מאַמע, װאָס מאַמע? דאָ זײַנען נאָר בײמער
נאָר בײמעלעך — טראַ־לאַ־לאַ־לאַ.

— „מען זעט!" — קײנער זעט ניט. „מען הערט"! —
קײנער הערט ניט,
דאָס װעלדל איז בלינד און געדיכט.
אומאַרעם מיך, זיסע. דו זעסט איך בין רױִק,
איך קוש דיך נאָר — טראַ־לאַ־לאַ־לאַ.

— דו ליבסט מיך? — „איך ליב דיך!" — דו שעמסט דיך?
— „איך שעם מיך!"
— אַ, ליב מיך און שעם דיך און שװײַג;
און זע, װי עם מישן זיך פֿעך־שװאַרצע קרױזן
מיט גאָלדענע... טראַ־לאַ־לאַ־לאַ.

*

די זון איז פֿאַרגאַנגען, דער בחור — פֿאַרשװוּנדן
און חוהלע זיצט נאָך אין װאַלד.
זי קוקט אין דער װײַטנס און מורמלט פֿאַרחלומט
דאָס לידעלע: טראַ־לאַ־לאַ־לאַ...

איטע

(פֿראַגמענט)

הערט אַ מעשׂה, װאָס פֿאַרלױפֿט זיך
אין אַ שטעטל, אין דער ליטע!
ס'איז אַ מײדל דאָרט געװיזן
און געהײסן האָט זי איטע.

אױגן — בלױע, הענטלעך — װײַסע,
און די צעפּ — װי שװאַרצע שלאַנגען;
װער עם האָט זײ נאָר דערזען;
דעם איז ס'חיות אױסגעגאַנגען.

דער פֿלעגט אומגײן װי אַ שאָטן
און פֿלעגט שעפּטשען: „איטע, איטע..."
הערט אַ מעשׂה, װאָס פֿאַרלױפֿט זיך
אין אַ שטעטל אין דער ליטע!

* * *

All the boys in the village
were dying for the girl;
They'd dream about her lips
and the rustling of her dress.

All of them were crazy about her—
from the druggist to the tailor,
from the synagogue-goer to the *feldsher*[43];
only sons and teachers.

All of them read and studied
about how to love a pretty girl.
All of them dreamt of Ita's lips
and the rustling of her dress.

* * *

But her father is a *hasid,*
and a girl obeys her father.
He says "No!" and doesn't want to hear
about modernist boys wearing fancy ties.

What he wants is a pious boy--
and who can tell him what to do!
The rabbi's son
has long been sighing and stroking his sideburns.

He sings sadly over the Talmud,
glances at Ita's father:
"Look—I'm a boy who studies Torah,
not some village magistrate in a fancy tie."

* * *

Along comes a student,
all the way from St. Petersburg,

---

43. A half-trained medical person, often previously a military "medic"

*

אַלע בחורים אין שטעטל
פֿלעגן שטאַרבן נאָך דעם מיידל;
פֿלעגן טרוימען אירע ליפן
און דאָס רוישן פֿון איר קליידל.

ס'האָבן זיך אין איר פֿאַרבולבעט
פֿון אָפטיקער ביז דעם שערער,
פֿונעם קלויזניק ביזקל פֿערשל,
בני-יחידימלעך און לערער.

אַלע „לעזן" און שטודירן —
ווי מען ליבט אַ שיינע מיידל;
אַלע טרוימען איטעם ליפן —
און דאָס רוישן פֿון איר קליידל.

*

נאָר איר טאַטע איז אַ חסיד —
און אַ מיידל פֿאַלגט דעם טאַטן —
מאַכט ער „באַס"... און וויל ניט הערן
פֿון משפילים מיט קראַוואַטן.

וויל ער דווקא אַ בן-טובֿים,
און ווער קען אים זאָגן דעות!
אַ, דעם מורה-הוראהס זונדל
זיפֿצט שוין לאַנג און גלעט די פאות...

טרוייעריק זינגט ער ביי דער גמרא,
כאַפט אַ קוק אויף איטעם טאַטן:
„זע... אַ בחורל מיט תּורה,
ניט אַ סאַלטיק מיט קראַוואַטן!..."

*

קומט צו פֿאָרן אַ סטודענטל —
אַזש פֿון „פייטערבאַרג" געקומען;

a young fellow with green pants
and a boutonniere in his lapel.

Walks around in the beautiful summer,
slinking around in all the streets.
Here a dog and there a Gentile girl—
he sits and plays and jokes.

One time he happens to meet Ita
and hands her his boutonniere.
Here's a wild fellow, a student,
come from St. Petersburg!

                                    *   *   *

Ita doesn't take the pretty gift,
and runs away,
but from then on, they say,
she can no longer sleep.

So they try to heal her,
pour out wax and water,
say spells against the Evil Spirit—
Ita says nothing and grows paler.

So pass three long weeks—
she doesn't eat, she doesn't sleep.
The fourth week—where's Ita?!
She's run away with the jokester.

Near The Church

Near the church stands a tree,
stands there all bent over.
The town rabbi is hanging there,
with his eyes all bulging.

O God, God, Gentile God—
are you asleep in Heaven?

א יונגאטש אין גרינע הויזן,
און אין לאץ א בינטל בלומען.

גייט דאם אום ביי גאט א זומער
שלינג און שלאנג אין אלע גאסן;
ווי א הונט און ווי א שיקסע —
זיצט ער, שפילט ער, טרײבט ער שפאסן.

דארף ער איין מאל טרעפן איטען, —
שענקט ער איר זײן בינטל בלומען...
אט, א הולטײ, א סטודענטל,
וואס פון פיטערבארג געקומען !

*

איטע האט דאס דאס שיינע שענקעכץ
ניט גענומען און אנטלאפן;
נאר פון דענסטמאל אן — דערצײלט מען —
איז זי מער שוין ניט געשלאפן...

האט מען זי גענומען היילן:
אויסגעגאסן וואקס אין וואסער,
אפגעשפראכן פון עין-הרע, —
איטע שווײגט און ווערט אלץ בלאסער.

אט אזוי דרײ לאנגע וואכן:
ניט גענעסן, ניט געשלאפן;
אויף דער פערטער וואך — ווי איטע !
מיט דעם לץ איז זי אנטלאפן...

לעבן קלויסטער...

לעבן קלויסטער שטייט א בוים,
שטייט ער אײנגעבויגן;
הענגט אויף אים דער רב פון שטעטל
מיט אויסגעפיקטע אויגן.

א, גאט, גאט, גויישער גאט,
צי שלאפסטו אין די הימלען ?

Your son is dead, your cross now rots,
and your clouds are molding.

Take the Jew down from the tree
and crown him as a leader!
And let the newly baptized world
bow down to the martyr.

דײַן זון איז טויט, דײַן צלם פוילט
און דײַנע וואָלקנס שימלען.

קום, נעם דעם ייִד אַראָפ פֿון בוים
און קרוין אים פֿאַר אַ פֿירער !
און זאָל די נײַ־געטויפטע וועלט
זיך בוקן דעם מאַרטירער...

DAVID EINHORN

(born in 1886 in Karelitz, in the Novogrudsk district of Russia;
died on March 2, 1973 in New York)

The last religious man has died.

On Sunday, March 4, 1973, when we were at the funeral of the famous poet, our
lips murmured quietly"

> *The last religious man has died--*
> *the lonely synagogue is locked.*
> *The windows are locked*
> *and embarrassed shadows fill them.*

Together with the deep feeling of sorrow at the death of the last religious man
was also the pain and sorrow that there remained so few observant people to lament him.

David Einhorn was immediately placed at the Eastern Wall[44] of modern Yiddish
poetry when his first poems appeared in 1904. His first book of poems, 46 pages
long and titled *Shtile Gezangen* (Quiet Songs), which was published in Vilna
in 1909, evoked tremendous enthusiasm among professional critics and among
Jewish youth, who were virtually enchanted by the quiet, romantic tone and deep
lyricism that emanated from the poems. Bal Makhshoves and Samuel Niger both
wrote in the same vein that Einhorn's poems were a new turning-point in modern
Yiddish poetry. The poems breathed the mood of the awakened generation of
Jewish boys and girls who were searching for a way to satisfy their individual
and national feelings. Einhorn's poetry became, as Jacob Glatstein expressed it
in his essay about the poet, "the autobiography of a lost and disappointed generation." Einhorn was its bard.

His poem *Mir Veln Farblaybn in Shul* (We'll Remain in the Synagogue), his
poems to Jewish girls, his *Di Blase Bas-Malke* (The Pale Princess), and his plea
to the white birch tree to pray for him too, because

---

44. I.e., was given a place of honor

I came here a lonely man from far away.
The God of these parts is strange to me,
and His language is strange to me.

were seized upon by the searching youth, who were disappointed after the failed revolution.[45]

Most of Einhorn's poems in the early years were published in the literary supplements of Bundist newspapers and magazines. Despite his deeply nationalistic, and at times religious tendencies, the poet remained close to the Bund, and Bundists sang and recited Einhorn's poems about "remaining in the synagogue" with the same love as they did the poems of Liessin, Winchevsky, Reisen, Edelshtat, and Rosenfeld.

For his closeness to the revolutionary movement of the Bund, Einhorn was arrested in 1912 and imprisoned for half a year. The poet maintained his relations with the Bund till the second World War, though he was never an official party member. In a conversation with Jacob Pat in 1954, Einhorn said: "I was never a party person. In the chaos of Jewish life, the Old Guard of the Bund shone out to me. The people there stood very tall. The idea of social justice was always very dear to me."

In the same conversation, Einhorn, who at the time was carrying on a number of sharp, open battles with the Bund, said: "I never had to write anything for the Bund that I didn't want to write. I wrote freely what I thought and felt."

And he always felt like a deeply religious Jew, though even in that respect he was different from other people. At the same time as he fought against Jewish orthodoxy with all the fire of his publicistic talent, he sought to "achieve the purity of Jewish morality, the Bible." He expressed his belief in lines like these:

O God, I know You are with me.
You are with me
even when I deny You.

David Einhorn was also a publicist with a temper. His fiery articles between the two World Wars (published in the book *Shvarts-Royt* [Black-Red]) made an indelible impression on Jewish readers. His articles in the *Forverts*, of which he

---

45. The Russian Revolution of 1905

became a staff member in the 20's, as a foreign correspondent, also attracted the interest and affection of the general readership.

In 1940, Einhorn, thanks to the rescue work of the Jewish Labor Committee, came from his last home-city, Paris, to New York. He immediately became a regular staff member of the *Forverts*. Though in most of his articles and in his *Shmuesn Fun Zeydn Mitn Eynikl* (Conversations Between a Grandfather and His Grandchild) he called for a return to the traditional Jewish lifestyle, something with which many of the readers and staff members of the *Forverts* did not agree, he continued to command great respect.

In 1943, Einhorn published a collection of his poems in which he responded poetically to the Holocaust in Europe. About that book (*Ov HaRakhmim* [Merciful Father]), New York, 1943), Samuel Niger wrote that "Einhorn runs the gamut of Jewish national feelings, and one could create a modern prayer-book out of a collection of his poems on national themes." Niger also pointed out that in addition to Einhorn's previous motifs of sorrow and yearning, there had now been added new motifs of pity, hatred of the enemy, Jewish pride, and hope.

His last book, *Gezamlte Lider* (Collected Poems), published by the Workmen's Circle in New York, appeared in 1952. Einhorn begins the book, in which there is a selection from all his previous poetic creations, with a lengthy poem, *Gemore Nign* (The Gemore Melody), written in 1952. In that poem, the poet laments the disappearance of the traditional Jewish life, to which he had called for a return in recent years:

> *Your grandfather is dead now;*
> *the synagogue has been burned down,*
> *ravished, ravished*
> *at the hands of strangers and our own.*

But the poet consoles himself and calls on others to find consolation in the fact that

> *his dream remains eternal—*
> *it hangs before my eyes*
> *and sings to me in my blood,*
> *and wherever I may be,*
> *on whatever continent*
> *in which the blue sky can be found,*

wherever the eternal stars twinkle,
wherever lonely people
can find peaceful corners
to dream undisturbed,
to wait and remember
and sing out to God
the yearning of the world—
there can I erect my lonely tent.

In 1966, the famous poet and publicist retired from active work with the *Forverts*. From the beginning of 1972, the poet was a resident of the Workmen's Circle Home for the Aged in the Bronx; there he died on Friday, March 2, 1973.

The Last Religious Man Has Died

The last religious man has died.
The synagogue stands lonely,
the windows are closed,
filled with embarrassed shadows.

A sort of eternal sorrow
lies on the bare walls,
and two broken arms
lie beneath the priestly cross.

The last religious man has died—
there's no one to go up to the platform.
The Eternal Light flickers and goes out,
all alone in its corner.

And quietly on the steps to the Ark
the Divine Spirit stands lonely.
Her head is bowed and sad
and her dress is black as Night.

And it seems that her lips are murmuring
a quiet, last prayer,
and a voice is heard from the curtain:
"Too late, my faithful one, too late!"

We'll Remain in the Synagogue

We'll remain in the synagogue.
When the last person's steps have disappeared
and the wind has extinguished the Eternal Light,
we'll light the light again, my child.
It must not go out,
we must not forget
to light a *yortsayt* candle[46] to the Divine Spirit of the people--
we'll remain in the synagogue.

---

46. A candle lit to observe the anniversary of someone's death.

געשטאָרבן דער לעצטער בעל־תּפֿילה

געשטאָרבן דער לעצטער בעל־תּפֿילה.
פֿאַרשלאָסן שטייט איינזאַם די שול,
די פֿענצטער פֿאַרשלאָגן, און שאָטנס
פֿאַרשעמטע, זיי מאַכן זיי פֿול.

עס ליגט, ווי אַן אייביקער טרויער
אַריבער די נאַקעטע ווענט
און אונטער דער קרוין פֿון כהונה
פֿאַרבראַכענע רוען צווײי הענט.

געשטאָרבן דער לעצטער בעל־תּפֿילה,
ניטאָ ווער צום עמוד זאָל גיין.
עס לעשט זיך און צאַנקט דער נר־תּמיד
בײַ זיך אין זײַן ווינקל אַליין.

און שטיל אויף די טרעפּלער פֿון אָרון
די שכינה אַן עלנטע שטייט;
איר קאָפּ איז געבויגן אין טרויער
און שוואַרץ, ווי די נאַכט, איז איר קלייד.

און ס׳דוכט, אירע ליפּן זיי מורמלען
אַ שטילע, אַ לעצטע געבעט,
און ס׳הערט זיך אַ שטים פֿון פרוכת:
צו שפּעט, מײַן געטרײַע, צו שפּעט!...

מיר וועלן פֿאַרבלײַבן אין שול

מיר וועלן פֿאַרבלײַבן אין שול,
ווען די טריט פֿון דעם לעצטן אין ווײַט וועט פֿאַרשווינדן
און ס׳וועט דעם נר־תּמיד פֿאַרלעשן דער ווינט,
דאַן וועלן מיר ווידער זײַן ליכטל אָנצינדן,
מײַן קינד!
עס טאָר זיך נישט לעשן,
מען טאָר נישט פֿאַרגעסן,
צו שטעלן אַ יאָרצײַט דער שכינה פֿון פֿאָלק,
מיר וועלן פֿאַרבלײַבן אין שול.

The three daily prayers
we'll pray alone.
When the Sabbath bride comes,
don't cry, my child.
We must not be sad—
she has remained for us
our only friend from the past.
We'll remain in the synagogue.

The synagogue needs no crowds of thousands—
individuals have always guarded its beauty.
It will, like a mother, hug us and bless us
till the eternal night comes,
My child, after we're gone, the birds will sing
and the wind will mourn us at midnight.
In the evening, in the shine of the dying sunlight,
a dry blade of grass will whisper the closing prayer.
We'll remain in the synagogue.

Lullaby

Ay lyu-lyu, ay lyu-lyu—
Sleep, my dear one, and rest.
Lucky is he who has a mother,
and a cradle as well.

One can find anything,
get anything for money,
But a mother—there's just one;
not another one in the world

That's a gift from God
to whoever has the good fortune to have one.
Woe to him who has no mother
in this big, desolate world!

Ay lyu-lyu, ay lyu-lyu—
no matter how great the sorrow,

און שחרית, און מינחה, און מעריב פֿאַר אַלע
דאַן וועלן מיר דאַוונען און בעטן אַליין.
און ווען עס וועט קומען פֿון שבת די כּלה,
דאַן זאָלסטו פֿאַרמיידן געוויין,
מײַן קינד !
מען טאָר נישט באַטריבן,
זי איז אונדז געבליבן
דער איינציקער פֿרײַנד פֿון אַמאָל.
מיר וועלן פֿאַרבלײַבן אין שול.

די שול דאַרף קיין עולם פֿון טויזנטער מענטשן —
פֿון אייביק אַן היטן יחידים איר פּראַכט.
זי וועט, ווי אַ מאַמע, אונדז טוליען און בענטשן,
ביז וואַנען ס'וועט קומען די אייביקע נאַכט.
מײַן קינד !
נאָך אונדז וועלן זינגען די פֿייגעלעך שירה.
דער נאַכטווינט, ער וועט אונדז באַוויינען אין חצות,
פֿאַר נאַכט, אין דעם שײַן פֿון די פּורפּורנע שטראַלן
וועט סודן שטיל נעילה אַ טרוקענער גראָז.
מיר וועלן פֿאַרבלײַבן אין שול.

וויגליד

אַליע-ליוליע, אַליע-ליוליע —
שלאָף, מײַן טײַערער, און רו ;
ווײַל אין דעם וואָס האָט אַ מאַמען
און אַ וויגעלע דערצו.

אַלעם קאָן מען דאַך געפֿינען,
אַלעם קריגט מען דאַך פֿאַר געלט,
נאָר אַ מאַמע — זי איז איינע,
מער נישט איינע אויף דער וועלט.

דאָס איז דאַך אַ גאָטס מתנה,
וועמען עס איז נאָר באַשערט.
וויי איז דעם וואָס האָט קיין מאַמען
אויף דער גרויסער, וויסטער ערד !..

אַליע-ליוליע, אַליע-ליוליע —
ווי דער צער זאָל זײַן נישט גרויס,

one can always be rocked to sleep
in a mother's quiet lap.

Ay lyu-lyu, ay lyu-lyu—
no matter how heavy the sin,
it can always be washed away
by a mother's pure tears.

Sleep, my dear one, my beloved one—
close your eyes and rest!
Lucky is he who has a mother.
Ay lyu-lyu, ay lyu-lyu.

The BirchTree

Calmly, calmly, your leafy green head rocks,
my white birch tree, and prays endlessly—
each and every leaf quietly whispers a prayer.
Pray, little birch tree, for me as well.

I've come here lonely from afar-
the language of the god of these parts is strange to me--
he'll neither see my sorrow nor understand my prayer,
even though I pray, pray a lot.

From the distant West, a pink, gentle sunbeam
has stolen sorrowfully onto her slender branches
and lightly kissed the little leaves
that were dreamily listening to the nightingale.

A breeze has come from the brown fields
and has told legends to the leaves endlessly.
Deep in my heart, I've begun to yearn.
Pray, little birch tree, for me as well.

תּמיד קאַן מען אים פֿאַרװיגן
אין דער מאַמעס שטילן שױם.

אליע־ליוליע, אליע־ליוליע —
װי די זינד זאָל זײַן נישט שװער,
אָפּװאַשן װעט תּמיד קענען
זי דער מאַמעס רײנע טרער.

שלאָף, מײַן טײַערער, מײַן ליבער,
מאַך די אױגן צו און רו !..
װװיל איז דעם װאָס האָט אַ מאַמען
אליע־ליוליע, ליוליע־ליו...

די בעריאַזקע

רױק, רױק, שאָקלט איר געלאָקטע, גרינע קעפֿל
מײַן װײַסינקע בעריאַזקעלע און דאַװנט אַן אַ שיעור.
יעדעמ, יעדעם בלעטעלע אירם שעפּטשעט שטיל אַ תּפֿילה...
זײַ שױן, קלײן בעריאַזקעלע, מתפּלל אױך פֿאַר מיר !..

איך בין דאָ אַן עלנטער געקומען פֿון דער װײַטן,
פֿרעמד איז מיר דער גאָט און דאַן און פֿרעמד איז מיר
זײַן שפּראַך
נישט ער װעט מײַן טרױער זען און נישט פֿאַרשטײן מײַן
תּפֿילה,
כאַטש איך װעל מתפּלל זײַן, מתפּלל זײַן אַ סך.

פֿון דעם װײַטן מערב האָט זיך טרױעריק פֿאַרגנבֿעט
אין די דינע צװײַגעלעך אַ ראָזער, צאַרטער שטראַל
און אַ לײַכטן קוש געטאָן די בלעטלעך, די קלײנע,
װעלכע האָבן, דרעמלענדיק, געהאָרכט דעם נאַכטיגאַל.

פֿון די ברײטע פֿעלדער איז אַ װינטעלע געקומען
און דערצײַלט די בלעטלעך לעגענדן אַן אַ שיעור...
עפּעס האָט אין האַרצן טיף בײַ מיר גענומען בענקען :
זײַ שױן, קלײן בעריאַזקעלע, מתפּלל אױך פֿאַר מיר !.

JACOB ADLER

(Born on December 12, 1872 in Dinov, Galicia; died in Florida in 1974.

Few readers know that the talented B. Kovner, whom they know from his humoresques and humorous rhymes in the *Forverts*, began his literary career as an author of serious poems.

In 1907, a collection of his poems, *Zikhroynes* (Memories), appeared, and the name of the young poet, Jacob Adler, became recognized in the Yiddish world as a new and promising talent. The little book of poems was accompanied by a foreword by David Pinski, who praised the young poet whose poems were saturated with quiet, sad yearning and affection for his childhood years and the idyllic life of the small Jewish *shtetl*.

But Adler had started to write much earlier, in 1897, three years after his arrival in America. He published his first two socialist poems in the *Forverts*, under the pseudonym "Nesher"[47]. Subsequently, Adler's poems were printed in various publications in America, England, and Russia, and became very popular. In the collections of labor poems that were published in Russia and America in those years, together with the poems of other famous Yiddish poets were poems by Jacob Adler. We have before us the collection *Frayhayt: Revolutsionere Lider un Shirim* (Freedom: Revolutionary Poems and Songs), published by the Bund in Geneva in December 1905, and we find therein five poems by Jacob Adler.

In one poem, "dedicated to the Russian freedom-fighters," the poet calls out:

> *Let the storm blow, let the storm roar,*
> *and let the flames tear Heaven apart!*
> *Let the lightning shred the clouds*
> *and wake the universe from its eternal sleep.*
>
> *Let the thunder echo! Let the thunder roar*
> *and wake the sleepers like a thousand cannons!*
> *Let them awaken, united, together,*
> *and mount a fiery battle*
> *against those with full stomachs.*

---

47. The eagle

In another poem printed in the same collection, the poet pleads:

> *Shall I live, suffer, be patient, and wait,*
> *and gnaw the bones that fall*
> *from the table with the rich, delicious meals,*
> *and bend my head farther and farther down?*
>
> *Shall I sing them songs like a sycophant*
> *and praise the rich who live happily,*
> *or flee, save my life,*
> *and let my brother fall in battle?*
>
> *Or perhaps remain and hope and strive*
> *and fight with all my strength, my heroic power,*
> *and make the sparks glow even more strongly*
> *and help my brother win the battle?*

In these poems, just as in the later ones that were full of yearning and love for the lifestyle in the *shtetl,* one can recognize that behind them is a person with a rare taste for humor and a desire to make his readers laugh and forget their worries.

In a poem *Tsu Mayn Folk* (To My People), Adler sings:

> *I would lament you, my people,*
> *but I have no tears;*
> *I would light your way,*
> *but I am not a star.*
>
> *I would help you fight, my people,*
> *but I am tired and broken;*
> *I would give my body to you,*
> *but it's only bare bones.*
>
> *I wouldn't mind*
> *giving you my soul,*
> *but, my dear people, it has*
> *long since been torn to shreds.*

His poems, of which some have been incorporated into textbooks for children in the Yiddish schools, are distinguished by unusual rhythms and a certain playfulness, though they are about serious themes. In one of the best antiwar poems in Yiddish literature, under the title *Tsaytlid* (Song of the Time), he writes:

> *We'll not have any rye or wheat or barley—*
> *the broad fields have been dug for graves.*
> *We'll no longer have any sheep or cattle on the fields—*
> *the fields are occupied by corpses and ravens.*

We recall another of Adler's poems from our childhood, a poem that we consider also a true pearl of our poetry. It, together with others of Adler's poems, has entered the book lists of Yiddish schools, but the general readership does not know it. It has the theme of the yearning of the lonely Jewish immigrant for his *shtetl,* and is one of the most beautiful poems in Yiddish poetry:

> *Silver cloud, pearl cloud,*
> *don't rush, don't run away.*
> *Stop for just a moment—*
> *I want to ask a favor of you:*
>
> *when you float over*
> *those tall blue cliffs*
> *dreaming in the fog,*
> *and the fields full of young*
> *stalks of rye, and the creeks*
> *with the tiny silver ripples,*
> *and the big, deep ocean,*
> *come to my village,*
> *the quiet one.*

The poet further pleads with the silver cloud that when it arrives in his village, where a "broken-down cottage stands," and sees there his "faithful old mother," it should greet her and assure her that "when times get a little better, a little easier, I will surely not forget to sweeten her last few years."

With the blossoming of the humorous press in New York and the founding of the famous magazines *Der Groyser Kundes* (The Great Mischief-Maker) and *Der Yidisher Gazlen* (The Jewish Brigand) and other humorous publications, Adler went over to a light, humorous genre. From 1911 on, he was a regular staff member of the *Forverts*, where he began to publish his humorous series *Yente Telebende, Moyshe Kapoyer, Meyshe the Farmer, Tsaltshek Atereyse,* and hundreds of humorous poems and jokes. He used many pseudonyms: B. Kovner, *Khoyzik's Eynikl* (Mockery's Grandchild), *A Galitsianer*, *A Shtifer* (A Mischief-Maker), *Der Lets* (The Joker), and many others, but he became famous only as B. Kovner; that name was better known to the broad readership than his real name, Jacob Adler. His humorous poems, which he published under the name of B. Kovner, contain only sparks of the ebullient talent for humor that made him famous and beloved, but one can also quite often recognize in them the fine lyrical talent of Jacob Adler.

Cloud, Cloud

Silver cloud!
Pearly cloud!
Don't rush,
don't run away.
Just stop
for a moment—
I want to ask
a favor of you:
when you float
over those tall
blue cliffs
dreaming
in the fog,
and the field
full of young
stalks of rye,
and the creeks
with the tiny
silver ripples,
and the big
deep ocean,
come to my village,
the quiet one,
where white
little cottages
with gray
thatched roofs
stand in
little green gardens
decorated with
cherry trees,
apple trees,
pear trees,
and tall, slender
pine trees.

וואָלקן, וואָלקן

זילבער וואָלקן !
פּערל-וואָלקן !
נישט געאײַלט זיך,
נישט געלאָפֿן,
שטעל זיך אָפּ נאָר
אויף אַ רגע —
כ׳וויל אַ טובֿה
בײַ דיר בעטן :
ווען דו וועסט נאָר
איבערשווימען
יענע הויכע
בלויע פֿעלדזן,
וואָס זיי דרעמלען
אין די נעפּלען ;
און די פֿעלדער
מיט די יונגע
קאָרנזאַנגען ;
און די טײַכלעך
מיט די דראָבנע
זילבער-פֿאַלדן ;
און דעם גרויסן
ים, דעם טיפֿן —
זאָלסטו קומען
אין מײַן שטעטל
אין דעם שטילן,
ווו די ווײַסע
קליינע הײַזלעך
מיט די גרויע
שינדל-דעכער
שטייען אין די
גרינע גערטלעך,
אויסגעצירט מיט
קאַרשנביימער,
עפּלביימער,
באַרנביימער,
און מיט הויכע,
און מיט שלאַנקע
טאָנענביימער.

There, in the
quiet village,
in a broken-down
cottage
with closed
little windows,
with a well
in the garden
and a
cherry tree
near the window—

in that old
broken-down cottage
sits my old,
faithful mother,
with the tear-filled
eyes of exile,
and with wrinkles on her face
and a heart
with deep wounds,
a widow,
disheartened—
when you see,
O silver cloud,
my dear
good mother,
greet her heartily
in my name.

And don't forget
to tell her
that I yearn
for the quiet
little village
where my cradle
stood,
where she
rocked me to sleep
with a sweet children's song.

דאָרטן, אין דעם
שטילן שטעטל,
אין אַ שטיבל,
האַלב-צעבראָכן,
מיט פֿאַרקלעפּטע
קליינע שויבן,
מיט אַ ברונעם
אין דעם גערטל,
און אַ קאַרשנבוים
ביַים ברונעם,
און אַ קאַרשנבוים
ביַים פֿענצטער —

אין דעם אַלטן
חורבֿה-שטיבל
זיצט מיַין אַלטע,
טריַיע מאַמע,
מיט פֿאַרווייַנטע
גלות-אויגן,
און מיט קנייטשן
אויף דעם פּנים,
און אַ האַרץ מיט
טיפֿע ווונדן
אַן אַלמנה
אַ פֿאַרצאָגטע, — —
ווען דו וועסט, אַ
זילבער-וואָלקן,
זעןמיַין ליבע,
גוטע מאַמען,
גריס איר האַרציק
אין מיַין נאָמען.

און פֿאַרגעס נישט,
זילבער-וואָלקן,

איר צו זאָגן :
אַז מיר בענקט זיך
נאָך דעם שטילן,
קליינעם שטעטל,
ווו מיַין וויגל
איז געשטאַנען,
ווו זי האָט מיך
איַינגעשלעפֿערט
מיט אַ זיסן
קינדער-לידל.

Also don't forget,
silver cloud,
to tell her
that times
are hard,
that I can't
help her today—
when times
get a little better,
a little easier,
I will surely
not forget
to sweeten
her last
few years.

Silver cloud,
pearly cloud,
tell me—
will you not forget to tell
everything, everything
to my dear good mother.

Sabbath Evening

It's leaving now,
the holy Sabbath.
The house grows dark,
the house grows still.
Mama whispers:
"O God of Abraham."
She whispers the prayer
with heart and feeling.

אויך פֿאַרגעס נישט,
זילבער-וואָלקן,
איר צו זאָגן:
אז די צייטן
זענען שווערע;
אז איך קאָן איר
היינט נישט העלפֿן; —
ווען די צייטן
וועלן ווערן
עטוואָס בעסער,
עטוואָס גרינגער,
וועל איך זיכער
נישט פֿאַרגעסן
אירע לעצטע
ביסל יאָרן
צו פֿאַרזיסן.

זילבער-וואָלקן,
פּערל-וואָלקן,
זאָג מיר, וועסטו
נישט פֿאַרגעסן
אַלעם, אַלעם
איבערגעבן
מיין געטרייער
גוטער מאַמען?...

שבת בין-השמשות

ער גייט שוין אַוועק זיך,
דער הייליקער שבת
אין שטיבל ווערט פֿינצטער,
אין שטיבל איז שטיל;
עס שעפּטשעט די מאַמע:
„אך גאָט פֿון אברהם" —
זי שעפּטשעט די תּפֿילה
מיט האַרץ און געפֿיל.

"O God of Abraham,
Isaac, and Jacob—
accept my prayer
into Heaven's tent.
Send me sustenance
and grant me good luck—
may my dark world grow bright."

The sky grows dark,
clouds float by.
In the house it's dark
and sadly quiet.
But somewhere in a corner,
stuffed into a crack,
there chirps and chirps
a hidden cricket.

Starvation

We'll not have any rye or wheat or barley—
the broad fields have been dug up for graves.

We'll no longer have any sheep or cattle in the fields—
the fields are occupied by corpses and ravens.

The trees are loaded with apples and pears—
they'll rot and shrivel on the branches.

The youngest, strongest people stand in the fire—
there's not one to sow or plant or plow.

The fields are occupied by corpses and ravens—
we'll not have any rye or wheat or barley.

‏„אָך גאָט פֿון אַבֿרהם,
‏פֿון יצחק, פֿון יעקבֿ,
‏פֿארנעם דאָרט מײַן תּפֿילה
‏אין הימלס געצעלט —
‏און שיק מיר פרנסה,
‏און ריכט אויף מײַן מזל
‏און ליכטיק זאָל ווערן
‏מײַן פֿינצטערע וועלט...”

‏עס טונקלט דער הימל ;
‏עס ציִען זיך וואָלקנס
‏אין שטיבל איז פֿינצטער
‏און אומעטיק שטיל — —
‏נאָר ערגעץ אין ווינקל,
‏פֿאַרשטופֿט אין אַ שפּאַרע,
‏דאָרט טשירקעט און טשירקעט
‏פֿאַרבאָרגן אַ גריל...

הונגער

‏מיר וועלן קיין קאָרן, קיין ווייץ און קיין גערשטן
‏ניט האָבן —
‏די פֿעלדער, די ברייטע, זיי שטייען אין גריבער
‏צעגראָבן.

‏מיר וועלן קיין שאַף און קיין רינד אויפֿן פֿעלד מער
‏ניט האָבן —
‏די פֿעלדער, זיי זײַנען פֿאַרנומען מיט מתים
‏און ראָבן.

‏די ביימער, זיי שטייען באַלאָדן מיט עפּל
‏און באַרן —
‏זיי וועלן אַזוי אויף די צווײַגן פֿאַרפֿוילן,
‏פֿאַרדאַרן.

‏די יינגסטע, די קרעפֿטיקסטע מענטשן, זיי שטייען
‏אין פֿלאַקער —
‏ניטאָ ווער ס׳זאָל זייען און פֿלאַנצן אַ ן פֿירן
‏דעם אַקער.

‏די פֿעלדער, זיי זײַנען פֿאַרנומען מיט מתים
‏און ראָבן.
‏מיר וועלן קיין קאָרן, קיין ווייץ און קיין גערשטן
‏ניט האָבן —

H. ROISNBLAT

(born on May 15, 1878 in the village of Risoshe, in Podolya, Ukraine;
died on May 29, 1956 in Los Angeles)

One of the great wonders of American Yiddish poetry is the poet H. Roisnblat,
who came to America as a young boy of 12 and grew up here to become one of
the most powerful Yiddish poets. He was born in a village in Ukraine in which
there lived three thousand Ukrainians and about a dozen Jews. Those Jews had
deep roots in the Ukrainian earth and earned their bit of bread by the sweat of
their brow. "My great-grandfather, my grandfather, and my father," Royznblat
later told Jacob Pat in a conversation that was published in his *Shmuesn Mit
Yidishe Shrayber* (Conversations With Yiddish Writers), "were Ukrainian villagers who ran mills. When the Czar forbade Jews from owning mills in Russian villages, the 'entire village', including the dozen or so Jews, emigrated to
America." That was in 1891.

How great was the spiritual baggage of a 12-year-old boy who, as Roisnblat put
it in his conversation with Pat, "was slammed across the broad Atlantic Ocean
and was 'mixed here in a terribly large sack' which was poured out onto the very
shores of the Golden Land, the way one pours out freshly roasted chickens from
a colander: whoosh, whoosh, whoosh--go at God's command!"

That baggage was the same that most Jewish boys from the villages and towns
of Eastern Europe brought here to America: a bit of Torah and Rashi, a page of
Talmud, and a few accidentally browsed books.

But little Chaim from the village of Risoshe came here with something more:
a rare memory into which was engraved almost everything that his ears, eyes,
and heart had absorbed in his 12 years. He brought with him the Ukrainian landscape, the fruitful language of the village Jews, and a great poetic talent to bring
all of that to life in his later years.

He was heard to pray:

> *O God, my Lord, ignite my memory*
> *and lead me back to the shadowland of the sun.*

His memory was ignited in a remarkable way, and he did bring to life the mill and the Jews around it, the teacher and the tavern-keeper, and the local squire and the Gentiles. He never forgot them, as he said in his poem:

> *I'll never forget you,*
> *though you were a stepmother to me,*
> *my great, ripe Ukrainian earth.*

Jacob Glatstein indeed says in one of his essays about Roisnblat that "he became a poet with the secret power to remember poetically that which is readily forgotten. He has the hidden power to transform things that happened and things that almost or only barely happened and he shares his poetic experiences generously."

Roisnblat published his first poem in the *Forverts* on January 13, 1900.

Nokhem Borekh Minkoff, who wrote several interesting studies about Roisnblat, says that the theme expressed in that first poem was not an accidental one; it was repeated later on in several of his poems.

Here is Roisnblat's first published poem:

My Star

> *My old, wise grandmother used to tell me*
> *that there in the clear sky a star shines for me too.*
>
> *And not just an ordinary one—of all of them, it is the most beautiful;*
> *in the white kingdom of stars, it shines most brightly of all.*
>
> *I am searching for that star—I am searching for its bright shine.*
> *Many stars shine, but where can mine be?*
>
> *Over there shines a star with bright golden rays,*
> *and over there one trembles--a star has fallen.*
>
> *But no one weeps "Who knows what happened?"*
> *Only I, only I sit sadly and weep.*
>
> *O beautiful golden moon, O holy divine shine--*
> *tell which of the two might be my star.*

In his later books of poems, *Hrudes* (Clods of Earth), *Leym* (Clay), *Mayn Likhtike Nesiye* (My Radiant Journey), and *Odem's Kinder* (Adam's Children), and in his last book, *In Shenstn Tog Fun Harbst* (On The Most Beautiful Day Of Autumn), Roisnblat brought to life, in a masterly way, his village childhood, the Ukrainian countryside, and a gallery of figures that were unique in Yiddish poetry. He did so with light humor and the ebullient homespun language that he had preserved in himself. The literary critic B. Rivkin says about Roisnblat that "just like Sholem Aleichem, he takes his characters from language—the language virtually carves out the faces and figures."

His poems that are sung are among the most popular of Roisnblat's creations, but they are far from his best and most characteristic ones. *Don un Danye* (Don and Danye) is a folksy poem that became popular thanks to the beautiful, hearty melody that the composer Mikhl Gelbart created for it in the 1920's; the song was sung by yearning boys and girls in Europe and America, and was considered a folksong. The poem *Got Fun Avrom* (God of Abraham) is one of the most beloved and popular concert numbers of various Yiddish artists throughout the world; certainly that is largely due to the prayerful melody in which Sholem Secunda wrapped the words of the poem. Another popular song of Roisnblat's is *Vander Ikh Aleyn* (I Wander Alone), to which Mikhl Gelbart wrote the music.

However, the true pearls among Roisnblat's poems, in our opinion, are precisely those that are not sung.

In his last and most mature book, *On The Most Beautiful Day Of Autumn*, the poet says:

> *The farther I get from my childhood years,*
> *the greener, greener they become in my memory.*

Going back to his childhood years, however, didn't stop him from feeling the pulse of America and its energetic rhythms, its spacious landscape, and its spirit of Lincoln, Jefferson, Paine, and John Brown, whom he celebrated in many beautiful poems and songs.

The literary critic S. D. Singer, in his book *Dikhter Un Prozaiker* (Poets and Prose Writers), says correctly that "in his going along with and listening to the new Yiddish poetry, Roisnblat showed how much strength Yiddish possesses, even here on the rocky ground of our Jewish America."

America

On our ground wandered the spirits
of Lincoln, Jefferson, John Brown, and Paine.
In our land and beneath our sky,
Walt Whitman sang of Man and God and the sea;
and Emerson, of light and joy and good fortune;
and Poe, of love and yearning and death.
And you and I—children of another world—
have built our homes
on the shores of this beautiful land.
We wandered long and came here late, already late,
but the shores are still free and great.
And tomorrow—tomorrow they'll start to build new cities.
The sky will hang clear and pure above us,
and the white days will be long, long.

We build cities of stone and steel and iron,
with subways—steel worms
that nag at their bowels day and night;
with hundreds and thousands of trolleys
that crawl around like cockroaches in all the cracks,
and 'els' that run above black roofs,
smoking chimneys, and long lines of wet laundry.
On all our asphalt-gray streets,
bracketed by dreary lines of walls,
thousands of automobiles shriek, shriek, shriek
from dawn far into the night,
to the last thread of starlight.
We have cabarets, theaters, movies, restaurants, and hotels;
we have beautiful women, young dandies, old fools,
ragtime, jazz, and shimmy-dances.
We have poets, singers, artists, and actors,
and critics galore!
We have impudent dilettantes
and old 'girls' who smoke cigarettes,
wear men's clothing, and have short hair.

We have thousands of factories.
Millions of smoking chimneys support,
day and night, God's heaven over our heads.

אַמעריקע

אויף אונדזער ערד געוואַנדערט האָט דער גײַסט
פֿון לינקאַלן, דזשעפֿערסאָן, דזשאָן בראַון און פּײן.
אויף אונדזער לאַנד און אונטער אונדזער הימל —
געזונגען האָט וואָלט וויטמאַן וועגן מענטש און גאָט און ים,
און עמערסאָן — פֿון ליכט און פֿרייד און גליק,
און פּאָו פֿון ליבע, בענקעניש און טויט.
און דו און איך ? — קינדער פֿון אַן אנדער וועלט —
מיר האָבן אויף די ברעגן פֿון דעם שיינעם לאַנד
געבויט דאָ אונדזער נײַ געצעלט.
מיר האָבן לאַנג געוואַגלט און געקומען שפּעט, שוין שפּעט.
נאָר, — פֿרײַ און גרויס איז נאָך דער ברעג
און מאָרגן, מאָרגן נעמט מען בויען נײַע שטעט.
און לויטער העלנגען וועט דער הימל איבער אונדז
און לאַנגע, לאַנגע וועלן ציִען זיך די ווײַסע טעג.

מיר בויען שטעט פֿון שטיין און שטאָל און אײַזן,
מיט „סאַבוויײַס" — ווערעם שטאָלענע,
וואָס מאָטשען זייערע געדערעם טאָג און נאַכט :
מיט הונדערטער מיט טויזנטער טראַמווײַען,
וואָס קריכן, ווי מאַראַקאַנעס אום אין אַלע שפּאַרעס ;
מיט „עלם", וואָס טראָגן זיך אריבער שוואַרצע דעכער,
רויבנדיקע קוימענס, לאַנגע שורות נאַסע גרעט.
אויף אונדזערע אַספֿאַלט-גרויע גאַסן — אײַנגעקלאַמערט
צווישן כמורנע מויערן-שורות — שרײַען, שרײַען, שרײַען
טויזנטער און טויזנטער אָטאָמאָבילן
פֿון בראָך אויף מאָג ביז העט
צום סאַמע לעצטן פֿאַדעם שטערנליכט.
מיר האָבן קאָבאַרעטן, טעאַטערן, קינאָס, רעסטאָראַנען
און האָטעלן.
מיר האָבן שיינע פֿרויען, יונגע פֿראַנטן, אַלטע נאַרן,
„רענטיעס", „דזשעז" און „שימי"-טענץ.
מיר האָבן דיכטער, זינגער, מאַלער און אַקטיאָרן,
קריטיקער — גאָלאָר !
מיר האָבן פֿרעכע דילעטאַנטן, אַלטע פֿרײַלינס,
וועלכע רייכערן ציגאַרעטן,
טראָגן מאַנסבלישע בגדים, קורצע האָר.

מיר האָבן טויזנטער פֿאַבריקן.
מיליאָנען רויכנדיקע קוימענס האַלטן אונטער —
טאָג און נאַכט — גאָטס הימלען איבער אונדזערע קעפּ.

We forge plowshares, rifles, bells, keys,
window-bars, chains, wheels, rails, hammers, axes;
we weave silk, satin, velvet, carpets, cloth;
we dig coal, gold, and graves;
we sew dresses, shoes, shrouds, and sacks;
we polish cut-glass, diamonds, and various stones;
we pour silver, gold, and platinum—
jewelry for the beautiful women who decorate our land.

God of Abraham

O grandma dear, don't say "God of Abraham" yet.
What's your hurry today?
The sun hasn't yet set in the West.
O grandma dear, wait a little bit longer.

Don't disturb the joy of the holy Sabbath,
the quiet, holy calm.
You can't yet see any stars in the sky—
oh wait just another moment.

The "God of Abraham" harnesses us again
into the heavy everyday yoke—
to drag along our exile, the *kheyder*, the rabbi,
the burden and worries of the week.

But still grandma stands at the window, petrified—
she's deaf to my plea.
"O God of Abraham," and a tear
rolls down the dark window pane.

Don and Danye

Don has two little black side-curls,
and Danye has two golden braids.
Don is the genius of the village,
and Danye's the queen of the steppe.

מיר שמידן ; אַקער־אײַזנס, ביקסן, גלעקער, שלעסער,
גראַטעס, קייטן, רעדער, רעלסן, האַמערס, העק.
מיר וועבן — זײַדצײַג, אַטלעס, סאַמעט, טעפעכער, געוואַנט.
מיר גראָבן — קוילן, גאָלד און — קבָרים,
מיר נייען — קליידער, שיך, תּכריכים, זעק.
מיר שלײַפן — שניטגלאָז, דימאַנטן און שטיינער אַלערהאַנט,
מיר גיסן אויס פֿון זילבער, גאָלד און פּלאַטינום
צירונג פֿאַר די שיינע פֿרויען, וואָס באַצירן אונדזער לאַנד.

גאָט פֿון אַבֿרהם

אוי, באַבעניו, זאָג נאָך נישט „גאָט פֿון אַבֿרהם",
וואָס איז דאָס מיט דיר הײַנט דער איַיל ?
אין מערבֿ־זײַט איז נאָך די זון ניט פֿאַרגאַנגען,
אַ, באַבעניו, וואַרט נאָך אַ ווײַל.

צעשטער נישט דעם פֿרידן פֿון היילַיקן שבת,
די שטילע, די היילַיקע רו ;
מען זעט נאָך נישט שײַנען אין הימל קיין שטערן,
אוי וואַרט נאָך אַ רגעלע צו.

דער „גאָט פֿון אַבֿרהם", ער שפּאַנט אונדז צוריק אײַן
אין שווערן מאָג־טעגלעכן יאָך —
צו שלעפּן דעם גלות, דעם חדר, דעם רבֿין,
דעם עול און די דאגות פֿון וואָך.

דאָך בלײַבט ווי פֿאַרשטיינערט בײַם פֿענצטער די באָבע,
זי איז צו מיַין בעטן ווי טויב ;
„אוי גאָט פֿון אַבֿרהם" — און עס קײַקלט אַראָפּ זיך
אַ טרער אויף דער טונקעלער שויב.

דן און דאַניאַ

דן האָט צוווײ פֿאַהלעך שוואַרצע
און דאַניאַ צוווײ גאָלדענע צעפּ.
דן איז דער עלוי פֿון שטעטל
און דאַניאַ די מלכּה פֿון סטעפּ.

Don goes to synagogue at dawn,
his eyes half-closed with sleep.
Danye, with the sun on her brow,
drives her sheep out to the steppe.

Don meets the shepherdess
and mutely lowers his eyes.
Danye, embarrassed, smiles
and bows her head quietly.

Don sits and studies,
and the day somehow drags on endlessly.
It seems to him that the page is a meadow,
the letters a herd of sheep.

Danye guards her flock
of curly lambs, and thinks
about the beautiful side-curls—
curly and black as the night.

Don goes to the synagogue every day,
and Danye goes daily to the steppe.
Don has two little black side-curls
and Danye has two golden braids.

The Song of the Believer

A black darkness has descended on my house,
but I, I haven't closed my window.
After all, You taught me to love Your stars, God!
Should I forget and be afraid of the night?

Fear, like a plague, has tightly sealed my gate,
But I, I've let my door stand ajar.
All my life You've been my protector, God!
Should I now begin to be afraid to be alone?

I don't even have a lightning-rod on my roof
to repel Your lightning bolts.
After all, You've struck me so many times in my life, God!
Should I be afraid of a pain that lasts but an instant?

דן גייט באגינען אין קלייזל
זײַן אויג האַלב-פֿאַרכמאַרעט פֿון שלאָף,
דאַניאַ מיט זון אויף די ברעמען
צום סטעפּ טרײַבט אַרויס אירע שאָף.

דן גענגט אָן די פֿאַסטושקע
און לאָזט שטום די אויגן אַראָפּ.
דאַניאַ, פֿאַרשעמט טוט אַ שמייכל
און לאָזט שטיל אַרונטער דעם קאָפּ...

דן זיצט בײַם לערנען און ס׳ציט זיך
דער טאָג עפּעס לאַנג אָן אַ סוף,
ס׳דוכט אים : דאָס בלאָט איז אַ לאַנקע
די אותיות — אַ טשערעדע שאָף...

דאַניאַ זי הוט זיך איר סטאַדע
געקרײַזולטע לעמער און טראַכט
עפּעס פֿון פֿאָהלער שיינע,
געקרײַזולטע, שוואַרץ ווי די נאַכט...

דן גייט טאָג-טעגלעך אין קלייזל
און דאַניאַ טאָג-טעגלעך אין סטעפּ,
דן האָט צוויי פֿאָהלער שוואַרצע
און דאַניאַ צוויי גאָלדענע צעפּ.

דאָס ליד פֿון פֿרום-גלייביקן

אַ שוואַרצע פֿינצטערעניש האָט אויף מײַן הויז אַראָפּגעניַדערט,
נאָר איך, איך האָב מײַן פֿענצטער ניט פֿאַרמאַכט.
דו האָסט דאָך מיך געלערנט דײַנע שטערן ליב צו האָבן, גאָט !
זאָל איך פֿאַרגעסן... און זיך שרעקן פֿאַר דער נאַכט ?

דער פחד האָט, ווי אַ מגפה, מיר און טויער ענג פֿאַרריגלט,
נאָר איך, איך האָב מײַן טיר געלאָזן אָפֿן שטיין.
דאָס גאַנצע לעבן מײַנס ביסטו געוווען מײַן היטער, גאָט !
זאָל איך ערשט מורא האָבן זײַן מיט זיך אַליין ?

כ׳האָב אויף מײַן דאַך אַפֿילו ניט קיין בליץ-פֿאַרהיטער,
וואָס זאָל די פֿײַערפֿײַלן דײַנע אָפּשלאָגן צוריק...
דו האָסט דאָך מיך אַזוי פֿיל מאָל געשלאָגן אין מײַן לעבן, גאָט !
זאָל איך זיך שרעקן פֿאַרן שמאַרץ, וואָס נעמט אַן אויגנבליק ?

BARUCH VLADECK

(pseudonym of Baruch Charney; born on January 1, 1886 in Dukor,
near Minsk; died on October 30, 1938 in New York)

"He was a man. He was a personality. He was a world." That's how Vladeck eulogized Vladimir Medem in an article written in the *Forverts* of January 11, 1923, two days after Medem's death. Those words are tailor-made for Vladeck himself: he was a man, he was a personality, he was a world.

When B. Vladeck, in full bloom at the age of 52, suddenly died on October 30, 1938, a whole world that bore the name of B. Charney Vladeck, who was also known as "the second Lasalle" (and also as "the Jewish Lasalle" and "the young Lasalle"), "Bonye Brokhes," "Bontshe Shvayg's Grandson", "Moisei Vilner", and other names, was extinguished.

Abraham Liessin, his most intimate friend, read a poem at Vladeck's funeral that he had written on the death of his friend—the last poem by the poet, who passed into eternity three days later. In that poem, Liessin said:

He was, my people, a slave,
chained for eternity to the "reins" of your storm ship;
whether a storm was raging against us
or the hull of the ship was collapsing,
he could not release
the reins from his hand.

He chose slavery voluntarily,
chained himself to the difficult service while still young,
and in a knightly way and with a sweet smile,
wore the heavy chains for a lifetime
and steered constantly
toward some promised land.

He fought bravely against storm birds
with great effort, inspired,
till he fell, exhausted, at his post,
till the cold of death stopped his warm heart,

with the reins still in his hand—
chained to the end.

Vladeck acquired the reins of leadership when he was still very young. His literary, oratorical, and organizational talents propelled him to the front ranks when he was still a young revolutionary in Russia:

"Who is this Bonye Brokhes?" asked I.L. Peretz in a letter to the Bundist *Folkst-saytung* (People's Newspaper), in which Vladeck was publishing articles under that pseudonym. Peretz compared the unknown young writer to a hero in Greek mythology, Hercules, who cleaned out the Augean stables[48] in Greece. And Peretz predicted: "Vladeck will take a prominent place in Yiddish literature." Peretz's prediction did not come true. The reins of leadership led Vladeck in other directions: he became "the second Lasalle," who enchanted his listeners at general gatherings. He was the organizer of secret Bundist cells dedicated to overthrowing the brutal Czarist authority, and later became the "ambassador" of the Jewish and international labor movement in America, to which he emigrated in 1908.

However, he continued to weave his poetic talent into his daily practical work: his gentle dealings with people; the articles and essays he occasionally published; and his speeches, which brought him a legendary reputation.

When Vladeck's 50th birthday was celebrated in New York, two important anthologies were published under the direction of Ephim Jeshurin: one was a book titled *B. Vladek in Lebn un Shafn* (B. Vladeck—His Life and Writings), with an extensive biography of Vladeck, written by the poet and *Forverts* staff member Y. Kissin, and a selection of his literary creations; the other book, *B. Vladek in der Opshatsung fun Zayne Fraynd* (B. Vladeck, As Evaluated By His Friends) (174 pages in Yiddish and 50 pages in English) contained articles by the most important writers and personalities of the entire world.

When one reads Vladeck's poems, articles, and literary notes that were collected in the first anthology, one immediately senses that behind every line there was a sensitive, poetic personality that found expression in everything he did or wrote. Besides the poems and articles, the anthology also contained one of his dramas, *Moyshe Rabeynu, A Historishe Shpil in finf Bilder* (Moses, Our Teacher, A Historical Play in Five Acts.) This was a play in which Vladeck tried to place himself into the mind of Moses and into the minds of the masses who were being

---

48. A legendary place that was full of filth

led out of slavery to freedom but were not yet ready to receive it as free people. The play was published in the *Forverts* in 1920, and it evoked great interest in Yiddish literary circles.

In a number of the articles and appreciations published in the aforementioned books in honor of his 50th birthday, Vladeck was scolded in a friendly way because he had neglected his literary talent. Vladeck's elder brother, Samuel Niger, scolded him openly for "neglecting his easy, lively, and picturesque pen; for silencing his literary talent." Saul Ginsburg ended his article of greeting: "and as a member of the guild, I have another wish for him: that he should appear more often as a writer. That wish is not only for him but also for Yiddish literature and its readers. They will gain a lot thereby."

Mani Leyb, who dedicated a splendid sonnet to Vladeck, expressed the same thought in a poetic way:

> *In his first bright days, he exchanged*
> *the words of his poetry for the sharp words of action.*

and continued:

> *but when he is alone with his own blood and limbs,*
> *he hears his own lament in his blood,*
> *the unsung words of his poems.*

Among the others who contributed appreciations of Vladeck's great accomplishments to the second anthology were Sholem Asch, Zalman Schneur, Abraham Reisen, I.J. Singer, Dr Chayim Zhitlovski, Abraham Liessin, H. Leivick, David Pinski, Dr. Max Weinreich, S. Kazdan, Jacob Pat, David Einhorn, Viktor Alter, Comrade Noah, F. Kinski, Karl Kautsky, Upton Sinclair, and many others. There was also a moving greeting by Vladeck's younger brother, Daniel Charney.

They still tell interesting anecdotes about Vladeck's speeches, debates, and lectures to this day. The most popular one is about his answer to a Republican alderman when Vladeck was a member of the New York City Council. Professor Albert Einstein and Dr. Chaim Weitzman had come to New York, and a proposal was made to show the distinguished guests the traditional honor of giving them the keys to the city. But the Republican, Collins, who was known as somewhat of an anti-Semite, opposed the proposal, complaining that these were two "foreigners," and that they didn't deserve such an honor. At the same time, he presented himself as a true American whose great-great-grandfather had been secretary to Lord Baltimore, the founder of the city that bears his name. Vladeck then stood up and answered the anti-Semitic alderman as follows:

"Mr Collins's great-great-grandfather was secretary to Lord Baltimore. We all know what that means: he probably polished the lord's boots and served him in other ways. My great-great-grandfather and Weitzman's and Einstein's great-great-grandfathers were also secretaries to a lord: that was Moses, who carried out a mission from God and freed his people from slavery, and then, like a good secretary, transcribed God's Ten Commandments onto stone tablets."

After Vladeck's speech, the proposal to honor Weitzman and Einstein was adopted.

The popular song *Ikh Vil Nit Keyn Ayzerne Keytn* (I Don't Want to Wear Iron Fetters) was written by Vladeck in Russia, when he was still a Poale Zionist (he became a Bundist while he was in prison, in 1904.) Y. Kissin relates in the above-mentioned biography that people used to sing the song at Poale Zionist gatherings in Russia.

Among his other creations, a particular impression was made on us by a prose poem titled *Yisker* (Memorial) (published in the *Zukunft* in 1916), in which he says:

> *I want to memorialize souls:*
> *not of those who died in their own beds,*
> *surrounded by friends and family—*
> *their graves already have large, heavy headstones*
> *with golden letters;*
> *I want to remember those on whose graves*
> *rotted wooden boards are lying helter-skelter*
> *and who lie beneath fences,*
> *and those who hug the earth in crowded mass-graves,*
> *and those whose burial place is unknown.*
> *You've left us a heavy, heavy,*
> *threefold heavy legacy: poverty, chains,*
> *and looking into the holy future*
> *to witness your mute, endless suffering.*

I Don't Want to Wear Iron Fetters

I don't want to wear iron fetters,
I don't want to wear crowns of gold,
for slav'ry is ugly and bitter,
even if it's ordained by God of old.

I know not of fear of my "betters,"
I know not of bowing to God.
My heart is my slave and commander,
and my will is my comfort and my rod.

Let the cruel, ancient enemy curse me,
and let him sharpen his blade.
He'll sink into depths dark and dreary--
that's a promise that I've already made.

I spin out my thread from the sunbeams--
my banner is one where hope flies.
Of those who engage in the life-game,
only bold ones can end up with the prize.

The Voice That Spoke

The voice that spoke to Moses and Socrates
in the wilderness near the mountain and in the marketplaces of Athens—
that voice also speaks to me.
I see the whole world and each thing separately
and know that everything is clear and also wonderful,
and every door is open.
My pain is all the deeper because I see farther.
No crown deceives me and no gallows frightens me,
because he who spoke to Moses and Socrates
from the desert sky, loudly and through a thick lattice---
his voice also speaks to me.

איך וויל ניט קיין אײַזערנע קייטן

‏...איך וויל ניט קיין אײַזערנע קייטן,
איך וויל ניט קיין גאָלדענע קרוין,
די קנעכטשאַפֿט איז מיאוס און ביטער —
זי מעג זיין די גאָטהייט אַליין !

איך וייס ניט פֿון מורא פֿאַר לײַטן,
איך וייס ניט פֿון כּורעים פֿאַר גאָט,
מיין האַרץ איז מיין קנעכט און באַפֿעלער,
מיין ווילן איז אויך מיין געבאָט...

זאָל שילטן דער קליינלעכער שׂונא,
זאָל שאַרפֿן זיין טעמפיקן שווערד —
צו זינקען אין פֿינצטערן אָפּגרונט
איז אים פֿון מיין צוקונפֿט באַשערט...

איך שפין מיר מיין פֿאָדעם פֿון שטראַלן,
איך וועב מיר מיט גלויבן, מיין פֿאָן, —
פֿון די וועלכע שפילן אין לעבן
געווינט נאָר דער דרייסטער דעם קאָן...

די שטים, וואָס האָט געערעדט...

די שטים וואָס האָט געערעדט צו משהן און סאָקראַטען
אין וויסטעניש ביים ים באַרג און אויף די מערק פֿון אטען.
די שטים רעדט אויך צו מיר.
און כ'זע די גאַנצע וועלט און יעדע זאַך באַזונדער,
און וייס אַז אַלץ איז קלאָר און אַלץ איז אויך אַ וווּנדער,
און — אָפֿן יעדע טיר.
און טיפֿער איז מיין וויי, וויל וויַיטער איז מיין ראַיה,
און ס'לאָקט מיך ניט קיין קרוין, און ס'שרעקט מיך ניט
קיין תּליה,
ווײַל דער וואָס האָט געערעדט צו משהן און סאָקראַטען
פֿון מידבר-הימל הויך און דורך געדיכטע גראַטן,
די שטים רעדט אויך צו מיר.

PERETZ HIRSHBEIN

(born on November 7, 1880, in "Lipes Mill," near the village of Kleshtshel,
between Belsk and Visoke-Litevsk, in Grodno Province, Russia;
died on August 16, 1948,in Los Angeles)

Peretz Hirshbein earned his place in modern Yiddish literature as the first dramatist of Yiddish art plays, though he also made important contributions in almost
all the other fields of Yiddish literature: he wrote lyrical poems and composed
music to some of them; he wrote stories, novels, memoirs, and children's stories;
and he visited the most distant and far-flung communities on almost all the con-
tinents and described his impressions in newspaper articles and books. He even
composed music to the poems of other poets—the most popular one was to Berl
Shafir's *Oyfn Boydem Shloft Der Dakh* (Above The Attic Sleeps The Roof.)

In everything he did, Hirshbein was a poet of longing for beauty, exaltation,
and distant, beautiful dreams. His appearance, his way of walking and talking,
his manner of dress, and his relationships with people all breathed poetry. "As
people who knew Hirshbein will say," writes Jacob Glatstein, "he came to Yiddish literature with his imposing and majestic bearing, which often looked to
us like a frozen pose but was in reality the manufactured pose of a professional
artist in his time."

Though Hirshbein went his own way in Yiddish literature, he was, after all, as
Samuel Niger points out, "a representative of his generation…who not only
dreamed the dream of Zion, as well as the socialist dream of the new youth, but,
like other Yiddish writers at the beginning of the 20th century, devoted himself to
Reb Israel[49] and, of course, to himself."

It was for that reason, indeed, that "his efforts to raise himself from the bottom
up to the clouds, to the stars; his wavering between reality and dreams; his getting up and flying away in the midst of a stroll; and his interposing poetry with
prose" (Samuel Niger) were so characteristic of his creations and his way of life.

It seems to us that there is no one for whom the well known expression "if you
want to understand a poet, you have to go to his country" is more appropriate
than Hirshbein. His childhood around the water-mill; the healthy small-townish-
ness that he absorbed there from his grandfather, with his "blue, red, and berry-

---

49. i.e., the people of Israel

tinted melody"; his mother's love of nature; and the goodness and piety of his uncles, those healthy and earthy Jews—all of that later sang out from his work. There, around "Lipes Mill," the young, dreamy boy heard many weird stories, legends, and folk-beliefs, and later wove them into his creations. Hirshbein's symbolism, his secretiveness, and the riddles in some of his plays are more likely ascribable to what he heard as a child than to the influence of Maeterlinck and Strindberg from Western European literature, as many literary critics would have it. He carried those mystical moods and thoughts within himself, as David Pinski has correctly written:

"He received them from his surroundings and observed the secretiveness of his father's mill. As a child, he must have heard voices behind the rushing sounds of the water that drove the mill, and he grew up to still hear voices behind everyday noises, bumped into them more than he heard them. He got used to responding to ideas: somewhere deep within him, somewhere far away in him, an idea would arise and he would react to it as if the idea were clear and distinct."

We do indeed see riddles and symbolic images in his *Tsvishn Tog un Nakht* (Between Day And Night), *Oyf Yener Zayt Taykh* (On The Other Side Of The River), and *Oyfn Sheydveg* (At The Crossroads), and even in his folksy comedies, in which the village Jews and farmers of *Grine Felder* (Green Fields) and their full-blooded real lives sang out.

Most literary critics who have written about Hirshbein (and there is a large and extremely interesting literature about him and his works) have tried to divide the period of his creativity into an earlier period of symbolism and a later period of folksy realism. In truth, we think, these two motifs were interwoven in all of his creations. Even in his first drama in Hebrew, *Miriam*, Hirshbeyn tried to penetrate the depths of the reality of poverty in Vilna by presenting a fallen girl who has been caught in the web of the underworld. When the play was staged in Buenos Aires in 1900, it shook up the entire Jewish public. Under the influence of that drama and the lamentations of the many unhappy, seduced girls that could be found in the theater, people began to strike at the denizens of the underworld and drive them out of public Jewish life. It is believed that this was the first great blow in the successful battle that the Argentinian Jews undertook against the "foul ones" who had flooded Jewish life in Argentina.

Also in the famous play *Neveyle* (The Dead Horse), which has been performed hundreds of times by professional and amateur group throughout the world, one can see Hirshbein delving into the real world of people who feel superfluous, and beneath the thick skin of the horse-skinner, Mendel the Horse, one can hear the beating and yearning of a warm human heart.

In his *Dem Shmid's Tekhter* (The Blacksmith's Daughters), *A Farvorfn Vinkl* (A Faraway Place), *Grine Felder* (Green Fields), and *Der Puster Kretshme* (The Empty Tavern), we see, in the guise of bucolic idylls, the yearning of simple Jews for goodness and Torah, the struggles between the Evil Spirit and the Good Spirit, and the constant victory of the human love and goodness that are deep within every person.

* * *

In 1904, three years after he had published his first Hebrew poem, the 24-year-old Peretz Hirshbein, like most young writers of that time, knocked on the door of I.L. Peretz in Warsaw. After Peretz read Hirshbein's two plays *Miriam* and *Shvorim* (Interrupted Sounds), both in Hebrew, he said to the young writer: "You are a dramatist…we lack dramatists. I expect a lot from you."

Peretz advised him to remain in Warsaw. He introduced him to Bialik and other writers and helped him to get opportunities to give Hebrew lectures so he could support himself.

Hirshbein writes:

> *What more could I have asked for at that time, though those were only my first steps, my beginnings. In Vilna, I still very often wandered to the streets around the Great Synagogue and satisfied my yearnings with the sounds of Torah that issued loudly from the open synagogue windows; in Warsaw, in the Jewish streets around the liquor stores, I often heard the "Buy, buy!" of the Jewish street-vendors. Which of the two cities needed Yiddish or Hebrew poets or Yiddish or Hebrew dramatists?"*

Hirshbein didn't receive a satisfactory answer to that question till quite a few years after he had begun writing and publishing his plays. The first productions of his plays were in Russian, and although they brought him a reputation, they brought sorrow along with the joy:

> *Success as a writer should begin among one's own. The fact that the first serious production of a play of mine had to be in Russian and not in the original language, Yiddish, elicited more yearning than joy in me.*

But Hirshbein reforged his yearning for Yiddish theater into deeds. In 1905, the Hirshbein Troupe, the first Yiddish art theater among Jews, was created in Odessa. Hirshbein was the founder, producer, and director, and was also an actor. The Troupe traveled to various cities and villages in Russia, and staged not only Hirshbein's plays but also plays by Sholem Asch and other writers.

Hirshbein writes about that period (which lasted two years) that it was not just a matter of staging Yiddish theater but also

> *of awakening in the audience a relationship to the language and the content;*
> *of speaking the language being acted as beautifully and clearly as possible.*
> *On the professional stage of the time, stuttering and babbling and crippling*
> *the folk-language was considered part of comedy, but in our case, in con-*
> *trast, much weight was placed on the clarity of the language.*

But the young actors were not only consumed with transmitting the purity and clarity of the Yiddish language but even more with the whole idea of establishing Yiddish theater "as a legitimate child of Yiddish culture." It was not an easy job. The general audience was used to light, entertaining plays presented in a Germanized Yiddish that people had never spoken but that the "paper heroes" declaimed on the stage. The Hirshbein Troupe, on the other hand, presented portraits of life: the struggles of the individual and the community and the problems of Jewish life.

Hirshbein recounts: "Not only were they different for the public, which was looking for, and still today looks for, pleasure in operettas and trashy theater, but it was new for the actors themselves." And that too was Hirshbein's historic accomplishment: thanks to his troupe and his plays, intelligent boys and girls who saw in Yiddish theater a folk-mission, an exalted mission to which they dedicated their young lives, began streaming to the theater.

One would have to write separately about Hirshbein's journeys and his beautiful descriptions, which opened the doors and windows of the great world to tens of thousands of readers. We will just end our essay about Hirshbein with a few lines from a little known poem of his, which fits him just as it does the majority of writers whose "pearls" we have collected in this book:

> *I've planted a garden by myself—*
> *magical trees grow there.*
> *It's simply enormous*

and every branch bears fruit.
The door and gate are open to all
to ask for fruit from the garden.
I ask people to come here,
to give me their hands and their hearts,
to walk freely in my garden,
and to enjoy its fruits and joys.

An Angel Weeps

An angel weeps, an angel weeps
and covers the earth with dew.
Beloved mine, beloved mine,
I yearn for you, I do.

My pillow's padded with down
and I lie abed on straw.
Beloved mine, beloved mine—
my yearning for you is still raw.

I'll Mourn

I'll mourn all my life—
woe is me and alas!
I've stirred up a spark in the ashes
and blown it into the wind.

I've hung on the window
Red and blue threads.
Let him come and extinguish the fire—
my heart is beating so.

He comes to my window—
my door is open.
I've stirred up a spark in the ashes—
woe is me and alas!

Oceans Roar
(fragment)

Oceans roar, waves pound
night and day.
Hearts languish, lives lament,
lament.

Old ways—they mislead
old lives to the edge.
New ways—they decorate

אַ מלאך וויינט

אַ מלאך וויינט, אַ מלאך וויינט
און באַדעקט די גראָז מיט טוי.
ליבסטער מײַנער, ליבסטער מײַנער,
איך בענק נאָך דיר אַזוי...

עס איז מײַן בעט מיט פּוך געבעט
און איך װאָלגער זיך אויף שטרוי.
ליבסטער מײַנער, ליבסטער מײַנער,
איך בענק נאָך דיר אַזוי...

קלאָגן װעל איך...

קלאָגן װעל איך מײַן גאַנץ לעבן:
װײ איז מיר און װינד —
כ'האָב אין אַש אַ פֿונק פֿאַרשאַרט,
בלאָזט אים אויף דער װינט.

כ'האָב בײַם פֿענצטער אויפֿגעהאַנגען
פֿאָדעם רויט און בלוי —
זאָל ער קומען ס'פֿײַער לעשן,
ס'קלאַפּט מײַן האַרץ אַזוי...

קומען קומט ער צו מײַן פֿענצטער —
אָפֿן איז די טיר...
כ'האָב אין אַש אַ פֿונק פֿאַרשאַרט,
װײ און װינד איז מיר...

ימען רוישן
(פֿראַגמענט)

ימען רוישן, כװאַליעס שלאָגן,
נעכט און טעג,
הערצער שמאַכן, לעבנס קלאָגן,
קלאָגן.
אַלטע װעגן — זײ פֿאַרפֿירן
אַלטע לעבנס צו אײן ברעג;
יונגע װעגן — זײ באַצירן

your dreams and lead them
to the edge.

My stars shine more brightly
over my path.
May morning come sooner,
sooner.

Flash more brightly, my flames,
my dreams along my way!
Flash more brightly, mountains and oceans—
my heart burns in my flames
my dreams along my way!

Stars Are Now Dying

Stars in the skies are now dying
and men now are dying on Earth,
those with a glorious future
and those doomed to sorrow from birth.

Rivers meet rivers meet rivers—
mixed waters flow into the Main,
but people and lives pass away
alone with their separate pain.

When a star falls away from the sky,
it traces a radiant swath,
but people and lives pass away
on a lonely and silent dark path.

A Little Story

There was once a Jew with a Jewess—
poor as church-mice they were.
They had two little daughters
but not a cent to their names.

דײַנע טרױמען און זיי פֿירן

דײַנע טרױמען צו אַ ברעג.

מײַנע שטערן שײַנען העלער

אױף מײַן װעג.

זאָל דער מאָרגן קומען שנעלער,

שנעלער.

פֿלאַקערט העלער מײַנע פֿלאַמען,

מײַנע טרױמען אױף מײַן װעג !

פֿלאַקערט העלער בערג און ימען,

ס׳ברענט מײַן האַרץ אין מײַנע פֿלאַמען,

מײַנע טרױמען אױף מײַן װעג.

עס לעשן זיך שטערן

עס לעשן זיך שטערן אין הימל,

עס לעשן זיך לעבנס אױף דר׳ערד.

פֿאַר װעמען ס׳איז ליכטיק זײַן גורל

און װעמען ס׳איז טרױער באַשערט.

עס טרעפֿן זיך טײַכן מיט טײַכן

און גיסן אין ים זיך אַרײַן,

און מענטשן און לעבנס פֿאַרגײַען

אַלײן אין דעם אייגענעם פּײַן...

און פֿאַלט װען אַ שטערן פֿון הימל,

דאַן האָט ער זײַן ליכטיקן װעג,

און מענטשן און לעבנס פֿאַרגײַען

אַלײן אױף אַ פֿינצטערן שטעג...

אַ מעשׂהלע

געװען אַ מאָל אַ ייִד מיט אַ ייִדענע,

קבצנימלעך גרױסע װי די װעלט ;

האָבן זיי טעכטערלעך צװײי געהאַט,

נאָר אָן אַ גראָשן געלט...

Ah, where to get dowry at least
to marry off their daughters?
Listen, just listen to what happened—
it's not a laughing matter.

A guest comes for Sabbath
and they open the door wide for him.
And he is, he is
the prophet Elijah.

So they prepare all good things for him,
make a place for him.
After *havdole,*[50] he departs quietly,
leaving a blessing behind.

Pitchers of milk, rivers of wine, an ocean of money
good fortune brought them.
They became as stingy as can be—
no Jew should know from it!

The great punishment came
for the terrible sin—
the milk and wine ran out,
and from the money just broken pottery remained.

---

50. The blessing that concludes the Sabbath

אײ, װוּ נעמט מען כאָטש נדן,
די טעכטער חתונה מאַכן ?
הערט נאָר, הערט, װאָס איז געשען —
אַ מעשׂה גאָר ניט צום לאַכן.

קומט אויף שבת אַן אורחל ;
עפֿנט מען בריַיט די טיר פֿאַר אים,
און געװוען איז דאָס, אײ, געװען —
אליהו הנבֿיא.

גרײט מען אים פֿון אַל דאָס גוטס,
דאָס אָרט פֿאַר אים געלאָזן ;
נאָך הבֿדלה שטיל אַװעק,
אַ ברכה איבערגעלאָזן.

עמער מילך, טײַכן װיַין, רענדלעך אַ ים
האָט דאָס מזל זײ געבראַכט ;
איז געװאָרן קאַרג פֿאַר זײ די װעלט,
ניט פֿאַר קיין יִידן געדאַכט.

געקומען איז די גרױסע שטראָף
פֿאַר דעם חטא דעם האַרבן ;
אויסגערונען מילך און װיַין,
פֿון רענדלעך נאָר אַ שאַרבן.

H. LEIVICK

(pseudonym of Leyvik Halper; born on December 1, 1888 in Ihumen in the
province of Minsk; died on December 23, 1962 in New York)

In one of his many autobiographical poems, H. Leivick talks about himself thus:

While still in my childhood,
at a time when all children play,
I lived with myself alone,
distant from other people,
like something hidden from everyone.

I already saw then
how people suffered in silence.
I incorporated the silence into myself
and imagined myself far into old age:
something greater, more wonderful
would come of the suffering.

That theme, the suffering of mankind and the belief that "something greater,
more wonderful would come of the suffering" runs like a red thread through all
the creations of this great writer.

Leivick has often been designated the conscience of our literature. He was more
than that--he was the conscience of the people who created the literature. Samuel
Niger (who, by the way, first met Leivick in 1906 in the Minsk Prison, where
they were both prisoners) says about him: "One feels the breath of generations
breathing in his creations; one also feels the breath of our generation. One knows
that Leivick, who so often listens to the voices of the past, has visions of the
future. One knows that he is both traditional and revolutionary…a poet of conscience, he doesn't seek to rock us to sleep but to awaken us…he wants us, like
him, to seek and find the sense in human suffering."

Niger ends his book about Leivick with these words:

That is one of the reasons that the Yiddish reader has such honest respect
for him and gives him so much attention and affection. He is the great ques-

294

tioner of our generation...he is our own restlessness, our prayerful voice,
our deep silence.

Leivick very early became a voice of the suffering of the people around him, and
he sought in various ways to ease it, abolish it. Even while he was still in the yeshiva, his ear and his heart were awake to everything that was happening around
him. "Years later," he told Jacob Pat in New York, "the news of Hirsh Lekert's
attempted assassination of the governor of Vilna, von Wahl, made a tremendous
impression on me in the yeshiva." That event engraved itself deeply on his mind,
and he returned to that theme more than once in later years, in his poems and in
a drama.

As a 17-year-old boy, he became connected to the revolutionary Jewish labor
movement, which was trying to end the suffering of his people and of all humanity. He was fascinated by the fiery words of the Bundist speakers at the secret
meetings in the forest, and he became one of those who wanted to rebuild the
world on new and just foundations. At one of the meetings (in 1905), he was
arrested and sent to prison. Because he was still a minor, he was freed after one
week. But instead of going back to the yeshiva, he went to Minsk, where he organized a strike of servant-girls. Leivick was arrested a second time and was incar-
cerated in the Minsk Prison, where he waited two years for his trial. In prison, he
began to publish a newspaper titled *Der Turme Glok* (The Prison Bell), and in it
he published his first poem. The poem reached his free comrades and they sent it
to New York, where it was printed in the weekly *Tsaytgayst* (Spirit of the Times),
which the *Forverts* was publishing at the time. The first lines of the poem were:

Winds are frolicking, weeping, blowing,
whistling angrily, howling furiously.
Fear creeps into my heart, deep into me,
and sucks up my blood.

The fear, however, was not the kind that could force him to surrender. At the
trial, he refused a defense attorney. He declared to the presiding judge:

I don't want to defend myself because I don't want to deny anything. I was
completely aware of what I was doing. I am a member of the Jewish revolu-
tionary party, the Bund. I am doing everything I can to overthrow the tsarist
autocracy and the bloody hangmen, and you as well (quoted from his conversation with Jacob Pat in the book *Shmuesn Mit Yidishe Shrayber* (Conversations With Yiddish Writers), New York, 1954.)

Leivick was sentenced to four years of prison, to be followed by permanent exile to Siberia. Many years later, in 1939, he told the children in the Yiddish schools in America how he received the sentence: He knew that "prison" meant hard labor, chains, prisoner's clothing, whipping and cells, and hunger and illness. After that, the snows of Siberia—permanent exile. At the same time, however, the words "prison" and "Siberia" attracted him and called to him: "So many thousands are already 'there,' are suffering and being tortured there—let me go there too. Let me taste it too. Let me be there for real, totally."

In prison, Leivick wrote his first drama, *Di Keytn Fun Moshiakh* (The Chains of the Messiah.) In that drama one can already find presages of all the themes we encounter later in all his poems, dramas, essays, and public lectures. "In that first drama," says Samuel Niger, "there is already an expression of the beginnings of Leivick's questioning of the order of things, of the tragic contradictions that he saw in it, and of the deeply moralistic feeling of responsibility with which all his poetry, the poetry of conscience, is suffused."

In 1913, Leivick succeeded in escaping from Siberia, and with the help of his comrades he came to New York, where his rich and creative life began. We say "rich and creative" because we know that the reader will understand that we don't mean a rich life in the material sense. It is well known that Leivick worked for many years in shops as a paperhanger to make a living for himself, his wife, and his two sons.

"At the premiere of my drama *Shmates* (Rags)," Leivick recounts, "I came right from work. I barely managed to take off my overalls." It was, however, a rich spiritual life. He was creative, and each new book brought him a greater reputation and honors in the whole Jewish world.

Our Dream

In the desert wilderness,
the Messiah stands in chains.
He stands and waits in hope
till Mankind is ready,

with heart and brain,
with yearning gaze,
for him to come
and bring freedom and happiness.

In our village,
this is how the old folks told the tale—
they would keep saying:
"I hope the time will come soon!"

And I, as a boy, used to hear
the words of the old folks
and think quietly to myself
that the time had already come long ago.

And if everyone has to be ready,
I'm ready at any moment
to go to the Messiah in the desert
and free him from his chains.

Just let people tell me
how to get to the desert--
but no one can tell me,
for no one knows where it is.

So I used to pray in my heart:
"Let my words reach you.
No one knows where to find you,
so just come by yourself."

"For you can see that everyone,
young and old, is waiting for you.
They send their hearts to you
and are looking as hard as they can."

אונדזער חלום

אין דער וויסטעניש פֿון מידבר
שטייט משיח פֿאַרשמידט אויף אַ קייט,
ער שטייט און וואַרט אין האָפֿענונג
ביז מענטשן וועלן ווערן גרייט.

מיט זייער האַרץ און מוח,
מיט זייער פֿאַרבענקטן בליק,
אַז ער, משיח, זאָל קומען
און ברענגען פֿרייהייט און גליק.

אַזוי פֿלעגן ביי אונדז אין שטעטל
דערצײלן די אַלטע לײַט,
און יעדעם מאָל פֿלעגן זיי זאָגן:
אַ, הלוואַי קומט שוין די צײַט.

און איך, אַ ייִנגל, פֿלעג הערן
די רייד פֿון די אַלטע לײַט,
פֿלעג איך טראַכטן פֿאַר זיך אין שטילקייט,
אַז ס'איז שוין לאַנג געקומען די צײַט.

און אויב איעדער דאַרף גרייט זײַן —
בין איך יעדע רגע גרייט
צו גיין צו משיח אין מידבר
און באַפֿרייַען אים פֿון דער קייט.

נאָר זאָלן די לײַט מיר זאָגן
ווי קומט מען צום מידבר צו. —
אָבער קיינער קאָן מיר ניט זאָגן,
ווייַל קיינער וויסט ניט אַוווּ.

פֿלעג איך תפֿילה טאָן אין האַרצן:
— זאָל מיַן וואָרט צו דיר דערגיין,
קיינער וויסט ניט ווּ דיך געפֿינען —
טאָ נעם און קום אַליין.

ווייַל וועסט דאָך — עס וואַרטן אַלע
אויף דיר, פֿון קליין ביז גרויס,
זיי טראָגן דאָס האַרץ דיר אַנטקעגן,
און קוקן זייערע אויגן אויס.

That's what I used to pray—
I remember it from my childhood.
Even now, when I'm all grown up,
I never stop praying.

Even now I dream the dream
of freeing the Messiah from his chains.
I look for him everywhere
and I'm always ready for him.

And when I can't find him,
I cry out from every road:
"I'm waiting even though you tarry—
I'll wait till the end of my days."

The dream of my youth
is stronger than the reality of old age.
Let reality itself become
the dream of a new generation.

A Jewish child should never
stop being ready,
never stop looking for the footprints of the Messiah,
to free him from his chains.

Somewhere Far Away

Somewhere far away, somewhere far away,
lies the forbidden land.
Silvery blue the mountains there,
untrodden yet by any man.
Somewhere deep, somewhere deep,
buried in their earthen height,
treasures great await us there,
treasures hidden from our sight.

Somewhere far away, somewhere far away,
a prisoner lies alone all day.

אַזוי פֿלעג איך טאָן תּפֿילה, —
כ'געדענק עס פֿון קליינווייז אָן. —
אַפֿילו איצט, ווען איך בין אַ גרויסער,
הער איך ניט אויף די תּפֿילה צו טאָן.

אויך איצט חלום איך דעם חלום
צו באַפֿרייען משיחן פֿון קייט,
איך זוך אים איבער אַלע וועגן,
און בין שטענדיק פֿאַר אים גרייט.

און אַז איך קאָן אים ניט געפֿינען —
רוף איך פֿון יעדן וועג:
— איך וואַרט אַפֿילו אַז דו זאַמסט זיך,
וועל וואַרטן ביזן סוף פֿון די טעג.

דער חלום פֿון יונגע יאָרן
איז שטאַרקער פֿון אַלטער וואָר.
די וואָר אַליין זאָל ווערן
דער חלום פֿון אַ ניַיעם דור.

אַ ייִדיש קינד זאָל קיין מאָל
ניט אויפֿהערן צו זיַין גרייט
צו זוכן די טריט פֿון משיח
און אָפּבינדן אים פֿון דער קייט.

ערגעץ ווײַט

ערגעץ ווײַט, ערגעץ ווײַט
ליגט דאָס לאַנד דאָס פֿאַרבאָטענע,
זילבעריק בלאָען די בערג
נאָך פֿון קיינעם באַטראָטענע;
ערגעץ טיף, ערגעץ טיף
אין דער ערד איַינגעקנאָטענע,
וואַרטן אוצרות אויף אונדז,
וואַרטן אוצרות פֿאַרשאָטענע.

ערגעץ ווײַט, ערגעץ ווײַט
ליגט אַליין אַ געפֿאַנגענער,

On his head the shine
of setting sun now fades away.
Somewhere someone wanders 'round,
his legs deep in the snow, and
cannot find the hidden road
that leads to the forbidden land.

Yiddish

My cradle stands near Minsk, in Ihumen;
my chains lie in Siberia, where, in the archives,
the poem that I worked on in New York
circles around Buenos Aires, Moscow, and Tel Aviv.

The poem from New York, via Vilna and Warsaw,
plows new life in Tel Aviv too.
Above all the treasures I've inherited
go the lines from one of my mother's letters.

My mother's Yiddish, with great big Ns—
your writing is still overflowing with blood, Mama;
there's also a brother and a sister
who receive you with a No in Russian and Hebrew.

For that reason, I purify you even more jealously,
with affection, my bright jargon.
I see a book of pedigree opening
and a white banner fluttering over you.

In the light of the book, it gets as hot as fire--
your shouted song, your smallest letter.
Woe to those who don't love you,
to those who would lock you into a prison.

אויף זײַן קאָפ שטאַרבט די שײַן
פֿון זון דער פֿאַרגאַנגענער;
ערגעץ וואַגלט ווער אום
טיף אין שניי אַ פֿאַרשטײענער,
און געפֿינט ניט קיין וועג
צו דעם לאַנד דעם פֿאַרבטענעם.

ייִדיש

מײַן וויג שטייט לעבן מינסק, אין איהומען,
מײַנע קייטן ליגן אין סיביר, ווז, אין אַרכיוו,
דאָס ליד, וואָס איך האָב אין ניו-יאָרק פֿאַרנומען,
קרײַזט אַרום בוענאָס-אײַרעס, מאָסקווע, תּל-אָבֿיבֿ.

דאָס ליד פֿון ניו-יאָרק, דורך ווילנע, וואַרשע,
אַקערט אויף נײַ לעבן אויך אין תּל-אָבֿיבֿ.
איבער אַלע אוצרות, וואָס כ'האָב געירשנט,
גייען אויף די שורות פֿון מײַן מאַמעס אַ בריוו.

מײַן מאַמעס ייִדיש מיט נונען גרעסטע —
מיט בלוט איז פֿאַרפֿלייצט נאָך, מאַמע, דײַן כּתב.
פֿאַראַן אויך אַ ברודער, פֿאַראַן אויך אַ שוועסטער,
וואָס נעמען דיך אויף מיט אַ „ניעט", מיט אַ „לאָוו".

דעריבער ליטער איך מיט מער נאָך אײיפֿער
אין ליבשאַפֿט דיך, מײַן העלער זשאַרגאָן.
איך זע ווי ווי עס עפֿנט זיך אַ יחוס-ספֿר
און פֿלאַטערט איבער דיר ווי אַ ווײַסע פֿאָן.

אין ליכט פֿון ספֿר ווערט הײַם ווי פֿײַער,
דײַן קלענסט געזאַנג, דײַן מינדסטער אות.
אוי ווי וויי צו די וואָס האַלטן דיך ניט טײַער,
צו די וואָס וואַרפֿן דיך הינטער אַ טורמעשלאָס.

Forever

The world takes me around with arms long and prickly,
and throws me in pyres that burn all the day.
I burn and I burn but the fires don't consume me—
I pick myself up, stride again on my way.

In fact'ries that I stride through, I fall 'neath the giant wheels.
With courage, I blow up the steam pipes today.
I lay myself down as a brand new foundation—
I pick myself up, stride again on my way.

Just see: now I'm a horse, in harness of leather;
my raging young rider is whipping away.
I slice through the ground like a sharp-bladed farm plow—
I pick myself up, stride again on my way.

I sow all of my poems—I sow them like grain seeds;
they sprout and they grow just like grain stalks today.
But I still lie here like a twisted old bramble--
I pick myself up, stride again on my way.

I live here in a dungeon, blow open the cell-door;
above me the freed men are joyful today.
They leave me here bleeding, alone in the doorway--
I pick myself up, stride again on my way.

My clothes bloodily soaked, and dragging my weary limbs,
with purified love I am coming this day.
I come to a house and collapse on the doorstep—
I pick myself up, stride again on my way.

אייביק

די וועלט נעמט מיך ארום מיט שטעכיקע הענט,
און טראָגט מיך צום פֿײַער, און טראָגט מיך צום שַײטער;
איך ברען און איך ברען און איך ווער ניט פֿאַרברענט, —
איך הייב זיך אויף ווידער און שפּאַן אַוועק ווײַטער.

איך שפּאַן דורך פֿאַבריקן און פֿאַל אונטער ראָד,
איך רײַס אויף די דאַמפֿן מיט קראַפֿט מיט באַנײטער,
איך ליג זיך אַוועק, ווי אַ נײַער יסוד, —
און הייב זיך אויף ווידער און שפּאַן אַוועק ווײַטער.

אָט שפּאַן איך זיך אײַן אין געשפּאַן פֿון אַ פֿערד,
און איבער מיר בײַטשט אַ דערצאָרנטער רײַטער;
ווי אַן אַקער אַ שאַרפֿער איך גראָב דורך די ערד, —
איך הייב זיך אויף ווידער און שפּאַן אַוועק ווײַטער.

איך זיי מײַנע לידער, ווי קערנער מען זייט,
זיי שפּראָצן, זיי וואַקסן, ווי זאַנגען און קרײַטער;
און איך אַליין ליג ווי אַ דאַרן פֿאַרדרייט, —
איך הייב זיך אויף ווידער און שפּאַן אַוועק ווײַטער.

איך וויין אין אַ תּפֿיסה. איך רײַס אויף די צעל,
עס טרעמט איבער מיר צו זײַן גליק דער באַפֿרײַטער,
און מיך לאָזט ער ליגן אין בלוט בײַ דער שוועל, —
איך הייב זיך אויף ווידער און שפּאַן אַוועק ווײַטער.

אין בלוט מײַנע קליידער, — די פֿיס קוים איך שלעפּ,
איך קום מיט אַ ליבשאַפֿט פֿון לעצטן געלײַטער;
איך קום צו אַ שטיבל, איך פֿאַל אויף די טרעפּ — — —
איך הייב זיך אויף ווידער און שפּאַן אַוועק ווײַטער.

MOYSHE-LEIB HALPERN

(born on January 3, 1886 in Zlotshev, eastern Galicia;
died on August 31, 1932 in Brooklyn, New York)

If Moyshe-Leib the poet should say
he saw Death amid the waves today,
in a mirror-image sort of way,
in the morning, around ten o'clock, let's say—
would anyone who heard
take Moyshe-Leib's word?

And if Moyshe-Leib should say
he waved to Death from far away,
at the very time that crowds of folks
were swimming joyfully, telling jokes—
would anyone who heard
take Moyshe-Leib's word?

And if Moyshe-Leib should swear to our face
that he was greatly drawn to Death,
the way a bridegroom's drawn with yearning breath
to the window of his betrothed's place—
would anyone who heard
take Moyshe-Leib's word?

And if Moyshe-Leib should describe Death this way:
beautifully colored, not dark or gray,
is how he looked amid the waves today,
this morning at ten, let's say—
would anyone who heard
take Moyshe-Leib's word?

No one, no one wanted to believe the poet that Death was so near, and that at any moment he would meet him for his last encounter, from which he would not come back anymore.

The poet and literary critic Eliezer Greenberg points out in his comprehensive book *Moyshe-Leyb Halpern in Ram fun Zayn Dor* (Moyshe-Leib Halpern in the

Frame of His Generation) that Halpern made a strong impression with his question marks and his constant doubts, and not with ready answers.

Upon leafing through the first pages of his poems, the reader immediately feels that speaking to him is a poet whose "life is a wild, desolate war" with himself. "He often puts on a mask," writes Greenberg in the above-mentioned book, "and speaks about himself via the mouth of other characters, but the skilled reader recognizes the disguised poet in them anyway. The skilled eye and ear grasp immediately that behind the mask of the unnamed figures is hidden none other than the restless Moyshe-Leib himself. He was himself both the arrow and the target, and the result was, as the Irish poet William Butler Yeats put it, 'that from fighting with others, one creates rhetoric, but from fighting with oneself, one creates poetry.'"

Yes, all his life Moyshe-Leib Halpern was at war with himself. But Greenberg correctly points out, at the end of his book, that "while painting his own portrait, he indirectly painted in the contours of his entire lost generation."

Moyshe-Leib Halpern was not the first, and certainly not the only poet who painted the portrait of the lost generation to which he belonged. Like every true and great poet, however, he did so with his own paints and colors, with his own melody.

No one painted with such sarcasm a picture of the great city he hated:

> *Such a garden,*
> *where the tree has barely seven leaves,*
> *and it seems to me it thinks:*
> *"Who brought me here?"*
> *It's the kind of garden*
> *where, with a magnifying glass,*
> *one can see a bit of grass.*
> *Could that be our garden,*
> *such a garden in the morning sunlight?*
> *Of course it's our garden!*
> *What then—it's not our garden?*

And with the same pain and sarcasm, he paints for us the 'joys' in *Dos Goldene Land* (The Golden Land), a poem that is among the most beautiful pearls in modern Yiddish poetry:

308 Pearls of Yiddish Poetry

> *"Would you believe me, mama,*
> *that everything of yours is being transformed into gold,*
> *that gold is made from blood and iron,*
> *from blood and iron day and night?"*
> *"My son, one doesn't hide things from a mother—*
> *a mother recognizes and sympathizes.*
> *It seems to me that you haven't had enough bread,*
> *even there in the Golden Land."*

And the dialogue between mother and son continues till he can no longer hide his pain:

> *You're right, mother, we are separated—*
> *a golden chain and an iron chain;*
> *a golden chair in Heaven for you,*
> *and a gallows for me in the golden land.*

He felt lonely, lost, and superfluous in the great and alien city that he had come to hate, and in which he wandered around like a "captive lion" with the "restlessness of a wolf or a bear."

What didn't he try in the new land to which he came in 1908 from his home in Galicia, the village of Zlotshev? He was a waiter in a restaurant and a presser, and he tried his hand at other trades, but he was not suited for any kind of physical labor. He was constantly hungry, often slept on a park bench, and couldn't get a foothold on life. One finds portraits of that bitter time in his poems from that period, in which he says:

> *I pass my nights in poor little bars—*
> *a heavy grayness pervades my days.*

In 1912, he was invited by the editor Leon Khazanovich to Montreal, where Khazanovich had begun publishing a labor newspaper, the *Folks-Tsaytung* (The People's Newspaper). Halpern became the assistant editor, and carried out various assignments there. During the great strike of the men's tailors in 1912, he wrote and printed a poem about the strike that became very popular among the striking workers. It was recited and sung, and Halpern's name became popular.

The *Folks-Tsaytung*, however, had to cease publication after a short time, and Halpern didn't even have enough money to travel back to New York. A farewell banquet was arranged for him, at which the needed few dollars were raised so he could go back to New York.

In New York, Halpern contributed humorous and satirical poems to *Der Kibitser* (The Kibbitzer), *Der Kundes* (The Mischief-Maker), and other humor publications. He became close to the poetry group *Di Yunge* (The Young Ones) and published poems in their publications, poems that began to attract the attention of the better class of readers and critics. A particular stand-out was his poem *In Der Fremd* (In A Strange Land), in which he lamented his own fate and the downfall of his generation, which "goes around in the world like a blind man with his eyes open, and yearns and searches and inquires, but remains alone, like a child in its cradle and like the gray stone in the cemetery."

In 1915, upon the death of Peretz, Halpern published in *Literatur un Lebn* (Literature and Life*)* his great poem *Yitskhok Leybush Perets (*Isaac Loeb Peretz), which made a deep impression throughout the Jewish world. At the same time, he wrote and published his lengthy poem *Pan Yablonski* (Mister Yablonski) and his *Der Gasn-Poyker* (The Street Drummer), which became one of the most popular poems in modern Yiddish poetry. Not only did professional reciters and actors like to read that poem at their performances, but also ordinary readers knew it by heart and often hummed to themselves:

Thus did I rip,
rip, rip
my head through a wall,
across highways and byways
throughout the land,
with my teeth.
Chop the stone!
Chop the stone and remain alone!

* * *

There is not another poet about whom Yiddish poets have written as many poems as they have about Moyshe-Leib Halpern. In dozens of poems, Yiddish poets lamented the premature death of their brother, the rebel. Writers and critics wrote books and articles. They tried hard to interpret and explain, and proposed many theories, but no one explained the poet as well as he himself did in his poetry. No one painted a portrait of Halpern that was as clear and sharp as the one he himself painted in his powerful poems.

My Portrait

I've summer freckles, like the stars—
my hair is black and mixed with gray.
Yes, I am not so handsome, dear—
that's clear and certain, let me say.

Broad nose and Devil's eyebrows black—
my teeth are sharp and wolfish wild.
But bright blue are my poet's eyes—
they're gentle and their gaze is mild.

For dancing, I have clumsy feet--
they've very, very little skill.
My big, unlovely, gawky ears
can't tell good music, never will.

But from my warmly beating heart
I sing as well as I know how,
and to the rhythm of my heart
the whole world's dancing with me now.

An eagle has large, beating wings,
and I have long and strong arms.
My life is love and struggling too--
my blood cries out my charms.

Gingili

O Gingili, my bloody heart—
who is the youth who dreams in the snow
and drags his feet like blocks of wood
in the middle of the street at night?

It's that brat Moyshe-Leib,
who'll freeze some day
while he fantasizes
about summer flowers.

מײַן פּאָרטרעט

זומער-שפּרענקלעך פֿיל װי שטערן,
האָר געמישטע שװאַרץ מיט גרױ.
יאָ – אַז איך בין ניט קײן שײנער –
דאָס איז זיכער, שײנע פֿרױ.

ברײטע נאָז און טיַװאָלסברעמען,
צײן און ליפֿן װעלפֿיש װילד;
– אָבער אױגן האָב איך בלױע –
אױגן בלױע, גוט און מילד.

ס׳האָבן מײַנע פֿיס צום טאַנצן
װײניק, װײניק װאָס טאַלאַנט –
און די גרױסע אױערן מײַנע
הערן מוזיק װי די װאַנט –

אָבער מיט אַ האַרץ װאָס האַמערט
זינג איך מיר, װי מיר געפֿעלט.
און צום האַמערטאַקט פֿון האַרצן
טאַנצט די גאַנצע שײנע װעלט.

– האָט דער אַדלער פֿליגל גרױסע –
האָב איך ברײטע שטאַרקע הענט.
האָט דאָס לעבן קאַמף און ליבע –
האָב איך בלוט װאָס שרײַט און ברענט.

גינגילי

אַ, גינגילי, מײַן בלוטיק האַרץ,
װער איז דער יונג װאָס טרױמט אין שניי
און שלעפּט די פֿיס װי קלעצער צװיי
אין מיטן גאַס בײַ נאַכט?

דאָס איז דער תּכשיט משה-לײב,
װאָס װעט אַ מאָל דערפֿרירן
בעת ער װעט פֿון פֿרײלינגצװיט
און בלומען פֿאַנטאַזירן;

And when he is already lying in the snow
and not moving any more,
he'll still be dreaming even then
of strolling in fields of grain.

So the brat Moyshe-Leib dreams
and the watchman sings "tri-li-li";
the vagabond answers "kachoo,"
the dog goes "arf, arf, arf "
and the cat goes "meow."

O Gingili, my bloody heart—
who's creeping back and forth in the snow
and thinks he's sitting near the fireplace
in the middle of the street at night?

It's that brat Moyshe-Leib,
who's too lazy to think about things;
he's freezing in the snow and sees before him
a closed palace
with himself as king there,
guarded by watchmen,
and all his years will pass
like suns in the evenings.

So the brat Moyshe-Leyb yearns
and the watchman sings tri-li-li.
The vagabond answers "kachoo",
the dog goes "arf, arf, arf "
and the cat goes "meow."

O Gingili, my bloody heart,
who's all twisted up
and hopping around in the lantern-shine
in the middle of the street at night?
It's that brat Moyshe-Leyb,
who starts to dance in the snow
so his feet won't freeze completely;
meanwhile, he sees the snow upon him
sparkling like flowers in the sunshine,

און וועט ער ליגן שוין אין שניי
און זיך שוין מער ניט רירן, —
וועט ער אין טרוים נאָך דעמאָלט אויך
אין זאַנגגענפֿעלד שפּאַצירן.

טרוימט דער תּכשיט משה-לייב,
זינגט דער וועכטער טרי-לי-לי,
ענטפֿערט דער באָסיאַק האָפּטשי,
מאַכט דאָס הינטל האַוו-האַוו-האַוו,
מאַכט דאָס קעצל מיאַו.

אָ, גינגילי, מײַן בלוטיק האַרץ,
ווער קריכט אין שניי אָהער, אַהין,
און זעט זיך זיצן בײַם יַם קאַמין
אין מיטן גאַס בײַ נאַכט?

דאָס איז דער תּכשיט משה-לייב
וואָס פֿוילט זיך צו פֿאַרטראַכטן;
ער פֿירט אין שניי און זעט פֿאַר זיך
אַ פּאַלאַץ אַ פֿאַרמאַכטן,
און זיך אַליין דעם קעניג דאָרט
פֿון שומרים אַ באַוואַכטן
און אַלע זײַנע יאָר פֿאַרגיין
ווי זונען אין פֿאַרנאַכטן.

בענקט דער תּכשיט משה-לייב,
זינגט דער וועכטער טרי-לי-לי,
ענטפֿערט דער באָסיאַק האָפּטשי,
מאַכט דאָס הינטל האַוו-האַוו-האַוו,
מאַכט דאָס קעצל מיאַו.

אָ, גינגילי, מײַן בלוטיק האַרץ,
ווער קאַרטשעט זיך אין דרײַען אײַן
און האָפּקעט בײַם יַם לאַמטערן-שײַן
אין מיטן גאַס בײַ נאַכט?
דאָס איז דער תּכשיט משה-לייב,
וואָס שטעלט אין שניי זיך טאַנצן,
כּדי עם זאָלן אים די פֿיס
ניט אײַנפֿרירן אין גאַנצן;
דאַבײַ זעט ער דעם שניי אויף זיך
ווי צוויט אין זונשײַן גלאַנצן

and girls with loose hair
decorated with wreaths of fire.

So he dances, that brat Moyshe-Leib,
and the watchman sings "tri-li-li."
The vagabond says "kachoo,"
the dog goes "arf, arf, arf"
and the cat goes "meow."

O Gingili, my bloody heart,
is there a rooster in the town?
Who crowed there
in the middle of the street at night?

It's that brat Moyshe-Leib,
who has nothing to worry about,
and because he thinks that daylight
is hidden somewhere
and he thinks
they've choked the last rooster,
he crows himself and says
good morning to himself.

So he crows, the brat Moyshe-Leib,
and the watchman sings "tri-li-li."
The vagabond says "kachoo,"
the dog goes "arf, arf, arf"
and the cat goes "meow."

The Sun Will Set

The sun will set behind the mountain
and love will come along,
silently will come along
to sorrow, which sits on a golden stone
and weeps for itself, all alone.

The sun will set behind the mountain
and the golden peacock will come flying,

און מיידלעך מיט צעלאָזטע האָר
באַצירט מיט פֿײַערקראַנצן.

טאַנצט דער תכשיט משה־לייב,
זינגט דער וועכטער טרי־לי־לי,
ענטפֿערט דער באָסיאַק האָפּטשי,
מאַכט דאָס הינטל האַוו־האַוו־האַוו,
מאַכט דאָס קעצל מיאַו.

אַ, גינגילי, מײַן בלוטיק האַרץ,
צי איז דען דאָ אין שטאָט אַ האָן ?
ווער האָט דאָס אַזאַ קריי געטאָן
אין מיטן גאַס בײַ נאַכט ?

דאָס איז דער תכשיט משה־לייב,
וואָס האָט ניט וואָס צו זאָרגן,
און ווײַל אים דאַכט זיך אַז דער טאָג
האָט ערגעץ זיך פֿאַרבאַרגן,
און ווײַל אים דאַכט זיך אַז מען האָט
דעם לעצטן האָן דערוואָרגן,
צעקרייט ער זיך אַליין און זאָגט
צו זיך אַליין גוט־מאָרגן.

קרייט דער תכשיט משה־לייב,
זינגט דער וועכטער טרי־לי־לי,
ענטפֿערט דער באָסיאַק האָפּטשי,
מאַכט דאָס הינטל האַוו־האַוו־האַוו,
מאַכט דאָס קעצל מיאַו.

די זון וועט אַרונטערגיין...

די זון וועט אַרונטערגיין הינטערן באַרג,
וועט קומען אַ שטילע די ליבע צו גיין,
וועט קומען אַ שטילע די ליבע צו גיין
צום אומעט, וואָס זיצט אויף אַ גאָלדענעם שטיין
און וויינט פֿאַר זיך איינער אַליין.

די זון וועט אַרונטערגיין הינטערן באַרג,
וועט קומען די גאָלדענע פּאַווע צו פֿליִ'ן,

the golden peacock will come flying
and will take us all along
to the place we yearn for.

The sun will set behind the mountain
and Night will come and sing lyu-lyu,
to eyes that are already closing,
to sleep in eternal rest.

The Street Drummer

When a bird sings happy and free,
the king trembles on his throne.
Trembling is not appropriate,
so I sing like the bird,
free and quick
like the wind.
I dance wantonly, blindly,
in one street and out another!
If I am sick and old and gray,
who cares? Ha, ha, ha!
For just a copper penny,
I beat my drum till it might burst,
and clash my cymbals,
and whirl 'round and 'round—
clang, clang, boom, boom, boom,
clang, clang, boom!

A witch girl comes
and a fire ignites in me,
so I start to whirl more wildly still
and clench my teeth and roar:
"Girl, come here—
give me your hand and give me a hug;
a couple's dance is hotter.
Some snake like you
abandoned me not long ago."
My heart is sick and bursts with pain,
so I beat my drum till it might burst,
and clash my cymbals

וועט קומען די גאָלדענע פאַװע צו פֿלי׳ן
און מיטנעמען וועט זי אונדז אַלע אַהין,
אַהין װוּ די בענקשאַפֿט װעט צי׳ן.

די זון וועט אַרונטערגיין הינטערן באַרג,
וועט קומען די נאַכט און וועט זינגען ליו-ליו,
וועט קומען די נאַכט און וועט זינגען ליו-ליו
אַריבער די אויגן, װאָס פֿאַלן שוין צו,
צו שלאָפֿן אין אײביקער רו.

דער גאַסן-פֿויקער

זינגט דער פֿויגל פֿרײַ און פֿרײלעך,
ציטערט אױף זײַן טראָן דער מלך,
ציטערן איז ניט כּדאַי,
זינג איך, װי דער פֿויגל, פֿרײַ,
און געשװינד
װי דער װינט,
טאַנץ איך הפֿקר, טאַנץ איך בלינד,
גאַס-אַרײַן און גאַס-אַרױס! —
בין איך קראַנק און אַלט און גראָ,
װעמען אַרט עס — האַ-האַ-האַ !
פֿאַר אַ קופֿער-גראָשן בלױז
פֿויק איך, אַז די פֿויק זאָל פֿלאַצן
און איך דזשינדזשע אין די טאַצן,
און איך דרײ זיך רונד-אַרום —
דזשין, דזשין, בום-בום-בום.
דזשין דזשין בום !

קומט אַ מײדל אַ מכשפֿה,
צינדט זיך אָן אין מיר אַ שׂרפֿה,
נעם איך זיך נאָך װילדער דרײיען,
און איך פֿרעם צונױף די צײן.
און איך ברום :
— מײדל קום,
גיב די הענט, און נעם אַרום,
הײסער טאַנצט זיך עס צו צװײי.
ס׳האָט אַזאַ װי דו אַ שלאַנג
מיך פֿאַרלאָזן ערשט ניט לאַנג.
קרענקט דאָס האַרץ און פֿלאַצט פֿאַר װײי —
פֿויק איך אַז די פֿויק זאָל פֿלאַצן
און איך דזשינדזשע אין די טאַצן,

and whirl 'round and 'round—
clang, clang, boom, boom, boom,
clang, clang, boom.

Children are laughing merrily, heartily,
so I don't get depressed.
"Move it, children! Faster, hup, hup!"
Again I slap my head,
again I spit!
Anyway,
with a jump everything passes.
I'm used to everything bad,
so I pinch a piece of bread from my pocket
and slurp from my flask.
My blood burns and my sweat runs
and I beat my drum till it might burst,
and clash my cymbals
and whirl 'round and 'round—
clang, clang, boom, boom, boom,
clang, clang, boom.

And thus I tear through,
tear through and gnaw through
with my teeth, as through a wall,
over highways and byways and countryside,
with my teeth.
Chop the stone!
Chop the stone and stay alone!
Dog and bearer, rogue and wind—
untrammeled through foreign lands!
I have no coat, I have no shirt,
I have no wife or child.
I beat my drum till it might burst,
and clash my cymbals
and whirl 'round and 'round—
clang, clang, boom, boom, boom,
clang, clang, boom.

און איך דריי זיך רונד־ארום —
דזשין, דזשין, בום־בום־בום.
דזשין דזשין בום !

לאכן קינדער לוסטיק, מונטער,
פאל איך ניט ביי זיך ארונטער,
רירט זיך יונגען ! פלינקער — האָפּ !
נאָך א מאָל א זעץ אין קאָפּ.
נאָך א שפרייַ !
סייַ ווי סייַ
מיטן שפרונג גייט אלץ פאָרבייַ.
צוגעוווינט צו אל דאָס בייז,
קנייפ איך א שטיק ברויט פון מאָש
און איך זשליאָקע פון דער פלאש.
ברענט דאָס בלוט און רינט דער שוויים —
פויק איך אז די פויק זאָל פלאצן
און איך דזשינדזשע אין די טאַצן,
און איך דריי זיך רונד־ארום,
דזשין, דזשין, בום־בום־בום.
דזשין דזשין בום !

אָט אזוי זיך דורכגעריסן,
דורכגעריסן, דורכגעביסן
מיטן קאָפּ ווי דורך א וואנט,
איבער שטעג און וועג און לאנד
מיט די ציין —
האָק דעם שטיין !
האָק דעם שטיין און בלייַב אליין !
הונט און שלעפער, לומפ און וויינט.
הפקר, הפקר דורך דער פרעמד !
האָב איך ניט קיין ראָק, קיין העמד,
האָב איך ניט קיין ווייַב, קייַן קינד.
פויק איך אז די פויק זאָל פלאצן
און איך דזשינדזשע אין די טאַצן,
און איך דריי זיך רונד־ארום —
דזשין, דזשין, בום־בום־בום.
דזשין דזשין בום !

MANI LEIB
(pseudonym of Mani-Leyb Brahinski)
(born on December 20, 1883, in Niezhin, district of Chernigov;
died on October 4, 1953, in the Liberty Sanitarium of the Workmen's Circle
in Liberty, New York)

Wonder upon wonder,
everywhere, in everything!
In our black bread
and our white salt,

and in the blue water
that slakes our thirst,
and the red fire
that warms us with its glow,

and in the child's laughter
that echoes from its mother's lap,
and in little children
who grow up to be big.

Oh wonder upon wonder,
wonders without end;
and among all the wonders,
children, we sing!

The poet Mani Leib went around in our world like a big child with wide-open eyes, and everything he saw or heard elicited from him wonderment, new and previously unheard musical sounds, and a feeling of beauty:

In poor houses, there is so much beauty, he says in one of his poems. In another poem, we see him stand astonished as he says:

Beauty on the wandering earth
weeps ashamedly from every place;
I bring you a bottleful
of the beauty of the word.

320

"Beauty of the word"—he was the first in Yiddish poetry who conjured up from the Yiddish word all its musical charms and nuances, and gave us poems that before him had been different; who (as Itsik Manger puts it) announced that "the Yiddish word is on the way to a masterliness that can be compared to the great beauty in Yiddish literature." "But Mani Leib's poetry," Manger continues, "went one step farther…each motif that he touched with his finger began to vibrate with a finely nuanced melodiousness that was an absolute wonder."

Jacob Glatstein also writes: "No one before him had dared to handle Yiddish words so gently…a line of Yiddish carried on itself a yoke, like a camel. It never went out into the street without the protection of deep secrecy, wisdom, a wink, or a sly dig. He began to treat Yiddish words like little bells. He touched a word lightly and the word rang even before it spoke."

Not only words but also silence sings in him:

> *I ran from crazy outcries*
> *in the park. Now no one goes there.*
> *With my hands folded thus, with quiet weary steps*
> *I walk around on silent, empty avenues,*
> *and, weary from the moon's magical rays,*
> *I remain silent and trembling.*
> *I stand and listen, happy, and can understand*
> *why the rustling yellow leaves fall.*

The poet is happy. He can understand "why the yellow leaves fall," and the reader, just like the poet, is enveloped by the white, magical moon-rays and the quiet melody that comes from the falling leaves.

David Einhorn, the first great lyrical poet in modern Yiddish literature, also spoke admiringly about Mani Leyb's musicality and mastery of language: "To refine a folk language," he wrote, "to make it an instrument of beauty, is not easy. It's like polishing diamonds. Mani Leib, from the poor houses, gifted by God with sound, color, and word, with eyes open to everything that is beautiful, was able to make the Yiddish language an instrument for the finest and most delicate things, which is something that other folk languages have long had to wait for."

This mastery of language can be seen not only in his lyrical, purely individualistic poems but also in the social themes, in his ballads and children's poems, in everything that came from his God-blessed pen. His social poems, therefore, affect us not like those of Winchevsky, Edelshtat, and Bovshover, with their direct calls to battle, not with the groans and lamentations of Rosenfeld and Reisen, but with the sound of the words and with the deep impression of the poetic pictures that penetrate into our souls.

One of Mani Leib's poems about the sweatshop is often mentioned in literary criticism as one of the best creations of social poetry by our poets. How different it is from the formulaic shop poems, and yet—how strong and lasting the impression remains:

On Fifth Avenue, in a white building,
in a white building on the thirteenth floor,
girls sew and wait in the pallor of sorrow
for the lazy signal of the evening bell.

But the bell is sleeping lazily in a swamp of hours,
and the day lies ill in the stone of the wall.
The needles weep and lament wounds,
and the silk rustles, rustles in girlish hands.

White silk, pink silk, purple and blue,
and the needles weep softly, quiet and muffled;
and the sun in the windows, in the pallor of sorrow,
creeps along hot arrows of green dust.

And the needles weep and lament wounds,
and the silk rustles, rustles in girlish hand;,
and the day lies ill in the wounds of hours,
in girlish hands and the stone of the wall.

When one reads this poem, one feels the full sorrow of the seamstresses, "who wait in the pallor of sorrow for the signal of the evening bell," which "is sleeping lazily in a swamp of hours." By means of only sixteen lines, the poet paints a picture that engraves itself permanently in the soul of the reader. You even see that "the day lies ill in the stone of the wall," and hear the quiet weeping of the girls and their needles, which weep and lament wounds, and the silk, which "rustles, rustles in girlish hands."

* * *

Mani Leib was one of the group *Di Yunge* (The Young Ones), who appeared in American Yiddish literature before the first World War. Some of the other poets in the group were Zishe Landau, Reuben Iceland, and Abraham-Moyshe Dillon. Samuel Niger characterizes the group and their way in Yiddish poetry thus:

"They did not wish to work any longer in the thrall of social or national motifs. Their poetry was the opposite of that other kind that dominated in American Yiddish poetry when it was going out into the streets to the masses. At that time, poets didn't believe in pure, personal lyricism...so *Di Yunge* came and, as in all times of revolt, turned the stick over to its other side. They denied themselves social poetry, just as the older generation had not felt it was right to concern themselves with the individual."

The critic Noah Steinberg wrote in 1917: "Mani Leib is the truest poet among our new poets...incomparable individual charm sings out from him...Mani Leib is one of the first of us who has immersed himself in his own self."

We were not used to such lines in American Yiddish poetry as:

> *She plays. I weep. Her long, tremulous fingers,*
> *like pale countrymen yearning in the dark—*
> *yearningly they search and blunder about and find,*
> *and my children weep—they weep, my children.*

The readers may not understand who the woman is that is playing, and why the poet and his children weep, but he immediately feels that a true poet is speaking to him with his own language and his own rich interior world, and he receives them with curiosity and reverence.

With time, Mani Leib's poems became more laden with content, with Jewish folklore. In a conversation with Jacob Pat, Mani Leib explained: "For me, going to the source, to the wellspring of *yidishkeyt,* meant going to Jewish folklore. I went to the prayers of our mothers, to the purity of folksong, to the quality of idiom."

Mani Leib wrote a number of wonderful ballads in which he revived the folk figures Elijah the Prophet, the *lamed-vovniks*[51], and the wise men of Chelm. The poems are deeply Jewish in their content and poetically new in their form.

---

51. The legendary 36 hidden good men, because of whose goodness God allows the world to continue to exist

Mani Leib's talent sang out especially in his children's poems, which became the most beloved poetic creations in Yiddish schools throughout the world. Composers wrote music to them and famous painters painted illustrations for them. Children, young people, and many adults knew his beautiful poems by heart: *Blimelekh Krentselekh* (Little Wreaths of Flowers), *Yingl Tsingl Khvat*, *Der Fremder* (The Stranger), *Di Noyt* (Poverty), and many others. To this day, Mani Leib's poems are the most beloved creations among the Yiddish teachers in Yiddish schools.

When Mani Leib was sixty years old, the Yiddish cultural community in America (at the initiative of Jacob Pat) gave him a gift: a house in which he could live and work in comfort.

The last years of his life were very productive, though his old illness, tuberculosis, often chained him to his bed. His poems and sonnets, which he published in the *Forverts* and in literary magazines, elicited new praise and recognition for the poet. As people were preparing to celebrate his 70th birthday party, Mani Leib again became seriously ill and had to go to the Deborah Sanitarium and later to the Liberty Sanitarium, where he died on October 4, 1953.

A number of poets wrote poems in which they lamented the death of Mani Leib. Among them was H. Leivick, who wrote:

> *Your death I lament with the slender flute of your poems,*
> *and with their beauty I conceal my weeping.*
> *At the end, we were close brothers*
> *who swore that our poetry would not die.*

I Am...

I am Mani Leib, famous far and wide,
from Brownsville to Yehupets, far away.
All the cobblers say I'm a good cobbler,
and all the poets? I'm a good poet, they say.

                              *   *   *

A boy at the workplace, at the heavy cobbler's last,
on moonlit nights, long ago, long ago--
a poem like a prayer came to my heart,
and the awl fell away from my hand.

The first Muse came graciously
and kissed the cobbler boy's lips,
and I experienced the sweet shudder
that gave voice to the mute tongue.

And my tongue became a clear spring--
my song resounded to other places,
my narrow world became open to me,
and my bread and toil became sweet to me.

The cobbler boys, the faithful apprentices,
were amazed when I sang with gusto.
My song pleased their bitter hearts,
but they didn't know why I was singing.

And incited by the sorrow of their toil-filled life,
they kept on mocking me
and gave me a permanent nickname:
"*gram-shtram latutnik*[52]," "*gram-shtram* poet."

May you live and be well, my dear brothers,
my fellows of the workplace—it doesn't bother me.
In my heart is the Muse—in my breast are poems.
I go to poets to be a poet.

---

52. Patcher

איך בין...

איך בין מאַני לייב, ווייט און ברייט אַ באַוווּסטער,
פֿון בראָנזוויל ביז יעהופּעץ — העט;
מיט אַלע שוסטער — אַ גוטער שוסטער,
מיט אַלע פּאָעטן — אַ גוטער פּאָעט.

אַ ייִנגל ביַים ווערקשטעל, ביַי דער שוועֶרער קאָפּילע,
אין נעכט פֿון לבֿנות — אַ מאָל, אַ מאָל,
איז צו מיַין האַרצן אַרונטער אַ ליד ווי אַ תּפֿילה,
און פֿון דער האַנט איז געפֿאַלן די אָל.

דאָס איז גנעדיק די ערשטע מוזע געקומען
און געק שט די ליפּן ביַים שוסטעריונג,
און איך האָב יענעם זיסן שוויידער פֿאַרנומען,
וואָס גיט דאָס וואָרט צו דער שטומער צונג.

און מיַין צונג איז געוואָרן צו אַ קוואַל אַ קלאָרן,
און מיַין ליד האָט אויפֿגעהילכט ווי פֿון ניט־הי,
און מיַין ענגע וועלט איז מיר אָפֿן געוואָרן,
און זיס איז געוואָרן מיַין ברוֹיט און מי.

די שוסטעריונגען, די געטריַיע געזעלן,
זיי האָבן געגאַפֿט ווי איך זינג מיט גוסט.
זייער בימער האַרץ איז מיַין ליד געפֿעלן,
נאָר צו וואָס איך זינג האָבן זיי ניט געוווּסט.

און גערייצט פֿון אומעט אין מיזאַמען לעבן,
האָבן זיי מיט חוזק מיך אויסגעשפּעט,
און אויף אייביק אַ צונאָמען מיר געגעבן:
„גראַם־שטראַם לאַטוטניק", „גראַם־שטראַם פּאָעט".

איז זייט מיר געזונט, מיַינע טיַיערע ברידער,
ביַים ווערקשטעל מיט אַייך — גייט מיר ניט אַיַן.
אין האַרצן די מוזע, אין בוזעם לידער —
איך גיי צו פּאָעטן אַ פּאָעט צו זיַין.

And when I came to the poets,
a little bird just hatched from the egg,
they received me with great honor
and I became one of them.[53]

Ah poets, singers—free as the birds!
Inspired and pale and with our song
we sang of new beauties,
like beggars let loose at the fair.

We sang and drowned out the world,
our hearts overwhelmed by one tiny town after another,
We sang our lungs out and swallowed our hunger,
and not one of us has left this world.

And God, who feeds even the worm—
His grace to the poet was not great.
So I went back, barefoot and poor,
to my workplace to eat my bread and sweat.

And thanks to you, Muse, for your great gift,
though there's no bread in your granaries.
At the cobbler's last, with only pure intentions,
let me serve till my last hour.

And let my name be famous far and wide,
in Brownsville, Yehupets, and even farther,
and I'm thankful I'm not a poet who's a cobbler,
but a cobbler who's a poet.

At the Riverside

On the other side of the river, the sun has already set.
On the other side of the river, a girl is walking,
with yearning in her heart and tears in her eyes,
looking for girlish happiness.

---

53. In this and the next two paragraphs, Mani Leib appears to be alluding to his poetry group, *Di Yunge*

און אַז איך בין צו די פּאַעטן געקומען, —
אַ פֿויגל אַ קליינס און אַקאַרשט פֿון איי —
האָבן זיי מיט גרוים כּבֿוד מיך אויפֿגענומען,
און איך בין געוואָרן איינער פֿון זיי.

אַך, פּאַעטן, זינגער, ווי די פֿייגל פֿרייע ! —
באַגייסטערט און בלייך און מיט אונדזער ליד,
מיר האָבן געזונגען פֿון שיינקייטן נייע,
ווי די בעטלער הפֿקר אויף אַ יאַריד.

און מיר האָבן געזונגען און די וועלט פֿאַרקלונגען,
די הערצער באַצווונגען פֿון העק צו העק,
געריסן די לונגען און דעם הונגער געשלונגען, —
אַז ניט איינער פֿון אונדז איז פֿון דער וועלט אַוועק.

און גאָט, וואָס ער שפּייזט אַפֿילו דעם וואָרעם,
איז זיין גנאָד צום פּאַעט געווען ניט גרוים,
בין איך מיר צוריק אַוועק באַרוועס און אָרעם
צום ווערקשטעל עסן מיין ברויט אין שווייס.

און אַ דאַנק דיר, מוזע, פֿאַר דיין גרוימער מתּנה,
כאָטש אין דיינע שפּייכלערס איז קיין ברויט ניטאָ.
און ביי דער קאַפּילע נאָר מיט ריינער כּוונה
זאָל איך דיר דינען ביז מיין לעצטער שעה.

און מיין נאָמען זאָל זיין און ברייט און וויַיט אַ באַוווּסטער,
אין בראָנזוויל — יעהופּעץ און ווייטער, העט —
און אַ דאַנק, וואָס איך בין ניט קיין פּאַעט אַ שוסטער,
וואָס איך בין אַ שוסטער אַ פּאַעט.

ביַים טיַיך

אויף יענער זייט טיַיך איז די זון שוין פֿאַרגאַנגען,
אויף יענער זייט טיַיך איז אַ מיידל געגאַנגען
מיט בענקשאַפֿט אין האַרצן און טרערן אין בליק
צו זוכן איר מיידלשן גליק.

And seven times seven little blue flowers
she picks by the light of the moon
and throws them into the river's stream:
"Swim straight, my flowers, straight!"

"Swim straight to far away, to where the rivulets run—
my happiness you'll probably find there.
And when you find my happiness there,
swim back, little flowers, quickly!"

Night casts a fog over the river.
The girl stands bowed down at the riverside,
looks long, long at the rivulets,
and shrugs her shoulders wearily.

The rivulets run, run—
the flowers find nothing there;
no flower comes back.
Weep, little girl, you have no happiness!

Yiddish

The world is full of language,
for every creature speaks.
Each creature in its own way,
each sound a meaning seeks.

The clouds speak with thunder,
the sun with fire and flame,
the woods with trees a-rustle,
the ocean's sparkle speaks its name.

The beast knows only roaring,
the bird knows only song;
the springs just softly whisper,
the cornstalks hum along.

The flow'rs speak with perfume
and colors endless, bright;
the tiniest of insects
goes buzzing in the night.

און בלימעלעך בלויִנקע זיבן מאָל זיבן
האָט זי בײַ דעם שײַן פֿון לבֿנה געקליבן
און האָט מיטן שטראָם זיי געלאָזן אין טײַך :
— שווימט גלײַך, מײַנע בלימעלעך, גלײַך !

שווימט גלײַך, ווײַט אַהין, ווו די וואַסערלעך רינען,
מסתּמא מײַן גליק וועט איר דאָרטן געפֿינען,
און אַז איר וועט דאָרטן געפֿינען מײַן גליק —
שווימט, בלימעלעך, גיכער צוריק !

די נאָכט האָט דעם טײַך מיט אַ נעפּל פֿאַרצויגן.
בײַם טײַך איז דאָס מיידל געשטאַנען געבויגן
און האָט אין די וואַסערלעך לאַנג, לאַנג געקוקט
און שווער מיט די אַקסלען געצוקט...

די וואַסערלעך זײַנען גערונען, גערונען...
די בלימעלעך האָבן דאָרט גאָרנישט געפֿונען,
קיין בלימעלע איז ניט געקומען צוריק.
וויין, מיידל, דו האָסט ניט קיין גליק !

ייִדיש

די וועלט איז פֿול מיט ריידן, –
עס רעדט דאָך יעדע זאַך,
און יעדער אויף זײַן שטייגער,
און יעדער אויף זײַן שפּראַך.
דער וואָלקן רעדט מיט דונער,
די זון מיט פֿײַער–פֿלאַם;
דער וואַלד מיט גרינעם רוישן,
מיט ברויזן רעדט דער ים.
מיט ברומען רעדט די חיה,
דער פֿויגל – מיט געזאַנג;
מיט פֿליסטערן – די קוואַלן,
מיט שאָרכען רעדט די זאַנג;
מיט אַלע טויזנט פֿאַרבן
און ריחות רעדט די בלום;
די פֿליגעלע די מינדסטע
רעדט אויך מיט איר געזשום.

But Man, the crown of all the world,
the wise one, he alone
speaks every sort of language,
of plains and even stone.

In many different languages
he speaks to you and me,
and only his ears hear them
and only his eyes see.

Wherever there's a people,
a language is there too.
In England they speak English
as Russians Russian do.
In Spain it's charming Spanish,
Chinese in old Cathay,
Romanian in Romania,
in Turkey the Turkish way.

And Jews speak Yiddish
all through the great wide world,
wherever in their peaceful way
their banners are unfurled,
in Africa, the hot place
and Siberia, cold as space.*

And Jews speak Yiddish,
a language lovely, plain.
To understand another Jew
is easy, without pain.

---

* These last two lines are continuously sung with this poem, but are not shown here in the Yiddish text

דער מענטש נאָר מיט מיט זײַן חכמה –
פֿון אַלעמען די קרוין –
ער רעדט מיט יעדן לשון,
אויך פֿונעם שטיין פֿון פֿלוין.

אויף זיבעציק לשונות
פֿאַרשטייט דער מענטש און רעדט,
וואָס נאָר עס הערט זײַן אויער,
וואָס נאָר זײַן אויג דערזעט.

און ווי אַ פֿאָלק מיט מענטשן,
איז דאָ אַ שפּראַך בײַ זיי:
אין ענגלאַנד רעדט מען ענגליש,
און רוסיש אין ראָסײַ;
אין שפּאַניע רעדט מען שפּאַניש,
כינעזיש אין קיטאַי,
וואָלאַכיש אין וואָלאַכיע,
און טערקיש אין טערקײַ.

און ייִדן רעדן ייִדיש
אין אַלע עקן וועלט,
ווו נאָר אַ ייִד אין פֿרידן
שטעלט אויף זײַן רו־געצעלט.

און ייִדן רעדן ייִדיש,
און ייִדיש איז דאָך שיין,
און גרינג אַ צווייטן ייִדן
פֿאַרשטיין ווי זיך אַליין.

ZISHE LANDAU

(Born in Plotsk, Poland, in 1889; died in New York City in 1937.)

Zishe Landau was the "rebbe" of the group in Yiddish poetry that is known by the name *Di Yunge*, a group that led Yiddish literature out onto new artistic paths.

In 1906, when he was seventeen, Landau came to New York from his home city of Plotsk. He was descended from rabbis, *tsadiks*,[54] and scholars. Right after coming here, he made his literary debut with a poem in the socio-literary magazine *Tsaytgayst* (Spirit of the Times), which was published by the *Forverts* in those years. That poem, like other poems he published during the first five years after he came to America, was indeed in the spirit of the times: an emigrant's loneliness, yearning, the sweatshop, and struggle. Several years later, he became the *vegvayzer* [55] for *Di Yunge*, whose members were Mani Leib, Joseph Rolnik, Reuben Iceland, and others, and in their name he declared that with them, *Di Yunge*, true artistic poetry in Yiddish literature began.

In their writings, Landau and *Di Yunge* began a battle with the earlier poets from the previous generation, about whom they complained that they were more publicists than poets. Landau didn't even spare Peretz, and called him "the literatteur from Warsaw," because Peretz, like all other poets of his generation, was more concerned with the content than the form of poetry.

The first poems of *Di Yunge* indeed had little content, but they were distinguished by the beauty and musicality of the Yiddish word. When other poets later began making compromises and began joining beautiful form with content in their poems, Landau still sang about "porcelain marquis," "girls like half-moons," and "blue-green beads." Even he, however, came a bit later to poems that joined beauty to substance. He began to sing the praises of his ancestors, from whom he had inherited the greatest Jewish pedigree, and he wrote a series of magnificently beautiful poems about the Bal Shem Tov, Rabbi Naftoli Ropshitser, and the "Strikover Rebbetsin." He began immersing himself in Yiddish folk-poetry, and introduced a folksy Yiddish charm into his poems:

> *The dear queen in the story*
> *and I stroll o'er the land,*

---

54. Literally, saints; here referring to *hasidic* rebbes.
55. One who shows the way, the guide, the leader.

and the sweet, white billy kid
nibbles grass blades from my hand.

In the poem *For Our Destroyed Jewish Life*, written after the First World War, he virtually prophetically foresaw the great Jewish Holocaust of later years: "I weep for you, our mother Vilna, and for Kolomej and Brod." In another poem, he says: "And still you do not wish to see the day when Germany enslaves the world."

Landau, "The Man of Song," as he called himself, brought to Yiddish poetry a large number of beautiful pearls, which will remain in the rich treasure of our literature. His poem *In Der Fintster Zaynen Dayne Oygn Shener* (In the Darkness, Your Eyes are More Beautiful), was very widely read both here and in Europe.

I'm the Man of Song

I strolled through the city
and saw nothing at all,
as if before my eyes
there stood a blank wall.

No such wall was there, though—
the street was completely free.
Just houses, street, and people
that I'd chosen not to see.

It wasn't some deep sorrow
that blotted out my sun.
A spring inside my heart
had simply overrun.

And what I understood then,
what I then perceived,
was for my understanding
alone by Fate conceived.

My blood, a deep and flowing stream,
a river flowing free,
is one with generations
before and after me.

I've something more to tell you,
but telling would be wrong,
for you are men of action
and I'm the man of song.

For Our Destroyed Jewish Life

For the Jewish life we had, now destroyed,
I fall and pray for Your *gnod*![56]
I weep for our mother, Vilna,
for Kolomej and for Brod,

---

56. Grace or mercy

איך בין דער מאַן פֿון ליד

איך בין אין גאַס געגאַנגען
און גאָרניט ניט געזען.
ווי ס'וואָלט פֿאַר מײַנע אויגן
אַ גרויע וואַנט געוועזן.

ס'איז ניט קיין וואַנט געוועזן,
דער וועג געוועזן איז פֿרײַ,
נאָר גאַס און לײַט און הײַזער
גיי איך כּמעט פֿאַרבײַ.

ס'איז ניט געוועזן טרויער,
וואָס האָט מײַן ליכט פֿאַרשטעלט.
אין טיפֿעניש פֿון האַרצן
אַ קוואַל האָט אויפֿגעקוועלט.

און וואָס איך האָב פֿאַרנומען,
און וואָס איך האָב געהערט –
צו הערן און פֿאַרנעמען
איז מיר געוועזן באַשערט.

מײַן בלוט אַ שטראָם אַ טיפֿער,
אַ פֿאָדעם אָן אַ קנופּ,
איז איינס פֿאַר טויזנט דורות
איר פֿאָר, איר נאָך מײַן גרוב.

כ'האָב נאָך אײַך וואָס צו זאָגן,
נאָר זאָגן וועל איך ניט.
איר זײַט די לײַט פֿון מעשׂים,
איך בין דער מאַן פֿון ליד.

פֿאַר אונדזער חרובֿ ייִדיש לעבן

פֿאַר אונדזער חרובֿ ייִדיש לעבן,
פֿאַל איך און נעם פֿאַר דיַן גנאָד.
איך וויין אויף אונדזער מאַמע-ווילנע,
אויף קאָלאָמעע און אויף בראָד.

for Warsaw, Kovno, Kalish, and Lemberg,
for cities large and small ones too,
for all the enemy's destroyed so far
and the destruction to ensue,

for every dirty Jewish alley,
for every store I cry and mourn,
for every bar and pawnshop and tavern,
for every measure falsely sworn,

for every happy Jewish home
amid the homes of Gentile folk,
for everything that once was ours
that's gone and vanished in the smoke.

Clean and bright is all that's Jewish—
that modest life shall rise again!
Rock to sleep with quiet words
the saddened souls of men.

The Song of the White Kid

Unblemished as the moon,
like my mother's name white,
fresh as the streams of springtime,
I come to you tonight.

With words delicate, I tell
of distant vistas white as milk.
From pastures lush and green,
I bring the trembling silk.

The dear queen of the story
and I stroll o'er the land,
and the sweet, white billy kid
nibbles grass blades from my hand.

My gorgeous peacock now has spread
his golden wings above the plains.
The night lies locked up tight
and fear lies in its chains.

װאַרשע, קאָװנע, קאַליש, לעמבערג,
אױף גרױסע און אױף קלײנע שטעט,
װאָס ס׳איז דער שׂונא שױן באַפֿאַלן,
װאָס שפּעטער נאָך באַפֿאַלן װעט.

פֿאַר יעדן ייִדיש שמוציק געסל,
אױף יעדער קראָם װײן איך און קלאָג,
אױף יעדער שענק, לאָמבאַרד און קרעטשמע,
אױף אונדזער פֿאַלשער מאָס און װאָג;

אױף יעדן ייִדיש פֿרײילעך הײזל,
װאָס אין אַ גױיש שטעטל שטײט –
אױף אַלץ װאָס געװען איז אונדזערס
און מיט רױך אַצינד פֿאַרגײט.

ס׳איז רײן און העל אַלץ, װאָס ס׳איז ייִדיש!
דאָס אָר׳מע לעבן בױ צוריק!
און די פֿאַראומערטע נשמות
מיט אַ ניטדאַאיק װאַרט פֿאַרװיג.
(געשריבן בעת דער ערשטער װעלט–מלחמה)

דאָס ליד פֿון װײַסן ציגעלע

װײַס װי מײַן מאַמעס נאָמען,
װי די לבֿנה רײן,
פֿריש װי די פֿרילינגס–שטראָמען
קום איך צו אײַך צו גײן.

איך טראָג פֿון װערטער דינע
די מילך–פֿאַרהױכטע װײַס,
איך טראָג פֿון װעלדער גרינע
דאָס ציטערדיקע זײַד.

די מלכה פֿון דער מעשׂה
מיט מיר אינאײנעם שפּאַנט,
דאָס ציגעלע דאָס װײַסע
צופֿט גרעזולעך פֿון מײַן האַנט.

מײַן פֿאָװע האָט די פֿליגל
די גאָלדענע צעשפּרײט;
די נאַכט ליגט אונטער ריגל,
די שרעק ליגט אױף אַ קײט.

ISRAEL JACOB SCHWARTZ

(born on September 5, 1885, in Petroshun, in the Kovno district;
died on September 22, 1971, in New York)

In his great autobiographical poem, *Yunge Yorn* (Youthful Years), the poet tells how his father, the rabbi of the Lithuanian village of Petroshun, Rabbi Yitskhok Ayzik, sent him to America in 1906, accompanied by the words: "Be a Jew!" The young son and poet never forgot those words of his father's. They floated over him in the new and strange land and reminded him, not only of his father but of entire generations who had called out: "Don't forget our path through the world—be a Jew!"

Schwartz recounts:

> *Generations cried over me:*
> *"My child, remain a Jew.*
> *May your father's legacy and song*
> *be deeply observed in your heart."*

It was no time to sing about his father's legacy—the old way of life had collapsed and no new one had been created. There had been attempts: the Jewish socialist movement had looked for, and to some extent found, new forms of *yidishkeyt*, but Schwartz was afraid of them—he was afraid of a life in which all the traditions of generations of Jews were rejected, forgotten. In one of his first poems, he says:

> *No Sabbath candles*
> *are lit on your table...*
> *the grayness of the week*
> *never disappears from your house.*

> *Your children grow up strangers,*
> *without a spark of belief;*
> *you don't say "I confess"*
> *with them, with hands upraised.*

> *And your seder night*
> *has long not decorated your house;*

340

and the weeping of kol nidre
doesn't move your heart.

And therefore, when you die,
no angel will lament,
and your child won't say
kadish at your grave.

It was not easy to sing so Yiddishly and individualistically at the time when Schwartz entered Yiddish literature. It was the time of the social poem, of immigrant loneliness, of battle. When *Di Yunge*, a group that Schwartz joined, arrived, they exchanged the social poem for individualistic-romantic themes, but seldom for Jewish national ones.

In his essay about Schwartz, Jacob Glatstein points out correctly that "Mani Leib, Zishe Landau, Reuben Iceland, and Moyshe-Leib Halpern brought neo-Slavic and neo-Germanic tones to Yiddish poetry, but Schwartz remained faithful to the Hebrew and Yiddish poem, which received in him a good chemical mixing and became the rhythm of his blood and his thoughts."

For that reason, it is understandable that Schwartz devoted so much time and effort to translating and singing in Yiddish the poems of poets from medieval times: Shloyme Ibn Gavirol, Moyshe Ibn Ezra, and Yehuda Haleyvi. He later put together two anthologies of Sabbath-themed poems from the old and new literature, and repoeticized into Yiddish most of the poems of the great modern Hebrew poets Chernikhovski and Bialik.

Concerning those translations, Samuel Niger wrote that Schwartz was "successful in singing along with the poets. When one reads his Yiddish repoeticization of Bialik and other poets, one feels that it isn't just somehow poured from one vessel into another…No, it's played on a new instrument, and the player, the so-called translator, is part of the melody."

Schwartz's greatest contributions to Yiddish poetry are his American themes. He was perhaps the first who felt his deep roots in the new home:

My roots have burrowed into the depths
and new poems have rung out in my head.

He perceived not only the loneliness of the immigrant and his yearning for his old home, but also the beauty and splendor of the new home, and he began to celebrate them with previously unheard poems:

> *O great North America, strong earth,*
> *in the blessed plenty of your rich autumn,*
> *my heart is filled with a paean to you.*
> *God grant that your great tranquility shall not be disturbed,*
> *ever. I never grow weary*
> *of singing your splendor, fruitfulness, and plenty.*
> *One prayer I have in my heart, one plea:*
> *that your apples should taste of my poetry.*

The prayer was heard. Schwartz became the first poet who brought into Yiddish poetry the spaciousness of the American landscape; its fields and plantations; its Negroes, with their suffering and yearning; and the Jewish pioneers, with their struggle to root themselves in the New Earth. His *Kentucky* appeared in 1925 and was immediately recognized as one of the most significant works in Yiddish literature, and as the beginning of the Yiddish epic in America. Rivkin wrote correctly: "*Kentucky* is a book of earth and earthly beauty."

A Legacy

Generations have wept over me:
"My child—remain a Jew;
may your father's legacy and suffering
be preserved in your heart.

"I was not punished with gold,
but God gave me my spirit.
I carry many generations in me—
He doesn't deny us His grace.

"I am weary, I am old, you are young;
go forth—may God protect you, my child;
may your soul emerge still pure
from life's temptations and sin.

"Do not forget our course through the world—
be a Jew"…he said no more,
but his eyes shone and glowed
with hope and silent prayer.

In the synagogue, the eternal light burned
with its flickering, sorrowful light.
I bent over with awe and fear,
my face in the Holy Ark's curtain.

Parting

We've parted from our old home—
a storm wind has blown us here from far away.
Some have left an old mother behind,
and others their father's grassy grave.

But the hearts of all are pained,
and each is choked with silent tears,
has packs on his shoulders and children at his side,
in strange streets with memories from far away.

א ירושה

איבער מיר האָבן דורות געוויינט:
...„מיַין קינד, דו זאָלסט בליַיבן אַ ייִד.
זאָל דיַין טאַטנס ירושה און לייד
אין דיַין האַרצן טיף ווערן געהיט.

„כ'בין מיט גאָלד ניט געוואָרן געשטראָפֿט,
נאָר מיט גיַיסט האָט באַשאָנקען מיך גאָט;
איך טראָג דורות און דורות אין האַרץ,
ער פֿאַרמיַידט ניט פֿון אונדז זיַין גענאָד.

„איך בין מיד, איך בין אַלט — דו ביסט יונג,
גיי פֿאַרוים, גאָט באַשירעמט מיַין קינד;
און דיַין זעל זאָל געליַיטערט אַרוים
דורך נסיונות פֿון לעבן און זינד.

„ניט פֿאַרגעס אונדזער גאַנג איבער וועלט —
זיַין אַ ייִד". — ער האָט מער ניט גערעדט.
נאָר זיַין בליק האָט געלויכטן, געגלים,
מיט בטחון און שטילן געבעט.

ס'האָט אין שול דער נר-תמיד געצאַנקט
מיט זיַין ציטערדיק טרויעריק ליכט;
כ'האָב מיט יראה און אַנגסט זיך געבוינג,
אין פּרוכת פֿאַרהילט מיַין געזיכט.

צעשיידונג

מיר האָבן זיך פֿון אונדזער אַלטער היים געשיידט —
אַ שטורעמווינט האָט אונדז אַהער פֿון וויַיט פֿאַרווייט.
ס'האָט איינער ווו אַן אַלטער מאַמען דאָרט געלאָזן
און איינער האָט אַ טאַטנס קבֿר צווישן גראָזן.

נאָר איטלעך איינעם האָט דאָס האַרץ מיט ווי געדריקט
און איטלעך איינעם האָבן די אָבן טרערן שטום געשטיקט;
מיט פּעקלעך אויף די פּלייצעם, קינדער בײַ די זיַיטן,
אין גאַסן פֿרעמדע מיט זכרונות פֿון דער וויַיטן.

One has brought a packet of earth here,
or an old book that his grandfather shed a tear on,
with a silent sorrow, an age-old sorrow,
and echoes of heavy sighs in his ears

Torn away like a branch of an old tree,
we began to build our new home.
The old stock is back there, broken-hearted,
with the great, broad ocean between.

And like a young tree that sprouts
from a hard, cold cliff, without a mother's love,
one that takes along exhausted branches—
thus was our time of blossoming.

Years have gone by. New sap
has streamed with life through the saplings.
The roots have dug down deep
and new songs have rung out on its crown.

The New Home

The land here is fat and fruitful—
it bears treasures in its heart.
The land here is fresh with youth—
it's rich and big and smart.

The land here is full of riches:
iron, copper, steel, and gold.
Silvery waterfalls flow down quickly
from the mountains to valleys of old.

Our land has deep rivers;
fish-filled rivers are clear.
Its mountains reach to the sky
its valleys are fresh and dear.

The land is flooded with sunlight;
green are its broad fields.

און עמעץ האָט אַהער געבראַכט אַ בינטל ערד,
אַן אַלטן ספֿר פֿון זיַין זיַידנס אויג באַטרערט;
אַ שטילן צער, אַ דורותדיקן אַלטן טרויער,
אַ ווידערקול פֿון שווערע זיפֿצן אין זיַין אויער.

און אָפּגעריסן, ווי אַ צווײַג פֿון אַלטן בוים,
גענומען האָבן מיר זיך בויען אונדזער ניַיע היים;
דער אַלטער שטאַם איז דאָרט, דאָס האַרץ פֿאַרשניטן,
דער גרויסער, ברייטער ים־אָוקינוס אין דער מיטן.

און ווי אַ ביימעלע אַ יונגס, וואָס שפּראָצט אַרויס
פֿון האַרטן, קאַלטן פֿעלדז, אַן מוטערס שויס,
וואָס נעמט מיט צווײַגלעך מיט פֿאַרחלשטע זיך ציַין —
אַזוי איז דאָ געווען אונדזער ציַיט פֿון בליַין.

און יאָרן זיַינען זיך געלאָפֿן. ניַיע זאַפֿט
האָט דורכן שפּראָצלינגבוים געשטראָמט מיט לעבנסזאַפֿט;
די וואָרצלען האָבן זיך געגראָבן אין דער נידער
און אויפֿן קאָפּ געקלונגען האָבן ניַיע לידער.

די ניַיע היים

ס׳איז דאָס לאַנד דאָ פֿעט און פֿרוכטבאַר,
אוצרות טראָגט עס אין זיַין שויס;
ס׳איז דאָס לאַנד דאָ פֿריש אין יונגס,
ס׳איז דאָס לאַנד דאָ ריַיך און גרויס.

ס׳איז דאָס לאַנד דאָ פֿול מיט אוצרות —
איַיזן, קופּער, גאָלד און שטאָל;
ס׳פֿאַלן זילבער־וואַסערפֿאַלן
פֿון די בערג אַראָפּ אין טאָל.

אונדזער לאַנד האָט טיפֿע טיַיכן,
קלאָרע טיַיכן פֿול מיט פֿיש;
אירע בערג דערגרייכן הימלען,
אירע טאָלן זיַינען פֿריש.

ס׳איז מיט זון דאָס לאַנד באַגאָסן —
זיַינע פֿעלדער זיַינען גרין.

Quick and strong are its daughters,
proud and courageous the sons it yields.

Virginia gives its tobacco,
California, its wine,
and in Florida, oranges
glow red in the sunshine.

Ships steam in the harbors;
trade grows far and wide.
People come by the millions,
stream here from every side.

Its gigantic factories
never seem to tire.
From the Atlantic to the Pacific,
our great song rings out with fire.

Blue Grass
(from the poem *Kentucky*)

The broad plains of Kentucky—
I already feel their gentle breath,
their sun has already illuminated me,
and their trees have shaded me.
And I, a child of wandering
who has experienced God's world in Lithuania,
with its sad forests and charming blue rivers—
I, on the threshold of my youth,
find myself in the maelstrom of New York,
at the banks of the yellow Hudson
where all the broad world's currents
join together.
And I have learned to love
the great, eternal, wild restlessness:
I've been a spray from its waves,
a flash of its lightning.
It has become very dear to me,
with its winners and losers,

פֿלינקע, שטאַרקע — זײַנע טעכטער,
שטאָלץ און מוטיק — זײַנע זין.

ס׳גיט ווירדזשיניאַ איר טאַבאַקאָ,
קאַליפֿאָרניע — איר ווײַן,
און אין פֿלאָרידאַ — מאַראַנצן
גליִען רויט אין זונענשײַן.

אין די האָפֿנס דאַמפֿן שיפֿן —
ס׳בליט זײַן האָנדל גרוים און ווײַט,
און מיליִאָנען מענטשן קומען,
שטראָמען דאָ פֿון יעדער זײַט.

זײַנע ריזיקע פֿאַבריקן
ווערן קיין מאָל גאָר ניט מיד...
פֿון אַטלאַנטיק צום פּאַסיפֿיק
קלינגט איין גרוים רײזנליד !

BLUE GRASS
(פֿון דער פֿאַעמע קענטאָקי)

די ברייטע פֿלאַכן פֿון קענטאָקי —
שוין פֿיל איך זייער צאַרטן אָטעם ;
שוין האָט מיך זייער זון באַלויכטן,
און ס׳האָט מיך זייער בוים באַשירעמט.
און איך, אַן אייניקל פֿון וואָנדער,
וואָס האָט גאָטם וועלט דערשפּירט אין ליטע
מיט אירע אומעטיקע וועלדער
— און בלויע חנעוודיקע טײַכן —
איך האָב זיך אויף מײַן שוועל פֿון יוגנט
אין מאַלשטראָם פֿון ניו-יאָרק געפֿונען,
בײַם גרויסן ברעג פֿון געלן האָדסאָן,
וווּ ס׳גיסן זיך צונויף די שטראָמען
פֿון גאָר דער גרויסער וועלט דער ברייטער.
און כ׳האָב זיך אויסגעלערנט ליבן
דעם גרויסן אייביק ווילדן אומרו :
געוווען אַ שפּריץ פֿון זײַנע וואָלן,
אַ בליץ צווישן זײַנע בליצן.
ביז טײַער איז ער מיר געוואָרן
מיט זײַנע זינגער און באַזינגטע,

its fortunes and misfortunes,
its riches and poverty,
its stifled groans and rejoicing.
I love its rosy autumn in the parks
full of copper and bronze
and its warm blue skies.
I love the seashore in New Jersey,
where the waves pound eternally
and turn from green
to light blue and dark blue
topped with pearly peaks.
And now, when my hair is graying,
I stand on the Kentucky plains,
with their soft blue skies
and broad, endless distances,
with fresh, bright mornings,
broad green tobacco fields,
and blue meadows.
And in the nights, studded with nearby stars,
there come to my balcony
the whinnying of horses
and the soft and gentle sound of mandolins,
interrupted merrily
by the unique resounding laughter
of big, black Negro children.

מיט זײַנע אומגליקן און גליקן,

מיט זײַנע רײַכטימער און דלות,

מיט זײַן פֿאַרשטיקטן קרעכץ און יובֿל.

איך ליב זײַן רעזן האַרבסט אין פֿאַרקן

פֿון קופֿער און פֿון בראָנדז געגאָסן,

מיט זײַנע וואַרעם-בלויע הימלען.

איך ליב דעם ים-ברעג פֿון ניו-דזשוירזי

ווו אייביק שלאָגן אָן די וואַלן

און גיסן זיך פֿון גרין אַריבער

אין העל-בלוי און אין טונקל-בלויען

באַזוימט מיט פֿערלדיקע שפֿיצן.

און איצטער, ווען מײַן קאָפּ נעמט גרויען,

שטיי איך אויף די קעגנטאַקער פֿלאָכן

מיט זייער וווילכן בלויען הימל

און ברייטער, נישט-געצוימטער ווײַטסקייט,

מיט פֿרישע ליכטיקע פֿרימאָרגנם,

מיט גרינע ברייטע טאַבאַק-פֿעלדער

און לאָנקעס בלויעלעד-גרינע גראָזן.

און אין די נעכט, פֿאַרשטערנט-נאָענט,

דערגייט מיר דאָ אויף מײַן גאָניק

פֿון פֿערד דאָס הירזשן, און די קלאַנגען

פֿון מאַנדאָלינען, ווייכע, צאַרטע,

וואָס ווערן אונטערבר. אָכן לוסטיק

מיט אייגנאַרטיק הילכיק לאַכן

פֿון גרויסע שוואַרצע נעגער-קינדער.

MOYSHE NADIR

(pen name of Isaac Reiss)
(born in March 1885, in Narayev, eastern Galicia;
died on June 8, 1943, in Woodstock, New York)

I have many enemies—too many—
good, dear enemies!
I have feelings for you
like those for my own face.
There needs but be a word
between you and me,
and it cuts like a knife
the road between you and me,
the road that leads to your house.

But when you sigh and groan,
the bony knife hurts.
I'm a slave to the free word—
tears spurt from the silent goblet.

Yes, Moyshe Nadir made many enemies during the fifty years of his creativity. His "pen and rifle" didn't leave anyone out. In his poems, humoresques, feuilletons, books of theater reviews, essays, and articles, he fought with the whole world. But the biggest battle was the one he fought with himself. Only to his close friends and his lyrical poems did he entrust the fact that the same Moyshe Nadir who had so often and so arrogantly proclaimed to the world that "my hands have shed this blood" himself suffered greatly, and possibly caused more pain to himself than he did to others:

My washcloth sometimes knows the kind of deception
that takes place at the corners of my eyes.

In the same poem, Nadir tells how he boasted that his "soul often goes around without underwear," and that he wore

Colorful ties
and clothing of the finest wool.
I have the best table- and bed-manners

352

and women love my impudence,
my gray hat that sits so wantonly
on my young, gray head.

In his *Ani Mamin* (My Credo), which he wrote in 1940, several months after he had broken with the communist press, he tells about himself in true Nadiresque style:

> *What kind of dybbuk[57] possessed me, I cannot understand in retrospect. So manifoldly complicated is Man that he will often do things because he is afraid that they are beyond his strength. Chekhov has a story in which a man is supposed to have a duel with someone and is so afraid of death that he commits suicide. Whom did I not curse out, and at whom did I not energetically throw my suicidal pen? Perhaps it was my conscience that cried out: "Cry loudly and you won't hear how something is crying out loudly in me."*

And therefore, in the same confession, he pleads with everyone with whom he has waged war:

> *Forgive me, I beg you, if you can.*
> *I assure you that the whip that struck you*
> *has done more damage to me than to you.*
> *As I've said before:*
> *"Because it hurts me so much, I hurt you so much."*

But not everyone wanted to or could forgive Moyshe Nadir. Not everyone believed that this was now his real face and not a new mask, as L. Feinberg testified in his Introduction to the book *I Confess*, which was published after Nadir's death:

> *And when Moyshe Nadir saw the deep abyss before him, the bankruptcy of his dream of world salvation, and split with the movement to which he had devoted the most beautiful and fruitful years of his life, there were cynics, and even nasty people who again didn't believe him: "Hah! A new mask!"*

Forgiven or not, no one, it seems to us, denied that Moyshe Nadir was and has remained one of the most original and talented of the writers in modern Yiddish literature.

---

57. The spirit of a dead person that enters and controls a living person

He came to America as a young boy of thirteen, in 1898, with his parents and four siblings. "By my fourteenth year," he says in his *Moyde Ani* (I Confess), "I had already had a taste of the sweatshop, of poverty…in my life. I had served in all the occupations—I jumped from trade to trade."

It was difficult for the sensitive young boy Yitskhok Rayz (Isaac Reiss--Moyshe Nadir's real name) to forget his village Narayev and to find a place in big New York, where "nearly everyone is everyone's enemy and one has to enter life like entering the army: to fight." So in 1904 he went back to Europe, "where life at that time had, if not a more beautiful content, at least finer forms."

But he couldn't remain long in Europe either. As he writes, he began to long, not only for American bananas, tomatoes, and hot chocolate but also "for the democratic ways of the East Side, the glitter of Broadway, the American spaciousness and freedom."

In 1910, he, together with Jacob Adler (B. Kovner), began to publish a humor weekly, *Der Yidisher Gazlen* (The Jewish Brigand*)*. He also contributed to other humor weeklies. In 1915, his first book, *Vilde Royzn* (Wild Roses), appeared under his new name, Moyshe Nadir. It was not only a new name but a new style: miniatures that were, as he himself later put it, "wanton, sad, fresh, genteel coarseness." The book was very successful, and the name Moyshe Nadir became famous and even beloved. In 1918, he became a member of the staff of the Philadelphia daily newspaper *Di Yidishe Velt* (The Yiddish World), and later of *Der Tog* (The Day), where he wrote literary-philosophical miniatures in a column *Fun Mentsh Tsu Mentsh* (From Man to Man). In them were expressed not only wisdom but also great talent for wordplay and language renewal. When the communist *Morgn Frayhayt* began appearing, Nadir (together with Moyshe-Leib Halpern) was drawn into the communist web, and began to serve the "new God" with all his talent. Of course, true Nadir tones, which were lyrical and sentimental, shone through in his articles, poems, and humoresques, but he tried to suppress them "because I recognized my profound disbelief," as he recounted later about his communist years. "I forcibly hardened an iron belief, a steely discipline."

In 1926, Nadir spent nine months in Soviet Russia. There he saw "bureaucracy and poverty," but he didn't want to see them. As he tells it, he yelled at himself: "Communism may not be suitable for you, Moyshe Nadir; you love to work, eat, and sleep behind closed doors and curtained windows." But for most people, he continues, "freedom consists chiefly of the possibility of being free from absolute starvation and physical suffering…and they have no need of curtained windows." And he continued to serve communism with all his body and soul and with all his talent.

Only when the Hitler-Stalin pact of September 1939, which ignited World War II, became known did Moyshe Nadir leave the communists and begin to publish articles and poems of great regret. He explained at that time: "For each drop of blood that I have shed with my pen, I have paid with two drops of my own heart's-blood."

In one of his last poems, Nadir pleaded:

> *O hurry to me, friend Lord!*
> *My eye sinks, my pen falls.*
> *Who is dying in me? A stranger—*
> *only his hand is recognizable to me.*
> *I wait and wait alone—*
> *will God come toward me?*
> *At least two or three steps toward my doorstep?*
> *I carry snow-flowers to him in my soul.*
> *Shema Yisroel—the end of the poem;*
> *that's how every Jew must die.*

* * *

Concerning Moyshe Nadir's contribution to Yiddish literature and the Yiddish language, which he enriched, much has been written. We want to pause here at his song *Der Rebbe Elimeylekh*, which has been considered a folksong. Even by the year 1922, the folklorist and anthologist S. Bastomski had incorporated the song into his anthology in the Vilna *Pinkes* (Chronicle) (reprinted in *Baym Kval* [At The Well], Vilna 1923.) There it is listed as an anonymous folksong, received from someone in Soviet Russia in 1921. In M. Kipnis's 80 Folkslider (80 Folk Songs) (Warsaw, 1925), the song was also printed anonymously, as one received from someone in Bialystok. After that, it was printed in dozens of poetry anthologies, without an author. As late as 1969, the song was printed as an anonymous folksong in the anthology of Yiddish songs *Es Brent, Brider, Es Brent* (It's Burning, Brothers, It's Burning), which was printed (in German translation) in Berlin.

Emil Sekulets, the well known folklorist from Rumania (now living in Israel), in his book *Yidishe Folkslider* (Yiddish Folk Songs) (Budapest, 1959) writes that the song, with a musical arrangement by Z. Zilberts, first fell into his hands in 1948, and he found out that the author of the famous song was Moyshe Nadir. Incidentally, Sekulets also says that in Russia the song is sung in Russian, and that its name was changed from *Der Rebbe Elimeylekh* to *Dyadya*[58] *Eli*. Who the composer of the music was, says Sekulets, is still unknown.

Moyshe Nadir published the song in his book *A Lomp Oyfn Fentster* (A Lamp In The Window), which appeared in 1929 in New York. There, on page 4, we find the song *"The Rebbe Elimeylekh,* words and music by Moyshe Nadir." (In 1927, sheet music for the song was published in an arrangement by Abe Ellstein.) Anyone who knows a little about English folklore can easily recognize that Moyshe Nadir took the theme from the well known song *Old King Cole*. The first lines of the English song are: *"Old King Cole was a merry old soul, and a merry old soul was he. He called for his pipe and he called for his bowl, and he called for his fiddlers three."*

Moyshe Nadir's *Rebbe Elimeylekh*, however, is not a translation and is not even an adaptation of the English song. It is an original Yiddish song that was created, one might say, under the influence of the English song.

One of our readers, Moyshe Merenshteyn of the Bronx, has written correctly about this: "They say that Moyshe Nadir took his *Rebbe Elimeylekh* from the English folksong *Old King Cole*. But see what a wonderful Yiddish song he has made out of it, a song that was one of the most popular Yiddish folksongs because it was so truly Jewish and original."

Nadir's original text has been folklorized and has many variations. As far back as 1921, people apparently sang a folklorized version that was the most widespread one and was the most frequently reprinted one.

---

58. Russian for "uncle"

How Slowly

How slowly, how slowly I fall,
and how long
the last embers burn!
I'm a bit of the sun
that falls down
into the eternal Grand Canyon.

My song—
the last one;
sparkling head
of an empty well.

O life of mine,
O mother—
I'm as lonely
as a bunch of weeds
on the sand plains
of Utah;

as lonely as a dog
sleeping on the prairie;
as lonely as a nest
on a burned-down wall;
as lonely
as the May moon
over the silvery mountains
of Arizona.

ווי לאַנגזאַם

ווי לאַנגזאַם, ווי לאַנגזאַם איך פֿאַל !
און ווי לאַנג די לעצטע
האַלעװועשקעס ברענען !
איך בין אַ בלעטעלע מיט זון,
װאָס פֿאַלט אַראָפּ
אין אײביקײטס גרענד-קעניאָן.

מײן ליד —
דער לעצטער.
גלימצעדיקער קאָפּ
פֿון אַן אויסגעשעפּטן
קװאַל.

אַ, לעבן מײַנס,
אַ, מוטער,
איך בין אײנזאַם
ווי אַ בינטל װילדע גראָז
אויף די זאַמד-פֿעלדער
פֿון יוטאַ.

אײנזאַם ווי אַ הונט אַ שלאָפֿנדער
אויפֿן פּרײַרי-לאַנד ;
אײנזאַם
ווי אַ נעסט
אויף אַן אָפּגעברענטער
װאַנט.
איך בין אײנזאַם,
ווי די מײַ-לבֿנה.
אויף די
זילבער-בערג
פֿון אַריזאָנאַ.

I and Moyshe-Leib

Moyshe-Leib doesn't want to die in Zlotshev—
I don't want to die anywhere.
He'll have to die, Moyshe-Leib,
in Zlotshev or *somewhere.*

The hour will come—
the lights in our eyes will go out
even though we have such fine bows
for the fine fiddles.

That, my dear comrade, will be
the quiet end of both of us.
The same end, Moyshe-Leib,
as with *my* grandfather and *your* grandfather.

The sun will stand still,
and all the radiant girls,
and we'll have to be so good
as to close our eyes.

The Rebbe Elimeylekh

When the Rebbe Elimeylekh
started getting very *freylekh*[59],
very *freylekh* started getting Elimeylekh.
So he put his festive hat on,
and his satin gown brand new
and he sent for his fiddlers, the two.

And the fiddle-happy fiddlers
fiddled oh so happily,
oh so happily they fiddled all night long.
And the fiddle-happy fiddlers
fiddled oh so happily,
oh so happily they fiddled every song.

---

59. Literally, "happy"—here implies "drunk." The Yiddish word is retained to create an otherwise impossible rhyme.

איך און משה-לייב

משה-לייב וויל ניט שטאַרבן אין זלאַטשעוו.
איך וויל ניט שטאַרבן אין ערגעץ.
מען וועט מוזן שטאַרבן, משה-לייב,
אין זלאַטשעוו אָדער אין ערגעץ.

די שעה וועט קומען, וועט אויסגיין
די זון אין אונדזערע אויגן,
כאָטש מיר האָבן צו פֿײַנע פֿידלען
אַזוינע פֿײַנע בויגנס.

דאָס וועט זײַן, מײַן ליבער חבֿר
דער שטילער סוף פֿון אונדז ביידן.
דער זעלבער סוף, משה-לייב,
וואָס פֿון מײַן זיידן, און דײַן זיידן.

מ׳וועט לאָזן שטיין די זון
און אַלע ליכטיקע מוידן,
און מ׳וועט מוזן אַזוי גוט זײַן
און צומאַכן די אויגן.

דער רבי אלימלך

אַז דער רבי אלימלך איז געוואָרן זייער פֿריילעך,
איז געוואָרן זייער פֿריילעך אלימלך.
האָט ער אָנגעטאָן דאָס היטל, און דעם שבתדיקן קיטל,
און געשיקט נאָך די פֿידלער די צוויי.

די פֿידלדיקע פֿידלער האָבן פֿידלדיק געפֿידלט,
און פֿידלדיק געפֿידלט האָבן זיי.
די פֿידלדיקע פֿידלער האָבן פֿידלדיק געפֿידלט —
אָט די פֿידלדיקע פֿידלער די צוויי.

When the Rebbe Elimeylekh
started getting yet more *freylekh,*
yet more *freylekh* started getting Elimeylekh.
So he took off all his *tfiln*[60]
and put on his reading *briln*[61]
and he sent for his drummers, the two.

And the drumming-happy drummers
drummed away so happily,
oh so happily they drummed the whole night long.
And the drumming-happy drummers
drummed away so happily,
oh so happily they drummed their merry song.

When the Rebbe Elimeylekh
started getting still more *freylekh,*
still more *freylekh* started getting Elimeylekh.
So he said his pray'r *havdole*[62]
with his colleague Reb Naftole,
and he sent for his cymb'lists, the two.

And the cymbal-happy cymb'lists
cymbaled oh so happily,
oh so happily they cymbaled all night long.
And the cymbal-happy cymb'lists
cymbaled oh so happily,
oh so happily they clanged their lusty song.

When the Rebbe Elimeylekh
started getting very *freylekh,*
very *freylekh* started getting Elimeylekh.
So he yawned a mighty yawn,
said: "Enough, it's nearly dawn,"
and he sent all the players back home.

But the Rebbe's drunken players
didn't want to end their night,
so they danced around the floor with all their might.

---

60. Phylacteries
61. Glasses--the Yiddish word is retained to create an otherwise impossible rhyme.
62. The prayer that ends the Sabbath

אַז דער רבי אלימלך,

איז געוואָרן זייער פֿריילעך,

איז געוואָרן זייער פֿריילעך, אלימלך,

ער האָט אויסגעטאָן די תּפֿילין,

און אויסגעווישט די ברילן.

און געשיקט נאָך די פֿידלער די צוויי.

די פֿידלדיקע פֿידקלער, וכו׳.

אַז דער רבי אלימלך,

איז געוואָרן זייער פֿריילעך,

איז געוואָרן זייער פֿריילעך אלימלך,

האָט ער אָפּגעמאַכט די הבֿדלה,

און דער גבאי ר׳ נפֿתּלי,

איז געלאָפֿן נאָר די צימבלער די צוויי.

די צימבלדיקע צימבלער, וכו׳.

אַז דער רבי אלימלך,

איז געוואָרן זייער פֿריילעך,

איז געוואָרן זייער פֿריילעך אלימלך,

ער האָט געטאָן אַ גוטן גענעץ

און געזאָגט: „מ׳דאַרף שוין מיין ניט!"

און געשיקט די קאָפּעליע אַהיים.

די שיכּורע קאַפּעליע פֿון רבין מלך־עליע,

האָט אויסגעשטעלט דעם דלות אַ פֿייג.

די פֿריילעכע קאַפּעליע האָט געהאָפּקעט ביז דער סטעליע

און זיך פֿאַרביטן מיט די קלאַפּער־געצייג.

די פֿידלדיקע פֿיקער האָבן צימבלדיק געפֿידלט,

און בראָנפֿנדיק גענאָסן זיך מיט וויין.

די לוסטיקע קלעזמאַרים מיט פֿלעשער אונטערן אָרעם,

האָבן געהוליעט ביזן העלן טאָג אַריין.

And they got their tools mixed up,
didn't know the down from up,
and they played all the rest of the night.

And the fiddle-happy drummers
fiddled oh so cymbal-ly,
oh so cymbal-ly they fiddled all night long.
Drank the whiskey, drank the wine,
feeling oh so very fine,
and they kept on playing happy, lusty song.

ZALMEN SEGALOWICZ

(born on February 26, 1884, in Bialystok;
died on February 19, 1949, in New York)

It is symbolic that the last creation that came from Zalmen Segalowicz's pen was a story about how lonely he felt in the big, multimillion-person city of New York. Several days after his sketch about the telephone that didn't ring was printed in the *Forverts,* the poet suddenly died in his New York hotel room, which was the last stop in his wanderings throughout the world.

Eybik Eynzam (Ever Lonely)—that's what Segalowicz called an autobiographical novel that he published in Warsaw at precisely the time when his popularity was the greatest that a Yiddish writer could hope for. All reports from the hundreds of libraries in the cities and town of Poland in the years between the two World Wars show that Segalowicz's book were the most widely read. His novels *Ever Lonely*, *Dos Anarkhistishe Meydl* (The Anarchist Girl), and *Undzer Froy* (Our Wife), from the trilogy *Zelik's Yorn* (Zelik's Years*)*, just like his other novels and stories *Di Vilde Tsilke* (Wild Celia), *Roykh Fun a Lyulke* (Pipe Smoke), *Shmendriks* (The Foolish Ones), and many others were grabbed up by thousands of young readers. No less popular were his romantic poems and longer poems, such as *In Kazmerzh* (In Kazmerzh[63]), *Regina, Reyzele Dem Shoykhets* (Reyzele The Slaughterer's Daughter), and others.

But he always felt lonely, alone.

Professional literary critics did not recognize Segalowicz. They threw up to him that his writing was too light, that he catered to the tastes of petit bourgeois girls and boys who were not interested in the burning problems of life but only in their personal feelings and experiences. "One doesn't feel in his work," one critic wrote, "the pulse of this turbulent era." Another critic wrote that "Segalowicz rocks the reader to sleep with sentimental tones, doesn't arouse deeper feelings in him, and doesn't aim for the heights." What was most criticized was Segalowicz's prose, the novels and stories. With respect to his poetry, even such a hard, sharp critic as I. Rappoport believed that "he has left his mark on Yiddish poetry." Rappoport strongly praised his poem *In Kazmerzh,* saying that it was "something new in Yiddish poetry, a true romantic creation whose verses sparkle and flow like the waves of the Vistula on a moonlit night."

---

63. Name of a village in Poland

Leo Finkelstein wrote about that same poem that with it "the poet has purchased citizenship in Yiddish literature."

The poet and critic Melekh Ravitsh wrote: "In my opinion, Segalowicz is first of all a poet...his poem-cycles *In Kazmerzh* and *Regina* are pearls of Yiddish lyricism." Segalowicz's ballad *Reyzele The Slaughterer's Daughter*, which the poet wrote in 1910, was also received with great praise by readers and critics. A melody was put to it, and though it has many verses, the song was sung a lot.

People also sang many of Segalowicz's other songs. Boys and girls liked to sing his *Mirke's Libe* (Mirke's Love), which begins with these verses:

> *Dark black eyes are full of fire—*
> *yours are black, my dear.*
> *And you've hurled great sparks of fire*
> *into my heart, I fear.*

> *Call me Judith or Shulamis,*
> *seek me far and near.*
> *A bold young man is what I crave—*
> *if you are bold,come here.*

Also very popular was his poem:

> *Who is singing there on the other shore—*
> *who is singing so secretly?*
> *Young shepherdesses*
> *are driving their herds home.*

Segalowicz loved the Polish countryside, the Vistula, the mountains, and the valleys, which now every poet saw, but for him they were a constant poetic inspiration. In *In Kazmerzh,* his love for that countryside is expressed in a highly artistic way when he says:

> *There mountains snake along, full of sweet valleys,*
> *many green tunnels overgrown with forests;*
> *a clear spring speaks to us of youth,*
> *though the village and everything here are old.*

> *I don't know why I have such yearning—*
> *my youth was passed in the smoky city.*

The noise of the city attracts me to the rustling of the trees—
in the forest I am calm, in the fields I am free.

I love to have the sky over my head,
the open sky, a blanket of blue—
I love to bend the flowers in the evening,
in the evening when they drink their fill of dew.

This sentimental and romantic poet was destined to become the lamenter and be-wailer of our great Holocaust. The carefree singer of *Reyzele The Slaughterer's Daughter*, *Mirke's Love*, and the loves of boys and girls in Jewish Poland was transformed into the great scribe of the Jewish people. Through burning cit-ies and countries, the poet saved himself and lived in Tel-Aviv during the War. During those seven years, a witness recounts, "he went around like a mourner, didn't go to the movies or theater, and also avoided cafes with music. His newer works, not yet published anywhere, he recited from the manuscripts. His listen-ers were professors from the Jerusalem universities, poets, lawyers, students, and ordinary people. Through his recited poems, he transmitted to his listeners his sorrow and his mourning for the tortured Jews of Poland.

His lengthy poems *Nishto Itster Dortn* (Not There Now) and hundreds of oth-ers were living headstones for the unmarked graves of his beloved Polish Jews. "With songs of mourning," writes Jacob Glatstein, "Segalowicz gave Yiddish great consolation and wrote a Yiddish *Lamentation* into our ancient book." And Samuel Niger summarizes the poet's life with the following evaluation: "Sega-lowicz did not change in essence. The air was shaken as if by an earthquake, and the *leitmotif*[64] of his poetry and prose suddenly became deeper, broader, higher…the weeping of generations became his. The poet was torn out of his own life's ground; waves of chaos seized him, and he heard in himself--and we all heard-- his new and mighty, but also not silent and still true, voice from out of the depths."

---

64. Theme

Reyzele, the Slaughterer's Daughter
(fragment)

Reyzele the slaughterer's daughter is beautiful
has a youthful, carefree heart.
She sings and enjoys life,
as a swallow enjoys the morning.
Her hair crowns her head,
her eyes are full of charm—
she's always proud,
won't bow down to anyone.
Reyzele the slaughterer's daughter is beautiful—
everyone admires her.
More than one mother wishes
she would be her son's bride.

But the slaughterer is pious
and is also quick to anger.
When his daughter combs her hair,
he starts to bite his lips.
Her singing while combing
and her laughter annoy him.
He quarrels with her mother
because she stands up for Reyzele.
"She's completely spoiled," he says.
But Reyzele knows no worries—
she wants to sing and dance.
So the slaughterer gets full of fear
when his daughter goes strolling—
he's sure that Satan will seduce her in the end.

Every little flower has its Spring!
Reyzele is growing up more and more.
Rains fall, winds blow—
she's always free and merry.
She comes to her mother
and entrusts her with a sweet secret,

רייזעלע דעם שוחטס

(פראגמענט)

שיין איז רייזעלע דעם שוחטם,
האָט אַ יונג האַרץ אַן זאָרגן,
זינגט און פֿרייט זיך מיטן לעבן,
ווי אַ שוואַלב מיט דעם פֿרימאָרגן.
עם באַקרוינען איר די לאָקן,
פֿול מיט חן זײַנען די אויגן,
און אַ שטאָלצע איז זי שטענדיק
ווייל פֿאַר קיינעם זיך ניט בייגן.
שיין איז רייזעלע דעם שוחטם,
עם באַוווּנדערן זי אַלע —
ניט איין מאַמע וועט זיך ווינטשן,
זי זאָל זײַן איר זונם אַ כּלה...

נאָר דער שוחט איז אַ פֿרומער
און דערצו אַ גרויסער פֿעסן,
ווען זײַן מאַכטער קעמט די לאָקן,
הייבט ער אַן די ליפן בײַסן.
עם פֿאָרדריסן אים די לידער,
וואָם זי זינגט בעתן קעמען,
עם פֿאָרדריסט אים איר געלעכטער...
און ער קריגט זיך מיט דער מאַמען,
ווײַל די מאַמע האַלט מיט רייזלען
— דו צעלאָזסט זי עם אין גאַנצן !...
רייזל אַבער ווייסט קיין זאָרג ניט :
זי וויל זינגען, זי וויל טאַנצן.
איז דער שוחט פֿול מיט מורא,
ווען זײַן מאַכטער גייט שפּאַצירן;
ער איז זיכער, אַז דער שׂטן
וועט זי סוף-כּל-סוף פֿאַרפֿירן...

יעדעם בלימל האָט זײַן פֿרילינג !...
רייזל וואַקסט דערווײַל מער אונטער.
ס'גיסן רעגנם, ס'בלאָזן ווינטן —
זי איז שטענדיק פֿרײַ און מונטער.
אָפֿט מאָל קומט זי צו דער מאַמען
און פֿאַרטרויט אַ סוד אַ זיסן,

and her mother pleads fearfully:
"Just don't let your father know!"
And her father knows nothing as yet.
But everyone in Kazmerzh knows:
Reyzele is going with Motele,
and is already called "Motl's bride."

Gone
(fragment)

We are sick from not forgetting.
We must weep and trust—
the emptiness of the "gone"
will press on us and crush us.
Gottlieb, Schipper, and Stern are gone,
and Aaron Einhorn, the wise.
Stupnitski is also gone--
the editor Uger, from Lodz, is gone.
Menakhem Kipnis, such a fine fellow—
I can still hear him singing *Brayne*;
a fine fellow and dear storyteller,
with all his folk tunes.
Yiddish actors, many groups,
all of whose names are dear to me.
Gone is Isaac Somberg—
such a talent, so much fire!
Such a talent, Abraham Ostshega,
with his Jewish sculptures.
I see and feel it constantly—
a world wiped away without a trace.

Gone the pious Hillel Zeitlin
and his son, my friend Elkhanon.
The peoples won't blush—
and again Jesus and the Madonna.
And again the brain struggles
with science for the murderers.
Where shall we get the strength and super-strength
to slap the world in the face?

און די מאַמע בעט מיט פּחד :
— זאָל דער טאַטע כאָטש ניט וויסן !
און דער טאַטע וווייסט נאָך גאָרנישט.
נאָר אין קאַזמערזש וווייסן אַלע :
רייזל גייט אַרום מיט מאַטלען
און זי הייסט שוין „מאַטלס כּלה".

נישטאָ

(פֿראַגמענט)

מיר זײַנען קראַנק פֿון ניט פֿאַרגעסן,
מיר מוזן וווינען און פֿאַרטרויען,
עס וועט אונדז פֿרעסן און צעפֿרעסן
די ליידיקייט פֿון די „נישטאָען"...
נישטאָ מער גאָטליב, שיפּער, שטערן,
און אָהרן אײַנהאָרן דער קלוגער.
סטופֿניצקי אויך נישטאָ שוין מערער,
נישטאָ פֿון לאָדזש רעדאַקטאָר אוגער.
מנחם קיפּניס, אַזאַ וווילער —
איך הער נאָך איצט זײַן זינגען : „ברײַנע",
אַ יאַט, אַ טײַערער דערצײַלער
מיט אַלע פֿאָלקס-ניגונים זײַנע.
אַקטיאָרן ייִדישע, פֿיל קרײַזן,
וואָס יעדער נאָמען איז אונדז טײַער,
נישטאָ שוין מער דער סאַמבערג אײַזיק —
אַזאַ טאַלאַנט, אַזוי פֿיל פֿײַער.
אַזאַ טאַלאַנט... אַבֿרהם אָסטשעגאַ
מיט זײַנע ייִדישע סקולפּטורן...
איך זע און זע עס פֿיל יעדער רגע :
אַ וועלט פֿאַרוויישט פֿון אַלע שפּורן.

נישטאָ דער פֿרומער הלל צייטלין,
דער זון זײַנער, מײַן פֿרײַנד אלחנן.
די פֿעלקער וועלן זיך נישט רוימטלען —
און ווידער יעזום און מאַדאָנאַ.
און ווידער מאַטערט זיך דער מוח
מיט וויסנשאַפֿט פֿאַר די גזלנים...
וווּ נעמט מען קראַפֿט און איבער-כּוח
אַ פּאַטש צו טאָן דער וועלט אין פּנים ? ...

My heart is over-filled with names:
Ringelblum, the historian.
Oh how much joy and how many names
wiped away, with their wives and children—
my lovable neighbor Zagan
and Mikhl Klepfisz, who achieved a great reputation,
and Lazar Klog and Liss and Kagan—
came from the people and died with the people.

And Man! How will you
greet Nature and boast
of your initiative and knowledge?
O world! If you don't hear us
and help us with our revenge,
may you, like we, be destroyed
by murder and war.

Mirke's Love (Black Eyes)
(fragment)

Dark black eyes are full of fire—
yours are black, my dear.
And you've hurled great sparks of fire
into my heart, I fear.

Call me Judith or Shulamis—
seek me far and near.
A bold young man is what I crave—
if you are bold, come here.

Only bold boys will I flirt with,
toying with their joy.
You I'll torture with my love,
then conquer—you're no boy!

Your gifts to me and your flow'rs
I gave away today.
I have told just everyone
of your mischievous way.

מײַן האַרץ איז איבערפֿולט מיט נעמען:
דער רינגעלבלום — געשיכטע־שרײַבער.
אוי, וויפֿל פֿרייד און וויפֿל נעמען
אַראָפּגעוויישט מיט קינדער, ווײַבער,
דער האַרציקער, דער שכנא זאַגאַן
און מיכל קלעפּפֿיש — רום דערוואָרבן,
און לאָזער קלאַג און לים און קאַגאַן —
פֿון פֿאָלק אַרויס — מיט פֿאָלק געשטאָרבן.

און מענטש! ווי וועסטו זיך באַגריסן
מיט דער נאַטור, און ווי זיך גריסן
מיט אינטוזיע און מיט וויסן...
אַ, וועלט! אויב דו וועסט ניט דערהערן —
ניט העלפֿן אונדז אין דער נקמה —
זאָלסטו, ווי מיר, פֿאַרטיליקט ווערן
פֿון מערדערײַ און פֿון מלחמה...

מירקעס ליבע

(פֿראַגמענט)

שוואַרצע אויגן האָבן האַבן פֿײַער —
דײַנע זײַנען שוואַרץ,
האָסט געוואָרפֿן הייסע פֿונקען
אין מײַן מיידלש האַרץ.

רופֿסט מיך יהודית, רופֿסט שולמית,
זוכסט מיך אומעטום —
איך האָב ליב אַ דרײַסטן בחור,
ביסטו דרייסט, דאָן קם!

נאָר דעם דרייסטן וועל איך רייצן,
שפּילן מיט זײַן גליק;
כ׳וועל דיך פֿײַניקן מיט ליבע,
זײַ אַ העלד — באַזיג!

דײַנע בלומען און מתּנות
האָב איך הײַנט צעטיילט,
דײַנע ווילדע שטיפֿערײַען
אַלעמען דערציילט.

Now the girls will laugh at you
and say: "Call me no more."
Now you'll sit long hours and wait
outside my cottage door.

But you simply do not see
me gaze at you all day.
You're my love, and dear to me,
though now I have my way.

You have gone away from me—
all peace has left me too.
Others come, but none of them
is dear to me like you.

Can it be my lovely dream
has made a fool of me?
Can it be you will not come--
I'll have to wait and see.

With the colors of my sorrow,
I have painted you.
But your eyes, your dear black eyes,
they burn me through and through.

You'll yet come and you'll yet feel
the yearning I feel here.
Dark black eyes are full of fire,
and yours are black, my dear.

איצטער וועלן אַלע מיידלעך
אָפּלאכן פֿון דיר,
איצטער וועסטו לאַנגע שעהען
װאַרטן ביַי מיַין טיר...

נאָר דו זעסט נישט; דורכן פֿענצטער
לויפֿט דיר נאָך מיַין בליק;
ביסט מיר ליב נאָך, ביסט מיר טיַיער,
כאַטש איך קװעל פֿון זײג.

ביסט אַװעק... נאָר נישט געפֿונען
האָב איך מער מיַין רו;
ס׳קומען אַנדערע, נאָר קיינער
ליבט מיך ניט װי דו.

קען דאָס זיַין דען, אַז מיַין חלום
האָט מיך אָפּגענאַרט?
קען דאָס זיַין, דו זאָלסט נישט קומען?
װיפֿל טעג איך װאַרט...

מיט די פֿאַרבן פֿון מיַין אומעט
מאָל איך אויס דיַין בילד,
נאָר די אויגן, דיַינע אויגן
ברענען אַזוי װילד...

װעסט נאָך קומען, װעסט נאָך פֿילן,
װי עס בענקט מיַין האַרץ;
שװאַרצע אויגן האָבן פֿיַיער —
דיַינע זיַינען שװאַרץ...

ISAAC KATZENELSON

(born in 1886 in Karelitz, district of Minsk; lived and worked in Lodz;
died in Auschwitz in 1944)

I believed you, heavens, celebrated you
in my every poem, my every song.
I loved you as one loves a woman—
she's gone now, dissipated like foam.
When I was very young,
I compared the sun to my hopes;
thus do my hopes fade away,
thus is my dream extinguished.

So sang the poet Isaac Katzenelson, who, together with his wife and their three sons, was driven from his home city Lodz into the Warsaw ghetto and then into the concentration camps of southern France, from which he was sent to Auschwitz.

In the ghetto and the camps he was destined to see and live through a sunset that was very different from the one he had celebrated in his youth, in the famous poem *Di Zun Fargeyt in Flamen* (The Sun Sets in Flames), which was one of the most beloved songs of Jewish youths in Poland. He saw the downfall of his people, and very different poems ripped themselves out of his soul, poems that will remain the most powerful accusations against the world that permitted the cruel destruction of his people.

Until the outbreak of the second World War, Katzenelson was famous as a Hebrew-Yiddish dramatist and a poet whose poems bubbled with the lust for life and with love of Nature and Jewish children. Some of his children's poems were included in his anthology *Gezang un Shpil* (Songs and Games) (Warsaw, 1920), one of the earliest song and game collections for Jewish children, with music by Israel Glatstein. The poems were sung by thousands of Jewish children in Poland, the same children that he saw later when they were

The first to die, the Jewish children, all of them;
mostly without parents, ravaged by cold, hunger, and suffering;
holy Messiahs, sanctified by suffering.

These were his children, who used to play unworriedly and sing the songs he had created for them:

> I am a little tailor,
> and they call me Mister Big Guy.
> This is how I draw a thread
> through a needle's eye.

> I am a little cobbler,
> and they call me Reb Mikhl.
> This is how I take the awl
> and poke it through the shoe.

These were the same little children he had taught to play "creatures":

> I am a little bee,
> I am a little eagle.

and

> I am a little angel,
> and I've come from Heaven.
> I'm looking for a little child
> who's sleeping sweetly.

It was his little angels that he saw abandoned by God, and he called on Heaven to open and let in "the children of my tortured, murdered people, because each of my children, killed, can be a god for them."

Some twenty years earlier, he had arranged those little Jewish children in rows to go on a happy, singing, march. He used to consider each child a dear treasure, and he says mischievously:

> One and two
> and three and four—
> what we are
> we are, not more.

And here, in the ghettos of Lodz, Cracow, and Warsaw, and in the Vitel and Drancy concentration camps, and in Auschwitz, he had had to look on as the "best in the world, the most beautiful that the dark world possessed," a million Jewish children, were killed.

The Katzenelson family was famous in pre-War Lodz. The poet's father, Jacob Benjamin, was himself a Hebrew-Yiddish writer and a founder of the Hebrew-Yiddish schools and orphan asylums. The school in Lodz was built on the most modern pedagogical foundations, and Isaac was the one who put together the poems, stories, and games for the students. He wrote Hebrew textbooks, wrote plays and directed them with the children, grew close to the pioneer movement, and twice visited Palestine, where he lived on a kibbutz and took an active part in its cultural work.

Katzenelson's Hebrew and Yiddish dramas were staged by the Habimah in Moscow, by Rudolf Zaslavski, by the Vilna Troupe, by Peretz Hirshbein, by Maurice Schwartz (*Fatima*, November 1920, in the Irving Place Theater), and by many other theatrical troupes. Zalmen Zylberczweig, in his *Leksikon fun dem Yidishn Teater* (Lexicon of the Yiddish Theater) (Volume 5, 1967, pages 4686-4726) mentions seven Yiddish plays and 23 Hebrew ones that Katzenelson wrote. That includes the dramas he wrote in the ghettos: *Iyuv* (Job*)*, *Eyl Nehares Bovl* (God of the Rivers of Babylon), etc.)

Witnesses say that Katzenelson was very productive during the time of the occupation. His close friend the commandant of the Vilna ghetto uprising, Yitskhok (Antek) Zukerman, says that in the ghetto Katzenelson wrote a very large number of songs, poems, and dramas. Some of them were sung, for example the song *Aroys a Yid in Gas* (*A Jew Went Out Into The Street)*, which was about the death of the folk-poet Hershele Danilowicz, for whom the composer Israel Glatstein composed music, and a song, *Bay di Taykhn fun Bovl* (By The Rivers of Babylon), in which the poet says:

> *Hunted, tormented, our hearts broken,*
> *we crept to the rivers of Babylon.*
> *Shamed, depressed, tears flowing like rivers—*
> *does anything compare to our misfortune?*

In Camp Vitel, he kept a diary in Hebrew throughout his stay. "In its pages," writes David Maisel in his Foreword to the collection *Dos Lid fun Oysgehargetn Yidishn Folk* (The Song of the Murdered Jewish People) (New York, 1948),

"Katzenelson makes clear his state of mind, which often borders on insanity. He begins to write things down and breaks off; he wants to make 'the great accounting,' but he feels he doesn't have the strength to do so 'because he is about to go out of his mind.' Katzenelson writes: 'I wake up crying out: Woe, woe! What I dreamed happened! How, God, I called out trembling--why was my people exterminated? Why and when did it die for no reason? Not in battle, not in conflict—young and old, there's no one left!'"

Several months later, at the beginning of October in 1943, he began to write his *Song of the Murdered People*, which he finished on January 18, 1944.

On April 17th of that same year, Katzenelson and his son Tsvi (his other two sons and his wife had been killed previously) were led out of Camp Vital to Auschwitz, where he died a martyr. Later, after the liberation, some of his creations were dug up from the ground where they had been hidden in bottles, and they became a living memorial to the cruel suffering of our people, a memorial that calls on us never to forget and never to forgive.

"Through his lamentations," writes the poet Aaron Zeitlin, "the martyr Isaac Katzenelson has become a survivor. He will rise eternally from the ashes to demand an accounting."

Elegy

The sun fades away in flames—
we can barely see it now, it seems.
Thus fades away my hope
and thus fade away my dreams.

The night, the night is dark—
the night is black and mute.
So appears my mourner's sorrow
and my mourner's heart, to boot.

World, O world, don't worry—
day will be reborn!
But my sorrow is eternal—
eternally I mourn.

To Heaven
(fragment)

That's how it began, in the very beginning...
Heaven, tell me why! Do tell me why!
Why do we deserve to be so shamed upon the great Earth?
The Earth is deaf and mute—seems to have closed its eyes.
But you, Heaven, looked on from high, from above,
and didn't turn a hair!

Mila Street

There's a street in Warsaw called Mila Street.
Oh tear out your hearts
and put stones in your breast instead.
Oh tear the moist eyes out of your head
and put pieces of pottery on them[65],
as if you didn't see and didn't know.
Stop up your ears and don't hear—deaf!
I'm about to tell you about Mila Street.

---

65. A custom with dead people

עלעגיע

די זון פֿאַרגייט אין פֿלאַמען.
די זון — מען זעט זי קוים.
אזוי פֿאַרגייט מײַן האָפֿנונג,
אזוי פֿאַרלעשט מײַן טרוים.

די נאַכט, די נאַכט איז פֿינצטער,
די נאַכט איז שטום און שוואַרץ ;
אזוי זעט אוים מײַן טרויער,
אזוי זעט אוים מײַן האַרץ...

וועלט, דו וועלט, דו זאָרג ניט —
באַלד לײַכט אויף דײַן טאָג !
אייביק איז מײַן טרויער,
אייביק איז מײַן קלאָג.

צו די הימלען

(פֿראַגמענט)

אזוי האָט זיך עס אָנגעהויבן, באַלד אין אָנהייב...
הימלען, זאָגט פֿאַר וואָס ? אַ, זאָגט פֿאַר ווען ?
פֿאַר וואָס, אַ, קומט עס אונדז אזוי פֿאַרשעמט צו ווערן
אויף דער גרויסער ערד ?
די ערד טויב-שטום האָט וו פֿאַרמאַכט די אויגן...
איר הימלען, אָבער, איר האָט דאָך געזען,
איר האָט זיך צוגעקוקט פֿון אין דער הייך, פֿון אויבן,
און ניט איבער זיך געקערט !...

די מילאַ-גאַס

(פֿראַגמענט)

ס'איז דאָ אַ גאַס אין וואַרשע, דאָס איז די מילאַ-גאַס, אַ רײַסט
ארוים די הערצער זיך פֿון ברוסט
און לייגט אָנשטאָט די הערצער שטיינער דאָרט אַרײַן. אַ,
רײַסט ארוים פֿון קאָפּ די אויגן נאַס
און לייגט ארויף אויף זיי שאַרבוינעס, ווי איר וואָלט עס ניט
געזען און ניט דערפֿון געוווּסט —
פֿאַרשטאָפּט די אויערן און הערט עס ניט — טויב ! איך גיי
דערצ ײַלן פֿון דער מילאַ-גאַס.

There's a street in Warsaw called Mila Street.
Who's that crying? And so softly. Not I—I don't cry, no!
Mila Street rises above all tears.
No Jew is crying. If Gentiles saw it,
they would all break out
into terrible, bitter weeping.
But on that day in Mila Street, on that very day,
there were no Gentiles in the ghetto.

Just Jews and Germans—Jews, Jews, Jews!
So many, and even more.
They've already killed
three hundred and fifty thousand Jews from Warsaw.
The old ones were shot in the cemetery,
and the others were led out of the city
to the Treblinkas. And Mila Street is full
and overfilled, like the railroad cars. Look and be astonished!

Our March

One and two and three and four,
what we are, we are—not more.
Though we are just young and small,
we must walk like heroes all.

Chorus[66]:

Step forward, your best foot forward—
we'll march together and never tire.
Let's stride on proudly like little soldiers,
with heads held higher, higher, higher.

Step one foot and then one more,
quite erect and proud we all.
Stride with pride and certainty—
hold your heads up straight and tall!

---

66. The chorus is not present in the original version of this poem, as published; it was added by Yiddish music teachers in the United State to make the poem more enjoyable and singable for children in Yiddish schools and camps

ס׳איז דא א גאס אין ווארשע — די מילא־גאס. ווער וויינט?
און שטיל אזוי? ניט איך, איך וויין ניט, ניין!
די מילא־גאס שטייגט איבער אלע טרערן. ס׳וויינט קיין ייד
ניט. גויים. ווען זיי וואלטן עם געזען,
זיי וואלטן דעמאלט אויסגעבראכן אין א מוראדיקן אלע, אין
א ביטערן געוויין,
א גוי איז אבער אין דעם טאג פון מילא־גאס, אין טאג אין
יענעם, אין יידישן אין געטא ניט געווען.

יידן נאר און דייטשן... יידן! יידן! יידן! אזוי א סך און
מערער נאך — מען האט
דרײַ הונדערט פופציק טויזנט יידן פון אײן ווארשע,
ווארשעווער דערהרגעט שוין —
די אלטע אויסגעשאסן אויפן בית החיים, די איבעריקע אלע
ארויסגעפירט פון שטאט
אין די טרעבלינקעס — און די מילא־גאס איז פול,
איז איבערפולט ווי די וואגאנעם, קוק און שטוין!

אונדזער מארש

אײנס און צווײ און דרײַ און פיר,
וואם מיר זײַנען — זײַנען מיר!
כאטש מיר זײַנען יונג און קליין,
ווי די העלדן דארף מען גיין!

א פיסל איבער א פיסל,
און שטיפער, שטיפער – שטיפער א ביסל.
און שפאן, שפאן שטאלץ, שפאן שטאלץ און זיכער –
די קעפלעך העכער, העכער, העכער.

א פום לעם א פיסל,
און שטײַפער א ביסל;
שמראם, שטאלץ און זיכער,
די קעפעלעך העכער!

Chorus:

Though we are just young and small.
we must walk like heroes all!
What we are, we are—not more;
one and two and three and four.

Chorus:

Five and six and seven, eight—
do not weep, it's not too late.
Don't just stand there in one spot—
forge ahead, for fools we're not!

Chorus:

We don't need to ask the way,
we're familiar quite with it.
Whether fresh and greening fields
or in forests dark, moonlit.

Chorus:

Don't just stand there in one spot—
forge ahead, for fools we're not!
Do not weep, it's not too late—
five and six and seven, eight.

Chorus:

Nine and ten, eleven, twelve—
see a farmer, say "Good-day!"
See a bird and bid him: "Fly!"
See a leaf that blows our way.

כאַטש מיר זײַנען יונג און קליין
ווי די העלדן דאַרף מען גיין !
וואָס מיר זײַנען — זײַנען מיר ;
איינס און צוויי און דרײַ און פיר.

פינף און זעקס און זיבן, אַכט, —
נישט געוויינט און נישט געלאַכט.
נישט געשטאַנען, נאָר נישט שטיין,
נישט געלאָפן, גיין, נאָר גיין !

מיר דאַרפן נישט פרעגן,
מיר ווייסן די וועגן ;
אין פריש-גרינע פעלדער,
אין טונקעלע וועלדער !

נישט געשטאַנען, נאָר נישט שטיין,
נישט געלאָפן — גיין, נאָר גיין !
נישט געוויינט, און נישט געלאַכט,
פינף און זעקס און זיבן, אַכט !

נײַן און צען און עלף און צוועלף —
טרעפסט אַ פויער — זאָג : גאָט־העלף !
טרעפסט אַ פויגל — זאָג אים : פלי !
טרעפסט אַ בלימל — זאָג אים : בלי !

Chorus:

March and march along our way,
bang the drums and sing all day.
High our banners, proud and true—
what better could our troop now do?

Chorus:

See a bird and bid him: "Fly!"
See a leaf that blows our way.
Nine and ten, eleven, twelve--.
see a farmer, say "Good-day!"

Chorus:

מאַרש, מאַרש, געגאַנגען,
מיט פּויק און געזאַנגען !
מיט פֿענער, אײַ פֿענער !
וואָס קען שוין זײַן שענער !

טרעפֿסט אַ פֿויגל — זאָג אים פֿלי !
טרעפֿסט אַ בלימל — זאָג אים : בלי !
טרעפֿסט אַ פֿויער — זאָג : גאָט־העלף !
נײַן אין צען און עלף און צוועלף.

MOYSHE BRODERZON
(born on November 23, 1890, in Moscow;
died on August 17, 1955, in Warsaw)

The name Moyshe Broderzon became known in Yiddish literature at the time of and just after the first World War. It was a time of extinguished hopes, bloody days when human dreams and ideals were being trampled on the battlefields of Europe; of years when gnawing doubts often drove people to raw and lawless deeds and speech. The same was true in literature, the eternal mirror of life.

It was the time of *Di Khalyastre* (The Gang), of which Broderzon was a cofounder, a time when people often tried to use loud outcries to silence their own weeping and the weeping of a disappointed generation. In those days, Peretz Markish proclaimed that "our measure is not beauty but honor," and said proudly: "I belong to nobody! I am beyond rules, with no beginning and no end." Honor and lawlessness were favorite expressions in the Yiddish poetry of that time.

At the same time, Broderzon, a poet of his generation, sang in one of his first songs:

> *The coil of contradiction wraps and unwraps itself,*
> *and I find a starting thread and lose it.*

From contradictions and doubts it is only one step to despair and uncertainty: "To whom should I reveal the rents in my heart?" he asks in one of his poems, and he finds no answer. So it was no accident that one of his early books of poetry bears the name *Shvarts-Shabes* (Black Sabbath). Black Sabbath poems they were, wrapped in depression and despair:

> *Whoever has seen the Black Sabbath in its depths*
> *will always, always be haunted by it.*
> *It has in it an angry strength, an accursed power.*
> *It has its cruelly thundrous words that astonish,*
> *and chain one's body and soul to the place*
> *that draws creativity from the earth.*

But Broderzon didn't want to be ruled completely by the "angry strength" of the Black Sabbath of that time. In the same poem, he pleads that he wants to try "to begin from the beginning, from ABC":

and to begin to feel again the blue light...
may a faint smile play upon my countenance.
I want to begin with first words: daddy, mama...
and find some sort of new words,
to endow them with a new, happy meaning,
to beautify them, to endow them
with the charm of a new day.

Broderzon sought to free himself and his generation from the Black Sabbath despair and find a new beginning, to raise themselves high above the "deeply depressed day," all the way to the stars, as he says in his song to the stars:

We youths—we, a joyful, song-filled gang,
we're traveling an unknown road
in deeply depressed days
and nights of fear.

The "new beginning" and the joy that should "be fruitful and multiply" was found by Broderzon in the renewed cultural-societal life that began to build in post-War independent Poland and in his home city, Lodz, to which he returned from Moscow. The Jewish folk person didn't want to let the clouds of doubt and chaos that the storm of war had brought hang over him very long. He set out to build the cultural institutions, workers' homes, children's schools, and libraries for adults.

Broderzon was carried along by the healthy streams of life. "Hatred can burn a world to ashes," he says in a poem. So he wanted to free himself and his surroundings from that hatred, and he pleads in the same poem: "Meanwhile, my child, play a little Chopin for me." He wants to divert himself from that world of hatred that can burn into a world of ashes. And where else can one do that as well as in the pure world of children?

It's the beginning of the new Yiddish schools. The children need new poems, joy, and laughter. Broderzon, just like his fellow Lodzer Isaac Katzenelson, begins creating for children. His poems are playful—they rhyme lightly, naturally so that they practically plead to be sung:

Little Tsipele
bit her lipele.[67]
"O Tsipele, why are you crying?
Would you like an apple."
Oh no, no, no...
who says I am crying?"

With his poems, he led them out to broad, blossoming fields and let them drink their fill of spaciousness and beauty:

Fields are greening, forests are rustling.
We walk with full baskets—
no end of flowers.
We are embraced and crowned
by youthful wreaths
in gaudy decoration.

Broderzon wrote plays for children, operettas, and marionette shows, and that playfulness and light versification brought him to his other great love: Yiddish theater. He helped to create the Yiddish *Kleynkunst*[68] Theater, at first as a marionette theater, *Khad Gadyo*[69], which presented well known personalities from the Yiddish cultural and literary community; later (in 1926) the *Kleynkunst* theater *Ararat* was born.

Broderzon wrote dozens of charming poems in a folksy style, which (thanks to the music of Henekh Kon, David Bergelson, and other composers) were grabbed up by Jewish actors and singers throughout the world. Many of these little theater songs that he wrote are still sung today, and are often considered folksongs. One of them, *A Gut Morgn Dir, Hirsh Dovid* (Good Morning to You, Hirsh David), has been sent to us by our readers in various versions. Others are *Yidn Shmidn Zingen* (Jewish Smiths Sing), *Men Ruft Mikh Moyshe Gimpl* (They Call Me Moyshe Gimpel), *Vaser-Tregers* (Water-Carriers), *Klingen Gleker, Klingen Glokn* (Bells Are Ringing), *Di Khorogrande* (The Choral Group), and many others that Yiddish actors all over the world have taken great pleasure in putting into their repertoires.

---

67. An affectionate diminutive for "lip", usually applied to small children; the Yiddish word is retained here for the sake of rhyme.
68. Approximately equivalent to "cabaret"
69. Literally, "one goat"; refers to the well known Passover song

However, Broderzon did not waste all his poetic talent in playing with children's songs and theatrical couplets. In 1939, a few months before the outbreak of the second World War, his last book, *Yud*[70], containing 50 poems, was published in Lodz. Black unrest fluttered in the poet's heart. It was still before the Holocaust, but a sort of strange premonition was oppressing the poet's heart. Black Sabbath was bobbing up again in his soul. He sensed the fearsome death that was approaching the Jews, and just like his fellow Lodzer Katzenelson, who a few years later cried out from his secret hiding-place to Heaven because it was silent, Broderzon, even before the catastrophe began, addressed Heaven with a cry of sorrow and rage:

The yellow patch has flamed before and behind—
the heart and marrow have burned and been consumed.
The sun and the yellow patch have flared up, enraged--
the sun has ravished every day with light.

How could it look on at all the cruelty?
How could it listen to the mortal outcries?
How could the sun demand of itself
to be transformed into a well of sorrow and woe?

Those lines were written even before the sun was witness to all the cruelty that was inflicted beneath its light, just as the following lines by Broderzon, in which the poet so prophetically foresaw the death of our millions of brothers and sisters in Poland, were written even before Treblinka and Maidanek:

I hear precisely and clearly the counting of the minutes,
the clanging of machinery, the senseless measurement.
I'm not clear about it, but I feel that
a diabolical machine hovers over my days.

Any minute it will explode, explode insanely.
Who knows—with the gases of wailing or with laughter-dynamite?
Here I stand and cannot move from the spot—
the diabolical machine is already within me.

A few months later, the diabolical machine, driven by the two bloody world-burners Hitler and Stalin, had already passed, with insane energy, through the cities and towns of Poland. The insanity had indeed exploded. Moyshe Broder-

---

70. The tenth letter of the Hebrew alphabet

zon ran, along with tens of thousands of other Jews. He ran to the East. He hoped, like many others, who ran with him in that direction, that perhaps he would find rest there till the bloody stain passed by. After all, the bells of Moscow had rung so resoundingly throughout the world about the "bright Paradise" in which Jewish poets were living "in the free sixth of the world."

Within a few months, Broderzon had already published a poem to October[71] in the *Bialystoker Shtern* (Bialystok Star). That's what the poem was called: *October*. We remember a few lines from it:

> *I've looked deeply into your shining eye, October,*
> *and I've seen such humanity.*
> *You are the author of the happiest and most beautiful things,*
> *and auspicious was your origin and being.*

Did Broderzon really believe when he wrote those lines in besieged Bialystok that October was a synonym for great humanity? It was already after Izzi Kharik, "the youngest son of October," as Soviet literary criticism had crowned him, had 'disappeared' and it was no longer permitted to mention his name in Bialystok, as in the rest of October land. It was already after the disappearance of Moyshe Kulbak, after Max Erik, after Dr. I. Zinberg, etc., etc.

It is possible that he, the naïve poet really believed it, but it didn't take long before the "great humanity" rewarded the poet for his belief: like all the other Yiddishly creative people in Soviet Russia, Broderzon was dragged into October's slave-camps and prisons, where he languished for seven years.

Broderzon couldn't understand it:

> *Where shall I run to from myself out of pain and sorrow?*

he asks in one of the poems he created in that cruel time. He is ashamed of mankind, which has become "like an animal, a forest creature":

> *The shame is terribly great,*
> *the crime is serious,*
> *when Man is like a forest creature, an animal.*
> *Who knows who is guiltier?*

---

71. Referring to the October (i.e., Bolshevik) Revolution, thus to Soviet Russia

Ill and broken, Broderzon expected the new Khruschev regime to liberate him and 'rehabilitate' him while he was still alive, not like his comrades Markish, Der Nister, and all the other tortured Yiddish writers. He had the good fortune to go back to Poland, where his talent blossomed again and his name grew great. The Yiddish cultural world hoped that that would be only his first step on his journey to the great, free world.

But the hope was not fulfilled. A short time thereafter, on August 17, 1956, his sick and weakened heart stopped. His grave was in the Warsaw cemetery till 1970, but his widow, Sheyne-Miriam, did not want to leave Broderzon's body in Polish earth, so she, with the help of Yiddish writers and cultural organizations, moved it to Israel.

To The Stars

We youth, we joyously singing band,
are traveling on an unknown road
during deeply depressing days
and during nights of fear.
Per aspera ad astra![72]

Stars become tears
and tears become stars;
deaf men start to hear,
dead men begin to have desires,
and all good things come true

Is the road difficult that leads to the stars?!
Hey—don't think about it so much!
What is destined for us will happen!
Happiness will bear fruit and increase
and the skies will be willing to listen
and swear holy faithfulness.
Ha, ha! Meanwhile, bears dance.

Per aspera ad astra!
We're traveling on an unknown road,
during deeply depressing days
and during nights of fear,
we youths, we joyously singing band.

From the Poem 'Yud'
(fragment)

My name is a letter, a symbol,
the quietest of all the letters and symbols, large and small.
I am a letter, a symbol of the highest, deepest accomplishment,
and of not being able to remain on a side road.

On that side road, all the bridges have been blown up;
ahead and behind—shattered.

---

72. Through difficulties to the stars!

צו די שטערן

מיר, יונגען, מיר — אַ פֿריילעכע, צעזונגענע כאַליאַסטרע,
מיר גייען אין אַן אומבאַוווּסטן וועג,
אין טיפֿע, מרה־שחורהדיקע טעג,
אין נעכט פֿון שרעק —
Per aspera ad astra!

און ס'וועֶרן שטערן — טרערן,
און טרערן ווערן — שטערן,
און טויבע הייבן אָן צו הערן,
און טויטע הייבן אָן באַגערן,
און אַל דאָס גוטס — מקוים ווערן;

— ס'איז שווער דער וועג, וואָס פֿירט צו שטערן ??
היי, וויניקער אַ ביסל קלערן !
וואָס ס'איז באַשערט, וועט אונדז באַווערן !

די פֿרייד מ'זיך פֿרוכפֿערן און מערן,
און הערן וועלן הימלען גערן,
און בקדושה טרײַהייט שווערן;
כאַ־כאַ — דערוֶוויילע טאַנצן בערן !

Per aspera ad astra!
מיר גייען ! גייען מיר אין אומבאַוווּסטן וועג !
אין טיפֿע מרה־שחורהדיקע טעג,
אין נעכט פֿון שרעק —
מיר, יונגען, מיר — אַ פֿריילעכע, צעזונגענע כאַליאַסטרע !

פֿון דער פּאָעמע ,,י"

(פֿראַגמענט)

דער נאָמען מיינער איז אַן **אות** — אַ צייכן,
דער שטילסטער פֿון די אַלע אותיות און די מופֿתים גרוים
און קליין —
איך בין אַן אות, אַ צייכן פֿון דעם העכסטן, טיפֿסטן גרייכן
און פֿון נישט קאָנען בלײַבן אויף אַן אומוועג שטיין.

און אויף דעם אומוועג אויפֿגעגאַריסן זײַנען אַלע בריקן,
אויפֿגעשווידֶדערט — פֿאַרנם, אויפֿגעציטערט — הינטער מיר :

Can eternal wandering be my remedy
when I lose track of myself as I wander?

It's a letter *tof*: the road itself, the deepest mysteries of the Torah,
and the letter of the unachieved splendor of the Messiah.
My royal road, a *Via Dolorosa*,[73]
to the long, tumultuous, flooded night.

Yes, that's my name: *yud,* a symbol standing for the number "ten,"
and my sorrow is tenfold greater.
I am a letter—a people is prepared
to suffer further punishment and pay the price for it!

Flowers
(fragment)

Fields green, forests rustle—
we walk with full baskets
of innumerable flowers;
we walk embraced
and crowned with young flowers,
in gaudy decoration.

We sing and jump and dance,
and our eyes shine with happiness,
flowery and pure.
Whoever wants to be crowned with flowers
should come to us, to us—
should come to us.

We'll give him everything!
And we'll dance again in fields,
set out for distant places!
Set out quickly, quickly,
for we are all children,
little flowers ourselves!

---

73. Painful road—an allusion to Christ's long and painful walk to his execution while carrying the heavy cross.

מאַ זאָל דאָס וואָגלען אייביקע באמת זיַין מיַין תּיקון,
בעת די שפּורן אייגענע אין וואַנדער איך פֿאַרליר?

ס׳איז אַ ת — דער העג אַליין — די סתרי־תּורה ורזין דרזין,
און אות פֿון נישט דערגאַנגענער משיחות־פּראָכט,
דער דרך־מלך מיַינער — אַ ווײַס דאַלאַראָזאַ
אין לאַנגער, טומלדיקער און מבֿולבלדיקער נאַכט!

יאַ, ס׳איז דער נאָמען מיַינער — „יוד” — אַזאַ אַן צייכן,
אַ מספּר צען, און צען מאָל גרעסער איז מיַין צער:

איך בין אַן אות — אַ פֿאָלק איז זיך מכין —
נאָך עונש אָפּקומען — צי׳ לאַדענען אויף זיך דעם שׂכר
דערפֿאַר!

בלומען

(פֿראַגמענט)

פֿעלדער גרינען, וועלדער רוישן —
גייען מיר מיט פֿולע קוישן
בלומען אָן אַ שיעור...
גייען מיר אַרומגענומען
און באַקראַנצט מיט יונגע בלומען
אין דעם בונטן ציר...

זינגען, שפּרינגען מיר און טאַנצן
און פֿון גליק די אויגן גלאַנצן
בלומענדיק און רייַן!
ווער באַקראַנצט ווייל זיַין פֿון בלומען,
זאָל צו אונדז, צו אונדז זאָל קומען,
קומען זאָל צו גיין!

מירן אָפּגעבן אין גאַנצן!
און אין פֿעלדער ווייַטער טאַנצן,
לאָזן ווייַט זיך גיין!
לאָזן ווייַט זיך גיך, געשווינדער,
ווייַל מיר זיַינען אַלע קינדער —
בלימעלעך אַליין!

Jewish Smiths Sing

Jewish smiths sing—
singing is the most important thing.
Iron bars, ring, ring,
and spray sparks and pieces.

Hey, hey—things are good for the smith,
good is the smith's life.
His steel and iron limbs
ignite our courage.

Sorrow and rage glow—
want to be free.
We have to reforge
our swords into plows.

Hey, hey--things are good for the smith,
good is the smith's life.
His steel and iron limbs
ignite our courage.

Little Tsipele

Little Tsipele
bit her *lipele*.
O Tsipele, why are you crying?

Is an apple what you want?
Oh no, no, no—
who says I'm crying?

Little Tsipele
clamped her mouth shut.
O little Tsipele, why are you crying?
Is it two apples that you want?
Oh no, no, no—
who says I'm crying?

ייִדן שמידן

ייִדן שמידן, זינגען,
זינגען איז דער עיקר ;
קלינגען אײַזנס, קלינגען,
שפריצן פֿונקען שטיקער.

היי, היי, ווייל דעם שמידער,
ווייל איז אים און גוט,
זײַנע שטאָל- און אײַזן-גלידער
צינדן אונדז דעם מוט.

מענטשן, נעבעך, בלינדע
אין דער פֿינצטער טאָפן,
דאַרף מען זיי אַצינדער
פֿאָדקעווועם צוקלאַפן.

היי, היי, ווייל דעם שמידער...

צער און צאָרן גליִען,
ווילן דווקא פֿרײַ זײַן,
דאַרף מען איבערשמידן
שווערד אויף אַקער-אײַזן.

היי, היי, ווייל דעם שמידער...

ציפעלע

עס האָט די קליינע ציפעלע
פֿאַרבים זיך אַ ליפעלע...
— אוי, ציפעלע, וואָס וויינסטו ?

אַן עפעלע — דאָס מיינסטו ?
— אוי, ניין, ניין, ניין,
ווער זאָגט עם, אז איך ווייין ?

עס האָט די קליינע ציפעלע
פֿאַרקניפט דאָס מויל — אַ קניפעלע...
— אוי, ציפעלע, וואָס ווייינסטו ?
צוויי עפעלעך, דאָס מיינסטו ?
— אוי, ניין, ניין, ניין,
ווער זאָגט עם, אז איך ווייין ?

And her head shakes,
together with her pigtail.
O little Tsipele, why are you crying?
Is it three apples you want?
Oh no, no, no!
I want a kiss, nothing more!

Hirsh David

Good morning, Hirsh David!
Good morning, Zerah!
I heard you had the good fortune
to sell out all your pot cheese.

Not just the pot cheese,
but all the dairy food—
I sold out completely.
Let's put our hands on our shoulders—
Let's dance!
Ay-di, didl-di, di,di,di.

O Hirsh David, how's your wife—
I mean your Sarah Khaye?
The old girl cuts her hair
according to the latest fashion.
She's taken off her wig,
her Jewishness altogether—
demons are going to dance
over the chimneys and roofs.
Ay-di, didl-di, di-di-di.

I have a daughter, a good girl—
you have a son, Ephraim;
they'll make a fine couple,
so let's write a marriage contract.
Ha, ha, ha--
I'll give them
a total of two hundred in silver!
Through fields and forests Jews will dance,
ay-di, didl-di, di-di-di.

און ס'טרייסלט זיך איר קעפּעלע
צוזאמען מיט איר צעפּעלע.
— אוי, ציפּעלע, וואָס ווײנסטו ?
דרײַ עפּעלעך — דאָס מיינסטו ?
— אוי, ניין, ניין, ניין !
איך וויל אַ קוש — נישט מײַן !

הירש דוד

— אַ גוט־מאָרגן דיר, הירש־דוד !
— אַ גוט־מאָרגן, זרח !
— כ'האָב געהערט, האָסט מיט מזל
אויספֿאַרקויפֿט דעם צוואָרעך.

— נישט דעם צוואָרעך,
נאָר דאָס מילכיקס,
אויספֿאַרקויפֿט אין גאַנצן,
לאָמיר לייגן האַנט אויף אַקסל,
לאָמיר טאַקע טאַנצן !
אײַ־די דידל־די,
די־די־די...
— אַ, הירש־דוד, וואָס מאַכט דײַן ווײַבל,
כ'מיין דײַן שׂרה־חיה ?
אָט די קאַבילע זי שערט זיך
לויט די מאָדעם נײַע.
אויסגעמטאַן פֿון זיך דאָס שטײַטל
ייִדישקייט אין גאַנצן —
איבער קוימענס, איבער דעכער
גייען שדים טאַנצן.
אײַ־די, דידל־די, די־די־די...

— כ'האָב אַ מויד, אַ פּשר קעלבל,
דו אַ זון, אפֿרים,
מ'וועט זיי מאַכן אַ געוועלבל,
לאָמיר שרײַבן תּנאים.
כאַ־כאַ־כאַ, צוויי מאות זילבער
גיב איך זיי אין גאַנצן,
איבער פֿעלדער, איבער וועלדער
וועלן ייִדן טאַנצן.
אײַ־די, דידל־די, די־די־די...

ITSIK MANGER

(born on May 28, 1901, in Czernowitz, Bukovina;
died on February 20, 1969, in Israel)

Anyone who saw the poet Itsik Manger in pre-War Poland, where thousands of Jewish workers and ordinary people followed his every move and turn with their loving eyes and recited and sang his songs to him; anyone who remembers the packed halls where he appeared and where gray, humdrum days and nights were magically transformed into pure holiday; anyone who saw the reception that Jewish New York gave the poet when he finally got there after the War; and anyone who read how the Israeli *Sabras* felt Manger to be their poet and made his mischievous *Megillah* poems their own and began to sing them; also had to remember a picture from Manger's *Noente Geshtaltn* (Nearby Images).

In that book, Manger leads us through the streets of Jassy, where Abraham Gold-faden, the father of Yiddish theater, is strolling around. Porters, wagon-drivers, and shopkeepers standing in front of their shops take their hats off to him. Through the open windows, sounds reach him—people are singing. A mother rocks her child to sleep:

Sleep, sleep, my little Sarah—
it's your mother rocking you, little Sarah.

A chorus of seamstresses in a shop hum: "Turn, little wheel—this is not a game." A cobbler's apprentice raps with his little hammer and hums in accompaniment: "*A little scoundrel walks in the street. He's not capable of learning anything--he goes around idly and does what one is not permitted to do.*" Old Goldfaden looks up to the open windows and smiles--they are singing his songs, songs from *Akeydes Yitskhok* (The Sacrifice of Isaac), *Bar Kokhba*, and *Di Kishef-Makherin* (The Witch).

This description of Goldfaden's triumphant stroll through the streets of Jassy had to come to mind when one heard or read about Manger's success wherever he went. With how much joy and pride should a Yiddish poet's heart fill when he walks "with quiet steps, a king without a country," when he goes to distant countries and cities and encounters there thousands of readers who know and sing his songs and receive him joyfully, like a good and dear friend.

404

The song about "the king without a country" wandered across oceans and countries on the wings of Manger's golden peacock, and found a warm spot in the hearts of many, who, when

they feel sad, sing the songs
and the beautiful, hearty ballads
of Itsik Manger, O faithful comrade!

The love between poet and people has always been mutual. From the first steps that Itsik Manger took fifty years ago, he devoted himself to the creations of his people, to its proverbs and stories, to its poems and images. "There is no greater poet among the Jewish people," Manger once said at an evening lecture about folk creation, "than the people itself."

Anyone who knows Manger's artistic ways knows that that wasn't just the rhetorical affectation of a speaker who wanted to raise his prestige among his listeners, but represented the poet's artistic credo during all fifty years of his creativity.

"The more I immerse myself in the meaning of poetry, the clearer the importance and seductive beauty of folk poetry becomes to me," wrote Manger in one of his brief Introductions to his poems. Manger loved folk poetry, not only Yiddish poetry but also the poetry of other peoples, so he gave Yiddish readers a gift in the 1930s: a small, pure anthology of his translations of poems "that other peoples sing." He dedicated the book to the young Yiddish poets, with the intention that "the beauty of foreign folk poems might serve to reveal the beauty of our own Yiddish folk poetry."

Manger remained faithful to the folk treasure he had taken over from his father, the "splendid jokester and master tailor," from his brother Note, the tailor's apprentice, and from his mother, who had "revealed to him the wonderful beauty of Yiddish folk poetry." But Manger wanted not only to *preserve* the treasure but also to enrich it. I. L. Peretz's call: "Don't just write in Yiddish--Yiddish must be *created* and one must see with Yiddish eyes so that the Yiddish soul-words will be heard," received their true artistic fulfillment in Manger's creations. Even when he is singing about the eternal themes that poets sing about in all languages and all eras: love and weeping, stars and the night, and life and death; and even when

he gets sentimental over a glass of wine
and sings Rumanian doynes[74],
the most beautiful ones anywhere,

even then one can hear in his poems the *Jewish* melodies, because they are root-ed in our rich folk idiom, in comparisons and images, and in metaphors and rhythms.

The poet's love of Yiddish folksong brought him to Yiddish ballads. We say *Yiddish* ballads and not ballads in Yiddish because even before Manger we had had Yiddish poets who wrote ballads. Manger, however, was among those who not only raised that poetic form—the ballad—to truly artistic heights, but also clothed it in true Yiddish garments.

Once there was a story—
the story was sad and beautiful.

Thus does Manger begin his ballad about his brother, *Note Manger Der Shnay-deryung (*Note Manger The Tailor Boy), who later died of starvation in Siberian exile. And one feels immediately that with that first line of the well known folk-poem, the poet has brought his brother Note closer to every one of us.

Or his ballad about the Petlura pogroms[75], which Manger begins with these two lines:

Under Yankele's tiny little crib
lies the slaughtered golden kid.

With these paraphrased lines from the Yiddish lullaby that generations of Jewish mothers had sung, and into which they had woven their hopes and dreams, the poet awakened feelings and associations that he wouldn't have been able to by any other means: *"unter yankele's vigele/ ligt gekoylet dos goldene tsigele* (under Yankele's tiny little crib/ lies the slaughtered golden kid)—to what tragic sym-bolism the poet raised our old Jewish golden kid!

In his poem *The Sacrifice of Isaac* too, we feel that through word-play the poet manages to build a bridge from today to the eternal path of generations of Jews to various kinds of sacrifices all over the world.

---

74. A particular Rumanian dance.
75. Pogroms in 1941, attributed to the Ukrainian General Petlura

Say to your grandfather: "Isaac, do you remember,
so many years ago,
when the angel revealed himself to us
and you were saved?"

Now he regrets it, the ancient God,
and he demands the sacrifice of me,
though I've lived so many times
and died so many times.

We also see that same mixture of past and present, fantasy and reality, in Manger's famous Bible and Megillah poems. The poet takes the ancient patriarchal figures from the Bible and the Megillah, transfers them to our cities and towns, and brings them to life as our neighbors. The holy fathers and mothers become homespun Jews and Jewesses like the ones we meet every day in the *shtetl,* in stores and in synagogue. They become closer to us because they are more human.

Rare humor shines out from the poems. When Father Abraham scolds Lot for getting drunk every night, he says to Lot:

That's all right for Manger, the tailor-boy,
but it's not all right for you;
you have two daughters to marry off
and you're a wealthy Jew.

Or when Jacob sings a serenade under Rachel's window:

Oh, I must wait, Rukhtshe darling,
for you for seven years.
Oh, how I love your beautiful eyes
and your black hair!

Manger's poem appeals to the ordinary reader because of the folksy charm that radiates from it, and it is also close to the refined reader of poetry because of the artistic heights to which he raises it. We are often enchanted and blinded by the rich and multicolored veil of artistry in which the poet has wrapped the song of previous generations of folksingers.

Manger was not, as many believed, an easy singer, a bird that sings any meaning and thought "as long as it rhymes." Because of the light and playful songs that people seized upon and started singing as folksongs:*Rabeynu Tam* (Dear Rabbi Tam), *Yosl Ber Dint in Militer* (Yosl Ber Serves In The Military), etc., many did not immediately perceive the deepness of his poetry. In reality, Manger was one of the most conscious of poets—he knew exactly what he wanted and why he sang one way and not another.

In one of his poems, he says:

> *Poet, arise—assume your duties;*
> *the crowns are yours.*
> *Don't let them fade away in silent graves*
> *where the dead live.*

In his light and playful way, he assumed his duties. He clothed the ancient crowns, the folk motifs, with new flowers. In one of his poems, he recounts how there came to him in his sleep

> *the tiny cripples from all the annual fairs,*
> *with drums, harmonicas, and balalaikas;*
> *with God on their lips, legends, stories, and nursery tales,*
> *and demanded that I sing to them.*

And he sang to them. He took them out of the "silent graves," from the yellowed parchment sheets of the ancient holy books, from the old theatrical plays, and from the folk memory, and wove them into the old-new Yiddish melodies that he left us through the years.

Let Us Sing

Let us sing quite simply
of all that is homey and dear:
of old beggars who curse the frost
and mothers who bless the fire;
of poor brides who stand with candles
in front of blind mirrors late at night,
each of them looking for the familiar face
that laughed at her profession of love;

of fortune-tellers who speak double-talk
and fleece you out of your last penny;
of abandoned wives who curse the world
and go out through the back door;

of servant girls who work bitterly hard
and hide the best morsels of food
for the soldiers who come at night
so the proprietors won't see them.

Let us sing quite simply
of all that is homey and dear:
of poor mothers who curse the frost
and beggars who bless the fire;

of servant girls who give birth to bastards
in the summer, behind strangers' doors,
and tremble in fear of the police,
who can throw them in prison for that;

of sewing machines that screech loudly
on Fridays, in the courtyards;
of thieves who have bungled
and have to flee across the rooftops;

of rag pickers who dig around in the garbage
and think they'll find treasures there;
of poets who believed the stars in vain
and went out of their minds.

לאָמיר זשע זינגען

לאָמיר זשע זינגען פּשוט און פּראָסט
פֿון אַלץ, וואָס איז היימיש, ליב און טײַער :
פֿון אַלטע בעטלער, וואָס שעלטן דעם פּראָסט
און פֿון מאַמעס, וואָס בענטשן דאָס פֿײַער.
פֿון אָרעמע כּלות, וואָס שטייען מיט ליכט
פֿאַר בלינדע שפּיגלען שפּעט בײַ נאַכט,
און יעדע זוכט דאָס נאָענטע געזיכט,
וואָס האָט איר ליבע אויסגעלאַכט.

פֿון גורל-וואָרפֿער, וואָס רעדן פֿאַרשטעלט
און נאָרן די לעצטע גראָשנם אויס
בײַ עגונות, וואָס שעלטן די וועלט,
און גייען דורך הינטערטירן אַרויס.

פֿון דינסטן, וואָס האָרעווען ביטער-שווער
און באַהאַלטן דעם בעסטן ביסן
פֿאַר די זעלנער, וואָס קומען בײַ נאַכט,
די באַלעבאַטים זאָלן נישט וויסן.

לאָמיר זשע זינגען פּשוט און פּראָסט
פֿון אַלץ, וואָס איז היימיש, ליב און טײַער :
פֿון אָרעמע מאַמעס, וואָס שעלטן דעם פּראָסט
און פֿון בעטלערס, וואָס בענטשן דאָס פֿײַער.

פֿון מיידלעך, וואָס וואַרפֿן זומערצײַט
ממזרים הינטער פֿרעמדע טירן
און ציטערן פֿאַר מונדירטע לײַט
וואָס קענען דערפֿאַר אין תּפֿיסה פֿירן.

פֿון קאַטערינקעס, וואָס סקריפּען שווער
פֿרײַטיק בײַ טאָג, אין אָרעמע הויפֿן,
פֿון גנבֿים, וואָס האָבן פֿאַרפּאַסט,
און מוזן איבער די דעכער אַנטלויפֿן.

פֿון שמאַטע-קלויבער, וואָס גראָבלען אין מיסט,
און מיינען : זיי וועלן אַן איצר געפֿינען,
פֿון דיכטער וואָס האָבן געגלייבט אומזיסט
די שטערן — און זענען אַראָפּ פֿון זינען.

Let us sing quite simply
of all that is homey and dear:
of old folks who curse the frost
and children who bless the fire.

The Broder Singers

I jumped up into the wagon of the Broder singers
and rode along with them a way,
through cities and towns, through singing years,
through rootless wanderings, through hunger.

To tell the truth, it was easier for me
with those first joyful Yiddish actors.
Birds sing to the fields and crickets to the rye,
and to the Jews, we sing—the Broder singers.

In Jewish inns, in taverns along the way,
in the autumn when the rain pounds on the shutters,
we stop to sing and recite.

At long wooden tables, ordinary Jews eat and listen—
they sigh with their cares and laugh through their tears,
and outside in the rain the wagon waits for us.

The Sacrifice Of Isaac

Rock me, rock me, blind Fate—
I am dreaming with open eyes
and see a great silver bird
come flying across the ocean.

What the silver bird is bringing me,
God only knows.
Perhaps it's my grandfather's *kiddush*-cup,
with sweet Erets Yisroel wine

But who has mentioned my grandfather's name?
Here, striding toward me, is my grandfather,

לאָמיר זשע זינגען פּשוט און פּראָסט
פֿון אַלץ, וואָס איז היימיש, ליב און טײַער;
פֿון אַלטע לײַט, וואָס שעלטן דעם פּראָסט,
און פֿון קינדער, וואָס בענטשן דאָס פֿײַער.

„בראָדער זינגער"

כ'בין אַרויפֿגעשפּרונגען אויפֿן וואָגן פֿ'ן די „בראָדער זינגער"
און בין מיט זיי אַ מהלך וועגנם אָפּגעפֿאָרן,
דורך שטעט און שטעטלעך, דורך זינגענדיקע יאָרן,
דורך וואָגל, דורך הפֿקר און דורך הונגער.

דעם אמת געזאָגט, ס'איז מיר געווועזן גרינגער
מיט אַט די ערשטע פֿרײַלעכע ייִדישע אַקטיאָרן,
פֿאָר די פֿעלדער זינגען פֿייגל. די גרילן — פֿאָרן קאָרן,
און פֿאָר די ייִדן זינגען מיר — די „בראָדער זינגער".

אין ייִדישע אכסניהם, אין קרעטשמעם בײַ די וועגן,
האַרבסטצײַט, ווען אין די לאָדנם פּויקט דער רעגן,
שטעלן מיר זיך אַפּ כּדי צו זינגען און צו זאָגן.

בײַ לאָנגע הילצערנע טישן זיצן פּראָסטע ייִדן און זיי הערן,
אַט זיפֿצן זיי פֿאַרזאָרגטע און אַט לאַכן זיי מיט טרערן,
אין דרויסן אויפֿן רעגן וואַרט אויף אונדז דער וואָגן.

עקידת איציק

ווינג מיך, וויג מיך, בלינדער גורל,
איך חלום מיט אָפֿענע אויגן,
און זע — אַ גרויסער זילבערנער פֿויגל
קומט איבערן ים געפֿלויגן.

וואָס טראָגט פֿאַר מיר דער זילבערנער פֿויגל,
איין גאָט אין הימל קען וויסן,
אפֿשר מײַן זיידנם קידוש-בעכער
מיט ארץ-ישׂראל-ווײַן זיסן?

נאָר ווער האָט דערמאָנט מײַן זיידנם נאָמען?
אַט שפּאַנט צו מיר דער זיידע,

the wagon driver of Stoptshet:
"Itsik, the sacrifice is ready."

And his eyes burn at me
like two autumn stars.
His gray beard is full of wind
and seven big tears.

My grandfather leads me by the hand,
past cities and villages and graves.
The cities are small, the villages large,
and we walk over the graves.

My grandfather asks: "Itsik, do you remember,
so many years ago,
when the angel revealed himself to us
and you were saved?

"Now he's having regrets, the old God,
and is demanding the sacrifice from me,
though I've already lived so many times
and died so many times.

"Let there be an end to it. I don't need His grace
and let Him in Heaven not think so—
Itsik, it's a good thing your mother is dead
and is saved the trouble of weeping."

My grandfather leads me by the hand,
past cities and villages and graves.
The cities are small and the villages are large,
and we walk over the graves.

On The Road Stands A Tree

On the road stands a tree,
bowed in contemplation.
All the birds have flown away
from their leafy station.

דער בעל-עגלה פֿון סטאָפּטשעט:
„איציק, ס'איז גרייט די עקידה".

און זײַנע אויגן ברענען אויף מיר,
ווי צוויי האַרבסטיקע שטערן,
זײַן גראָע באָרד איז פֿאַרלאָפֿן מיט ווינט
און מיט זיבן גרויסע טרערן.

פֿירט מיך דער זיידע בײַ דער האַנט
איבער שטעט און דערפֿער און גריבער —
די שטעט זענען קליין, די דערפֿער גרויס
און מיר שפּרײַזן איבער זיי אַריבער.

זאָגט דער זיידע: „איציק, געדענקסט —
צוריק מיט אַזוי פֿיל יאָרן —
ווען ס'האָט זיך דער מלאך צו אונדז אַנטפּלעקט
און דו ביסט ניצול געוואָרן?

איצט האָט ער חרטה, דער אַלטער גאָט
און ער מאָנט בײַ מיר דעם קרבן,
כאַטש כ'האָב שוין אַזוי פֿיל מאָל געלעבט
און בין שוין אַזוי פֿיל מאָל געשטאָרבן.

אַ סוף, אַן עק, איך דאַרף נישט זײַן זײַן גנאָד
און זאָל ער אין הימל נישט מיינען —
איציק, ס'איז גוט וואָס דײַן מאַמע איז טויט
און זי וועט פֿאַרשפּאָרן צו וויינען".

פֿירט מיך דער זיידע בײַ דער האַנט
איבער שטעט און דערפֿער און גריבער —
די שטעט זענען קליין, די דערפֿער גרויס
און מיר שפּרײַזן איבער זיי אַריבער.

אויפֿן וועג שטייט אַ בוים

אויפֿן וועג שטייט אַ בוים
שטייט ער אײַנגעבויגן,
אַלע פֿייגל פֿונעם בוים
זענען זיך צעפֿלויגן.

Three flew East, three flew West,
the rest flew South together,
left the tree there by itself
to brave the stormy weather.

"Mother dear," I said to her,
"please don't try to stop me.
My intentions are, you see,
to be a bird there on the tree.

"I'll sit there upon the tree—
croon it softly into sleep;
through the winter comfort it—
sing to it 'O tree don't weep.'"

Mother says: "O dearest child,"
 and she weeps a bitter tear,
"on the tree you'll freeze to death—
that's my deep and solemn fear."

So I say: "O mother dear—
please don't weep, your eyes get red.
In the twinkling of an eye,
I'll be a bird, just as I said."

Mother weeps: "O Itsik dear,
take this shawl in God's sweet name.
It will help to keep you warm,
and you can perch there all the same.

"Take galoshes with you too-
Winter's cold, with wind and rain.
Put your wool cap on your head
so my cares won't be in vain.

"Take your winter-vest as well—
put it on to warm your breath.
I'm sure you do not want to be
a guest within the house of Death."

דרײַ קײן מיזרח, דרײַ קײן מערב,
און דער רעשט קײן דרום.
און דעם בוים געלאָזט אַלײן,
הפֿקר פֿאַרן שטורעם.

זאָג איך צו דער מאַמע: „הער,
זאָלסט מיר נאָר נישט שטערן,
וועל איך, מאַמע, אײנס און צווײ
באַלד אַ פֿויגל ווערן.

„איך וועל זיצן אויפֿן בוים
און וועל אים פֿאַרוויגן
איבערן ווינטער מיט אַ טרײסט,
מיט אַ שײנעם ניגון".

זאָגט די מאַמע: „ניטע, קינד",
און זי ווײנט מיט טרערן.
„קענסט חלילה אויפֿן בוים
מיר פֿאַרפֿרוירן ווערן".

זאָג איך: „מאַמע, ס'איז אַ שאָד
דײַנע שײנע אויגן" —
און איידער וואָס, און איידער ווען,
בין איך מיר אַ פֿויגל.

ווײנט די מאַמע: „איציק קרוין,
נעם, אום גאָטעס ווילן,
נעם כאָטש מיט אַ שאַליקל,
זאָלסט זיך נישט פֿאַרקילן.

„די קאַלאָשן נעם דיר מיט,
ס'גײט אַ שאַרפֿער ווינטער —
און די קוטשמע טו דיר אָן,
ווײ איז מיר, און ווינד מיר.

„און דאָס ווינטער-לײַבל נעם,
טו עס אָן, דו שוטה,
אויב דו ווילסט נישט זײַן קײן גאַסט
צווישן אַלע טויטע". —

I try to flap my laden wings—
too many things she's put on me.
I haven't got the strength I need
to lift them up onto the tree.

And I look so sadly now
into my mother's tearful face.
Her love did not allow me to
become a bird and take my place.

Lonesome

No one knows just what I say,
just what I am looking for.
Seven mouselings and a mouse
sleeping on the floor.

Seven mouselings and a mouse—
make eight if I am right.
I put on my old felt hat
and say to all "Good night."

I put on my old felt hat
and get up to go.
Where to go so late at night,
I really do not know.

In the square I find a bar—
"Fool" it calls and winks.
"I've a cup of gold for you—
lots of wine to drink."

Open I the bar-room door,
quickly stumble in;
shout my greeting out to all
through the noise and din.

No one knows just what I say,
just what I am looking for.

כ'הײב די פֿליגל. ס'איז מיר שווער,
צו פֿיל, צו פֿיל זאַכן,
האָט די מאַמע אָנגעטאָן,
דעם פֿײגעלע דעם שוואַכן.

קוק איך טרויעריק מיר אַרײַן
אין דער מאַמעס אויגן :
ס'האָט איר ליבשאַפֿט נישט געלאָזט
ווערן מיך אַ פֿויגל.

אײנזאַם

קײנער ווייסט נישט וואָס איך זאָג,
קײנער ווייסט נישט וואָס איך וויל —
זיבן מײַזלעך מיט אַ מויז
שלאָפֿן אויפֿן דיל.

זיבן מײַזלעך מיט אַ מויז
זענען, דוכט זיך, אַכט —
טו איך אָן דעם קאַפּעלוש
און זאָג : „אַ גוטע נאַכט".

טו איך אָן דעם קאַפּעלוש
און לאָז איך זיך גיין.
וווּ זשע גייט מען שפּעט בײַ נאַכט
אײנינקער אַלײן ?

שטײט אַ שענק אין מיטן מאַרק,
ווינקט צו מיר : „דו יאָלד !
כ'האָב אַ פֿעסעלע מיט ווײַן,
אַ פֿעסעלע מיט גאָלד".

עפֿן שנעל איך אויף די טיר
און איך פֿאַל אַרײַן :
„אַ גוט-יום-טובֿ אַלע אײַך,
ווער איר זאָלט נישט זײַן !

קײנער ווייסט נישט, וואָס איך זאָג,
קײנער ווייסט נישט, וואָס איך וויל —

Two old drunks with just one flask
are sleeping on the floor.

Two old drunks with just one flask
seem to me make three.
Should I be the fourth one here?
No sir, not for me!

I put on my old felt hat
and get up to go.
Where to go so late at night,
I really do not know.

I'll Take Off My Shoes

I'll take off my shoes in sorrow,
and come back to You
just as I am, all worn out,
and let You look at me.

My God, my Lord, my Creator—
purify me in Your radiance.
I'm lying before You on a cloud--
rock me, rock me to sleep.

Speak kind words to me
and tell me I'm Your child,
and kiss the signs of my sin
off my forehead.

After all, I've fulfilled Your mission
and have spread your divine song,
so is it my fault
that Jew and song accidentally rhyme?[76]

Is it my fault
that beautiful and weeping accidentally rhyme,[77]

---

76. The Yiddish word for song is *lid*, and the Yiddish word for Jew is *yid*, so in Yiddish, song and Jew rhyme.
77. In Yiddish, the respective words are *sheyn* and *geveyn*.

צוויי שיפורים מיט אַ פּלאַש
שלאָפֿן אויפֿן דיל.

צוויי שיפורים מיט אַ פּלאַש
זעֶנעֶן, דוכט זיך, דרײַ.
זײַן אַ פֿעֶרטעֶר דאָ אין שפּיל
לוינט זיך ? — נישט כּדאי.

טו איך אָן דעם קאַפּעֶלוש
און איך לאָז זיך גיין.
וווּ זשעֶ גייט מעֶן שפּעֶט בײַ נאַכט
אייֶנינֶקעֶר אַליין ?

כ'וועֶל אויסטאָן די שיך...

כ'וועֶל אויסטאָן די שיך אין דעם טרויעֶר,
— און קומעֶן צו דיר צוריק —
אַט אַזוי ווי איך בין אַ פֿאַרשפּילטעֶר,
און שטעֶלן זיך פֿאַר דײַן בליק.

מײַן גאָט, מײַן האַר, מײַן באַשאַפֿעֶר,
ליִַטעֶר מיך אויס אין דײַן שײַן —
אַט ליג איך פֿאַר דיר אויף אַ וואָלקן,
פֿאַרוויג מיך און שלעֶפֿעֶר מיך אײַן.

אין רעֶד צו מיר גוטעֶ ווערטעֶר,
און זאָג מיר אַז איך בין „דײַן קינד".
און קוש מיר אַראָפּ פֿונעֶם שטעֶרן
די צייֶכנם פֿון מײַנעֶ זינד.

איך האָב דאָך געֶטאָן דײַן שליחות
און געֶטראָגן דײַן געֶטלעֶך ליד —
צי בין איך דעֶן שולדיק, וואָס ס'גראַמט זיך,
על־פּי טעֶות „ייִד" מיט „ליד".

צי בין איך דעֶן שולדיק, וואָס ס'גראַמט זיך
על־פּי טעֶות „שײַן". מיט „געֶוויין".

and that yearning, real yearning,
always wanders alone?

Is it my fault, radiant One,
that I am now beaten and weary
and lay this weary song
at Your feet?

My God, my Lord, my Creator—
purify me in Your radiance.
I'm lying before You on a cloud—
rock me, rock me to sleep.

I Wandered For Years

I wandered for years in foreign places—
now I'm going back to wander at home,
with one pair of shoes, one shirt on my body,
and a staff in my hand—how can I do without it?

I won't kiss your dust like that great poet,
though my heart, too, is full of song and weeping.
What do you mean, kiss the dust?! I *am* the dust,
and who, I ask you, kisses himself?

I'll stand agape before the blue sea of Galilee,
wearing my garments of poverty,
a wandering prince who has found his blue,
and whose dream has always been blue.

I don't want to kiss Your blue,
but just to stand there for no reason, as in a silent *shmone esre*[78].
What do You mean, kiss the blue?! I *am* the blue,
and who, I ask you, kisses himself?

I'll stand deep in thought before Your great desert
and listen to the age old tread of the camels

---

78. Eighteen Blessings, part of the daily prayer

און די בענקשאַפֿט, די אמתע בענקשאַפֿט,
וואָגלט כּסדר אַליין ?

צי בין איך דען שולדיק, דערלויכטער,
וואָס כ'בין איצט דערשלאָגן און מיד,
און לייג דיר אַוועק צופֿוסנס,
דאָס דאָזיקע מידע ליד ?

מײַן גאָט, מײַן האר, מײַן באַשאַפֿער,
לײַטער מיך אויס אין דײַן שײַן —
אָט ליג איך פֿאַר דיר אויף אַ וואָלקן,
פֿאַרווייג מיך און שלעפֿער מיך אײַן.

כ'האָב זיך יאָרן געוואַלגערט

כ'האָב זיך יאָרן געוואַלגערט אין דער פֿרעמד,
איצט פֿאָר איך זיך וואָלגערן אין דער היים.
מיט איין פֿאַר שיך, איין העמד אויפֿן לײַב,
אין דער האַנט דעם שטעקן — ווי קען איך זײַן אָן דעם ?

כ'וועל נישט קושן דײַן שטויב ווי יענער גרויסער פּאָעט,
כאָטש מײַן האַרץ איז אויך פֿול מיט געזאַנג און געוויין.
וואָס הייסט קושן דײַן שטויב ? איך בין דײַן שטויב.
אין וואָר קושט עס, איך בעט אײַך, זיך אַליין ?

כ'וועל שטיין פֿאַרגאַפֿט פֿאַר דעם כּנרת בלאָ,
אין מײַנע בגדי דלות אָנגעטאָן,
אַ פֿאַרוואָגלטער פּרינץ, וואָס האָט געפֿונען זײַן בלאָ,
און בלאָ איז זײַן חלום פֿון תּמיד אָן.

כ'וויל נישט קושן דײַן בלאָ, נאָר סתּם אַזוי
ווי אַ שטילע שמונה-עשׂרה וועל איך שטיין —
וואָס הייסט קושן דײַן בלאָ ? איך בין דײַן בלאָ
און וואָר קושט עס, איך בעט אײַך, זיך אַליין ?

כ'וועל שטיין פֿאַרטראַכט פֿאַר דײַן מידבר גרויס
און הערן די דורות-אַלטע קעמלטריט,

who rock Torah and merchandise
across the sand on their humps, and to the old wander-song
that trembles hotly glowing across the sand,
dies away, thinks better of it, and tries never to fade away.
I won't kiss Your sand—no and ten times no!
What do You mean, kiss Your sand? I *am* the sand,
and who, I ask you, kisses himself?

וואָס וויגן אויף זייערע הויקערס איבערן זאָמד

תּורה און סחורה, און דאָס אַלטע וואַנדערליד,

וואָס ציטערט איבער די זאָמדן היים צעגליט,

שטאַרבט אָפּ, דערמאָנט זיך און וויל קיין מאָל ניט פֿאַרגיין.

כ׳וועל נישט קושן דײַן זאָמד, ניין און צען מאָל ניין !

וואָס הייסט קושן דײַן זאָמד ? איך בין דײַן זאָמד,

און ווער קושט עם, איך בעט אײַך, זיך אַליין ?

JACOB GLATSTEIN

(born on August 20, 1896, in Lublin;
died on November 19, 1971, in New York)

Of course anything can happen in an instant,
but it would be a terrible injustice
to take me away so young.

The terrible injustice happened. In the midst of the jubilee celebrations in honor of his 75th birthday, Jacob Glatstein was suddenly taken from us forever, on the night of November 19, 1971.

If one had to summarize in a single sentence the multifaceted creative life of this poet, literary critic, publicist, and essayist, one couldn't find more suitable words than those that he alone had said about himself in a poem:

In everything my eyes have seen,
I was there.
In everything about my poetry,
I was a participant.

As a "participant," he went around the streets of New York not only "as a singer filled with deep faith, with his Yiddish songs," but as one involved in the Yiddish cultural-societal struggle with every fiber of his being, as activist, spokesman, and fighter. He was a blessed artist who could express his thoughts, moods, and convictions on various instruments, and he could play all of them with the same virtuosity.

His essays and publicistic articles bubbled with the same wisdom and keenness as his lyrical poems. He was just as creative, inventive, and provocative orally as he was in writing. In everything, he was as he had presented himself to the Yiddish reader for the first time with his first book of poems: Jacob Glatstein.

In the more than fifty years of his creativity, Glatstein raised himself to the level of our national poets, who, with their poetry, had made a place for themselves not only at the Eastern Wall[79] of our literature but also in the pages of our history. One cannot pass by the time of the eve of Treblinka and Maidanek and not men-

---

79. Figuratively; the expression here means "a place of honor."

tion the alarm-call by this Yiddish poet, who, as early as 1938[80], was knocking on the door of the world, which had closed its eyes and was ignoring the oncoming Holocaust of our people. That was an alarm, a protest, and, at the same time, a call to the millions of Jews over whose heads the sword of Damocles was hanging to take strength and to seek consolation and hope within themselves and within the eternal history of martyrdom.

> *Though everything is devastated,*
> *I cover myself with your dust,*
> *O sad Jewish life.*

Glatstein was saying a prayer to his people, which the world had forced to say "Good night, world." In the face of the ghetto, the yellow patches, and the oncoming Holocaust, the poet was nevertheless consoling that it was just an angry, passing night, and that "green leaves will yet rustle on our withered tree."

Dozens of articles throughout the world were written at that time about Glatstein's poem *A Gute Nakht, Velt* (Good Night World). Most of them expressed criticism and resentment that the poet "was calling us back to the ghetto." But when we look back to that era in retrospect, we know that the poem wasn't really a call to lock ourselves back into the ghetto but an expression of belief in the spirit of our people, which emerged intact and exalted from all the oppression and torture that the world inflicted on us. It is a historical document about an era that only a poet of great understanding and courage could have created, when in response to the world's "cold compresses of sympathy" he could throw into its face such proud words as:

> *Good night, electricity-arrogant world—*
> *back to my kerosene, my tallow-candle shadows,*
> *eternal October, tiny stars;*
> *to my crooked streets, humpbacked lanterns,*
> *torn old scrolls and Biblical studies,*
> *Talmud and its difficult passages;*
> *to glorious Yiddish,*
> *to the sacred Law, to deep meaning, to duty, to justice.*
> *World, I stride with joy to the quiet ghetto lights.*

The poem is also, in great measure, a key to the entire poetic persona of Jacob Glatstein. Few of our writers were so clearly bound to world literature and its

---

80. The year his poem *Good Night, World* was written

culture as Glatstein was; he was perhaps one of our most "wordly" Yiddish writers, who "felt at home" in the American and also in the world culture, and in its music and art, its literature and history. But he was, in spite of that (or should one rather say *because* of that?) one of our most Jewish writers, who, despite being new and modern in form, was deeply rooted in Jewish folk-tradition, its psyche and its idiom.

It didn't bother him much when his poems were labeled "provincial." To this, he answered:

> *Others have put their emphasis on the world—*
> *I, on the Jew.*
> *So they'll make hash of my poems some day—*
> *they'll opine*
> *that I was provincial*
> *and fell into the abyss*
> *because I lost sight*
> *of our broad Gentile surroundings.*
> *But a Jewish academic*
> *will remember my name*
> *and will quote me,*
> *help himself to one of my lines.*
> *A hundred years from now,*
> *wherever I may be floating around,*
> *my lips will say piously:*
> *"That's what it means to rise and live,*
> *to be immortal*
> *in the small dear vineyard*
> *of my people."*

Glatstein himself and his poem *Relevant* (Relevant) were both relevant to the problems of our time. He felt pain at the "generational rift" and complained in many of his poems about those who wanted to cut the thread that bounds them to previous generations of their people. In one of his poems, he complains to present-day Jewish grandchildren:

> *I haven't fled as far*
> *from the Lord*
> *as you have*
> *from your grandfather.*

In another poem, he responds to the enthusiasm for ecumenism with these bitterly sarcastic lines:

Little Jew, my jewel, do not fear the bells
and incense. Our murderers
will soon forgive us
for our bit of life
that is always in their way, a stumbling-block.

For two thousand years,
they've sentenced you to wander
under the shadow of their bloody cross.
The bells sound—they say
that they're ready now
to relieve you of the terrible burden
of their compassionate cross.

But he could also rage at and punish his own people, virtually like a prophet, when "with murder in its eyes, it girded itself with bow and arrow" and committed dark crimes during the Kibiyeh episode.[81] "It is difficult " he says, "to forgive such dark heroism," and he turns to those who have "turned away from pity" and have "stained the parchment of my life" with the following harsh words:

Don't go into world-imprisonment
with bloody chains on your wrists.
Even on the field of battle,
in the dark, shadowed night,
our sons must be radiant Jews,
not marauding murderers.

At an intimate party in honor of Glatstein's 75th birthday, a few days before his sudden death, fellow-writers took particular note of the remarkable fact that Glatstein had achieved such verbal virtuosity precisely at a time when "our children play in deaf-and-dumb language," as Glatstein put it, and when "Yiddish words are sad precious stones that are lying extinguished in heaps of dust."

---

81. An attack in 1953 by Jewish military forces against Arab villagers, which caused many deaths; though the attack was in retaliation for a previous hand-grenade attack of Arab infiltrators against a Jewish village, many in the Jewish community, like Glatstein here, criticized it severely.

When Sholem Aleichem wanted to write the way people spoke, he went out into the street and listened to the language of the Jew, which he then described. But whence came "the joy of the Yiddish word" that bubbled up in all the themes and charms of Glatstein's language? After all, the Jew from Lublin was all of seventeen years old when he began to walk through the New York streets as a "deeply faith-filled singer with torn shoes and bare hands."

The answer can be found in Glatstein's poems. He saw himself, like the entire Yiddish literature in America, as "the guardian at the forest gate who is guarding a great treasure," and he called on himself and all the other guardians of Yiddish: "Let us strengthen the tiny little people with the speech of our remembered Jewish scene, and with our shaky memories of Yiddish speech spoken at the Mount Sinai of Jewish villages." Glatstein preserved in himself the Yiddish speech of generations of Jews in Jewish villages, and he also renewed it with new and wonderful sounds and charms.

* * *

At the jubilee celebration that we held in honor of the poet, his face was shining. He expressed his great joy that so many Jews had come to help him carry his youthfulness. "Only a Yiddish poet can be worthy of such an honor," he said. He did indeed look young, as in the poem he recited:

> *I don't yet recognize my own limits—*
> *I wouldn't change places with the youngest person.*
> *My face is not yet engraved*
> *with the scars of aged wisdom.*

It never occurred to anyone, and certainly not to him, to recall the last lines of that same poem, in which he says:

> *Of course, anything can happen in an instant,*
> *but it would be a terrible injustice*
> *to take me away so young.*

As Glatstein said to I.L. Peretz, so can we too say:

> *You Yiddishized*
> *our thrust to the outside,*
> *brought a holiday atmosphere*
> *and beauty to our substance.*

Speak Yiddish To Me

Speak Yiddish to me, my Jewish land,
and I, naturally, will speak Hebrew to you.
Abraham and Sarah are coming toward me
from the Cave of the Patriarchs.

God help me, dear grandpa and grandma—
Abraham is walking silently in the street.
"Don't take it to heart, Yankl,"
says Sarah. "He's an expert on all languages.

"It's taken for granted here—
a man should not speak Yiddish.
But a woman
has something to say about Yiddish,
so I say to you: 'God help you, my child—
All good things to you.'"

"Believe me, Yankele, there will come a time
in the tree-shaded land of raisins and figs
when every Hebrew child
will stop not speaking Yiddish.

"And when they burst into speech,
and they will, it will be a pleasure to hear it.
That will happen, Yankele, my child—
I can swear an oath to you about it."

Grandfather Abraham, from across the street,
winks to me and waves his shawl.
Oh speak Yiddish to me, my Jewish land,
and, naturally, I will speak Hebrew to you.

A Father To His Son

My son, I've led your blind fingers
over Yiddish writing as if over Braille.
I've secretly fed you

רעד צו מיר ייִדיש

רעד צו מיר ייִדיש, מײַן ייִדיש-לאַנד,
און איך וועל צו דיר רעדן עבֿרית ממילא.
אבֿרהם מיט שׂרהן קומען מיר אַנטקעגן,
פֿון דער מערת המכפּלה.

— גאָט-העלף, זיידע-באָבעשי.
אבֿרהם גייט שװײַגנדיק די גאַס אַריבער..
— נעם זיך ניט צום האַרצן, יאַנקעלע,
זאָגט שׂרה, ער איז מבֿין כּל דיבור.

ס׳איז אַזוי דאָ אַנגענומען.
אַ מאַנסבּיל דאַרף ייִדיש שטומען.
אָבער אַ ייִדענע פֿון ייִדיש-טײַטש
האָט אויך עפּעס װאָס צו זאָגן.
זאָג איך דיר גאָט-העלף, מײַן קינד,
זאָלסט מיר אַל דאָס גוטס פֿאַרמאָגן.

גלייב מיר, יאַנקעלע, ס׳ועט קומען אַ צײַט,
אין כּאַמישאַסער-לאַנד פֿון ראָזשינקעס און פֿײַגן,
אַז אַלע עבֿרית-קינדער
וועלן אויפֿהערן ייִדיש שװײַגן.

און אַז זיי וועלן זיך צערעדן,
וועלן זיי, וועט אַ נחת זײַן צו הערן,
אַזוי וועט געשען, יאַנקעלע, מײַן קינד,
אַ שבֿועה קען איך דיר שווערן.

דער זיידע אבֿרהם פֿון יענער זײַט גאַס,
וויינקט צו מיר און פֿאַכעט מיט דער פּאַטשיילע.
אַ, רעד צו מיר ייִדיש, מײַן ייִדיש-לאַנד,
און איך וועל צו דיר רעדן עבֿרית ממילא.

אַ פֿאָטער צו זײַן זון

מײַן קינד, כ׳האָב געפֿירט דײַנע בלינדע פֿינגער
איבער ייִדישן שריפֿט װי איבער ברעליל.
כ׳האָב דיר אײַנגעגעבן,

teaspoonfuls of *yidishkeyt.*
You made a face
as if it were castor oil--
you never understood what I was saying.
My child, I vaccinated you
to protect you against the outside.

I fed you Yiddish day in and day out—
sculpted your body with love and affection.
You always wondered
how a father could be so cruel,
how he could make a child's wounds
angrier and rawer.
My child, I gave you
substance and Jewish perseverance.

Now you're wandering away—
the outside has pulled you away.
You're drawn to the mountains,
and the valleys call to you.
You're fleeing—your father's Torah has grown stale.
But all your yearning limbs
cry: *shema yisroel.*[82]

Good Night, World

Good night wide world,
big, stinking world--
not you but I lock the gate.
With my long black coat
and my fiery yellow patch,
with a proud step and at my own command,
I go back to the ghetto.
Erase and stamp out all traces of assimilation—
I am wallowing in your garbage.
Praise, praise, praise
O crippled Jewish life;

---

82. The last prayer of a Jew facing imminent death.

בגנבֿה, עס-לעפֿלען יודישקייט.
האסט זיך געקרומט
ווי ס׳וואלט געווען ריצנאייל
האסט קיין מאל נישט פֿארשטאנען וואס כ׳בין געווען אויסן.
מײַן קינד, כ׳האב דיר געשטעלט פֿאקן,
צו באוואָרענען דיך קעגן דרויסן.

כ׳האב דיך טאָג-אײַן טאָג-אויס געיײַדישט.
געשניטן דײַן לײַב מיט ליבשאַפֿט, מיט צובונד.
האסט זיך תמיד געחידושט
ווי אַ טאַטע קען זײַן אזאַ אכזר,
ווי ער קען דעם קינדס וווּנד
מאַכן וווּנדיקער און רויער.
מײַן קינד, כ׳האב דיר אײַנגעגעבן
האָפֿט און יודישן דווער.

איצט בלאַנדזשעסטו אַוועק.
ס׳האָט דיך די פֿרעמד פֿאַרשלעפֿט.
ס׳ציט דיך צום באַרג,
ס׳רופֿט דיך דער טאָל.
אַנטלויפֿסט. דעם טאָטנס תורה איז אויסגעװװעפֿט.
אָבער אַלע דײַנע פֿאַרבענקטע אבֿרים
שרײַען שמע ישראל.

אַ גוטע נאַכט, וועלט

אַ גוטע נאַכט, ברייטע וועלט,
גרויסע, שטינקענדיקע וועלט.
נישט דו, נאָר איך פֿאַרהאַק דעם טויער.
מיט דעם לאַנגן כאַלאַט,
מיט דער פֿײַערדיקער, געלער לאַט,
מיט דעם שטאָלצן טראָט,
אויף מײַן אייגענעם געבאָט —
גיי איך צוריק אין געטאָ.
וויש אַפֿ, צעטרעט אַלע געשמדטע שפּורן.
כ׳וואַלגער זיך אין דײַן מיסט,
לויב, לויב, לויב,
צעהויקערט יודיש-לעבן.

anathema, world, upon your unclean cultures.
Though everything is devastated,
I cover myself with your dust,
O sad Jewish life.

Pig of a German, hateful Polack,
thieving Rumania, land of swilling and gorging;
flabby Democracy, with your cold-compresses of sympathy.
Good night, electricity-arrogant world—
back to my kerosene, my tallow-candle shadows,
eternal October, tiny stars;
to my crooked streets, humpbacked lanterns,
torn old scrolls and Biblical studies,
Talmud and its difficult passages;
to glorious Yiddish,
to the sacred Law, to deep meaning, to duty, to justice.
World, I stride with joy to the quiet ghetto lights.

Good night. I contribute to you, O world,
all my would-be saviors.
Take the Jesus-Marxes—choke on their courage;
Devil take you for a drop of our baptized blood.
And though the Messiah tarries,
my anticipation rises day by day:
green leaves will yet rustle on our withered tree.
I need no comforting—I'm going back to my four walls,
back from Wagner's pagan music to the humming of *khasidic* melodies.
I kiss you, O disheveled Jewish life—
the joy of coming back weeps within me.

חרם, וועלט, אויף דײַנע טריפֿהנע קולטורן.
כּאטש אַלץ איז פֿאַרוויסט,
שטויב איך זיך אין דײַן שטויב,
טרויעריק ייִדיש לעבן.

חזירישער דאָטש, פֿײַנטלעכער ליאַך,
עמלק־גנבֿ, לאַנד פֿון זויפֿן און פֿרעסן.
שלאַברע דעמאָקראַטיע, מיט דײַנע קאַלטע
סימפּאַטיע־קאָמפּרעסן.
אַ גוטע נאַכט, עלעקטריש־צעחוצפּהטע וועלט.
צוריק צו מײַן קעראָסין, חלבֿנעם שאָטן,
אייביקן אָקטאָבער, דריבנע שטערן,
צו מײַנע קרומע גאַסן, הויקערדיקן לאַמטערן,
מײַנע שמות, מײַן סוואָרבֿע,
מײַנע גמרות, צו די האַרבע
סוגיות, צום ליכטיקן עבֿרי־טײַטש,
צום דין, צום טיפֿן מײַן, צום חובֿ, צום גערעכט,
וועלט, איך שפֿאַן מיט פֿרייד צום שטילן געטאָ־לעכט.

אַ גוטע נאַכט. כ'גיב דיר, וועלט, צושטײַער
אַלע מײַנע באַפֿרײַער.
נעם צו די יעזוסמאַרקסעס, ווערג זיך מיט זייער מוט.
קראַפּיר איבער אַ טראָפּן פֿון אונדזער געטויפֿט בלוט.
און איך האָב.האָפֿן, אַז כאַטש ער זאַמט זיך,
גייט אויף טאָג־אײַן טאָג־אויס מײַן וואַרטן.
ס'וועלן נאָך רוישן גרינע בלעטער
אויף אונדזער בוים דעם פֿאַרקוואָרטן.
איך דאַרף קיין טרייסט נישט.
איך גיי צוריק צו דלד אמות.
פֿון וואָגנערס געץ־מוזיק, צו ניגון, ברומען.
כ'קוש דיך, פֿאַרקאַלטנט ייִדיש־לעבן.
ס'וויינט אין מיר די פֿרייד פֿון קומען.

Grandchild Generations

O dear Jewish grandchild-generations,
generations of play and mischief,
I'm having trouble with your handwriting—
I'm going blind
from the future hieroglyphics.
And though everything is printed beautifully,
the letters are all chewed up
and are even more irritating
than worn out, thousand-year-old papyri.

On the surface, everything looks
clear and understandable—
now it's all coming clear to me.
Seems to me it's not hard—
it's even similar
to Yiddish or Hebrew.
A cozy tear, a smile flashes—
it makes sense and has meaning.
Now you've got it!
But soon it turns into a complete scrawl.

Grandchild of mine, wait a moment—
what's the rush
to run away from me so soon?
First a dozen years
have to pass
to give you time and understanding
to live for us both.
I haven't fled
as far from God
as you are fleeing from your grandfather.

אייניקל-דורות

אַ טײַערע, ייִדישע אייניקל-דורות.
דורות פֿון שפּיל און שטיפֿן.
כ׳מאַטער זיך איבער אײַער שריפֿט.
כ׳בלענד זיך די אויגן
איבער צוקונפֿטיקע היראָגליפֿן.
און כאַטש אַלץ איז שיין געדר.קעט,
זײַנען די אותיות פֿאַרצוקט,
און נאָך גרעסערע פֿאַרדרוסן
ווי אָפּגעריבענע טויזנטיאָריקע פּאַפּירוסן.

אויבנאויף זעט אַלץ אויס
קלאָר און פֿאַרשטייִש.
אָט ווערט מיר ליכטיק
אין די אויגן.
ס׳דאַכט זיך ס׳איז נישט שווער,
ס׳איז ענלעך אַפֿילו,
אויף ייִדיש, העברעיִש.
ס׳גיט אַ בליץ אויף
אַ היימישע טרער, אַ שמייכל,
אַ זין, אַ פּשט, אַ שׂכל.
אָט האָט איר עם !
אָבער באַלד ווערט דערפֿון —
לאָפּעטעס מיט קאַטשערעס.

אייניקלעך מײַנע, וואָרעם אַ ווײַלע,
וואָס איז ס׳געאײַל,
פֿון מיר אַזוי גיך צו אַנטלויפֿן ?
ס׳דאַרף דאָך לכל-הפּחות פֿאָרלויפֿן
אַ צענדליק יאָר,
וואָס זאָל געבן
אָרט-צײַט און פֿאַרנעם,
צו לעבן פֿאָר אונדז ביידן.
איך בין אַזוי ווײַט נישט אַנטלאָפֿן
פֿון בעל-שם,
ווי איר אַנטלויפֿט פֿון אײַער זיידן.

My Father-Mother Language

The flashbulb of my father's *git vokh*[83]
after the last shadowed minutes
of holy Sabbath humming—
that's Yiddish to me.
The first yearned-for star
and my mother's accompanying tears
for the dear, hearty Sabbath that is going away
and the dear week that is coming—
to your good health, to life, to good luck,
to blessings, and to making a good living.

The worried hands for my mother's
"God of Abraham,"
which, throughout the week,
were taking down the iron bars
of the clothing-shop;
my father's wavering voice,
which separated quiet holiness
from the talkative holiness of the weekdays:
his *havdole* was a blessing
on the entire week
of lively, tumultuous,
warm Yiddish.

The singing melody of my Torah with Rashi,[84]
of my Talmud translation,
the song of all the interpretations and gestures,
the flaming fire of my great teachers,
my examiners,
burning faith in a better world,
and also in my deniers and explainers--
you were the whole *hasidic* kingdom,
my father-mother Yiddish.
You talked to God so simply--
you were the noble companion

---

83. "Good week," to greet the incoming workaday week, as opposed to *git shabes*, to greet the Sabbath.
84. The most famous commentator on the Torah, from the 12th century.

מײַן טאַטע־מאַמע־שפּראַך

דער בליצלאַמפּ פֿון טאַטנס גיטװאָך,
נאָך די לעצטע פֿאַרשאַטנטע רגעם
פֿון הייליקן שבתדיקן ברומען —
איז פֿאַר מיר ייִדיש.
דער ערשטער אויסגעבענקטער שטערן,
דער מאַמעס באַגלייטנדיקע טרערן
צום ליבן האַרציקן שבת װאָס גייט אַװעק
און צו דער ליבער װאָך װאָס טוט קומען —
צו געזונט, צום לעבן, צו מזל,
צו ברכה און צו אַ גוטער פּרנסה.

די זאַרגעװודיקע הענט פֿון דער מאַמעס
גאָט פֿון אבֿרהם,
װאָס האָבן אויף דער פֿולער װאָך
אַרונטערגענומען די אײַזערנע שטאַבעס
פֿון דער קליידער־קראָם.
דעם טאַטנס צעפֿלאַקערט קול,
װאָס האָט אָפּגעשײדט שטילע הייליקייט
פֿון דער ריידעװודיקער הייליקייט פֿון חול.
זײַן הבֿדלה איז געװען דער קידוש
אויף אַ גאַנצער װאָך
פֿון לעבעדיקן, טומלדיקן
און װאַרעמען ייִדיש.

געזאַנגיקער ניגון פֿון מײַן חומש מיט רש״י,
פֿון מײַן גמרא־טײַטש,
ליד פֿון אַלע מײַנע פּשטלעך און תּנועות,
פֿלאַם־פֿײַער פֿון די גרויסע מלמדים מײַנע,
פֿון מײַנע פֿאַרהערערס,
ברענענדיקע אמונה אין אַ בעסערער װעלט,
אויך פֿון מײַנע לייקענערס און אויפֿקלערערס.
דאָס גאַנצע מלכות־חסידיש
ביסטו געװוען, מײַן טאַטע־מאַמע ייִדיש.
האָסט זיך אַזוי פֿראָסט געזאָגט מיט דעם בעל־שם,
ביסט געװען דער איידעלער חבֿר

of the yearning Bratslaver.[85]
How can I be false to you?
You're not just my mother tongue,
a language from my cradle,
but the seal of all my memories.
Partner language of my folk priesthood,
language of the poor workingmen,
our fatherly *git vokh*, flashbulb of our life—
none other did your mother's
"God of Abraham"
give you as a consolation.

---

85. Rabbi Nachman of Bratslav, the great-grandson of the Bal Shem and a distinguished *hasidic* scholar in his own right

פֿון דעם פֿאַרבענקטן בראצלאָווער.

ווי קען איך פֿעלשן אין דיר ?

ביסט מיר נישט בלויז קיין מוטערשפּראך,

קיין שפּראך פֿון וויגל,

נאָר דער זיגל פֿון אַלע מײַנע געדעכעענישן.

שותּפֿות־שפּראך פֿון מײַן פֿאַלקס־כּהונה,

לשון פֿון זײַן אָרעמער, פֿאַרהאַרעוועטער חיונה.

פֿאָטערלעכער גיטוואָך אונדזערער, בליצלאָמפּ פֿון אונדזער
לעבן,

נישט אַנדערש, ס׳האָט אונדז דער מאָמעם
גאָט פֿון אברהם
דיך פֿאַר אַ טרייסט געגעבן.

AARON GLANTZ-LEYELES

(Born in Voltshavek, Poland, in 1889; died in New York City in 1966.)

Aaron Glantz-Leyeles, like Zishe Landau, was the founder and spokesman of a new trend in Yiddish poetry. He was a personality who had a lasting influence on our entire Yiddish cultural community in America, and also outside of America: on literature, into which he introduced new poetic forms; on the Yiddish press, in which, with great courage and talent, he took on a dominant role as an independent fighter for the truths in which he believed; on the Yiddish and Yiddishistic cultural community, in which he was a practical activist who inspired the new efforts with his belief; and on the Yiddish secular schools, in which he was one of the pioneer teachers. Even before the appearance of the schools of the fraternal organizations, he created the first Yiddish secular school on Henry Street in New York, and later helped found similar schools in Rochester, Winnipeg, and Toronto. There was, in other words, not a single corner of Yiddish-secular cultural life in America that Leyeles didn't influence with his words, his deeds, and his thoughts.

But the main thing for which Leyeles is remembered in our literary history is for being the founder and spokesman of the combative group *In Zikh,* which he, together with Jacob Glatstein and Nokhem Borekh Minkoff, established in 1919. Those were the years when *Di Yunge*, with Zishe Landau, Mani Leib, and Reuben Iceland at their head, were involved in a struggle against "thought" poetry and also against the poets who wrote social and national poetry. The *Inzikhists,* who were also known as the *Introspectivists*, demanded a broadening of the themes of poetry so as to express not only an individual's moods and feelings, but also precisely thought, which *Di Yunge* had so strongly opposed. Their credo was, among other things, the use of simple words and that everything the poet sees around him can be a stimulus for poetry. There was no such thing, they claimed, as "poetic" and "non-poetic" words—all the words in human language could be used for writing poems. They also fought for free verse in poetry so that it could express the poet's thoughts precisely, not limited by rhyme and rhythm. The group was young and combative, and, just like *Di Yunge*, it denigrated many recognized poets of the day. A fierce war developed that lasted for quite a few years.

In a conversation with Jacob Pat many years later (*Shmuesn Mit Yidishe Shrayber/* Conversations with Yiddish Writers, 1954), Leyeles, in answer to the ques-

444

tion about what the battle with *Di Yunge* consisted of, answered as follows: "They concentrated only on mood. They ignored thought in their poetry. They had contempt for ideas—they didn't want to see an expression of national struggle in poetry. We turned our face toward life, towards the boiling cauldron of the world, the general and the Jewish world. One may write poems not only about workers and strikes but even about mayoral elections. We fought for true poetry that is simultaneously full of deep *yidishkeyt*."

Leyeles later revised more than one of his positions. His colleague Jacob Glatstein wrote about that: "He had considered free verse to be at a higher level than rhyme and regular rhythm, [but] in contradiction of all his declarations about new rhythms, he later began restraining his own outcries." Leyeles himself wrote about that in one of his poems:

> *Structure myself I must, though I love free verse*
> *and with it I've aired out our language and tongue,*
> *but now I'm afraid of free strides and swings*

That, already, was in the time of the Holocaust, when Leyeles, in his book *A Yid Oyfn Yam* (A Jew At Sea), in restrained but deeply felt poems, expressed the pain of all of us about what had happened to our people.

Every new book of poetry or drama that he published elicited great recognition in the literary world. Though the recognition didn't come immediately because "he had to fight a long and stiff-necked battle with literary judgments" (Leo Finkelstein), he achieved his recognition. Samuel Niger confessed that "Leyeles assisted in the modernization and urbanization of Yiddish poetic language, and had an influence with his dramatic poems and with the richness of his poetic forms."

Leyeles's poems on American motifs are unique in the Yiddish language. They are an inspired paean to the big city that no one sang before him: to New York, the Bowery, Columbus Circle, Battery Park, and the rivers that encircle New York. A special place is occupied by the poem *Amerike un Ikh* (America and I), in which the poet "sums up the fifty years" he lived and created in America, and the struggle he carried on:

> *I brought fiery battle into Yiddish poetry;*
> *I brought new rhythms and new rhymes;*
> *I breathed a new outlook on life,*
> *derived not only from melancholy evenings*

or from a narrow, lyrical, decorative frame.
Storms lashed at me,
exactly as if I had shattered the ancient holy Tablets.

Many critical essays, treatments, and dissertations have been written about Leyeles and his place in Yiddish literature. We quote here a paragraph from Isaac Bashevis's essay in his book *Penimer un Nemen* (Faces and Names):

> *Leyeles was a milestone in the development of Yiddish poetry...not everyone is fated to be the beginner of a new road that others later tread. Leyeles was a beginner, a renewer. Even others who had doubted him later made use of his beginning and his renewal. Many Yiddish poets who didn't pray from his poetic siddur, so to speak, have him to thank for the melodies and recitatives with which they sang out their own prayers.*

My Language

The last ones to write my language, my Yiddish
will belong to the noblest line.
They will bless each and every letter,
will give each word the longed-for flavor.

They will, with acidic, neat strictness,
guard the profundity and wisdom of the people,
and their pained, heroic yearning
will turn them into brightly orderly syllables.

They'll be faithful guardians and builders,
will mix cement from pure hearts,
will lay sorrow upon sorrow, like bricks,
and erect columns of dazzling silver.

They'll polish the varied blueness
of the sky over the Vaysl, the Dnieper, the San,
and folksy Yiddish sounds with the hereness
of the Hudson, La Plata, and Saskatchewan.

Understanding, quiet, self-controlled,
they'll look deeply into the heart of Time
and change from the last ones to the beginners,
the first ones at Fate's command, which gladdens and liberates.

To America

I love the proud skyline of Manhattan,
the rivers of the land, the age-old prairies.
I love the autos, the roads shining like parquet,
I love the dream of the reality called America.

I love the youthful energy and breathing free--
the hopeful voices, all kinds of languages,
the mixture of peoples, races, colors, and tribes
from the sunny South to the North's snowy mountains.

מיַין לשון

די לעצטע צו שרייַבן מיַין לשון, מיַין ייִדיש –
זיי וועלן געהערן צום נאָבלסטן שטאַם.
זיי וועלן אויף איטלעכן אות מאַכן קידוש,
באַטעמען דאָס וואָרט מיט דעם גלוסטיקסטן טעם.

זיי וועלן מיט ציטעריקער, ציכטיקער שטרענגסשאַפֿט
באַוואַכן דאָס עמקות און חכמה פֿון פֿאָלק,
און זייער צעוויַיטיקטע, העלדישע בענקשאַפֿט
אריַינטאָן אין זילבן מיט ליכטיקן טאַלק.

זיי וועלן זיַין שומרים געטריַיע און בויער,
און מישן פֿון הערצער, פֿון ריינע – צעמענט,
און לייגן, ווי ציגל, אַ טרויער נאָך טרויער,
און אויפֿשטעלן זיַילן פֿון זילבערנעם בלענד.

זיי וועלן צעבלישטשען ס'פֿאַרשידענע בלאָקייט
פֿון הימל בײַ זיַי וויַיסל, בײַ דניעפּער, בײַ סאַן,
און היימישע ייִדישע קלאַנגען מיט דאָקייט
פֿון האָדסאָן, לאָפּלאַטאַ און סאַסקאַטשעוואַן.

זיי וועלן – פֿאַרשטאַנדיקע, שטילע, באַהערשטע –
אַריַינקוקן טיף אין דעם האַרץ פֿון דער ציַיט,
און ווערן פֿון די לעצטע די אַנהייבערס, ערשטע
פֿון גורלס געבאָט, וואָס דערפֿרייט און באַפֿריַיט.

צו אַמעריקע

כ'האָב ליב די שטאָלצע הימל־ליניע פֿון מאַנהעטן,
די טויכן פֿון דעם לאַנד, די פֿריַירירס טויזנטיעריקע;
כ'האָב ליב די די אויטאָס, וועגן, גלאַנציק ווי פֿאַרקעטן,
כ'האָב ליב דעם חלום פֿון דער וואָר, וואָס הייסט אַמעריקע.

כ'האָב ליב דעם יונגן אימפּעט און דעם פֿריַיען אָטעם,
די שטימען האָפֿערדיקע, שפּראָכן אַלערליַיאיקע,
דעם אויסטויש פֿון פֿעלקער, ראַסן, פֿאַרבן, שבֿטים –
פֿון דרומס זונלאַנד ביז דעם צפֿונס בערגער שנייאיקע.

I've found here bread to eat and clothes to wear;
I've received here the greatest human gift:
the level gaze, the right to have a will of my own.
And I love you, O land, with tenderness and yearning.

After shame and fear, after patches[86] and the ghetto,
you are the last haven for the last hope.
Fate has given you a blessed, bright mission—
you will not yield to the enemy, the corrupter.

To You, Yiddish Poets

Yiddish poets, you closest brothers of mine,
brothers in the same loneliness, under the same yoke,
in the same lostness and catastrophe—
I write these lines to you, this song of songs,
my most intimate voice,
which will, despite everything,
ring out—today, tomorrow, and after that.
Listen through your searching, suffering, and hustling
to my words in structured and measured octaves.

Structure myself I must, though I love free verse
and with it I've aired out our language and tongue.
But now I'm afraid of free strides and swings—
our reality wails with funereal wails.
Frightened hang the dreams of the faithful—
they dare not spin hopefully, spin youthfully.
If there are no limits to suffering,
create with pain a fence in strictly structured form.

Our song of the Seventh Heaven,
our song of dew and need nourished in every land,
can it not bear fruit anew from every earth?
Oh, we're far from the basics—
our song, yesterday still a blade of grass, a little flower,
has now reached an adulthood that is seldom granted.

---

86. Referring to the yellow patches Jews were forced to wear in the ghettos

כ'האָב דאָ געפֿונען ברויט צום עסן, קלייד צו טראָגן,
כ'האָב דאָ באַקומען ס'העכסטע מענטשלעכע געשענקעניש:
דעם גראָדן קוק, דאָס רעכט אַ ווילן צו פֿאַרמאָגן,
און כ'ליב דיך, לאַנד, מיט צערטלעכקייט, מיט בענקעניש.

נאָך חרפֿה און גאַט שרעק, נאָך לאָטעס און נאָך געטאָ,
ביסטו פֿאַר לעצטער האָפֿענונג דער לעצטער האַבעריק.
דער גורל שטעלט דיר אַ געבענטשטע, העלע מעטע –
דו וועסט נישט נאָכגעגבן דער שׂינאה, דער פֿאַרדאָרבערקע.

צו אײַך דיכטער יידישע

דיכטער יידישע, איר מײַנע נאָענטסטע ברידער,
ברידער פֿון דעם זעלבן עלנט, פֿון דעם זעלבן יאָך,
פֿון דעם זעלביקן פֿאַרלוירעגניש און בראָך –
כ'שרײַב צו אײַך די שורות, אַזאַ ליד פֿון לידער,
מײַן אינטימסטע שטים, וואָס וידער אַלץ און וידער
קלינגען וועט אי היַינט, אי מאָרגן, און דערנאָך.
האָרכט מײַן וואָרט דורך אײַער זוכן, לײַדן, האַווען,
אין געצוימטע און געמאָסטענע אָקטאַווען.

צוימען מוז איך זיך, כאָטש כ'ליב די ריטמען פֿרײַע,
און איך האָב זיי מיט געלופֿטערט אונדזער שפֿראַך און צונג.
נאָר כ'האָב איצטער מורא פֿאַר צו פֿרײַען שפֿאַן און שוווּנג,
ס'יאָמערט אונדזער וואָר מיט יאָמער פֿון לוויה,
שרעקיק העטגען איצט די טרוימען די געטרײַע,
וואָגן ניט צו שפֿינען האָפֿערדיק, צו שפֿינען יונג.
ווען קיין גרענעץ איז נישטאָ פֿאַר די יסורים,
וויַיטיק–אויס אַ סיאָג פֿון שטרענג–געצוימטן פֿורעם.

אונדזער ליד פֿון זיבנפֿאַכעדיקן הימל,
אונדזער ליד, מיט טוי און נויט פֿון יערן לאַנד גענערט,
קען עס ניט באַפֿרוכפֿערן פֿונסנײַ נאָך יעדע ערד?
אַ, מיר האַלטן ווײַט נאָך אלף, בית און גימל,
אונדזער ליד, נאָך נעכטן ערשט אַ גרעזל, בלימל,
איז שוין אַ צעוואָקסנקייט וואָס זעלטן וועם באַשערט.

If a hand is pushing us down to the lowest depths,
let's sing today the brightest, loudest songs.

Let them, like timidly fluttering doves,
soar above the mountains and valleys of Time
to a time that is lazily indifferent, to a wanton time.
Let them knock on a doubter's windowpane
and tell about our wounded belief
and our need and struggle.
Perhaps a window will open somewhere
and the most alienated person will stretch out his arm.

אויב אונדז שטויסט אַ האַנט צו סאַמע לעצטער נידער,
לאָמיר זינגען היַנט די עלסטע, העכסטע לידער.

זאָלן זיי ווי פֿאַרכטיק–פֿלאַטערדיקע טויבן
זיך צעשוועבן איבער בערג און טאָלן פֿון דער ציַיט,
צו אַ זמן, וואָס פֿוילט אין גליַיכגילט, צו אַ זמן פֿאַרשיַיט.
זאָלן זיי אַ קלאַפּ טאָן אין אַ צוויַיפֿלערס שויבן,
און דערציַילן וועגן אונדזער ווונדער גלויבן,
און דערציַילן וועגן אונדזער גוט און אונדזער שטריַיט.
מעגלעך, ערגעץ וועט זיך עפֿענען אַ פֿענצטער,
און ס'וועט אויסשטרעקן זיַין אָרעם דער פֿאַרפֿרעמדטסטער.

RACHEL KORN

(Born in Podliski, Galicia, on January 15,1898;
died in Montreal, Canada on September 11, 1982.)

Rachel Korn wrote her first poems in the 20s, at a time when Yiddish literature was blossoming in Poland, a time of new schools and trends in poetry, a time of new creative streams that bubbled up from Jewish folk-life. She arrived with her own poetry, which immediately distinguished her from the richly folksy poetic generation.

It was poetry about the village earth that was her home and the home of generations of Jews. She arrived fresh and healthy, with "cherry branches in her hair," and she sang out about *Dorf* (The Village), *Royter Mon* (Red Poppies), and *Shnit (Harvests),* the names of her first books, between 1928 and 1941.

Village life and Nature were not new themes in Yiddish literature, but with few exceptions those who wrote about them were men who had fled from cities to villages, to the forests and fields, and they praised the beauty of Nature as outsiders. Reading the poems and stories of Rachel Korn, one is filled with joy at the rise of a poet who was herself deeply rooted in the village earth and environment and who could draw portraits of the landscape that did not exist in Yiddish literature before her:

> *the fresh black furrows*
> *lie submissive and weary under the autumn sun,*
> *like women giving birth for the first time*
> *who smile quietly out of their pain*
> *and are ready to give birth once again.*

One hears for the first time poems about real love of the forests and fields, of the autumn rains and winds. One tries, together with the poetess, to reach "the deep secrets of the village night" and of the village morning grayness" when

> *the first rosy-red rays of the sun bounce*
> *like squirrels from tree to tree,*
> *from branch to branch,*
> *closer and closer to the ground,*
> *and drown the abundance with dew.*

454

After the four books about the village and earthy motifs came eight more books, but now not about rootedness but about the homelessness and wandering of her refugee years in Great Russia. To the clear poetic portraits and the rich language were added wise thought and clever expression. She reached "*Yener Zayt Lid*" (The Other Side of the Poem) (the title of one of her poems) which few poets have the privilege of reaching. Her prayer that her words should not be shamed and have to go around in a borrowed, patched shirt as she sings out her sorrow was audible:

> *You've taken everything away from me and turned me into Job:*
> *every year, every day, every hour of my life,*
> *like something pawned and not to be redeemed.*
> *Amid the dust and ash of a burned-up skeleton,*
> *only the words, the poems, belong to me.*

The Spirit of Yiddish Poetry was merciful to her, and let her feel, to her last breath, the "taste of a word that is full of as-yet-unwept tears."

Just like her first poems about the village and the earth, her poems about home-lessness and sorrow have a prayerful tone:

> *My room is full of sorrow,*
> *as the field is with sheaves after the harvest.*
> *Who will inherit them, take care of them,*
> *the book and the field and the poems?*

With How Many Tears

With how many tears must I bathe my eyes
so I can once more see my mother's outstretched hands
and her face, framed by heavy blond braids,
as she turns to me and smiles.

With how much pain and suffering must I get drunk,
how many creases must plow my face,
so I can return, at least once, for a moment,
to our courtyard with its doves and its old well,

the well with a beard of dark-green moss
at which my mother used to stand, bent over in deep thought,
looking at the little white cloud-boat
over which the sun had cast a golden net?

But wait—Marishka is now turning the handle,
letting the wide bucket down deep into the water.
She drowns the little white cloud-boat,
and my mother's face fades away.

Kheshvan[87]

The fresh black furrows
lie submissive and weary under the autumn sun
like women giving birth for the first time
who smile quietly out of their pain
and are ready to give birth once again.

Crows have gathered for the party.
They take measured, mincing steps
and search with their wise black eyes for the dug-up worms,
shaking their heads like old aunts
when they chew pieces of cake with their toothless gums.
"The pain is not so bad—it's like a white rose,
and soon you'll have joy, soon,
even before swallows, with their sharp tails,
shear the first wool off the spring sky."

---

87. An autumn month in the Jewish calendar

אין וויפֿל טרערן

אין וויפֿל טרערן דאַרף איך אויסוואַשן די אויגן,
אַז כ'זאָל נאָך אײן מאָל זען מײַן מאַמעס
אויסגעשטרעקטע הענט
און איר פּנים אײַנגערעמט אין בלאַנדע, שוועארע צעפּ,
מיט אַ שטילן שמייכל אין מײַן זײַט געוואָענדט?

מיט וויפֿל לייד און וויי דאַרף איך נאָך שיכּור ווערן,
מיט וויפֿל קנייטשן נאָך צעאַקערן מײַן פּנים,
אַז כ'זאָל זיך אומקערן כאָטש אײן מאָל אויף אַ רגע
צו דעם הויף מיט טויבן און דעם אַלטן ברונעם?

דעם ברונעם פֿון אַ באַרד מיט מאָכן טונקל-גרינע,
וווּ ס'פֿלעגט מײַן מאַמע שטיין פֿאַרטראַכט און אײַנגעבויגן.
און נאָכקוקן דעם קלײנעם ווײַסן וואָלקן-שיפֿל,
איבער וועלכן ס'האָט די זון אַ גילדענע נעץ פֿאַרצויגן.

נאָר אָט, מאַרישקע דרייט שוין מיט דער קאָרבע
און לאָזט אַראָפּ דעם ברייטן עמער טיף אין וואַסער –
זי דערטרענקט דאָס קלײנע, ווײַסע וואָלקן-שיפֿל,
און מײַן מאַמעס פּנים ווערט אַלץ בלאַס און בלאַסער.

חשוון

די פֿרישע, שוואַרצע סקיבעס ערד
ליגן חכנהדיק און מיד אַנטקעגן אָסיענדיקער זון,
ווי די גאָווינערינס אין זייער ערשטער קימפּעט,
וואָס שמייכלען שטיל אַפֿער פֿון זייער ווייטיק
און זענען גרייט שוין נאָך אַמאָל צו ווערן מאַמעס.

עס זענען זיך צונויפֿגעקומען וואָרענעס צו דער שמחה,
שפּאַצירן מיט געצײלטע, טענצלדיקע שריט,
זוכן מיט שוואַרצע, קלוגע אויגן די אויסגעגראַבֿ'נע ווערים
און שאָקלען מיט די קעפּ, ווי אַלטע מומעס
בשעתן קײַמען שטיקלערך לעקעך מיט די בלאָע יאַסלעס:
"נישקשה, ס'איז דער ווייטיק, ווי די ווײַסע ראָסע,
און באַלד וועסטו דערלעבן נחת, באַלד,
נאָך איידער ס'וועלן שוואַלבן מיט די שאַרפֿע עקן
אַפּשערן די ערשטע וואָל פֿון פֿרילינגדיקן הימל."

Last Night I Felt

Last night I felt a poem on my lips,
a juicy fruit with hard-edged rind.
It flew away at dawn's first light—
left its aroma in my mind.

I hear the stammer of the things
that should have come to words in it,
but stand abandoned, hearts clamped shut,
beyond entreaty, oaths, or wit.

With every limb in frozen death,
with down-bowed head I cry,
for God bade me to do Creation,
and I have failed Him, who knows why.

The light of day is fading now—
the paper withers in my barren hand.
God's face He hides from me with clouds,
and in my house of shame I stand.

On The Other Side Of The Poem

On the other side of the poem is a meadow
on which there is a straw-thatched house.
Standing near, three silent pines—
standing quiet as a mouse.

On the other side of the poem is a bird,
all yellow-brown with breast of red.
It flies here every wintertime—
its color crowns a bush that's dead.

On the other side of the poem is a path—
it's sharp and thin, a hairline slit,

כ׳האָב היַינט ביַי נאַכט

כ׳האָב היַינט ביַי נאַכט געפֿילט אַ ליד אױף מיַינע ליפֿן –
עס איז געװעזן װי אַ פֿרי זאַפֿטיק–זיס און האַרב,
נאָר עס איז אסױגערונען אין מיַין בלוט ביַים טאָגס באַגין,
און ס׳גײיען מיר בלויז נאָך זיַין ריח און זיַן פֿאַרב.

זיַין שטילן ציטער הער איך אַלץ אין שטאַמלעניש פֿון זאַכן,
װאָס האָבן דורך דעם ליד געזאַלט נתגלה װערן;
זײ שטײען איצט פֿאַרלאָזטע, מיט פֿאַרמאַכטע הערצער,
און ס׳קענען זײ מער נישט עפֿענען קײן בעטן און באַשװערן.

ס׳װײנט מיט פֿאַרפֿרירטן טױט אין מיר אידער אבֿר,
און ס׳איז מיַין קאָפּ געבױגן אבֿלדיק צו דר׳ערד;
עס האָט מיך גאָט גערופֿן באַניַיען דעם בראשית,
און איך – איך האָב זיַין שטים פֿאַרפֿעלט און נישט דערהערט.

פֿאַרװיאַנעט איז דער טאָג שױן אין זיַן פֿריסטער שעה,
און אין מיַין האַנט עקרהדיק װעלקט ס׳װיַיסע בלאַט פּאַפּיר.
ס׳האָט מיט אַ כמאַרע גאָט פֿאַרשטעלט פֿאַר מיר זיַן פּנים,
און װי אַ פֿרעמדע שטײ איך איצט ביַי מיַין פֿאַרשעמטער טיר.

פֿון יענער זיַיט ליד

פֿון יענער זיַיט ליד איז אַ סאָד פֿאַראַן
און אין סאָד אַ הױז מיט אַ שטרויעינעם דאַך.
עס שטײען דריַי סאָסנעס און שװיַיגן זיך אױס,
דריַי שומרים אױף שטענדיקער װאַך.

פֿון יענער זיַיט ליד איז אַ פֿױגל פֿאַראַן,
אַ פֿױגל ברוין–געל מיט אַ רױטלעכער ברוסט.
ער קומט דאָרט צו פֿליִען יעדן װינטער אױף ס׳ניַי
און העַנגט װי אַ קנאָפּס אױף דעם נאַקעטן קוסט.

פֿון יענער זיַיט ליד איז אַ סטעזשקע פֿאַראַן,
אַזױ שמאָל און שאַרף װי דער דין–דינסטער שניט,

and someone barefoot, lost in time,
now softly walks the length of it.

On the other side of the poem wonders be,
even on a dull, dark day
that pulses, wounded, 'gainst the pane,
its fevered longing to display.

On the other side of the poem, mama may come out
and stand on the doorstep thoughtfully—
Then call me home, just as of old:
"Enough of games, come home to me!"

You

I am saturated with you,
like earth after a spring rain,
and my brightest day hangs
on the pounding pulse of your first word,
like a bee on the blossoming branch of a linden tree.

And I am above you, like the promise of plenty
when the wheat and rye even out in the fields
and lie with the hope of greenness
on the swept floors of the granary.

And my fingertips drip faithfulness onto your weary head,
like golden-yellow honey,
and my years,
the field your feet tread,

get fat and swollen
with pain, the pain of loving you,
my beloved husband.

און עמעץ, וואָס האָט זיך פֿאַרבלאָנדזשעט אין צײַט,
גייט דאָרט אום מיט שטילע און באַרװעסע טריט.

פֿון יענער זײַט ליד קענען וווּנדער געשען
נאָך הײַנט, אין אַ טאָג, וואָס איז כמאַרנע און גראָ,
ווען ער דופּקט אַרײַן אין דעם גלאָז פֿון דער שויב
די צעפֿיבערטע בענקשאַפֿט פֿון אַ וווּנדיקער שעה.

פֿון יענער זײַט ליד קען עמען מײַן מאַמע אַרויס,
און שטיין אויף דער שוועל אַ ווײַלע פֿאַרטראַכט
און מיך רופֿן אַהיים, ווי אַ מאָל, ווי אַ מאָל:
– גענוג זיך געשפּילט שוין, דו זעסט נישט? ס'איז נאַכט.

דיר

כ'בין דורכגעװעײקט מיט דיר, ווי ערד מיט פֿרילינגדיקן רעגן,
און ס'הענגט מײַן בלאָנדסטער טאָג
בײַם קלאַפֿנדיקן דופּק פֿון דײַן ערשטן וואָרט,
ווי אַ בין בײַם בליענדיקן צווײַג פֿון ליפּעס.

און כ'בין איבער דיר, ווי דער צוזאָג פֿון שפֿע אין דער צײַט
ווען אין פֿעלד גלעכט זיך אויס דער ווײץ מיטן קאָרן
און לייגט זיך מיט דער האָפֿענונג פֿון גרינקייט
איבער די אויסגעקערטע פֿאַדלאָגעס און שפּײַכלערס.

פֿון מײַנע שפּיצן פֿינגער טריפֿט געטרישאַפֿט אויף דײַן מידן קאָפּ,
ווי גאָלד–געלער האָניק,
און מײַנע יאָרן,
פֿעלד אויף וועלכן ס'טרעטן דײַנע פֿיס,
ווערן פֿעט און אָנגעשוואָלן
פֿון ווייטיק – דיך צו ליבן,
געליבטער מאַן.

KADYA MOLODOWSKY

(born in 1894 in Kartuz-Bereze, Poland; died on March 21, 1975)

Beginning with her book of poetry *Nights of Kheshvan*, which was published in 1927, the poet Kadya Molodowsky received recognition and praise from critics and readers. The women readers were especially moved by the feminine and maternal feelings that she expressed in her poetry. Her descriptions of the poverty and the sad situation in Dzhika Street and other streets in Warsaw were received with great empathy; readers identified with her sympathy for the needy children, among whom were the scrawny children she taught in the Yiddish schools. She depicted the workers and their strikes and illegal activities, and was impelled to march with them.

Kadya Molodowsky was born in Kartuz-Bereze, Poland, in 1894. She learned Torah and Talmud from her father the teacher, together with his other students, and she graduated from the Hebrew Teacher's Seminary in Warsaw. At the beginning of the 1920s, she lived in Kiev and was part of the community of the local writers. Later she went to Warsaw and became a teacher in the *Tsisho*-schools.[88] In 1935, she emigrated to New York. From 1950 to 1952, she lived in Israel. She then returned to America and renewed the magazine *Svive* (Community), which she had published previously. She died in 1975.

One of our favorite poems by Kadya Molodowsky is her *Eyl Khanun* (Merciful God), in which she prays to God to choose some other people:

Merciful God,
we are tired of dying;
for now, we no longer pray
to be victims...

and at the end of the prayer, she pleads:

and one more bit of grace to us,
merciful God—
take away from us the Divine Spirit of genius...

---

88. Yiddish-language schools sponsored by the Bund

The poem makes a powerful impression on the reader. How much stronger it was, one can imagine, when it was heard being read as an accompaniment to a dance performed by the brilliant artist-choreographer Pearl Lang. That was an unforgettable performance! Lang often read poems by her beloved poet Kadya Molodowsky to an audience.

Another moving poem by Kadya Molodowsky is *Light Your Candle*:

> *I may be the last of my generation--*
> *that's not my concern;*
> *it's not I that prepared the seeds of Time.*
> *My day, my only day,*
> *has merely been loaned to me,*
> *and I don't know when they'll want it back.*
> *When I was sixty or seventy,*
> *they told me:*
> *you are not superfluous;*
> *don't violate your only day—*
> *it's your today, your yesterday, and your forever.*
> *At whatever table they seat you,*
> *there light your candle and set up your pulpit.*
> *And even your candle has only been loaned to you.*
>
> *You are not the extinguisher and not the lighter;*
> *whether it's a bright day*
> *or one on which blind darkness has struck*
> *is not your concern—*
> *light your candle and be its guardian;*
> *your flame is part of the group of candles.*
> *You don't know who lit it or where,*
> *and while the candle burns*
> *you must carry both the light and the wounds.*

Kadya Molodowsky created a great deal of joy for children with her children's stories and poems. In the schools, children beamed with pleasure at such poems as *The Dark Cloth Coat*:

> *Then let my story now begin:*
> *not one about a sweet white goat*
> *but one about a handsome coat,*
> *a lovely, brand-new dark cloth coat.*

And the poet tells about a coat that is given to the children in the family to wear, from Shmuelik to Yosl Ber, to Beyla, to Hindl, till it comes to the brat Pantl, the youngest child, who tears it up till only the holes remain:

The very day he put it on,
he tore its corners—look and see!
The next day, not to be outdone,
he tore a hole right in the knee.
The evening of that selfsame day,
the collar's missing—something new!
And also two great gaping holes,
right at the elbows—howdja do!

The children took pleasure from other such poems: *Alka With the Blue Parasol* and *The Lady With the Little Dog*, in which

A lady comes to the train with a lot of luggage:
a little basket, a box, a little valise,
a pack, a sack, a little carton the size of a dot,
and a tiny dog.

A big dog jumps onto the train, and after three days of traveling they explain to the lady that during that time her tiny dog has grown into a big dog.

When the Jewish State came into being, Kadya Molodowsky wrote several books of poems about Jerusalem and the new Jewish land:

Whence comes the light throughout the world?
From Jerusalem comes the light throughout the world,
for it is there that the Shekhinah[89] resides—
so comes the light throughout the world.

Whence comes song throughout the world?
From Mount Zion comes song throughout the world,
for there the singer resides,
the Psalms of David—
so comes song throughout the land.

The grace throughout the world comes from Jerusalem, for it is there that the

---

89. The Divine Spirit, an aspect of God

prophets walked. Valor comes from the sands of Mount Sinai, for there the Ten Commandments were brought down on fiery tablets. And finally, the glow throughout the world comes from the stones of Jerusalem, for they:

> *washed them with tears,*
> *purified them with pain—*
> *so comes the glow throughout the world.*

Another beautiful poem about Israel is her poem *Psalm*, to which Malke Gottlieb wrote a charming melody, and which Ben Bonus used to sing; it is printed in our collection *Holidays*:

> Young were the birds in the ancient land.
> God planted a tree there
> with His right hand.
> The tree is blooming in the middle of the desert;
> blooming—that is a miracle!
> And a bird sings tunes there
> three times a day.

We first met Kadya Molodowsky in Camp Hemshekh[90], to which she had been invited to an evening event prepared for her by the children. The children received her with great praise and honor. They were thankful to her, as we all are, for the treasures with which she gifted us. She enriched Yiddish literature with a large number of songs, poems, stories, dramas, novels, and essays.

---

90. A children's camp in New York State, founded by the Bund for the children of Holocaust survivors.

Women's Songs
(fragment)

A.

The women of our family
will come to me at night, in my dreams, and say:
"With virtuous modesty, we have transmitted a pure blood
for generations,
brought it to you like a wine
guarded in the kosher cellars of our hearts."
And one will say:
I have remained an agunah[91]
since my cheeks were still like two red apples still on the tree,
and I've gnashed my white teeth, waiting,
through many a lonely night."
And I will give the grandmothers the following answer:
"Your sighs, which sounded like whistling whips,
have driven my young life out of the house,
fleeing from your wholesome pleading.
But you followed me wherever streets are dark,
wherever shadows fall,
and your quiet, choked weeping chases me
like the autumn winds,
and your words are silken threads that bind my brain.
My life is like a page plucked from a book,
with the first line torn off."

B.

I'll come to the man
who brought me my first womanly joy, and say:
"Man—I entrusted my silent looks to another
and laid my head next to his one night.
Now my sorrow is like the stinging of bees
around my heart,
and I have no honey to salve the wounds."
And the man will grab my braid
and I'll drop to my knees,
remaining at the doorstep,
like the woman turned to stone in Sodom.

---

91. An Orthodox Jewish woman whose husband has left her but hasn't divorced her; she cannot remarry and is therefore a "chained woman."

פֿרויען-לידער

(פֿראגמענט)

א׳

עס וועלן די פֿרויען פֿון אונדזער משפּחה

בײַ נאַכט אין חלומות מיר קומען און זאָגן:

מיר האָבן אין צניעות אַ לויטערע בלוט איבער דורות געטראָגן,

צו דיר עס געבראַכט ווי אַ ווײַן אַ געהיטן

אין כּשרע קעלערס פֿון אונדזערע הערצער.

און איינע וועט זאָגן:

איך בין אַן עגונה געבליבן, ווען ס׳זײַנען די באַקן – צוויי רויטלעכע עפּל –

אויף בוים נאָך געשטאַנען,

און כ׳האָב מײַנע ציינער די ווײַסע צעקריצט אין די איינזאַמע נעכט פֿון דערוואַרטונג.

און איך וויל די באָבעס אַנטקעגן גיין זאָגן:

אײַערע זיפֿצן האָבן ווי פֿאַקיקע בײַטשן געאַטעמט

און האָבן מײַן לעבן מײַן יונגן געטריבן פֿון שטוב צום אַרויסגאַנג,

פֿון אײַערע כּשרע בעטן אַנטלויפֿן.

נאָר איר גייט מיר נאָך, ווּ די גאַס איז נאָר טונקל,

ווּ ס׳פֿאַלט נאָר אַ שאָטן.

און אײַערע שטילע פֿאַרשטיקטע געוויינען יאָגן נאָך מיר ווי די האַרבסטיקע ווינטן,

און אײַערע רייד זײַנען זײַדענע פֿעדים אויף מײַן מוח פֿאַרבונדן.

איז מײַן לעבן אַן אויסגעפֿליקט בלאַט פֿון אַ ספֿר

און די שורה די ערשטע פֿאַרריסן.

ב׳

צו דעם וועל איך קומען,

ווער ס׳האָט דער ערשטער מיר מײַן פֿרויען–פֿרייד געבראַכט, און זאָגן:

מאַן,

כ׳האָב נאָך אײַנעם מײַן שטילן בליק פֿאַרטרויט

און אין אַ נאַכט לעבן אים מײַן קאָפּ געלייגט.

איצט האָב איך מײַן צער ווי בינען אָנגעשטאָכענע

אַרום מײַן האַרץ געבראַכט,

און האָב קיין האָניק ניט אויף לינדערן די ווּנד.

און ס׳וועט דער מאַן מיך אָננעמען בײַם צאָפּ,

וועל איך אַנידערברעכן זיך אויף בײַדע פֿיס,

און בלײַבן אויף דער שוועל, ווי די פֿאַרשטייגערונג פֿון סדום.

I'll raise my hands to my head,
as my mother used to do when blessing the candles,
but my fingers will stick out
like ten enumerated sins.

C.

For poor brides who were servant girls,
Mother Sarah draws sparkling wine
from dark barrels and casks.
To those who are fated to have a full pitcher,
Mother Sarah carries it with both hands,
and for those who are fated to have but a glassful,
she drops a tear into the wine.
And to streetwalkers
who are dreaming of white bridal slippers,
Mother Sarah brings pure honey
on small plates
to their tired mouths.

For poor brides from aristocratic families
who are ashamed to show their patched underwear
to their mothers-in-law,
Mother Rebecca brings camels
loaded with white linen.
And when the darkness spreads out before their feet
and all the camels kneel to the ground to rest,
Mother Rebecca measures out ell after ell of linen,
from the fingers of their hands
to their golden arm-bands.

For those whose eyes are tired
from looking at every neighbor child
and yearning for tiny hands,
and a small, soft body
and a cradle to rock,
Mother Rachel brings healing leaves
found on distant mountains,

איך וועל די הענט ארויפֿהייבן צום קאָפּ,
ווי ס'פֿלעגט מײַן טאַטע טאָן בײַם בענטשן ליכט,
נאָר ס'וועלן מײַנע פֿינגער שטיין
ווי צען געצײַלטע זינד.

ג'

פֿאַר כּלות אָרעמע, וואָס זײַנען דינסטמיידלעך געווען,
צאַפּט די מוטער שׂרה פֿון פֿעסער טונקעלע
און קרוגן פֿינקלדיקן ווײַן.
ווען מען ס'איז אַ פֿולער קרוג באַשערט,
טראָגט די מוטער שׂרה אים מיט ביידע הענט;
און ווען מען ס'איז באַשערט אַ בעכערל אַ קליינס,
פֿאַלט דער מוטער שׂרהס טרער אין אים אַרײַן.
און פֿאַר גאַסנמיידלעך,
ווען ווײַסע חופּה–שיכלעך חלומען זיך זיי,
טראָגט די מוטער שׂרה האָניק לויטערן
אויף קליינע טעצלעך
צו זייער מידן מויל.

פֿאַר כּלות אָרעמע, פֿון אַ מיוחסדיקן שטאַם,
וואָס שעמען זיך דאָס אויסגעלאַטעטע וועש
ברענגען צו דער שוויגער פֿאַרן אויג,
פֿירט די מוטער רבֿקה קעמלען אָנגעלאָדענע
מיט ווײַסן לײַוונט–לײַן.
און ווען די פֿינצטערניש שפּרייט אויס זיך פֿאַר די פֿיס,
און ס'קניִען אַלע קעמלען צו דער ערד צו רו,
מעסט די מוטער רבֿקה לײַוונט אייל נאָך אייל
פֿון די פֿינגערלעך פֿון האַנט
ביזן גאָלדענעם בראַסלעט.

פֿאַר די, וואָס האָבן מידע אויגן
פֿון נאָכקוקן נאָך יעדן שכנותדיקן קינד,
און דאַרע הענט פֿון גאָרן
נאָך אַ קליינעם קערפּערל אַ וויַיכס
און נאָך אַ וויגן פֿון אַ וויג,
ברענגט די מוטער רחל היילונג–בלעטער,
אויסגעפֿונענע אויף ווײַסע בערג,

and comforts them with quiet words:
"God may open your closed womb at any moment."

To those who weep at night on their lonely beds
and have no one to tell their sorrow to,
so they talk to themselves with parched lips,
to them Mother Leah comes quietly
and covers both eyes with her pale hands.

A Dark Cloth Coat

A tailor from Kamora town
had many kids, no Evil Eye—
just tiny kids, just poppy-seeds,
and with a cradle standing by.

Then let my story now begin:
not one about a sweet white goat,
but one about a handsome coat,
a lovely, brand-new dark cloth coat.

The coat was sewn by hand with care
from dark cloth—that's the rule.
'Twas for the eldest son named Shmuel
to wear each day to go to shul.

Our Shmuel wore it three long years,
and still it looked brand new.
And then he wore it one more year—
it still looked new and handsome too.

Our Shmuel put it on just right,
but one day found the waist too tight.

The whole Kamora was upset:
"A problem—something here's not right.
Our Shmuel put his cloth coat on
and found it feeling much too tight."

און טרייסט זיי מיט אַ שטילן וואַרט:
ס׳קאָן יעדע שעה גאָט עפֿענען דאָס צוגעמאַכטע טראָכט.

צו די, וואָס ווײנען אין די נעכט אויף אײנזאַמע געלעגערס,
און האָבן ניט פֿאַר וועמען ברענגען זייער צער,
רעדן זיי מיט אויסגעברענטע ליפן צו זיך אַליין,
צו זיי קומט שטיל די מוטער לאה,
האַלט בײדע אויגן מיט די בלײכע הענט פֿאַרשטעלט.

אַ מאַנטל פֿון אַ טונקעלן געוואַנטל

בײַ אַ שנײַדער אין קאַמאַרע
פֿול מיט קינדער, קיין עין–הרע,
קינדער פּיצעלעך ווי מאָן
שטייט אַ וויגל אויבן–אָן.

איצטער הייבט זיך אָן די מעשׂה,
נישט פֿון ציגעלעך קיין ווײַסע
נאָר אַ מעשׂה פֿון אַ מאַנטל
פֿון אַ טונקעלן געוואַנטל.

האָט מען אויפֿגענייט אַ מאַנטל
פֿון אַ טונקעלן געוואַנטל
פֿאָרן עלטסטן בחור שמואל
ער זאָל קענען גיין אין שול.

גייט אים שמואליק יאָרן דרײַ
איז דער מאַנטל שפּאָגל נײַ,
גייט אים שמואליק נאָך אַ יאָר
איז דער מאַנטל שענער גאָר.

איין מאָל שמואליק טוט אים אָן
איז דער מאַנטל קורץ אין שטאָן.

ווערט אַ טומל אין קאַמאַרע:
– נאָ דיר גאָר אַ נײַע צרה!
שמואליק טוט דעם מאַנטל אָן –
איז דער מאַנטל קורץ אין שטאָן.

So tell me, what can now be done?
Our Beyla now can have the fun.

Our Beyla wore it three long years,
and still it looked brand new.
He wore it then for one more year—
it still looked new and handsome too.

One day our Beyla gave a spit—
the coat's three seams just up and split.

The whole Kamora was upset:
"A problem—something here's not right.
Our Beyla gave a simple spit
and three coat seams just up and split.

So what's the matter—do I care?
The coat will go to Yosl Ber.

Our Yosl wore it three long years,
and still it looked brand new.
He wore it then for one more year—
it still looked new and handsome too.

One day he fell down on the stair
and tore off buttons everywhere.

The whole Kamora was upset:
"A problem—something here's not right.
He merely fell down on the stair
and now no buttons anywhere."

The family sat and figured out:
"Let Hindl wear the coat about."

Our Hindl wore it three long years,
and still it looked brand new.
She wore it here, she wore it there—
the coat was missing not a hair.

נו, איז מילא —
טוט שױן אָן דעם מאַנטל ביילע.

גייט אים ביילע יאָרן דרײַ
איז דער מאַנטל שפּאָגל נײַ,
גייט אים ביילע נאָך אַ יאָר
איז דער מאַנטל שענער גאָר.

אײן מאָל ביילע טוט אַ שפּײַ
פלאַצט אין מאַנטל נעטלעך דרײַ.

ווערט אַ טומל אין קאָמאַרע:
– נאַ דיר גאָר אַ נײַע צרה!
טאָמער ביילע גיט אַ שפּײַ
פלאַצט אין מאַנטל נעטלעך דרײַ?

װאָס זשע קען דאָ זײַן דער מער?
גייט אין מאַנטל יאָסל–בער.

גייט ער אין אים יאָרן דרײַ
איז דער מאַנטל שפּאָגל נײַ,
גייט ער אין אים נאָך אַ יאָר
איז דער מאַנטל שענער גאָר.

אײן מאָל פֿאַלט ער אױף די טרעפּלעך
און אַ סוף צו אַלע קנעפּלעך.

ווערט אַ טומל אין קאָמאַרע:
– נאַ דיר גאָר אַ נײַע צרה!
גיין און פֿאַלן אױף די טרעפּלעך
און פֿאַרלירן אַלע קנעפּלעך?

און עס פֿסקנט דאָס געזינדל:
זאָל שױן גיין אין מאַנטל הינדל.

גייט אים הינדל יאָרן דרײַ
איז דער מאַנטל שפּאָגל נײַ,
גייט זי אין אים נאָך אַ יאָר
פֿעלט דעם מאַנטל נישט קיין האָר.

One day a tumult in the house
and everyone is standing 'round.
Our Hindl's sobbing on the bed—
the coat-cuff's nowhere to be found.

Now everyone is shouting out:
"This girl will soon become a bride,
and look—she's sobbing on her bed!
How can you lose a cuff outside?"

The coat went to the youngest son—
our Pantl was the chosen one.

O Pantl, Pantl, what a brat!
He plays with every dog and cat!
He chases every cat he sees!
He fights, get beaten to his knees!
Meow and whistle, howl and bark—
Ma laughs and curses—what a lark!

So Pantl wore the dark cloth coat.
That bratty kid—he got our goat!

The very day he put it on,
he tore its corners—look and see!
The next day, not to be outdone,
he tore a hole right in the knee.
The evening of that selfsame day,
the collar's missing—something new!
And also two great gaping holes
right at the elbows—howdja do!

A tumult rose then everywhere:
"Oh woe is us, oh woe, oh dear!
That lovely coat, that handsome coat's
in childish, bratty hands we fear!"

One day our Pantl, no idler he,
came running, naked as a tree.
Then all, as far as eye could see,

אײן מאָל װערט אַ גרױסער טומל,
אַלע שטײען אין אַ רומל,
הינדל כליפּעט אױפֿן בעט –
האָט אָנגעװאָרן אַ מאַנקעט!

שרײַען אַלע, אַלע, אַלע:
– דאָס איז דאָך אַ מױד אַ כּלה,
ליגט און כליפּעט אױפֿן בעט!
װי פֿאַרלירט מען אַ מאַנקעט?

האָט שױן אָנגעטאָן דעם מאַנטל
איצט דער ייִנגסטער בחור פֿאַנטל.

פֿאַנטל, פֿאַנטל, אײַ איז דאָס אַ בחורעץ!
חבֿרט זיך מיט הינט און קעץ,
יאָגט זיך נאָך נאָך יעדער װאָגן,
שלאָגט זיך, װערט אַלײן געשלאָגן,
מיאַוקעט, פֿײַפֿט און שרײַט און בילט
און די מאַמע לאַכט און שילט.

האָט שױן אָנגעטאָן דעם מאַנטל
איצט אָט דער–אָ תּכשיט פֿאַנטל.

האָט ער באַלד דעם ערשטן טאָג
אָפּגעפֿליקט אַ גאַנצן ראָג,
און אױף מאָרגן אין דער פֿרי
אױסגעהאַקט אַ לאָך אין קני.
און דעם זעלבן טאָג פֿאַר נאַכט
אָן אַ קאָלנער אים געבראַכט,
מיט צװײי לעכער גרױס װי אױגן
אין די בײידע עלנבױיגן.

װערט אַ טומל אַ געשרײי,
– אַך און אָך און װינד און װײי!
אַזאַ מאַנטל, אַזאַ מאַנטל
פֿאַלט אַרײַן צום תּכשיט פֿאַנטל.

אײן מאָל פֿאַנטל איז ניט פֿױל,
קומט צו לױפֿן נאַקעט, הױל,
שרײַען אַלע פֿאַר אַ מאָל,

were angry, angry as could be.
"You naughty boy, what did you do?
Just where's your coat? Now tell us true!"

Our Pantl then just answered so:
"I'll tell you where the coat did go."

"I gave the right lapel away—
I gave it to our sweet black cat.
And then I gave the left lapel
to our white cat—and how 'bout that!"
And then he laughed—oh what a jest!
"Some time next week you'll see the rest!"

A tumult rose then everywhere:
"Oh woe is us, oh woe, oh dear!
That lovely coat, that handsome coat—
our Pantl's ruined it now we fear."

אַלע, אַלע אין איין קול:
– תכשיט, שגץ, פֿלעדערמויז,
װו דער מאַנטל זאָג נאָר אויס!

ענטפֿערט זיי דער װוילער יונג
מיט אַזאַ־אַ שאַרפֿע צונג:

– כ'האָב פֿון אים דעם רעכטן לאַץ
אָפּגעשענקט דער שװאַרצער קאַץ,
און דערנאָך דעם לינקן לאַץ
אָפּגעשענקט דער װײַסער קאַץ.
און די רעשטע, לאָך אויף לאָך,
ס'אָנקומען די צװייטע װאָך.

װערט אַ טומל אַ געשרײַ:
– אַך און אָך און װינד און װיי
אַזאַ מאַנטל, אַזאַ מאַנטל
פֿאַלט אַרײַן צום תכשיט פֿאַנטל!

REYZL ZHIKHLINSKI

(Born in Gombin, Poland, in 1910; died in California in 2002.)

Reyzl Zhikhlinski, who was the co-winner of the 1975 Manger Prize for Yiddish Literature (with Joseph Papyernikov), lived and wrote in New York City from1951 to 2000, two years before her death.. She is considered one of the most original female poets in Yiddish literature. When her first book, *Lider* (Poems), was published in Warsaw (with the blessing of the Pen Club and Itsik Manger, who wrote the Foreword), it was received by Yiddish literature critics with much praise. Jacob Glatstein wrote: "We here in America were surprised by Reyzl Zhikhlinski's musically free verse and by her original, cutting painterliness. Her poetry is a match for the modern poems in American Yiddish literature, and it is incomprehensible how the girl from Gombin has already been able to so skillfully dance over all banalities." (*In Tokh Genumen* [Taken as a Whole]).

When Zhikhlinski arrived in New York after her difficult refugee-years in Russia and then in Poland and Paris, Samuel Niger received her with a greeting-article, in which he wrote, among other things: "From her very first verse one could see that she lives in a world that she herself has dreamt up, that the secret she guards against revealing to us is her own secret…Reyzl Zhikhlinski has her own poetic language, for that which draws her to words is her own…"

What is the nature of Reyzl Zhikhlinski's uniqueness? The lines of her short poems are not always bound together understandably and logically, but they affect one with their mood and the emotional state that emanates from them, just as one is affected by the quiet musical tones that one's ear receives.

The poet Isaac Yanosovich writes about this: "When I start to read a poem by Reyzl Zhikhlinski, I often get the impression that the poet is sitting at the piano and playing the white keys with one finger. So comes one verse, a second one, a third one. And suddenly she starts accompanying herself with the other hand, and the previous verses become bound together, appear in a new light, and unexpectedly reveal a deep poetic world and recognition of it that grows into a symbol."

Yanosovich ends his essay about the poet with these words: "About Reyzl Zhikh-linski, it is irrelevant to use the epithet 'great'. About her one should say simply: 'Of such original, true poets we have only one. That is greater than 'great' .'"

On Rainy Days

On rainy days, people bend down closer to the ground
and think about their grandparents
who lived long lives;
clouds rest on their shoulders
and move on.
and everything around is the color
of before being born,
of after dying—
the deep purple of the asters,
the yellow brass antiques,
the ships floating by on the river,
the humpbacked, fog-shrouded bridges.

My Mother and the Oven

What did my mother
want from our oven?
She moved it around
every autumn—
dragged the oven from wall to wall,
from corner to corner,
made it higher, lower—
the white oven stood pale and silent.
The Gentile drank whisky
from a flask
and sang sad Slavic songs.
The clay shone on his big hands—
I was frightened by his shadow on the wall
and by the white shadow of the oven.

אין רעגנדיקע טעג

אין רעגנדיקע טעג בייגן זיך מענטשן
טיפער אַראָפּ צו דער ערד
און טראַכטן וועגן זייערע זיידעס
וואָס האָבן לאַנג געלעבט;
וואָלקנס רוען זיך אָפּ
אויף זייערע פּלייצעס
און ציען ווײַטער זייער וועג
און אַלץ אַרום האָט דעם קאָליר
פֿון פֿאַרן געבוירן ווערן
פֿון נאָכן שטאַרבן –
דער טיפּער לילאַ פֿון די אַסטרעס,
די געלע מעשענע אַנטיקן,
די שיפֿן וואָס שווימען אויפֿן טײַך פֿאַרבײַ
די פֿאַרהויקערטע, פֿאַרנעפּלטע בריקן.

מײַן מאַמע און דער אויוון

וואָס האָט מײַן מאַמע
געוואָלט אַרויסקלשוסֿן פֿון אונדזער אויוון?
זי האָט אים איבערגעשטעלט
אייעדן האַרבסט.
געשלעפּט אים פֿון וואַנט צו וואַנט
פֿון ווינקל צו ווינקל,
געמאַכט אים העכער,
קלענער,
דער קאַפֿל–אויוון איז געשטאַנען
בלויז, שטום.
דער גוי האָט געטרונקען בראָנפֿן
פֿון אַ פֿלאַש
און געזונגען לידער סלאַווישע, טרויעריקע,
דער ליים האָט געשײַנט אין זײַנע גרויסע הענט –
מיך געשראָקן האָט זײַן שאָטן אויף די ווענט
און דער ווײַסער שאָטן פֿון דער אויוון.

What Swims There In the Hudson?

What swims there in the Hudson
in the red light?
Who is crying there: "Save us,
we are sinking!"
They are my dead,
the cremated,
who are sinking again
in my memory.

Where Do the Words Disappear

Where do the words disappear
of the people
who talk to themselves
on the streets of New York?
Do they drop to the pavement
as mere dust?
Or perhaps they are wandering about, forever exiled
among the planets—
as white, lonely stars.
Where do the words disappear
of all the lonely people
who talk to themselves
in the big cities of the world?

Tadzio, Tadzio

Tadzio! Tadzio!
A mother called
her blond little *sheygets*[92] home
one evening
so many years ago.
But the Polish name,
the soft sound,

---

92. A Christian boy

וואָס שווימט דאָרט אויפֿן האָדסאָן?

וואָס שווימט דאָרט אויפֿן האָדסאָן
אין רויטן ליכט?
ווער שרײַט דאָרט – ראַטעווע,
מיר גייען אונטער –
דאָס זײַנען די טויטע מײַנע,
די פֿאַרברענטע,
וואָס גייען אונטער נאָך אַ מאָל
אין מײַן זכרון.

ווהין קומען אהין די רייד?

ווהין קומען אהין די רייד
פֿון די מענטשן
וואָס רעדן צו זיך אַליין
אויף די גאַסן פֿון דער שטאָט ניו-יאָרק?
פֿאַלן זיי אויפֿן ברוק אַראָפּ
בלויז שטויב?
אָדער בלאָנדזשען זיי אַרום אייביק
פֿאַרלוירן
צווישן די פּלאַנעטן –
קליינע, ווײַסע, עלנטע שטערן?
ווהין קומען אהין די רייד
פֿון עלנטע מענטשן
וואָס רעדן צו זיך אַליין
אין די גרויסע שטעט פֿון דער וועלט?

טאַדזשיאַ, טאַדזשיאַ

טאַדזשיאַ! טאַדזשיאַ!
אַ מוטער האָט גערופֿן
איר בלאָנד שגצל
אין אַ פֿאַרנאַכט אַהיים –
ציט אַזוי פֿיל יאָרן צוריק,
נאָר דער פּוילישער נאָמען,
דער וייכער קלאַנג

still falls like dew on my spirit,
the way it did
when I was a child.
Tadzio, Tadzio,
blond golden little *sheygets*—
did even you help slaughter Jews?

The Old-Age Home

The red brick home
for the aged
smiled to me this morning
with one bright, sunny wall—
an old smile
that can only be smiled by old people,
when one eye laughs
and the other one cries.
The other walls of the home,
with their curtained windows
in shadows, closed,
grieved ancient griefs
deeply hidden amid the bricks.

My Story Is Your Story

My story is your story,
neighbor across from me in the subway.
What you are thinking about
I have long since forgotten.
What will happen to you
happened to me long ago.
What you hope for
I smile about
with closed lips.
My fate is shown
in the blue veins on your hand—
yours you can read
in the deep wrinkles on my face.

פֿאַלט נאָך אַלץ מיט טוי אויף מײַן געמיט
אַזוי ווי אַמאָל,
ווען איך בין געווען אַ קינד
טאַדזשיאַ, טאַדזשיאַ,
בלאַנד, גאָלדן שגצל,
אויך דו האָסט געהאָלפֿן שעכטן ייִדן?

דאָס הויז פֿון די אַלטע

דאָס רויטע ציגלנע הויז
פֿאַר אַלטע לײַט
האָט צו מיר געשמייכלט אין פֿרימאָרגן הײַנט
מיט אײַן העלער זוניקער וואַנט –
אָן אַלטן שמייכל,
וואָס עס קענען נאָר שמייכלען אַלטע לײַט:
ווען אײן אויג לאַכט
און דאָס אַנדערע וויינט.
די אַנדערע ווענט פֿון הויז,
מיט די פֿאַרהאָנגענע פֿענצטער
פֿאַרשאָטנט, פֿאַרמאַכט,
האָבן געטרויערט אָן אַלטן טרויער
טיף אין זיך אַרײַנגעמויערט.

מײַן געשיכטע איז דײַן געשיכטע

מײַן געשיכטע איז דײַן געשיכטע,
שכן קעגן מיר אין סאָבווייַ.
פֿון וואָס דו טראַכסט
האָב איך לאַנג שוין פֿאַרגעסן,
וואָס דיך וועט טרעפֿן –
האָט שוין לאַנג מיט מיר געטראָפֿן,
אויף וואָס דו האָפֿסט –
פֿון דעם שמייכל איך
מיט צוגעמאַכטע ליפֿן.
מײַן גורל צייכענען
די בלויע אָדערן פֿון דײַנע הענט,
דײַנעם – קענסטו לעזן
אין די טיפֿע קנייטשן פֿון מײַן פּנים.

ABRAHAM SUTZKEVER

(Born in Smargon, near Vilna, on July 15, 1913;
died on January 20, 2010, in Tel Aviv, Israel.)

In the course of the years we have been publishing the Pearls, we have, on various occasions, reprinted the poems of Abraham Sutzkever and have written about the unique place he has occupied in our literature since 1937, when his first book of poems appeared. Even then the whole Yiddish literary world expressed great enthusiasm for the appearance of the young poet.

Much has been written already about the new poetic images and pictures that he introduced into Yiddish poetry, and especially about his linguistic virtuosity. He has conjured up new sounds, nuances, and rhymes from our Yiddish language, and has demonstrated the great richness of the language. We have already told how one of us (Y.M.), as a young man, was delighted by his neologisms and rhymes, and founded a circle of young readers who tried to read "Sutzkeverish."

Since that first book appeared in pre-War Poland, the poet has gifted us with another twenty, and each new book represents a new level of his creativity.

Abraham Sutzkever was born in Smargon, near Vilna, in the year 1913. The First World War broke out a year later, and his parents succeeded in fleeing from the burning city and settling in the Siberian city Omsk. When his father Hertz died suddenly in 1921, the orphaned family traveled back to Poland, to Vilna. There he became a member of the literary and artistic group Young Vilna, together with Chaim Grade, Shmerke Kaczerginski, and others. He studied there in a Talmud Torah, and later in a Yiddish-Polish gymnasium.[93] He began to write poems when he was very young, fifteen, but he first began to publish them in 1934, six years later. In 1941, he, together with all the other Jews of Vilna, were driven into the ghetto, and he joined the United Partisan Organization. He participated actively in the Yiddish cultural activities that were being conducted in the ghetto, wrote a lot, and received the first literary prize in the ghetto for his dramatic poem *Dos Keyver-Kind* (The Grave-Child).

Together with other Yiddish poets and cultural people, he was forced to work at sorting literary materials that were to be sent to Germany. However, Sutzkever, together with his friend and colleague Shmerke Kaczerginski and others, man-

---

93. A secular high school

486

aged, despite being watched closely, to save rare manuscripts and other rare books and bury them. Now these rare materials can be found in the archives of the New York YIVO.

When the Vilna ghetto was liquidated, Sutzkever escaped and joined a partisan group in the surrounding forests. In 1944, a special airplane took him to Moscow, where he appealed, on the radio, to Jews around the world to help conquer German fascism. Ilya Ehrenburg[94] published an article about him at that time entitled *Der Triumf Fun a Mentsh* (The Triumph of a Man). When the Nazi murderers were later tried by the International Tribunal, Sutzkever appeared as one of the witnesses to the Nazi crimes against humanity and against the Jewish people.

After the War, he lived and created in Poland, France, Holland, and Switzerland, and in 1947 he and his wife and child emigrated on the illegal ship *Patria* to Israel, where he immediately began playing a leading role in Yiddish literature as the editor of the journal *Di Goldene Keyt* (The Golden Chain), which he created thanks to financial support by Histadrut.

As this book was being prepared for publication, Abraham Sutzkever passed into eternity on January 20, 2010, after a long illness. His loss takes away from us the last surviving giant figure in Yiddish literature.

---

94. A renowned Soviet writer

Yiddish Words

Where stars grazed in the meadow like little goats,
where children studied and played in the Bible's glow,
where Yiddish words hatched in sunbeams,
now the light is a ruin where jackals bay.

Sunken ships in the ocean can leave some sign behind
so someone can swim between sharks' fins
to their treasure and bring up his beloved,
but the Yiddish words have sunk without a trace.

There is a time or non-time of resurrection,
and there I see the sunken Yiddish words
bestir themselves like little children wearing prayer shawls,
and the sunshine grows suddenly brighter with their sparks.

Around Lakes

Beneath the glow of Saturn,
'midst ancient arrowy fir trees,
my bare feet print their traces
around phosphorescent lakes.
I've come to this place
to wreath it lovingly with laurel—
for me, each clod of earth is like an altar
to which I bring my song as a sacrifice.
I'm reborn as a child
in the pale, quartz-veined countryside,
by the cold and crystal water
where forest dreams linger.

Let loneliness lead a soul by the hand—
I still walk faithfully through the wooded gates of Night.
Like the rush of wind in your viscera,
the life of everything I see rushes through mine,
even the images that hover nearby.

ייִדישע ווערטער

ווי שטערן ווי ציגעלעך האָבן אין פֿעלד זיך געפֿאַשעט,
ווי חומשדיק האָבן די קינדער גערוישט און גערש״ט,
ווי אויסגעפּיקט האָבן זיך ייִדישע ווערטער און שטראַלן,
אַצינד איז דאָס ליכט אַ רויִנע ווי ס'וווינען שאַקאַלן.

פֿאַרזונקענע שיפֿן אין ים קאָנען לאָזן אַ סימן,
אַז עמעצער זאָל צוווישן היַפֿישן־מעסטערס דערשוויִמען
צו זייערע אוצרות און ברענגען פֿון דעם – זיַן באַשערטער,
נאָר ס'זענען פֿאַרזונקען אָן סימן די ייִדישע ווערטער.

פֿאַראָן אַזאַ ציַיט אָדער אומצײַט פֿון תחית־המתים
און דאָרטן דערזע איך: ווי קינדערלעך אונטער טליתים
באַוועגן זיך ייִדישע ווערטער וואָס זענען פֿאַרזונקען
און ליכטיק ווערט פּלוצעם די זונשיַן פֿון זייערע פֿונקען.

אַרום אָזערעס

אונטער שיַין פֿון סאָטורן,
צווישן פֿרײַליקע יאָדלעס אוראַלטע,
קריץ איך אויס מיַנע באַרוועסע שפּורן
אַרום אָזערעס פֿאַספֿאָר־באַשטראַלטע.
יאָ, איך בין דאָ געקומען כדי איך
זאָל מיט ליבשאַפֿט די געגנט באַלאָרבן.
יעדער ערד איז פֿאַר מיר אַ מזבח
ווו איך ברענג מיַן געזאַנג פֿאַר אַ קרבן.
כ'וועל אויף ס'ניַי ווי אַ קינדהייט באַשאַפֿן
אין דער קוואַרצענער געגנט דער בלאַסער;
בײַ דעם קאַלטן בריליאַנטענעם וואַסער
ווו חלומות פֿון וויל דוועלדער גאָפֿן.

זאָל די אייַנזאַמקייט פֿירן
פֿאַר אַ האַנט אַ נשמה. אַ טריַיער
גיי איך נאָך דורך די וואַלדיקע טירן
פֿון דער נאַכט. ווי דער ווינטרוויש איז אײַער
רוישט אין אינגעווייד מיַינעם דאָס לעבן
פֿון דעם אַלץ וואָס איך זע; און אַסילו
פֿון די בילדער דערבייַ וואָס פֿאַרשוועבן.

I send a prayer to my own body
as if to strange, phantastical gods:
Make me whole, so I can resolve my simple earthly pleasures
on the steps of Night o'er which I clamber.
And I sink down by the shores of a lake.
See how my reflection, which in my inner confusion
I've been unable to fathom,
comes up to meet me from the quicksilver bottom.
Now it billows forth 'midst stars from the deep.
I see its contour encounter mine
and the two of us merge into a single body.
O heart of mine! Have you finally found a home
or have I sacrificed you for the sake of an instant of eternal beauty?

The Little Blue Horse

Your father still doesn't know, dear child,
whether God writes poems
and how many years old you were
long before you were born.
It's enough for him that he knows
that the little blue horse, your plaything,
freed from its reins, races in his veins,
overtakes Time and brings it back,
and whinnies out a magic spell
of rambling silver.

And if you're afraid, it's not his fault.
A hand belonging to no one now transforms
both of you into vanished images.
Your father is a fading old man in a cellar
and you are the protector of his world,
with the little blue horse at the head of your bed.

צו מײַן אייגענעם גוף טו איך תּפֿילה
ווי צו פֿרעמדע פֿאַנטאַסטישע געטער:

– מאַך מיך גאַנץ, איר זאָל קאָנען באַשײדן
מײַנע פּראָסטע און ערדישע פֿרײדן
איבער שטאַפּלען פֿון נאַכט ווי איך קלעטער.
און איך פֿאַל בײַ די ברעגן
פֿון אַן אָזערע. קוק, ווי דאָרט אונטן
פֿונעם קוועקזילבער-דנאָ קומט אַנטקעגן
מײַן געשטאַלט, וואָס איך האָב ניט דערגרונטן
זי געקענט אין מײַן איכיקן פּלאַנעטער.
איצטער קוואַלט זי אַרויס צווישן שטערן
פֿון דער טיפֿעניש. כ'זע ווי איר קאָנטור
טרעפֿט מיט מײַנעם זיך אויף און מיר ווערן
בײַדע איינס, אין אַ גופֿיקער איינקײט.
אָ דו הארץ מײַנס, צי האָסטו דערוואָרבן
שוין אַ היים, אָדער כ'ברענג דיך אַ קרבן
פֿאַר אַ רגע פֿון אייביקער שײנקײט?

דאָס בלויע פֿערדעלע

דײַן טאַטע ווייס נאָך אַלץ ניט, קינדעניו, צי גאָט שרײַבט לידער
און וויפֿל יאָר דו ביסט געווען העט-אײדער ביסט געבוירן.
גענוג אים אַז ער ווייס: דאָס בלאָע פֿערדעלע, דײַן שפּילצײַג,
באַפֿרײַט פֿון לייצעס, יאָגט אין זײַנע אָדערן,
דעריאָגט די צײַט און ברענגט זי אים צוריק
און הירושעט אויס אַ צויבערײַ פֿון בלאָנדזשענדיקן זילבער.

און שרעקסטו זיך, איז ניט זײַן שולד. אַ קײנעמסדיקע האַנט
פֿאַרוואָאַנדלט איצטער בײַדן אין פֿאַרשוווּנדענע געשטאַלטן.
דײַן טאַטע איז אַ זינקענדיקער זקן אין אַ קעלער
און דו – זײַן וועלט-באַשיצער מיטן פֿערדעלע צוקאָפֿן.

The little blue horse, your plaything,
races in his veins
with a crimson gallop.

The Same

The same man recognized himself
in the small face of the child in the white garden.
The child was blond, with sky-blue eyes,
and he—an aged, twisted wraith, burned out.

When he, with gaze as red as autumn,
saw the child at play in the snow
(the way a blind man sees
a slender ray of light in his black sleep)
his faded lips smiled with joy:

No, it isn't someone else—
it's me, my gold, my echo,
a sunburst of wondrous rebirth.
It's me alone, myself,
the same.

דאָס בלאָע פֿערדעלע, דײַן שפּילצײַג, יאָגט אין זײַנע אָדערן
אין פּורפּלנע גאַלאָפֿן.

דער זעלבער

דער זעלבער מענטש האָט זיך אַליין דערקענט
אין פּנימל פֿון קינד אין ווײַסן גאָרטן.
דאָס קינד איז בלאָנד, איז הימלבלאָ,
און ער – אַ רויך אַן אַלטער און צעקרימט, פֿאַרלאָשן.

בשעת ער האָט מיט האַרבסטיק–רויטע בליקן
דערזען דאָס קינד בײַם שפּילן זיך אין שניי,
(אַזוי דערזעט אין שוואַרצן שלאָף אַ בלינדער
אַ שטראַלכעלע אַ דינס),
האָבן זײַנע שקיעהדיקע ליפּן
צעשמייכלט זיך מיט פֿרייד:

ניין, ס׳איז ניט קיין אַנדערער,
ס׳איז איך, מײַן גאָלד, מײַן עכאָ,
אַ זונגעזאַנג פֿון וווּנדערלעכער נײַגעבורט,
ס׳איז איך אַליין, דער אייגענער,
דער זעלבער.

The Teacher Mira

In patches and tatters our clothes on us lie—
we're driven through streets to the ghetto to die.
Our houses, they bid us eternal goodbye—
we hear the decrees, but with hardly a sigh.

The graybeards march on with *tfiln* on brow—
a peasant goes by with his not-yet-grown cow.
A dying man's pulled in a cart by his wife—
a woman drags logs, for fire gives life.

And 'mid the whole group is our teacher, dear Mira,
who carries a child like a sack full of *lire.*
She carries one child, holds hands with another—
her pupils and she help encourage each other.

They get to the ghetto, and there is a gate
made of freshly hewn wood—a portent of fate—
and just like a sluice for the river's strong flow,
it opens and into the abyss we go.

They drive us past ruins, without bread or fire—
our bread is our books and The Book we admire.
We gather the children in broken-down rooms
and Mira starts teaching, though Death's specter looms.

She reads them from Sholem Aleichem a tale—
the children light up, their laughter's a gale.
She ties up their braids with a blue ribbon-bow--
a hundred and thirty her children in tow.

Our teacher, dear Mira, is just like the sun—
awake bright and early awaiting each one.
They come and she counts—no don't count them dear,
for twenty sweet children are no longer here.

די לערערין מירע

מיט לאַטעס אויף לײַבער, צעשניטן אין פּאַסן,
מע טרײַבט אונדז אין געטאָ, עס גייען די גאַסן.
די הײַזער באַגלייטן אויף אייביק געזעגנט,
און שטיינערדיק ווערט יעדער גזירה באַגעגנט.

אין תּפֿילין ווי קרוינען מאַרשירן די זקנים,
אַ קעלבעלע גייט מיט אַ דאָרפֿסקינד אין איינעם.
אַ פֿרוי שלעפּט אַ גוסס פֿאַרקלעמט אין די נעגל,
אַ צווייטער – אַ בינטעלע האָלץ אויף אַ וועגל.

און צווישן זיי אַלע – די לערערין מירע.
אַ קינד אויף איר אָרעם – אַ גאָלדענע לירע.
אַ קינד אויף איר אָרעם, בײַם העגטל – אַ צווייטן,
אַרום די תּלמידים, באַגלייטן, באַגלייטן.

און קומט מען צו ייִדישער גאַס, איז אַ טויער,
נאָך וואַרעם דאָס האָלץ ווי אַ קערפּער אַ רויער.
און גלײַך ווי אַ שליוז פֿאַר געטריבענע שטראָמען,
ער טוט זיך אָן עפֿן, פֿאַרשלינגט אין די תּהומען.

מע יאָגט איבער חורבות אָן ברויט און אָן פֿײַער,
דאָס ברויט איז אַ בוך, און דאָס ליכט איז אַ בלײַער.
פֿאַרזאַמלט די קינדער אין חרובער דירה,
עס לערנט זיי ווײַטער די לערערין מירע.

זי לייענט זיי שלום–עליכמס אַ מעשׂה,
עס פֿינקלען די קינדער און לאַכן בעת–מעשׂה.
זי פֿלעכט זיי מיט בלאָינקע סטענגעס די צעפּלעך
און צײלט איר פֿאַרמעג: הונדערט דרײַסיק די קעפּלעך.

צו גלײַך מיט דער זון איז די לערערין מירע
שוין וואָך און זי וואַרט. אויף די קינדערלעך אירע.
זיי קומען, זי צײלט. אָ, ניט צײלן זיי בעסער!
דורך נאַכט האָט דאָ צוואַנציק פֿאַרשניטן אַ מעסער.

Her skin's like a windowpane shadowed by night,
but Mira won't let children know their true plight.
She bites on her lip with courage anew—
she tells of Hirsh Lekert, heroic young Jew.

Nightime—the courtyards are gray everywhere,
as gray as the strands in our Mira's long hair.
Her blind mother's missing—a certain death-knell—
and seventeen children are missing as well.

When last night's wet bloodstains by sunlight are dried,
our Mira hangs flowers, the sorrow to hide.
Old Gerstein, the chorus director, comes in—
the world past the walls hears our joyous loud din.

Our song "Spring is Coming"—a glorious sound,
while axes and bayonets rattle the ground.
They're dragging us out by the roots of our hair—
we sing out our song as if they're not there.

Sixty are left, without sister or mother—
our teacher, dear Mira's first one then the other.
"The holiday's coming, my children, my dears—
let's put on a show and laugh through our tears."

The holiday's here, just forty remain—
they tread the stage-boards in shirts white and plain.
The stage looks so fresh in the sun's brilliant light;
it shines like a lake—what a beautiful sight!

While children are reading great Peretz's work,
the threatening Germans all 'round us still lurk.
The enemy's sending our children to Heaven—
morning reveals Mira's group is now seven.

And so, till an axe cut her down like a tree,
a flower was Mira, each child was her bee.
The flower's long since gotten wilted and gray,
but she'll bloom again on some wonderful day.

איר הויט ווערט אַ שויב אין פֿאַרנאַכטיקע פֿלעקן,
נאָר ס'טאָר זיי ניט מירע די קינדער אַנטפּלעקן.
פֿאַרבייסט זי אַ ליפּ און מיט גבֿורה באַנײַטער
דערציילט זי פֿון לעקערטן, מונטערט זיי ווײַטער.

דורך נאַכט האָט די גראָקייט באַצויגן די הייפֿן,
און גראָ ווערט דער לערערינס האָר אויף די שלייפֿן:
זי זוכט אינעם קעלער איר מאַמע די בלינדע –
צוזאַמען מיט איר פֿעלן זיבעצן קינדער.

ווען זון האָט די בלוטן געטריקנט, האָט מירע
באַהאַנגען מיט גרינס די פֿאַריתומטע דירה:
– געקומען דער לערער גערשטיין, מע וועט זינגען,
דער כאָר זאָל אַריבער די טויערן קלינגען.

שוין קלינגט עס: "ניט–ווײַט איז דער פֿריילינג". נאָר אונטן
די העק און באַגנעטן צעטרייסלען די גרונטן.
מע שלעפּט פֿאַר די האָר פֿון די קעלערס און לעכער.
"ניט–ווײַט איז דער פֿרילינג" פֿאַרקלינגט אָבער העכער.

שוין זעכציק פֿאַרבליבן אָן שוועסטער, אָן מאַמען,
די לערערין מירע איז אַלע צוזאַמען.
ס'איז נאָענט אַ יום–טובֿ, איז טײַבעלעך, קינדער,
אַ פֿאָרשטעלונג דאַרף מען באַווײַזן, געשווינדער!

צום יום–טובֿ – ניטאָ מער ווי פֿערציק, נאָר איטלעך –
מיט ווײַסינקן העמדל, מיט ליכטיקע טריטלעך.
די בינע איז פֿריש, מיט אַ זון, מיט אַ גאָרטן,
מע קען אַזש אין טײַכל זיך אויסבאָדן דאָרטן.

בײַם לייענען פּרצעס דריטע מתּנה
האָט אונטערגעזעגט דאָס געבײַ די סכּנה.
זיי האָבן געכאַפּט! און פֿאָרטאָג איז געבליבן
פֿון הונדערט און דרײַסיק נאָר מירע און זיבן.

אַזוי ביז די האַק האָט האָט צעשפּאָלטן די זינען,
איז מירע אַ בלום און די קינדערלעך – בינען.
שוין גראָ איז די בלום און פֿאַרוועלקט אירע גלידער,
נאָר מאָרגן אין טוי וועט זי אויפֿבלִיען ווידער.

Yiddish

Shall I begin at the beginning?
Shall I, like Abraham,
out of brotherhood smash all the idols?
Shall I let myself be translated while I'm still alive?
Shall I plant my tongue
and wait till it is transformed
into ancestral *Raisins and Almonds*?
What sort of facetious joke
is my brother-poet with the sideburns preaching:
that my *mame-loshn* will soon die?
A hundred years from now
we'll clearly still be able to sit
at the banks of the Jordan and carry on this discussion.
A question gnaws at me and gets under my skin:
if he knows precisely in what direction
the Berditshever's[95] prayer
and Yehoyash's poems and Kulbak's
are wandering toward extinction,
then let him tell me, please:
at what destination is the language going to die?
Perhaps at the Western Wall?
If so, I'll go there,
go and open my mouth,
and, like a lion clothed in fiery tinder,
I'll swallow the dying language,
swallow it and awaken every generation with my roaring.

Underneath Your Shining White Stars

Underneath your shining white stars,
stretch your great white hand to me.
All my words are tears of sorrow—
in your hand they wish to be.

---

95. Rabbi Leyvi Yitskhok of Berditshev, a Hasidic rabbi famous for putting God on trial for failing to answer his prayer for mercy and deliverance for the Jewish people

ייִדיש

זאָל איך אָנהײבן פֿון אָנהײב?

זאָל איך װי אַבֿרהם

אױס ברודערשאַפֿט צעהאַקן אַלע געצן?

זאָל איך זיך אַ לעבעדיקן לאָזן איבערזעצן?

זאָל איך איינפֿלאַנצן מײַן צונג

און װאַרטן ביז פֿאַרװאַנדלען

װעט זי זיך אין אבֿותדיקע

ראָזשינקעס און מאַנדלען?

װאָס פֿאַר אַ קאַטאָװעסדיקע

װיצן

דרשנט מײַן פֿאַעזיע–ברודער מיט די באַקנבאַרדן,

אַז מײַן מאַמע–לשון גײט באַלד אונטער?

מיר װעלן נאָך אין הונדערט יאָר אַרום אַ קענטיק זיצן

און פֿירן די דיסקוסיעס בײַ דעם ירדן.

װײַל אַ שאלה נאָגט און נאָגלט;

אױב ער װײס גענױ װוּ

די תּפֿילה פֿון בערדיטשעװער,

יהואשס ליד

און קולבאַקס

װאָגלט

צו דעם אונטערגאַנג –

טאָ זאָל ער מיר, אַ שטײַגער,

אַנװײַזן װוּהין די שפֿראַך גײט אונטער?

אפֿשר בײַ דעם כּותל מערבֿי?

אױב אַזױ, װעל איך דאָרט קומען, קומען,

עפֿענען דאָס מױל

און װי אַ לײב

אָנגעטאָן אין פֿײַערדיקן צונטער,

אײַנשלינגען דעם לשון װאָס גײט אונטער.

אײַנשלינגען, און אַלע דורות װעקן מיט מײַן ברומען!

אונטער דײַנע װײַסע שטערן

אונטער דײַנע װײַסע שטערן

שטרעק צו מיר דײַן װײַסע האַנט.

מײַנע װערטער זענען טרערן

װילן רוען אין דײַן האַנט.

See, their sparkle is now fading
as I watch from cellar black,
and I have no little corner
out of which to give them back.

Still I will, O dearest God mine,
all my treasure trust to Thee,
for it calls forth fire within me,
and on fire my days will be.

Only in the hidden cellar
can I find a murd'rous rest.
So I race 'cross roofs and higher,
and I search—from East to West.

But the weirdest things still chase me
on stairs and courtyards, howling near.
So I hang, a ruptured bass-string--
sing this tune to you, my dear.

Underneath your shining white stars,
stretch your great white hand to me.
All my words are tears of sorrow—
in your hand they wish to be.

A Wagonload of Shoes

The wheels are turning, turning—
what are they bringing with them?
They're bringing me a wagonload
of trembling shoes.

The wagon is like a wedding canopy
in the evening glow;
the shoes—a full load,
like people at a dance.

זע, עס מונקלט זייער פֿינקל
אין מײַן קעלערדיקן בליק.
און איך האָב גאָרניט קיין ווינקל
זיי צו שענקען דיר צוריק.

און איך וויל דאָך, גאָט געטרײַער,
דיר פֿאַרטרויען מײַן פֿאַרמעג.
ווײַל עס מאָנט אין מיר אַ פֿײַער
און אין פֿײַער — מײַנע טעג.

נאָר אין קעלערן און לעכער
וויינט די מערדערישע רו.
לויף איך העכער, איבער דעכער
און איך זוך: ווּ ביסטו, ווּ?

נעמען יאָגן מיך משוגה
טרעפּ און הויפֿן מיט געווײַ.
העָנג איך — אַ געפֿלאַצטע סטרונע
און איך זינג צו דיר אַזוי:

אונטער דײַנע ווײַסע שטערן
שטרעק צו מיר דײַן ווײַסע האַנט.
מײַנע ווערטער זענען טרערן
ווילן רוען אין דײַן האַנט.

אַ וואָגן שיך

די רעדער יאָגן, יאָגן,
וואָס ברענגען זיי מיט זיך?
זיי ברענגען מיר אַ וואָגן
מיט צאַפּלענדיקע שיך.

דער וואָגן ווי אַ חופּה
אין אָוונטיקן גלאַנץ;
די שיך — אַ פֿולע קופּע
ווי מענטשן אין אַ טאַנץ.

A wedding, a holiday?
or has someone struck me blind?
The shoes, such familiar ones,
I recognize anew.

The heels are tapping—
where to, where, where?
From the old Vilna streets
they're driving us to Berlin.

I need not ask "whose?"
but I get a clamp in my heart.
Oh tell me, shoes, the truth—
where are the feet?

Feet are stamping there
with buttons like dewdrops,
And here—where's the little body
and where is the bride?

Among all the children's shoes,
why don't I see any children?
Why doesn't the bride
put on her shoes now?

Among the children's shoes and other old shoes,
I recognize my mother's shoes.
She used to put them on
only on the Sabbath.

And the heels tap—
where to, where, where?
From the old Vilna streets,
they're driving us to Berlin.

אָ חתונה, אָ יום־טוב!
צי האָט מיך ווער פֿאַרבלענדט?
די שיך — אַזוינע נאָנטע
אויף ס'נײַ איך האָב דערקענט.

עס קלאַפּן די אָפּצאַסן:
ווּהין, ווּהין, ווּהין?
פֿון אַלמע ווילנער גאַסן
מע טרײַבט אונדז קיין בערלין.

איך דאַרף ניט פֿרעגן וועמעס,
נאָר ס'טוט אין האַרץ אַ רים:
אָ, זאָגט מיר, שיך, דעם אמת,
ווו זענען זיי די פֿיס?

די פֿיס פֿון יענע מױל
מיט קנעפּעלעך ווי טוי, —
און דאָ — ווו איז דאָס גופֿל,
און דאָרט ווו איז די פֿרוי?

אין קינדערשיך אין אַלע
וואָס זע איך ניט קיין קינד?
וואָס מוט ניט אָן די כּלה
די שיכעלעך אַצינד?

דורך קינדערשיך און שקראָבעס
כ'דערקען מײַן מאַמעס שיך!
זי פֿלעגט זיי בלויז אויף שבת
אַרױפֿציִען אויף זיך.

און ס'קלאַפּן די אָפּצאַסן:
ווּהין, ווּהין, ווּהין?
פֿון אַלמע ווילנער גאַסן
מע טרײַבט אונדז קיין בערלין.